KILLER DOCTORS

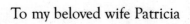
To my beloved wife Patricia

KILLER DOCTORS

THE ULTIMATE BETRAYAL OF TRUST

KENNETH J GIBSON

Neil Wilson Publishing • Glasgow

First published by:

Neil Wilson Publishing Ltd

www.nwp.co.uk

© Kenneth Gibson, 2012

The moral right of the author has been asserted.

A catalogue record for this book is available from

the British Library

ISBN: 978-1-906476-64-9

Ebook ISBN: 978-1-906476-59-5

Acknowledgements

Patricia Gibson for proof reading and

encouragement and Alison Prince for her contacts.

Designed by Melvin Creative

Printed and bound in the EU

CONTENTS

INTRODUCTION

I will use my power to help the sick to the best of my ability and judgement; I will abstain from harming or wronging anyone by it. I will not give a fatal draught to anyone if I am asked, nor will I suggest any such things.

NAMED AFTER HIPPOCRATES (460-377 BC) the Greek 'father of medicine', the Hippocratic Oath is traditionally taken by all doctors upon qualification. The oath sets out the moral precepts of their profession and commits them to a code of behaviour and practice. This document is often seen as a foundation stone of the western world's medical ethics.

What drives those doctors who choose to kill? Some, like Dr Shipman, are undoubtedly compelled by inner demons that lead them to murder. Others, such as Dr Palmer, are driven by insatiable greed or passion, for example Dr Crippen. Sexual passion and/or a lust for money undoubtedly played a part in a lot of these crimes. In some instances, the murderer was seriously ill. Dr Petiot could in no way be described as 'normal'. He was a psychopath deemed incurably insane in early life, yet he was able to mask his insanity long enough to qualify and practice as a doctor.

While motives may vary, opportunity and the esteem in which the medical professionals are held can greatly assist in obscuring crimes, particularly those committed on patients by people like Dr Adams. When someone is in a position of great trust and has the means to kill, then diagnose the cause of death and sign the death and cremation certificates, murder may be extremely difficult to discover, let alone prove. In addition, the respect the public has for the medical profession, their prestige and status in society makes few of us question them. Those who do may come up against bureaucratic intransigence, complacency, a failure to take the concerns of 'lesser mortals' seriously, colleagues 'closing ranks' or even attempts to bully them into silence.

Murderous doctors are, thankfully, few and far between, although there may have been a number whose crimes were never detected. The public in every society has a trust in medical practitioners inculcated since birth. Even the most vicious and sadistic of medical killers tend to have a coterie of supporters who categorically refuse to accept their guilt. In many instances, this is entirely understandable. A charming, well-educated, hard-working and highly skilled doctor who has saved one's own life or that of a family member or went out of his or her way to minister to one when sick is likely to provoke feelings of disbelief, even outraged and vociferous backing when accused of a crime seemingly totally outwith their character.

The doctors in this book are truly a varied bunch, yet most had one thing in common – an utter contempt for human life, life they took an oath to uphold, regardless of all other considerations. Perhaps Karl Brandt was close to the mark (for some at least) when he said of the Hippocratic Oath that: 'One may hang it on one's wall but no one pays any attention to it.'

Idealism attended by arrogance, even if warped, convinced Drs Brandt, Mengele et al that they had done no wrong, despite the bestial nature of their actions; wrapping themselves in their beliefs even until their own deaths, denying the world their contrition.

Doctors are highly intelligent and usually well-educated (Dr Petiot is a rare example of the former but not the latter). Even if a minority commit crimes that may seem inexplicable to you or me they will have a strong rationale and internal logic that justifies their actions. Like other human beings they are prone to the same human failings as others. That they are trained to save lives, not take them, makes any murder by a doctor, or for that matter, dentist, midwife, nurse or other caring professional particularly shocking. It is lucky for us then, that the overwhelming majority of practioners are dedicated to helping, healing and would not dream of harming anyone.

Among the doctors whose stories are outlined herein, are a dictator, a revolutionary and a variety of other assorted rogues of one shade or another. Probably only Dr Carl Austin Weiss cannot be so described.

Their methods of killing ranged from desk-bound murder to more direct involvement by destroying their victims using poison, arson, suffocation and a host of other imaginative and often sadistic ways. More often than not, the murderers' medical skills were specifically involved.

The doctors I selected for this book show the depths to which some travelled in deceiving their patients, spouse or those from the wider community. They and their innocent victims come from varied backgrounds, nationalities and time periods. Their crimes were committed in a number of countries, continents and societies.

Although only a tiny proportion of doctors ever deliberately harm, let alone kill, the cases described do not exist in isolation. Others that could have been added, had I wished to make this volume more extensive, might have included Dr Geza de Kaplany, a Hungarian who, in a fit of jealousy over imaginary infidelities, sadistically tortured, mutilated and murdered his 25-year-old model wife Hajna with acid and razors in San Jose, California, USA on 28 August 1962; Dr

Étienne Deschamps, a self-confessed occultist who in New Orleans, Louisiana, USA on 30 January 1889, raped and killed with chloroform 12-year-old Juliette Deitsche, a girl he had long abused; Dr Debra Green, an oncologist who on 24 October 1995 killed two of her three children in a fire at her home in Prairie Village, Kansas, USA and tried to poison her husband with ricin; Green Beret Dr Jeffrey MacDonald, who savagely beat and stabbed to death his 26-year-old pregnant wife and two young daughters in a frenzied attack on 17 February 1970, in Fort Bragg, North Carolina, USA; Dr Vladimir Pantchenko, a man paid by Mr Patrick O'Brien de Lacy to murder his brother-in-law Captain Vassilli Buturlin in order for de Lacy to inherit Buturlin's wealth. Dr Pantchenko killed Buturlin by injecting him with diphtheria toxin on 16 and 17 May 1910 in St Petersburg, Russia; Dr Ishii Shiro, a Japanese war criminal, who from August 1932 until the end of the Second World War, carried out medical experiments on Chinese, Korean and sometimes Western prisoners of war that were every bit as cruel and gruesome as those undertaken by the Nazis on their victims. Numerous other Japanese physicians were involved in attempting to develop biological weapons or better treatments of disease using human guinea pigs. Few were brought to justice after the war.

The list of deviant medical practitioners is by no means exhaustive. The stories of many others remain to be told.

A need to kill and have power over others as exemplified by Dr Shipman engenders a fear in many that other doctors, even the innocuous general practitioner, could betray our trust. Who knows, there may be others out there?

CHAPTER 1
Dr John Bodkin Adams: Got Away with Murder

DR JOHN BODKIN Adams was widely believed by police to be responsible for the death of upwards of 25 patients, yet not only did he allegedly 'get away with murder', he lived quietly and practiced medicine for many years thereafter. A portly Eastbourne GP and forger of prescriptions, Adams admitted prior to his trial to 'easing the passage' of patients who died in his care, an incredible 132 of whom mentioned him in their wills. How did it come about then that Dr Adams was able to escape justice, if in fact he was actually guilty?

Dr John Bodkin Adams was born on 21 January 1899 in Randalstown, County Antrim, Northern Ireland. His father, Samuel Adams, was a watchmaker, jeweller and lay preacher for the Plymouth Brethren and a local Justice of the Peace. His mother, Ellen Bodkin, was a shrewd businesswoman who invested her husband's modest income in property. The family soon prospered and in 1901 moved to Balinderry Bridge on the shores of Loch Neagh in County Tyrone. John had a younger brother, born in 1903, who died tragically of pneumonia 16 years later.

The family was strictly brought up in a God-fearing household and Adams always remained a Christian of the most upright and inflexible type throughout his life. Bodkin could never resist cakes or chocolate and soon became quite chubby, and as an adult became rather porcine.He rarely played with other children and became a 'mummy's boy', devoting himself to her completely until she died on 3 March 1943, leaving her son the tidy sum of £7,043.

At school Adams was not a particularly gifted pupil but he studied hard and secured a place at Queen's University Medical School, Belfast. There he socialised little, focusing entirely on his studies. It was hard for him to keep up with more brilliant, gifted colleagues and he soon suffered a nervous breakdown. Recovering, he graduated in 1921. A year later, after working as a house officer in a Bristol hospital, Adams joined a large practice in the English seaside town of Eastbourne, Sussex, as a junior partner to Drs Emerson and Gurney, earning half -a-crown (12.5p) for every home visit.

The practice Adams joined had advertised in an evangelical paper for a 'Christian young doctor-assistant with a view to partnership.' The practice had a lucrative private clientele in those pre-NHS days. Eastbourne, with a population of 70,000, was nicknamed the 'costa geriatrica', because of its preponderance of affluent retired people, predominantly women, attracted by the tranquillity of the town, its climate and attractive setting. Dr Adams settled in and progressed well. He had a reputation for hard work and began to work almost every night in an effort to build a clientele and reputation. By 1926 he gained a Doctorate in Philosophy, again from Queens, and later a Diploma in Anaesthetics. Despite such intellectual achievements, Adams was not always confident in his own ability and frequently called in specialists for second opinions. This helped reassure patients and made him popular with colleagues grateful for the fees.

In 1930 Adams was prosperous enough to buy a large villa, Kent Lodge, at 6 Trinity Trees, where he would live for the next half-century. The location was behind Eastbourne Grand Parade, conveniently only a few minutes from the Esperance Nursing Home. His by-now widowed mother and cousin Florence, came over from Ireland to keep house for him. In his home the deeply religious doctor would hold Bible classes on Sunday afternoons or instruct the local 'Crusaders'. He became joint chair of the YMCA, worshipped with the Plymouth Brethren and bought vestments for priests visiting the Esperance Nursing Home. A small, bespectacled man with grey-green eyes, only 5ft 5in tall (1.65m), the obese, jovial-looking doctor was piggy-eyed, with coarse hands and a double chin that drooped over his shirt collar. He was not in any way physically attractive and never married.

Dr Adams was dapper, with a penchant for expensive suits. He loved money but was no miser, just very careful. He never smoked, rarely drank and became a familiar sight in Eastbourne, travelling around for his first few years in town on a motorbike, looking somewhat out of place, given his portly figure.

Developing a passion for cars, four were in his garage at the time of his arrest, Dr Adams had an excellent bedside manner which charmed elderly patients and brought him into the affections of so many that he was soon receiving around £3,000 a year from grateful patients who had passed on. Not always did such bequests arrive without argument. In early 1936 Adams had to go to court when the niece, Amy Madge Horton, of one of his benefactors, Mrs Alice Whitton, contested a legacy of £3,000 he had received, claiming her aunt was 'not of sound mind' when changing her will in favour of Dr Adams. He won the case.

Early 1936 saw Adams engaged, to a Miss Norah O'Hara, daughter of Eastbourne's wealthiest butcher. It was not to last as Adams' mother looked down on her son's fiancée and quarrelled with her parents. Asked to choose between his mother and his intended, it was no contest. Adams sided with mummy and remained a confirmed bachelor. Other women were interested and, astonishingly, three swore they would never marry unless it was to him, despite his appearance. Possibly these women wanted to mother the Irish doctor – they could hardly have been attracted to him by animal magnetism!

The motive to kill for Adams was different from that of Shipman. He was as cold-blooded but not as compulsive a killer. Usually he murdered purely for modest financial gain.

* * *

Dr Adams was tried at the Old Bailey for the murder of Edith Alice Morrell, the 81-year-old widow of a Liverpool shipping merchant, six years earlier on 13 November 1950. There was considerable argument over which case should be brought. The prosecution brought this particular suit because they considered the evidence 'watertight' and that it would be 'open and shut'. The police were absolutely convinced of Adams' guilt but thought it would be hard to prove. Mrs Morrell's body had been cremated and so no forensic evidence could be provided and no corresponding experts brought to court to add their authority to the prosecution case. The Attorney General took the decision to try Adams on the Morell case because of what he considered 'overwhelming evidence', even without a body. It was a decision that even his junior counsel Mr Melford Stevenson expressed concern about.

Mrs Edith Morrell became a patient of Dr Adams on 5 July 1948. After suffering a stroke in Cheshire on 25 June that left her paralysed on her left side, she was driven by ambulance to an Eastbourne nursing home. Mrs Morell was moved frequently before she settled at Marden Ash, a house in Beach Head Road, on 30 March 1949.

Dr Adams wasted no time in introducing his new patient to morphine, on 9 July, and diamorphine (heroin) 12 days later. Mrs Morell was soon on the maximum daily dose of morphine, half-a-grain (7.8 grams), and a quarter grain of heroin, some 75% more than the maximum recommended. Over the next two years, Mrs Morell was calculated to have ingested 165 grains of morphine and 139.5 of heroin. It did not take long before Mrs Morell became seriously addicted. Needless to say, she was also wholly dependent on Dr Adams.

On 28 April 1949, Mr Hubert Sogno, Mrs Morell's solicitor, received a call from a 'rather anxious' Dr Adams who informed him that Mrs Morell wanted to change her will that very day. Visiting her, Sogno drew up a will that left £276 worth of dining-room silver to Dr Adams.

It was almost a year before Adams contacted Sogno again. On 8 March 1950, he arrived unannounced in the solicitor's office and informed him that Mrs Morell wanted to leave him a Rolls-Royce and jewellery box. Mr Sogno thought he should wait until the arrival of his client's son that weekend but Adams insisted that a codicil be added immediately. On 19 July a supplement to the will was added, leaving her house and chattels to Dr Adams if her son, Mr Claude Morell pre-deceased her. A further addition was made on 5 August leaving the Rolls to her GP again if Claude pre-deceased her.

On 12 September Dr Adams went on holiday. He would return four days later. In the meantime, Mrs Morell had acted swiftly to add another codicil on 15 September, this time cutting out Adams from her will. Resuming his vacation from 18-24 September it did not take long after his return to persuade the old, sick and ailing Mrs Morell to destroy the new codicil and, on 23 October, it was duly torn up. It was from this time forward that Mrs Morell began to decline rapidly, due no doubt to the ever-increasing quantity of drugs she now consumed. In the last five days of her life Mrs Morell allegedly consumed six grains of morphine by injection, 35 grains (90 tablets) of morphine and 37.75 grains (190 tablets) of heroin orally. It would be years before the exact circumstances of Mrs Morell's death would enter the public domain. In the meantime, Adams was free to kill again.

Sir Theobald Mathew, the Director of Public Prosecutions intended to try Adams for the murder of at least two other patients, Mr and Mrs Hullet, once a conviction was secured in the Morrell case. It did not happen but it was the deaths, within four months of each other, of Mr and Mrs Hullet that brought them and their GP to the attention of the police.

Mrs CJ 'Bobbie' Hullet became a patient of Dr Adams in 1950 after the death of her first husband, Mr Tomlinson. She was in her forties and an Eastbourne school head teacher. Deeply distressed by her husband's passing, Mrs Tomlinson allegedly declined physically and mentally. Dr Adams claimed credit for helping her and providing an introduction to Mr AJ 'Jack' T Hullet, a wealthy widower in his sixties. The couple soon married and remained patients of Dr Adams.

In November 1955, Mr Hullet had a serious operation and was nursed at home by his GP. On 13 March, he suffered a 'breathing attack' and Dr Adams was called. Arriving at 8.30pm Dr Adams put him to bed and at 10.30pm gave the patient an injection of hyperduric morphia. At 6.30am the following morning, Mr Hullet died in his sleep, leaving £700 to Adams and the rest of his fortune to Bobbie.

Widowed once more, Mrs Hullet was beside herself. Letters from April 1956 showed that she considered suicide but thought better of it. Dr Adams gave her sodium barbiturate, a normal dose of two tablets, 15 grains later reduced to 10, to help her sleep. On 19 July, suffering from a headache, Mrs Hullet took a massive dose of barbiturates at 10.00pm and fell into a coma. The following morning Adams visited and said he would 'let her sleep'. He drew the curtains but his patient slept on and he left. At 3.00pm Mrs Hullet's maid phoned Dr Adams to say she was worried. He could not attend but his colleague Dr RV Harris did. He diagnosed a cerebral haemorrhage. Told that Mrs Hullet was on sleeping pills, Harris asked Adams if a drug overdose was possible. Dr Adams replied that it was not.

Refusing to have his patient admitted to hospital, he stayed by her bedside injecting her with megamide, an known antidote to barbiturate. On Sunday 22 July he called the coroner to seek a private postmortem for his patient. The coroner thought this a surprising request, as Mrs Hullet was not yet dead!

But Mrs Hullet never emerged from her coma and died at 7.23am on Monday 23 July. Dr Harris refused to sign the death certificate and the coroner contacted the chief constable seeking an inquest. An autopsy revealed 115 grains of barbiturate in her body, despite no bottle being found by Mrs Hullet's bedside and Adams' categorical denials that his patient could possibly have stockpiled the drugs he had prescribed.

The tragic deaths of the Hullets had aroused suspicion. Mrs Hullet had left her estate of £137,302 to family and friends and her Rolls-Royce to Dr Adams, who had already benefited from a bequest from Mr Hullet. Mrs Hullet's will had only recently been drawn up, on 12 July, and executed five days before her overdose. A promise made by the late Mr Hullet to buy Adams a car had also been faithfully carried out, not by inclusion in the will but by Mrs Hullet writing her doctor a cheque for £1,000 on 17 July which he banked a day later. Adams had asked the bank to clear the cheque immediately. He was told it normally took three days. Adams asked for the cheque to be 'specially presented' so it would clear the following day. It was and it did. Had the cheque gone through the normal banking process it would not have cleared until 21 July. If Mrs Hullet had died before then, the cheque would not have cleared at all.

Friends of the Hullets included comedian Leslie Henson and the chief constable, Mr Richard Walker, a patient of Dr Adams himself, who began to make discreet enquiries into his GP. The doctor was found to have £125,000 in investments and £35,000 in his bank account.

The press were given a statement by the police and soon descended on Eastbourne. The inquest, held on 21 August, sought to find out the precautions Dr Adams had taken to ensure Mrs Hullet did not overdose on a drug that required only 50 grains to be lethal. Adams responded that Mrs Hullet had taken barbiturates he had not retrieved after her husband's death. He added that before going on his June holiday, he provided his suicidal patient with 36 tablets. His failure to provide suitable nursing care for Mrs Hullet, tell his partner of her depression or take any precautions, given her state of mind, were heavily criticised by the coroner, Dr AC Sommerville, who seemed to be aiming for an open verdict on the case, describing Dr Adams failure to contemplate barbiturate poisoning as 'extraordinary'. The jury declined to take the suggestion and returned a verdict of 'suicide.'

On 22 August 1956, the day following the inquest, the *Daily Mail* published a lurid tale of murder by poisoning of 'up to 400' wealthy patients in Eastbourne by Dr Adams over a 20-year period. Other newspapers picked up the story and soon the tubby Eastbourne GP was infamous throughout the UK as a serial poisoner. The *Daily Express*, perhaps to rile the *Daily Mail* or possibly because of a genuine belief in Adams' innocence, almost alone among the press, took the side of the beleaguered GP.

The police now began a full investigation. Detective chief superintendent Herbert Hannam of New Scotland Yard, detective sergeant Charles Hewitt and the local man, detective inspector Brynwel Pugh of Eastbourne Constabulary, made up the team. From the start, they believed Adams to be a monster, predator and murderer. In this they never wavered. That Dr Adams was a greedy 'legacy hunter' who actively pursued bequests from patients, there can be no doubt and he did not try to hide the fact. This may have made him unpleasant but not necessarily a killer.

The police searched for evidence against their suspect. They were soon amazed to find Adams a legatee in so many wills. Nonetheless, this was not proof of malice aforethought. Of the deceased, most had been cremated, destroying what evidence may or may not have existed. An astonishing 68% had died, according to the death certificates, primarily from cerebral thrombosis, a not unusual but hardly common end. It soon became clear that Adams was not very diagnostic-ally competent and may simply have misdiagnosed some of the illnesses from which his patients died. Negligent he certainly seemed but neither did this confirm him as a murderer.

On 1 October 1956, the three leading investigative officers interviewed Adams for the first of many times. On this occasion, the death of Mrs Morell was first raised. The police knew how much morphine and heroin Adams had prescribed but not the quantity injected. They hoped Adams would break, confess all and, if not, talk freely. He did not confess but he talked, talked and talked, occasionally bursting into tears. Adams said he had little use for money and that legacies were often in lieu of fees, although why his wealthy clientele did not always pay was not clarified. In any case, he could provide no details to confirm that fees were ever waived.

The suspect was forced to admit that he never divulged being a beneficiary of wills when signing cremation forms. Adams admitted to this saying: 'If I said I knew I was getting money under the will, they (the relatives) might get suspicious and I like cremations and burials to go smoothly.' This was a disclosure that revealed him as acting illegally. The police thought it significant at the time. In fact, the trial revealed it was standard practice among Eastbourne doctors in the 1950s. More damning for Adams was the revelation that he 'knew' Mrs Morell had left him her Rolls-Royce. Of course, she had not, but one could interpret this belief as a pecuniary motive for her murder, especially if Adams feared that his patient would change her mind and leave him nothing.

Frequently invoking the Bible, Adams denied regular usage of dangerous drugs such as opium and its derivatives. 'I very, very seldom ever use them', he said, contradicting himself by admitting to having given Mrs Morell 75 heroin tablets the day she died. As investigations proceeded, DCS Hannam soon discovered more and more about Adams' unsavoury money-grubbing and his possible victims.

Even in the 1930s it was rumoured that Adams walked around Eastbourne with a 'bottle of morphine in one hand and a blank legacy form in the other.' He prescribed highly addictive opiates to a host of elderly people who could then be manipulated by their unscrupulous dealer, Dr Adams. Once he was safely mentioned in a will, the patient could be relieved of any pain, stress, discomfort or their life by simply overdosing them. For the police, the difficulty in proving such a hypothesis was huge, many of the alleged 'victims', having simply ceased to exist following their cremation.

It had not always gone smoothly for Adams. Apart from the embarrassment caused by the Whitton case, he became increasingly arrogant and self-centred, causing him to make a serious miscalculation with his friends, the Mawhood's. Mr William Mawhood was a wealthy steel merchant who met Dr Adams in 1922 when the young doctor called to, unsuccessfully, set a broken leg. Mawhood took to Adams and became so friendly he loaned him £3,000 to buy his first home. Adams, as he did with many patients, would drop in unannounced at meal times and dine with William and his wife, Edith.

Mawhood introduced Adams to the 'country set' he socialised with and the doctor even accompanied him on pheasant shoots. As the friendship blossomed, Adams made numerous new well-heeled contacts ranging from landed gentry to patrons of the arts and successful business types, whom he happily added to his growing list of patients. With his partners now dead, Adams became the senior partner, recruiting three more doctors to what was now Eastbourne's most lucrative practice.

Years later, Adams would show how ungracious he was to the couple that had befriended him soon after his arrival in Eastbourne. As William Mawhood lay dying, Dr Adams asked Mrs Mawhood if he could be left alone with her husband. Suspicious, she listened at the door and heard Adams tell William to leave his estate to him and he would look after his wife. Outraged, Edith burst into the room and struck Adams with her brass-tipped walking stick, chasing him from her home. As he stumbled down the stairs, she threw the stick at him, missing but smashing a vase. Adams scurried for his car with Mrs Mawhood screaming at him never to set foot in her house again.

Dr Adams had behaved inappropriately and unprofessionally. At the very least he should have appeared before the General Medical Council (GMC). Undeterred, he continued to look for financial gain from his most vulnerable patients whenever possible.

Emily Mortimer originally intended to leave her assets to two nieces. The year she died, 1946, Mrs Mortimer changed her will to leave £3,000 in shares to Dr Adams. Shortly before her death on Christmas Eve, her nieces were cut out altogether, her entire estate of £5,000 being left to Dr Adams. Like most of Adams' patients, she too died of 'cerebral thrombosis', according to her death certificate.

One particularly sinister aspect was Adams' insistence that patients leaving him legacies stipulated specifically that they were to be cremated, not buried. Surely this was an attempt to destroy forensic evidence?

Nurse Osgood was looking after Mrs Annabelle Kilgour, a widow, in her home. As Mrs Kilgour had been feeling restless and unwell for several weeks, Dr Adams was called on the night of 27 December 1950. Before Nurse Osgood's very eyes a huge injection was administered, ostensibly so the patient could rest. 'This will keep you quiet', muttered Adams. It did. As he left, Mrs Kilgour fell into a coma and died the following day. Nurse Osgood accused Adams of killing her and he was terrified she would report him. He signed on Mrs Kilgour's death certificate that she died of 'cerebral haemorrhage'. The deceased bequeathed to Dr Adams some money and an antique clock.

A mere bought of flu could be fatal if consulting Dr Adams. Within a fortnight of doing so, in early 1951, Mrs Margaret Pilling fell into a coma. Her visiting daughter, Mrs Irene Richardson, was shocked to see her mother heavily drugged. After a showdown with Adams, she took her away to a house in Ascot and Mrs Pilling made a full recovery. Can there be any doubt as to her likely fate had Mrs Richardson not acted so?

Harriet Maud Hughes, a widow, was 66 when she died on 21 November 1951, as per usual from 'cerebral thrombosis', in the care of Dr Adams. A patient for only three months, she was seriously ill for weeks, recovering just long enough to visit the bank with Adams to enable the doctor to become executor of her will. The manager expressed some surprise at her choice but reluctantly agreed. She made two amendments to her will, one requesting cremation and bequeathing £1,000 to Dr Adams, another leaving £1,000 to a couple of friends of Adams, the Thurstons. It was a front. Adams kept 90% of the money left to the Thurstons and gave his friends a 10% 'commission' for use of their name.

Complaining of a pain in her stomach, sprightly 82-year-old Julia Bradnum called out Dr Adams on the morning of 27 May 1952. After five minutes alone with her GP she was dead, officially from 'cerebral haemorrhage'. A drug overdose was the probable cause. She had, needless to say, altered her will a few weeks earlier to benefit the doctor, following a previous visit when he apparently advised her the original was 'not legal'. Dr Adams asked Miss Mary Hine, a friend of Mrs Bradnum, to witness and sign the new will. When she tried to read it first he stopped her, insisting she simply sign and leave, which Miss Hine duly did.

Adams was named as Mrs Bradnum's sole executor in the will.

Mrs Lily Love, a niece of Mrs Bradnum, was very upset when her aunt died so suddenly, having been in good health and spirits only a few days previously and so, in the wake of Bobbie Hullet's death, she wrote to the chief constable to vent her suspicions. When the police exhumed Mrs Bradnum's body during their investigations into Adams, they were unable to identify the cause of death but ascertained it was not from a cerebral haemorrhage.

A Scottish spinster, Clara Neil-Miller, lived with her elder sister Hilda. Born only ten months apart, they moved to Eastbourne in 1940 following the death of their brother and last blood relative, residing in a residential home at 30 St John's Road. On 15 January 1953, Hilda died leaving everything to Clara. When Clara followed her on 22 February 1954, her estate of £5,000 went entirely to Dr Adams. When Clara's body was later exhumed she had not died of 'coronary thrombosis', as her death certificate stipulated, but pneumonia. This perplexed the police at first until they interviewed a Miss Welch, one of the guests at the rest home Miss Neil-Miller had lived and died in, who reported that Clara had suffered from influenza and called out Adams. He stayed with her for 45 minutes and left. The guest, on hearing no sound from her friend's room entered. There she was horrified to see, on a bitterly cold winter's night, her bed clothes pulled off, nightdress folded on her body to the neck and the windows of the room flung wide open to the elements. Miss Neil-Miller died the following morning. In the days before she died, Clara had made out two cheques to Dr Adams totalling £800.

Adams continued to hound his patients for legacies He was soon well known to bank managers and solicitors, visiting frequently when overseeing changes to wills. Once a patient had agreed, their lawyer was summoned forthwith. On one occasion, a near comatose patient, retired bank manager Mr John Priestly Downs, was so enfeebled he successfully signed with a cross only at the tenth attempt with Dr Adams guiding his hand. Mr Downs, a widower, had been a patient of Adams for only a month. Having suffered a fractured ankle after falling downstairs, he was left to his GP's tender mercies. Within two weeks of his accident, Mr Downs was in a drug-induced coma, emerging only briefly to alter his will in favour of Adams. A couple of weeks later, in May 1955, Mr Downs died, making his GP £1,000 richer.

During their investigations into Adams, the widowed sister-in-law of Clara Neil-Miller contacted the police. She had loaned the sisters money after her husband's death in 1940. The sisters were to preserve the capital, living off the interest, with the stipulation that the capital sum be returned to Mrs Neil-Miller upon their deaths. This did not happen. During the last year of Clara's life, her sister-in-law had sent 14 letters to her. None was ever answered. The police were able to confirm that the letters never arrived. The answer to the puzzle surely lay with the manager of Clara's residential home, Mrs Sharp. Only she could have been entrusted by Dr Adams to intercept mail and provide him with personal and financial details pertaining to her guests.

Mrs Elizabeth Sharp was duly questioned. After two interviews in which she appeared 'nervous and frightened', the police saw her as the key witness to Dr Adams' shenanigans. She knew much of what had gone on between Adams and his patients over the years and would be interviewed by DCS Hannam a third time when he returned from a week's conference with the Attorney General and Director of Public Prosecutions in London to discuss the case. Left to stew for a few days and consider her own position, the police were convinced Mrs Sharp would break. So, perhaps, did Dr Adams. In Hannam's absence, Mrs Sharp had 'taken ill', died and, on the express orders of Dr Adams, been cremated. The doctor, the police were convinced, had somehow got to and silenced a woman who could and would have incriminated him had she lived. It was a severe blow to Hannam but he pressed on, convinced he would soon have enough to hang his prey.

A search of Adams' surgery on 24 November at first revealed nothing and the doctor, who was present, denied having hidden anything about his person. In fact, he had taken and was carrying two bottles of hyperduric morphine. It looked very bad. Two days later, on Monday 26 November, Adams was arrested and charged the following morning with 13 relatively minor offences, including four false representations under the Cremation Act 1902. The immediate impact of this was that Adams was forced to surrender his passport. Interviewed again, Dr Adams used the phrase for which he would be come infamous: 'Easing the passing of a dying person is not all that wicked. Mrs Morell wanted to die. That cannot be murder.' Arrogantly, he added: 'It is impossible to accuse a doctor.' Here there was an admission that he deliberately killed his patient.

By 19 December 1956, the police had concluded their investigations. Adams was arrested at home and charged with murder. He responded: 'Murder? Murder? Can you prove it was murder? I do not think you can prove murder. She was dying in any event.' The interpretation of Adams' comments could be that he was more or less confessing, that he had indeed committed murder and was convinced no one could prove it or that he was shocked by the very suggestion. As he left with the police he remarked glumly to his receptionist: 'See you in heaven.'

In all, more than a dozen suspicious deaths were unearthed, with varying degrees of evidence pertaining to them. It would be for the Attorney General to consider which to pursue. As we have seen, he chose the Morell case.

On 14 January 1957, the Crown commenced committal proceedings against Dr Adams at Eastbourne on the charge of murdering Mrs Morell, also alleging that he murdered Mr and Mrs Hullet. Nine days later Adams was committed for trial at the Old Bailey for the murder of Mrs Morell.

Prior to commencement of the trial, the law on capital punishment was significantly amended. Passing into law on 21 March, four days into the Adams trial, the Homicide Act 1957 allowed for capital murder only in five categories. The cold-blooded poisoner was excluded, unless found guilty of two or more murders. Thus, Dr Harvey Hawley Crippen would not have hanged under such legislation. Adams would, but only if found guilty of murdering Mrs Morell and also one (or both) of the Hullets.

The trial opened on Monday, 18 March 1957. Lord Chief Justice Rayner Goddard normally presided over such cases but demurred and Sir Patrick Devlin (later Lord Devlin) was installed as trial judge. The Attorney General, Sir Reginald Manningham-Buller QC, MP (later Viscount Dilhorne) led for the prosecution, assisted by Mr Melford Stevenson QC and Mr Malcolm Morris. Mr Geoffrey Lawrence QC, assisted by Mr Edward Clarke, defended. Lasting 17 days, it was to be the longest murder trial ever held at the Old Bailey. The only time Adams said anything at the trial was to plead, 'Not guilty'.

In his opening address of just under two hours, Manningham-Buller asked the jury to first ignore press reports regarding Dr Adams. He then posed the rhetorical question as to why a stroke victim like Mrs Morell would be given not just sleeping draughts, but also morphine and heroin, two powerful and potentially lethal painkillers when she suffered no pain? The quantities of drugs involved were truly massive: 2,194 grains of barbiturates, 1,400 of sedomid, 171 of morphine and 145 of heroin in the five months before Mrs Morell's death. The quantity of opiates would peak in the last few days of Mrs Morell's life. Why if not to induce murder? The motive: financial gain by the accused. The Attorney General held up a syringe to dramatically convey the method used to murder Mrs Morell. The prosecution announced that the standard maximum dose of morphia was a quarter of a grain, yet only two days before her death her GP administered 18 grains, 72 times that amount. Adams must have known such a dose would be fatal. He was guilty as charged and the Crown would prove it!

First to testify were the chemists who supplied Dr Adams with the morphine and heroin that killed Mrs Morell. Four witnesses gave evidence, none of which was disputed by the defence. Its significance was the sheer volume of drugs dispensed to Dr Adams for the treatment of Mrs Morell in the last five days of her life, 79.5 grains of morphine and heroin, all dispensed by HR Browne, chemists, and signed for by the accused. The prosecution had to prove that injecting so much opiate would be lethal to Mrs Morell and that all of it was injected. To do so, the testimonies of 'on the spot' witnesses were required.

Sister Bartlett, sister Mason-Ellis, nurse Randall and nurse Stronach had looked after Mrs Morell in shifts, night and day, in the weeks leading up to her death. Over two days, the first to testify, nurse Stronach, explained that she and her colleagues had witnessed the tragic demise of Mrs Morell. Over a period of only six weeks, Dr Adams, in the quantities mentioned by Manningham-Buller in his opening address, had prescribed that elderly lady a vast amount of drugs. Nurse Stronach explained that whoever was on duty injected Mrs Morell with around a quarter of a grain of morphine at around 9.00pm. Later, around 11.00 pm, Dr Adams called and injected his patient with something, although she knew not what.

As well as the 18-grain dose on 11 November 1950, the prosecution contended that eight grains of morphine were injected on 8 November and 12 on the ninth as Adams steadily built up to a lethal dose. The short-term outcome of ingesting so many narcotics was, the nurse witnesses agreed, that Mrs Morell was permanently doped up, weak and rarely conscious, occasionally slipping 'in and out of a coma'. Such evidence appeared damning and, at even this early stage, a conviction seemed inevitable. The doctor's tenacious counsel thought otherwise. Although he loathed the man on trial, Lawrence was determined to provide his client with the best possible defence.

The nurses themselves apparently recorded in notebooks everything that occurred during Mrs Morell's final days. Unfortunately, they no longer had them or any clue as to their whereabouts. Teasingly, Mr Lawrence, cross-examining, lamented this. He then provided, to the amazement of the court, those very notebooks and thus the written record of Mrs Morell's treatment, not just as she was dying, but from 21 June 1949 until her death.

No one knew from where the eight record books of Mrs Morell's treatment had emerged and it was not revealed at the trial. In fact, Adam's legal team found them in his office. One might suppose that the books would aid the prosecution, as details of the drugs that ended the life of Mrs Morell were now available to the court. That Mr Lawrence presented such details was a clear statement that his client had nothing to hide. The police were made to look fools. They had a search warrant, the notes in question were labelled 'M' for Morell and in spite of that, the notebooks had not been found by them.

During further cross-examination of the nurses, Mr Lawrence revealed that in accessing their records, he was able to show that the quantities of drugs administered by Adams were nowhere near the amounts the witnesses stipulated. He also showed the jury written reports, signed and dated by the nurses that, contrary to memory, Mrs Morell had not slipped 'in and out of a coma' but sometimes 'sat upright, ate her breakfast and chatted'.

On day four of the trial, nurse Randall told the court how Dr Adams had given 5cc of the hypnotic paraldehyde to Mrs Morell on the night she died. Referring again to the notebooks, she conceded that when Dr Adams was on holiday in Scotland that September, Dr Harris had attended and actually increased the dose of morphine. She then admitted to not knowing the normal dose of paraldehyde, which was 5-10cc according to the British pharmacopoeia, and that she had erred when stating a few minutes previously that Mrs Morell had slipped 'in and out of a coma'.

In the witness box the nurses were forced to admit, with the notebooks before them, that they had given false testimony on a host of matters, including their recollections as to the physical and mental state of Mrs Morell in her dying days. No one doubted their integrity, but more than six years had elapsed and human memory is fallible. When confronted by book entries in their own hand-writing indicating that Adams was not the only person to inject Mrs Morell with drugs other than morphine, as surse Stronach had stated (all the nurses had injected Mrs Morell), it was clear the nurses' muddled statements would serve only to strengthen the defence.

Nurse Randall finished her evidence at midday on Friday, 22 March. She was followed later that day by the youngest of the nurses, Bartlett, who said little of impact. The last of the four was sister Mason-Ellis who could not detail, any more than her colleagues, what had happened to the drugs prescribed but not confirmed as given to the patient. For the outcome, it did not matter. The nurs-es, and more significantly the Attorney General, were forced to agree that the drugs detailed in the notebooks alone were used to treat Mrs Morell. While there would be conjecture as to what Dr Adams may or may not have done with the drugs prescribed but not used to treat Mrs Morell, it had no impact on the trial.

Cracks had appeared in the prosecution case. Despite this, the Crown believed that when Adams took the stand he would be destroyed under cross-examination. Many defendants insistent upon taking the stand to clear their name only succeeded in talking themselves onto the scaffold or into life imprisonment. Geoffrey Lawrence was more shrewd and refused to let his client hang himself, a wise move as Adams was by this time a frightened wreck and probably unlikely to withstand much pressure. The prosecution had clearly failed to anticipate this standard legal tactic. Banking on cross-examination to the exclusion of much else, they toiled. Still, they did have another ace to play. Mrs Morell's solic-itor was called to the stand.

Mr Hubert Sogno was a prime witness for the prosecution and informed the court Mrs Morell retained him from 1947 until her death. She apparently enjoyed making and changing her will and did so twice before becoming a patient of Dr Adams. Mr Sogno testified to the frequent comings and goings regarding Dr Adams, and the doctor's promptings to make changes that would benefit him. Nevertheless, after all the additions and deletions, Dr Adams' share of Mrs Morell's estate was £276 worth of silver, a mere fraction of the £157,000 she had left. True, the Rolls-Royce and other items had been left to Adams but only if Claude Morell died before the GP, an unlikely occurrence. The benevolence of Mrs Morell toward her doctor was modest compared to bequests made to her chauffeur of £1000, gardener £500, six charitable legacies ranging from £100 to

£1000 and three further personal gifts of £1000.

Mr Sogno's evidence had the effect of increasing the contempt of those who saw Dr Adams as a legacy hunter while filling them with puzzlement and doubt as to whether he would have committed murder for the trifling sum he inherited. Of course, Adams may have been under the impression that he was indeed to inherit the Rolls and much else besides.

As the police witnesses prepared to give testimony, a shot was fired across the prosecution's bow. Mr Lawrence made it clear that he would, on behalf of his client, tolerate no reference to other cases pending. Thus chastised, the Attorney General proceeded.

The police evidence was convincing, as they quoted from the mouth of Adams himself. The accused was portrayed as shaken and frightened. As a result he had proved incautious when arrested, the court being reminded of his seemingly incriminating comments at the time. Adams' response that day was portrayed almost as a gesture, not of defiance but surrender, as he imploringly asked an honest, open question. To the police, he was not making a rhetorical statement. Mr Lawrence disputed the police interpretation, the discussion ended inconclusively and the trial moved on.

In all such trials, expert medical opinion is vital to aid the prosecution of a case. In the Adams trial Dr Arthur Henry Douthwaite provided it. Dr Douthwaite was in his sixties, tall, handsome, courteous and possessed of considerable gravitas. He was recognised as the expert of his day on opiates. In evidence, Dr Douthwaite made it clear that opiates should never be used to treat a stroke victim unless severe pain was present and only one injection should be administered. Combination therapy using morphine and heroin was particularly detrimental to a sick patient's recovery, with probable side effects ranging from constipation to pneumonia. Addiction was the most obvious side effect. Douthwaite concluded that Mrs Morell's treatment was totally unjustified, addiction a certainty and the dosage administered, even if not the 79.5 grains announced by the Attorney General, could only have been given with the intention of killing the patient.

The notebooks revealed that on Mrs Morell's last five days of life, Dr Adams gave her less opiate than the nurses recalled or, was prescribed or witnessed. Even so, it still amounted to 10.5 grains of morphine and 16 of heroin. Dr Douthwaite again reiterated that, in his opinion, only the pursuit of murder could have led to the administration of such doses over that time period.

In counter-attacking, Mr Lawrence used Douthwaite's integrity to serve his client. Douthwaite was forced to agree that other doctors could deduce that Dr Adams did not intend murder and was merely looking out for the interests of his patient, reducing her distress and discomfort. Cleverly, Mr Lawrence had introduced 'reasonable doubt.'

The second doctor for the Crown, Dr Michael Ashby, was a consultant neurologist. He did not help the prosecution case much. Contradicting Dr Douthwaite, Ashby agreed with the defence assertion that Mrs Morell could have died of 'natural causes', albeit brought on by drugs she had been prescribed.

Calling his own witness, Mr Lawrence introduced a Dr John B Harman, a consultant physician from St Thomas' Hospital, London, who saw no link between the doses administered to Mrs Morell and her death. Dr Harman said he was 'not prepared to condemn' the doses of morphine administered to Mrs Morell adding that, as she had by her death become addicted, it would do more harm for her to endure the misery of withdrawal than take it until death. The defence noted that Mrs Morell had been given 5cc of paraldehyde on the night she died, to aid her suffering. Dr Douthwaite had earlier described such a dose as 'colossal'. Harman responded by saying: 'I never give less than 6cc'. To him, 5cc was 'not a large dose', and paraldehyde, 'a very safe drug'. His devastating riposte to the case against Dr Adams was that, as far as the death of Mrs Morell was concerned, he saw 'no necessity to link her death with the doses administered'. To Harman, the old lady's death had come principally from old age. The prosecution strongly counter-attacked but could not discredit or discomfit him, despite his inexperience with opiates. The defence brought no further evidence of importance and now rested.

In his closing speech, Mr Lawrence spoke for a man who invoked his right to silence. That Adams did not take the stand was a wise move, given how talkative he was when interviewed by the police. Adams did not take the stand counsel explained, 'because he had no case to answer'. A picture was presented of an innocent man deeply shaken by the ordeal of spending months in prison, 'day after day and night after night'. Dr Adams had no notebooks to illuminate the court with, nor recollections of a patient now long dead, the memory of whom had since faded. To Lawrence, the picture of his client risking all to murder a woman on the edge of death for a modicum of silver was 'too ludicrous'. He made it plain that the accused had given Mrs Morell opiates, 'not to ease pain or confuse her with wickedness in mind', but to compassionately enable the troubled, restless woman to sleep quietly and without distress. As for the quantity of drug used, Dr Adams 'could not know' the exact amount required to ease his patients suffering. The defence had become one of incompetence rather than malice aforethought.

It was after 3pm on Friday, 5 April when the Attorney General rose to speak. Turning to the jury, he began almost apologetically, suggesting that, 'It is not my duty ... to persuade you by my words of the guilt of the accused.' He then asked the jury to look on the evidence fairly to enable them to conclude that the death of Mrs Morell 'was secured by the deliberate acts of the accused'. As it was now late, he broke off his speech to resume the following week.

Manningham-Buller continued speaking the following Monday when the trial resumed. The evidence of Dr Harman was criticised and he postulated as to why the nurses had kept notebooks, which as they contained no incriminating entries, was by then a side-issue. It was the difference between what was recorded as injected on the one hand, which he appeared to accept during the trial, and the quantities prescribed and, he believed, administered in total, that was key for Attorney General. In this he tried to 'gild the lily' somewhat. The doses recorded and admitted had been enough to kill Mrs Morell, so exhausting this point may have served the purpose of showing Adams more strongly as a killer but placed an intolerable burden of proof on the prosecution. As any doctor of Adams' undoubted experience would have known that the drugs he administered on record would kill, he would have to be very foolish to take the further risk of obtaining drugs directly from the chemist to inject unseen.

Mr Lawrence could have objected to the Attorney General's line of attack but chose not to. In those days, until 1964, the prosecution had the last word in closing speeches and Manningham-Buller tried to take full advantage but he proved singularly unconvincing to the jury when his contribution was compared to that of Judge Devlin who followed him.

The summing up took three-and-a-half hours. The jury were told to ignore gossip and address the facts. As in all cases, the burden of proof lay with the prosecution and guilt had to be proven, 'beyond reasonable doubt'. In detail Judge Devlin explained that, if in response to a point made by the prosecution, the defence was able to advance an acceptable reason why the accused had acted in a particular way, the point in question could not be used to convict. He did add that if the defence had not contradicted prosecution evidence, for example the police evidence, then the jury must take it fully on board. The jury were also reminded that even if all of them considered Adams 'a rogue and a fraud', it did not make him a murderer. The jury had to agree that the prosecution had proven Mrs Morell had died an, 'unnatural' death, was killed by an act of murder and that it was Dr Adams intent to murder her.

The judge also told the jury 'as a matter of law' that 'there is no evidence on which you would properly come to the conclusion that any drugs were administered over and above the injections recorded in the nursing notebooks.' At a stroke, the evidence of nurse Stronach et al and Manningham-Buller's main thrust, could thus be safely disregarded. In most cases the judge is not a neutral spectator as the layperson might suppose. He leans towards one side or the other, more often than not the Crown. In this case it was clear that the Lord Chief Justice favoured acquittal, stating, 'Here the case for the defence seems to me to be manifestly strong.' Taking into account only the evidence before them and the judge's direction, the jury felt almost compelled to acquit and this they did in 44 minutes. On that day, 9 April 1957, Adams was discharged.

* * *

Years later Sir Melford Stevenson, as he became, still rued that Adams had 'gotten away.' The prosecution had, apparently, an 'absolute mountain' of material with which to cross-examine Adams. It was the gamble that Lawrence took in refusing to let his client take the stand that swung the case. In that regard, one must ask how it serves the public that a defendant cannot be cross-examined on statements made to the police, but the officer to whom he has given evidence can be cross-examined on that same piece of evidence.

The Attorney General acted immediately to bring proceedings for contempt against the importers and distributors of *Newsweek*, who had published an issue he considered might have prejudiced the jury unfairly against Dr Adams. It was hardly something that concerned the public. Across the country, the outcome of the trial caused widespread astonishment and anger. It was widely believed that Adams had got away with murder. In the House of Commons, Labour MP for Dudley, Mr George Wigg, raised the issue of Adams' acquittal on 15 April. Less than a week had elapsed since the trial and there was still extensive public shock and indignation that Dr Adams had unjustly escaped a life sentence and, had other cases been successfully pursued, the drop.

Mr Wigg asked the Attorney General if he would institute an enquiry into the 'conduct, preparation and organisation' of the prosecution. 'No', was the rather terse reply.

The government was clearly embarrassed at the outcome of the trial and Her Majesty's Loyal Opposition, once again in the person of Mr Wigg, raised the matter again on 1 May. Sir Manningham-Buller was questioned on: 'Whether he was aware that ... the case of Dr Adams has evoked discussion in terms which bring discredit upon the law and upon his office?' Other Labour MPs joined in the fray and the Attorney General was forced to defend his position during the ensuing two-hour debate.

The trial outcome was not at stake in the House of Commons. The Career of Manningham-Buller was. Speaking last, he defended his refusal to prosecute in the Hullet cases as he believed to do so would 'prejudice a fair trial' for Dr Adams. This would occur as some of the doctor's unpleasant, if irrelevant, characteristics could emerge and might be given undue weight by the jury. Normally a judge would rule on the admissibility of such information.

Why had he prosecuted in the Morell case anyway, when the police had the bodies of 11 other potential victims, none of whom had been cremated? 'System' was given as a significant reason for the choice of case. By this, what is meant is that evidence of system can be brought forward if a clear similarity can be shown between a crime for which an individual is charged and another that is 'strikingly similar'. The Attorney General argued that use of system in the Adams case would preclude a fair trial. Others might consider that a pattern of killing would appear, strengthen the Crown's case, leading to the conviction of a heartless killer who preyed on vulnerable old people, usually women. In choosing to act in the way he did, Manningham-Buller had weakened the prosecution, even if for the best of motives. He survived politically and eventually became Lord Chancellor.

The police were profoundly dismayed at the trial outcome. Despite their disappointment, there were plenty of other people who they believed Adams had murdered and another trial was expected to follow swiftly. Two more charges had been prepared and three other cases would soon be ready. However, embarrassed by the shambolic handling of the Morrell case, the Director of Public Prosecutions decided no more would be brought, despite the protests of Mr Melford Stevenson among many. The risk of another acquittal was just too great a danger for the authorities to face, with their prestige so greatly dented already. Instead, Adams would be charged with fraud.

On 30 June, Adams resigned from the National Health Service. On 26 July 1957, three months after his acquittal for murder, he was tried at Lewes Assizes on the 13 charges brought on 26 November the previous year. As well as those mentioned previously, they ranged from failing to keep adequate patient records to forging NHS prescriptions. The prosecution and defence counsels were veterans of Dr Adams' previous trial. Mr Melford Stevenson led for the prosecution, Mr Edward Clarke, the defence. Mr Justice Pilcher presided.

At the very least the police thought that Adams would be struck off, gaoled and therefore unable to drug and kill any more patients. They had carried out a huge investigation dating back ten years and provided a vast array of evidence. The defence argued only a few points, for example, the fact that few, if any, doctors were named routinely, if at all, as legacy beneficiaries on cremation certificates. Referring to a case that could not be raised during the murder trial, Mr Stevenson mentioned the case of Mr Downs, the patient who had died after signing his will with a cross after the doctor had badgered Mr Downs' solicitor to ensure he was mentioned in his patient's will. Yes, other doctors did not like to be named as will beneficiaries on cremation certificates. None of them actively pursued legacies with the determination, doggedness and sheer effrontery of Dr John Bodkin Adams.

Pleading guilty, Adams was fined £2400 and ordered to pay costs. Subsequently struck off the register by the GMC, he was not imprisoned as the judge took into account the time Adams already served on remand leading up to his murder trial.

No attempt was made to charge him with medical negligence, manslaughter or culpable homicide for the numerous patients he had killed through incompetence, even if one could believe him 'innocent' of murder.

On 4 September, Adams' authority to prescribe under the Dangerous Drugs Act was rescinded by the Home Office. However, this was not the end of the medical career of Dr John Bodkin Adams as a doctor removed from the register could still practice medicine; he simply could not declare himself qualified. Returning to Eastbourne, Dr Adams continued to work in private practice, with many former patients remaining on his books.

The Eastbourne public were divided. Some saw Adams as a man wronged, others that he had got away with the most heinous of crimes. As Adam's struggled to rebuild his reputation, he assisted poor patients for free and spent long hours helping out at a local hospital for no charge. He even loaned out the former Hullet Rolls-Royce to transport Eastbourne's Carnival Queen around town. It was held that: 'Many people wouldn't say a thing against Dr Adams.'

The reception Adams received from former colleagues was less welcoming. Few wanted anything to do with him and he was routinely cold-shouldered. To doctors, whose vocation was degraded by the accusations against Adams, he was considered an 'oafish bore', a 'disgrace to the profession' and 'simply inept.'

Inexplicably, especially to the friends and relatives of those he allegedly murdered, on 22 November 1961 the GMC readmitted Adams to the medical register, although the Home Office refused him a licence to dispense dangerous drugs.

Newspapers who accused Adams of having committed murder were now liable under the libel laws. In 1961 the Daily Mail apologised to him and withdrew all accusations after forking out an undisclosed sum. Up to and including 1969, Adams received monies from a number of publications that had offended against his 'good' name.

When the heat of publicity eventually dissipated, it was business as usual for Adams. A plaque was displayed outside his home advertising when patients and friends could drop by for 'sherry and conversation.' His medical practice prospered and legacies still occasionally came in. In May 1965, for example, he received a bequest for £2000.

Dr Adams cocked a snook at the authorities and retired in comfort to enjoy his ill-gotten gains while the police fumed on the sidelines, convinced their man had murdered repeatedly and never had to face the consequences. Adams led a lonely existence in his twilight years and eventually died peacefully at the ripe old age of 84 on 5 July 1983. He left an estate valued at £402,970 and 47 surviving friends and patients who loyally stood by him for more than a quarter of a century were the recipients of Dr Adams' own will and testament.

It has been speculated that it was possibly the murderous career of Adams that persuaded Dr Shipman that he too could get away with murder.

CHAPTER 2
Dr Karl Brandt: Life Unworthy of Life

*'Euthanasia is nothing more than a higher degree of humanity, the
highest level of human ethics, the strongest expression of the affir-
mation of life.'*

Dr Karl Brandt.

IN 1939, SEVENTY-five per cent of all doctors in Hitler's Germany were members of the Nazi Party. No other profession, social or economic group was so committed to the National Socialist cause. Why?

In 1933, Germany's Jewish community numbered somewhat less than 1%
of a population of 65 million, yet around 16.5% of all doctors were Jewish. While
a tribute to the educational attainment and professionalism of this talented
minority, such success bred jealousy, resentment and hatred among those who
saw the Jews as blocking the path to their own advancement, especially at a time
when many doctors were unemployed and found it hard to establish their own
practices or be accepted into one.

The Nazis offered a solution. By forcing Jewish doctors to treat only other
members of the small Jewish population, leading inevitably to the impoverishment and emigration of many Jewish doctors, millions of potential patients
became available to 'Aryan' practitioners, many of whom greedily swooped on
the large and lucrative practices reluctantly abandoned by their Jewish compatriots. In hospitals and universities, professorships, consultancies and other specialist posts were freed up by the departure of Jews, often leading to rapid promotion
for those who would otherwise have waited years or were unworthy on grounds
of merit alone.

At the same time as the Jews were being swept from their former bastions in
German medicine, the virulent Nazi ideology of Nordic Aryan racial superiority
gained ground quickly in the medical profession. 'Racial science', in which
alleged anthropological differences were blamed or credited with ethnic vices or
virtues, became highly respected in Germany. Eugenics, with supporters on the
left and right of the political spectrum in Europe and the USA, became the
orthodox political and medical belief system in Germany, as most illnesses were
considered to have a strong hereditary basis.

Eugenics, from the Greek 'well born' is a philosophy which was founded by

Sir Francis Galton in 1859 that seeks to improve human hereditary qualities, encouraging selective breeding of people based on positive attributes, or weeding out defects by discouraging 'defective' humans from reproducing. People deemed intellectually and physically 'valuable' according to eugenic principles, should be encouraged to have more children. Those considered 'inferior', such as the mentally or physically disabled, including deaf and blind people, should be discouraged or prevented from raising families. Gradually, as humanity improved in quality, hereditary defects would disappear and there would be less pain, misery and suffering in the world.

Eugenics was considered ideologically mainstream in the early 20th century. Alexander Graham Bell, the Scot who invented the telephone advocated that deaf people should not be allowed to marry or procreate, for fear of producing a 'deaf human race'.

The Nazi leadership believed the proportion of Germany's population suffering from inherited disease to be growing, threatening ultimately the health of the entire nation. Excluding ethnic groups deemed 'inferior' by the regime from sexual contact with Aryans became a cornerstone of Nazi policy. Jews and Gypsies were foremost among 'ethnic pollutants' to be dealt with. However, the Nazis were determined to weed out even 'racial' Germans who suffered from 'hereditary feeble-mindedness', a policy that ultimately resulted in the mass murder of thousands of Germany's weakest, most defenceless and vulnerable citizens.

Karl Rudolf Brandt was a German physician whose career rose meteorically in the Nazi years. Born in Muhlhausen, Alsace, on 8 January 1904 while that province was still part of Germany (1871-1919), he was the son of a Prussian army major. Having received his gymnasium diploma, the highly intelligent Brandt studied medicine at Jena, Freiburg, Munich and Berlin, where he graduated in 1928. Obtaining his medical licence on 1 July 1929, Brandt worked as an intern at Bergmannsheil hospital in the Ruhr industrial town of Bochum.

An enthusiastic supporter of the revolutionary nationalism promoted by Hitler, Dr Brandt joined the Nationalsozialistische Deutsche Arbeiterpartei (National Socialist German Workers Party or NSDAP) as the Nazis were formally called, on 1 March 1932 as member number 1,009,617. However, he was no 'paper' member, becoming active almost immediately and he soon headed the Bochum branch of the Reichsschutzbund (Realm Protection League) and the Sturmabteilung (Stormtroopers or SA) soon after.

In appearance Brandt did not particularly stand out from the crowd. Tall and slim with dark hair and eyes, like so many Nazis Brandt was anything but the blonde and blue-eyed 'Nordic' ideal. He was first noticed when treating Hitler's adjutant Wilhelm Bruckner and niece Geli Raubal, who was soon to commit suicide, following a car accident. By July 1934 Brandt was a member of the Schutzstaffel (Protection Squad or SS), with the position of Untersturmführer (second lieutenant) rapidly gaining promotion to Sturmbannführer (major). Formed initially to safeguard Hitler at rallies, the SS was a force that quickly evolved into a powerful security police organisation with the role of actively repressing enemies of the regime.

In 1934 Brandt also became 'escort physician' to Hitler. As the Führer's personal doctor, Brandt gained regular promotion in future years and was a frequent visitor, with his beautiful wife Anni, to the Führer's alpine retreat in the Obersalzberg, the Berghof. There he made many powerful friends not least of which was the grandiosely titled Reichsführer SS, Heinrich Himmler, who would one day save his life.

Many years later, while in American custody, Brandt wrote an amusing paper called *Women around Hitler* for his captors. In it, Brandt suggested that the Führer did not marry until the war was lost in order to 'keep the mystic legend alive in the hearts of the German people that so long as he remained a bachelor there was always the chance that any one of the millions of German women might attain the high distinction of being at his side.' In 1934, Hitler even announced in front of his mistress, Eva Braun, that, 'the greater the man, the more insignificant should be the woman.' Brandt believed their relationship was more like father and daughter than that of lovers. She was completely subservient to Hitler but, according to Brandt, treated her own sister 'like a personal maid'.

In 1935 Brandt transferred from Bochum to the Surgical University Clinic, Berlin, as an assistant medical director. At this time he also based himself at the SS-Hauptamt (SS Main Office).

Karl Brandt never 'personally' killed anyone. Unlike some 200 or more German physicians and psychiatrists, he would not experiment, dissect, inject or torture his victims. He was a Schreibtischmorder (desk murderer) – a man who fully participated in the Holocaust and Nazi euthanasia programme, yet who seldom came directly face to face with the countless victims of policies and procedures he enthusiastically supported and ensured were implemented.

In the winter of 1939, in a letter to Hitler's Chancellery, Herr and Frau Knauer, the parents of a deformed baby boy, explained the burden their family suffered from having to raise a defective child and asked that he be 'put to sleep'. It was not an isolated case. The Fuhrer received many such communications, urging that action be taken to relieve families of relatives who were an encumbrance.

Euthanasia is the painless termination of a patient's life with his/her consent. Also known as 'mercy killing', it is sanctioned in societies where it is believed to be more humane to let someone end their life if suffering from an incurable, distressing and agonising disease than let them endure without the possibility of a cure. Euthanasia as the Nazis understood it, was about eliminating people considered inferior, usually without any humane considerations whatsoever, for ideological and/or economic reasons. Euthanasia was a Nazi misnomer, a euphemism for murder. The victims were not terminally ill and most suffered no pain from their disabilities.

Hitler responded 'positively' to those who implored the implementation of a euthanasia programme. Dr Brandt was sent to Leipzig to see if the Knauers were telling the truth. Meeting the doctors who cared for the Knauer child, who was blind, had only one leg, part of an arm and was an 'idiot', he sought their opinion. As the Leipzig doctors could see no reason for preserving the 'creature's' existence, Brandt gave permission for the boy's life to be terminated. Hitler had given express instructions that the parents were not to feel guilty nor be subject to prosecution then or later for what had happened. Any legal proceedings that might arise would be quashed.

A Pandora's Box had been opened and soon party ideologues and fanatics would win an argument that had raged in the Nazi Party for years regarding euthanasia – that it should be implemented in full across Germany and, where necessary, without the consent of the families concerned. Support for killing disabled people had strong roots in Germany, especially in the scientific and medical community. In 1920, the legal scholar Karl Binding and psychiatrist Alfred Hoche had published their polemic entitled *Die Freigabe der Vernichtung Lebensunwerten Lebens* (Permission for the Destruction of Life Unworthy of Life). Millions, they argued, had died in the Great War and Germany no longer had the resources necessary to maintain the futile existence of incurably ill people.

In 1929, Hitler had made his views on euthanasia plain at the Nuremberg Rally. There he made it clear that if '700,000 or 800,000 of our weakest babies were destroyed at birth each year, then the remaining 200,000 might even make Germany stronger.' In 1931, Dr Hermann Simon of Guttersloh asylum defined the categories he, and the Nazis, deemed inferior. These included the insane, the physically handicapped and the 'imbecile'. Dr Simon was of the stark view that such people 'must die', not least because of their 'drain' on the resources of the Reich.

Others took an apposite stance. At a meeting of Bavarian psychiatrists in Munich, Professor Oswald Bumke accurately foretold a future under the Nazis when the 'logical consequences' of prioritising 'economic considerations' before ethical or humane reflection would mean the destruction not only of the crippled and mentally sick but disabled veterans, the elderly and anyone else deemed 'unproductive'.

Hitler had advocated killing the mentally ill in his earlier manifesto, *Mein Kampf* (My Struggle) written in Munich's Landsberg prison where Karl Brandt would one day hang. After taking power in 1933, Hitler prophesied that, should war break out, he would use it as cover to destroy the most helpless people in

Germany without he erroneously hoped, 'too much trouble' from the churches.

On 14 July 1933 the Gesetz zur Verhutung Erbranken Nachwuchses (Law for the Prevention of Hereditary Diseased Progeny) was passed, allowing for the sterilisation of those deemed genetically 'unfit' to reproduce. On 18 October 1935 the Gesetz zum Schutz der Erbgezundheit des Deutshcen Volks (Law to protect the genetic health of the German People) was passed. Known as the Ehegesundheitsgesetz (Marriage Health Law), this prevented marriage between a couple if either of them suffered from hereditary disease or mental illness. Before his or her wedding, prospective partners had to present a Marriage Fitness Certificate, showing no defective ancestry. This law built on earlier legislation to sanction the compulsory sterilisation of those believed to suffer from genetic disease, such as Huntingdon's Chorea, schizophrenia and idiocy.

Between 1934 and 1945, over 400,000 Germans were sterilised, decisions on their future being taken by a judge and two doctors in absentia. Those doctors could be from any medical discipline. Some 220 Hereditary Health Courts were established across Germany to carry out this work. A third of those sterilised were psychiatric patients, the rest 'socially worthless' people such as criminals, chronic alcoholics, the 'work shy' and people considered 'slow witted'. As with the euthanasia programme that came later, categories were catch-all and corralled people with no family history of congenital illness whatsoever. Many of those sterilised were discovered after the war to be completely 'normal' in every sense.

From 1933, a register of disabled individuals had been compiled, including those committed to institutions or special schools. There were also denunciations of people suspected of qualifying for the register, often by people who did so for base reasons, such as personal animosity. In 1934-35 alone, 388,400 people were identified, 80% of them by doctors, nurses, teachers and social workers. Ultimately, the goal was to have a eugenic register for the entire German population. Had Germany won the Second World War, no doubt the relatives of disabled people would also have found themselves subject to stringent laws that initially encouraged the sterilisation and ultimately led to the deaths of tens of thousands.

The Nazis wanted to create Volksgemeinschaft (National Unity), by eliminating all who did not conform to their ideals. From the beginning, excluded categories included the Jews, Gypsies and the physically and mentally handicapped. As the regime became more extreme others were marked down for destruction. Hitler was concerned that the Catholic church would cause difficulties if euthanasia was implemented on the scale he supported. An academic thesis, known as the Meinung (opinion) was written by Joseph Mayer, Professor of Philosophical Theology at the Catholic University of Paderborn suggesting that there would be no church opposition, thus emboldening the Führer.

The outbreak of war on 1 September 1939 signalled the ratchetting up of euthanasia in Germany. That very day Hitler signed the Euthanasie-Erlass (Euthanasia Decree). This instructed asylum directors to send a registration form for each patient in order for a panel of gutacher (experts) to decide who should be killed. Meanwhile, after the conquest of Poland was rapidly accomplished, Dr Karl Brandt was promoted to the rank of SS-Obersturmbannführer (Lieutenant-Colonel) in the Leibstandarte (bodyguard) Adolf Hitler division of the Waffen (armed) SS, enhancing his authority for the tasks ahead.

The euthanasia programme was carried out with 'the utmost secrecy' and called Aktion T-4, after the address of the office from which it was eventually administered, Tiergartenstrasse 4. Chief of the State Chancellery (Kdf), Reichsleiter Phillip Bouler and Dr Karl Brandt were in charge. Victor Brack, a senior Kdf official was given the job of organising the killings. His department's involvement was kept secret. The Reich Ministry of the Interior was therefore designated to carry out the required tasks, with Dr Herbert Linden, Head of State Hospital and Heredity, serving as liaison. The organisation that covered for T-4 was the Gemeinnützige Stiftung für Anstaltspflege (Charitable Foundation for Institutional Care). Despite his direct involvement in T-4, Dr Brandt continued with his medical practice and attending to Hitler.

Secrecy was required because, despite years of indoctrination during which the Geheime Staatspolizeiamt (Secret State Police or Gestapo) kept Hitler fully informed of public opinion, although supportive of sterilisation, Germans believed that those alive should be cared for. This was promised in the film Opfer der Vergangenheit (Victims of the Past), which pointed out that the genetically sick were innocent of what they had inherited from their parents.

Children were specifically excluded from T-4 but in October 1939 a special children's unit was established, reporting to Brandt's team to work in parallel with the destruction of adult psychiatric patients. Young people judged to lead 'ballast lives' were moved to 37 'children's centres' where 6,000 of them were murdered, dissected and studied. These included those with Down's syndrome, microcephaly, hydrocephaly, cerebral palsy, paralysis, the absence of a limb and spinabifida among other conditions.

German universities helped promote and organise the programme. Doctors were not coerced into participation and no sanctions were imposed on those who refused. Of course, from the very commencement of the Nazi regime, doctors, nurses and other 'care' staff were more likely to be promoted if they were dedicated Nazis who believed in Hitler's policies. In the early 1930s, the psychiatric profession in Germany was a caring one, seen to be at the forefront of humanitarian research. The grip of the Nazi Party and its influence on the appointments and promotions of those who sympathised with Nazi ideology soon changed psychiatry and other caring professions and vocations for the worse. Soon, Nazi bureaucrats and their medical comrades controlled all of Germany's asylums and ran them like concentration camps. Dr Walter Schmidt of Eichenberg asylum would strut around in SS uniform with a pistol at his side threatening to shoot any patient who might attempt escape. Meseritz-Obrawalde Director Walter Grabowski would patrol wards dressed in hunting attire accompanied by a large dog. Others would bully and cajole staff and patients alike, ordering killings or organising 'research'.

Many Nazi doctors involved in T-4 believed it should have begun years earlier. Some participated to avoid serving at the front, because salaries were higher and promotions easier to obtain. Ideology drove some on, ambition and self-interest many more. As for the underlings, many psychiatric nurses (mostly male) were not 'real' Nazis but had joined the NSDAP to retain their jobs. They were often de-sensitised to suffering and were gradually introduced to killing until they became full participants. Likewise, lower-ranked SS men, not always aware of why they were being posted to killing centres, were soon inculcated into the culture of murder, even if not at first directly.

One of the most enthusiastic participants in research and a keen collector of anatomical specimens was Professor Julius Hallenvorden of the Kaiser Wilhelm Institute for Neurology, who proudly assembled a collection of over 600 brains he removed or obtained from his colleague Dr Hans Heinze, Director of the Brandenburg-Gorden asylum just outside Berlin. When interrogated about his specimens after the war, Hallevorden showed great pride in them and complete indifference to their origin. 'Wonderful material in those brains', he said. They had 'beautiful mental defects, malformations and early infantile disease. I accepted the brains. Where they came from and how they came to me was none of my business.'

Each German child was identified by a nurse, doctor or midwife who, from 18 August 1939, were obliged to complete a form, for which they were paid 2 reichsmarks per report, specifying any deformed children in their care. Even after the war, killings continued, the last child being murdered in Kaufbeuren asylum three weeks after liberation by US troops.

The decision to kill a child was taken by a panel of three eminent referees, under the direction of 37-year-old Werner Heyde, Professor of Neurology and Psychiatry at the University of Wurzburg and a fanatical Nazi, Professor Werner Catel, Director of Leipzig University paediatric clinic, Dr Hans Heinze and Dr Ernst Wenzler, a consultant paediatrician who had invented an incubator for premature babies. All three were contacted by Brandt personally and received up to a hundred forms at a time. Without meeting any children, they decided who lived or died. In red a '+' was marked on the form if the boy/girl was to die, a '–' for life and a '?' on the rare occasion when further consideration was deemed necessary.

Compulsion could be used against the parents of children earmarked for death. Many were relieved to have the responsibility and embarrassment of a profoundly disabled child taken from them, especially if they had other mouths to feed in straightened wartime circumstances and were worn down by frequent and expensive visits to specialists. Some parents demanded euthanasia, some did not want to know or be part of the decision to end life. Others genuinely thought their child would be properly cared for. When a child was killed, thought was given to ensuring that some form of 'natural' end was listed on the death certificate, such as heart failure or pneumonia.

Parents sometimes tried to visit their children and were often shocked and distressed at the state of their son or daughter, as the patients in the childrens' centres were routinely starved, neglected and dirty. As a result, parents were dissuaded from visiting whenever possible.

Doctors and nurses in the killing institutions were paid bonuses monthly and at Christmas. At Kalmenhof clinic, staff were taken to the well-stocked wine cellars to commemorate every 50th death.

Dr Brandt fought to keep personal control of T4 alongside Bouhler and Brack, and from other leading Nazis especially the Gauleiters, Germany's regional governors. Eminent men were appointed who would carry out their tasks fervently and ruthlessly.

Thousands of adults were done to death initially in six specialised killing facilities. Even before the war, numerous meetings were held to consider how the destruction of Germany's most vulnerable citizens could be accomplished 'efficiently'. Eventually it was decided that gassing using carbon monoxide would be the method. Although Hartheim was chosen as a killing site in February 1939, the Renaissance castle of Grafeneck, already in use as an asylum, was the chosen site for the first exterminations. High in a remote part of the Swabian Alpine forest, isolated but with excellent road and rail links nearby, Grafeneck was the perfect location. In late 1939, armed SS men in civilian clothes constructed a gas chamber and crematoria, surrounding the castle with barbed wire.

Those who would carry out the Aktion were ideologically driven and known for their brutality. T4 became the main training ground for the extermination of the Jews. Franz Stangl, future commandant of Treblinka and Sobibor and Christian Wirth, who would command both those death camps and also Belzec, would, together with many of their underlings, learn their 'trade' at Grafeneck and the five other euthanasia centres; Bernburg, Brandenburg, Hadamar, Hartheim and Sonnenstein. The six sites were strategically placed across Germany. T-4 also established 24 intermediate asylums, where victims would be gathered before being transported to their deaths.

Not everyone at Grafeneck was an SS employee. Some of the staff were recruited locally. All were informed by Wirth that their task would directly involve the gassing and burning of 'mental patients that were a burden on

Germany'. The motto was, 'Silence or the death penalty'. Anyone revealing what went on 'would be shot'. Four categories were exempt from euthanasia – the families of T-4 operatives, those who had served in the armed forces, women decorated with the Mutterkreuz (mother cross), for having nine or more children and Hitler's personal circle.

Doctors were recruited to oversee the killings at each facility. By 9 September 1939, Dr Leonardo Conti, Reich Health Minister, had already given orders for all asylums to register their criminally insane, feeble-minded, foreign, epileptic, schizophrenic and senile patients.

In the lead up to war films were made as part of a systematic propaganda drive to provide the scientific, economic and ideological rationale for the euthanasia and sterilisation programmes. The first, Erbkrank, (Genetically Diseased) was made as early as 1934. Directors used light and shadow to pander to existing stereotypes and prejudices in portraying the mentally ill and disabled as demonic beasts and monsters. Watered down versions were shown in schools to 'condition' German children to the necessity of annihilating 'useless eaters' who burdened the Reich at a time when resources in terms of doctors, nurses, beds, money and medicine were needed to treat the ever-growing number of war casualties. Patients were falsely shown to live in beautiful and tranquil surroundings which many people contrasted with their own dreary and often squalid surroundings.

Lebensunwertes leben (life unworthy of life), created the 'humanitarian obligation' to snuff out those potrayed on propoganda posters as weakening the country's racial stock, each one costing the Reich, and therefore the German people, 60,000 reichsmarks over a lifetime. In fact, the work carried out by asylum patients often paid for their keep. Among the young, hatred of mentally and physically handicapped people was particularly strong, encouraged as it was by a regime determined to acclimatise its people to loathe anyone different or 'inferior' to themselves.

In occupied Poland SS units began the killing of psychiatric patients in September 1939. Around 12,850 Poles were murdered by the time the war ended. In Germany, while implemented slightly later, the programme was carried out with greater intensity. Until stopped by public outcry, 70,273 mentally and physically handicapped Germans were murdered by gassing. A further 20,000 perished by lethal injection, deliberate starvation or disease.

Transportation of patients was carried out by the Gemeinnütziger Krankentransport Gmbh (Charitable Patient Transport Company), known as 'Gekrat'. After being sent, usually by bus to killing centres, patients were usually despatched soon after arrival. They would be undressed, examined and their identity checked by a doctor who considered a plausible reason for death from 61 possible causes. After being weighed, photographed and sedated if 'causing a commotion', patients were given a number, supposedly to retrieve their clothing and were sometimes marked with ink, for autopsy purposes after death. Lead down into the cellars in batches of 50 or more, the unsuspecting victims were entrapped within the gas chamber, the valves turned on by a vergasungsarzte (gassing doctor) and killed. Terrified, the doomed would shout and scream for up to an hour before all was silent. Brenners (burners) then entered the chamber, tore gold teeth from the dead, disentangled the bodies and either burned them or sent those of 'scientific interest' for autopsy, where their brains were removed and sent to university clinics for study. Bones from cremated bodies were manually crushed with wooden mallets.

Families of the dead were sent ashes in a randomly filled urn with a letter explaining, 'with regret', the death of their loved one, signed by a doctor using an alias. For example, Dr Irmfried Eberl in charge of Bernberg called himself Meyer or Schneider. Eberl was yet another T-4 doctor who commanded a death camp. He became Treblinka's first commandant where upwards of 850,000 Jews were murdered.

After a while, the Nazis realised that a qualified medic wasn't really required to turn the gas valves and an orderly carried out the job. The farrago, that the entire operation was undertaken for 'medical reasons', was therefore soon dispensed with.

What went on in places like Grafeneck and Hadamar were no secret to local villagers who had to tolerate the smell of burning flesh and ash drifting over their community. In Hadamar near Limburg, more than 10,000 people were murdered from its first date of operation, 13 January 1941, until the killings 'officially' halted on 18 August that year, although children were exempted from even this temporary pause. Brandt had called Bouler personally, expressing the Fuhrer's wishes in this area. Relatives of the victims were starting to speak out. Many, naively thinking Hitler was unaware of what was going on, wrote to him with their concerns. Significantly, although they had some euthanasia sympathisers in their ranks, both the Lutheran and Roman Catholic churches began to denounce the killings. Of all clerics, Clemens Graf von Galen, Bishop of Munster, was the most outspoken. On 3 August he described from his pulpit, in meticulous detail, the T-4 programme. 'If one is allowed to kill unproductive people, woe betide those who become elderly and frail, lose their health and strength at work or return from the front as invalids ...'. His speech reverberated around Germany, aided by the Allies who, translating it in full, dropped millions of leaflets across the country. Officially, euthanasia stopped. Secretly, the killings continued. There was a brief pause for 'reorganisation'. When complete, categories of people suitable for euthanasia would include tubercular patients, vagrants, the 'work shy' and even the elderly. Hitler's lieutenants, not least of them Brandt, curried favour by suggesting ever more 'radical' solutions.

Isolated killing sites like Grafeneck and Brandenburg did not stay open long, closing in late 1940 – not because of second thoughts by the regime, but simply because the 'feeder' asylums that supplied their victims had run out of inmates. In places like Hadamar, near large population centres, the murders continued throughout the war.

In May and June 1940, a separate operation within T-4 had carried out the destruction of 5,000 Jewish psychiatric patients. Previous to this Jews were killed with other Germans. In preparation for their total annihilation, the killing of mentally-ill Jewish patients was prioritised.

Meanwhile, the propaganda drive continued. The film Ich Klage An (I Accuse) was released in 1940 and showed a woman with multiple sclerosis begging her doctor husband to kill her, while another doctor sombrely plays the piano in another room. The film was a huge hit, seen by almost 20 million Germans. For the purposes of indoctrinating and training T-4 operatives, it is known that much more sinister films were made, including one by the obscure director Herman Schweninger, which showed the gassing of inmates through a port hole in the door of the Sonnenstein gas chamber. Such footage has not actually been discovered although the script was found and in 1970 Schweninger admitted making the film.

Conditions in the asylums deteriorated for those considered 'unproductive'. With little money for psychiatric care, patients starved to death or existed in conditions of appalling squalor and neglect. They were left unwashed, often in their own filth and left to do as they pleased. The stronger preyed on the weak in the daily battle for survival and thousands died in winter from routine infections, the lack of heating and basic care. Doctors, nurses and orderlies, more often than not, took no interest in their plight. Active killing by lethal injection was commonplace.

Meanwhile, Dr Karl Brandt joined Hitler's personal staff in May 1940, where he stayed until the Führer had him arrested near the end of the war. Shortly before gaining this dubious honour, Brandt was appointed Professor of Medicine.

From April 1941, the T-4 centres killed ill and exhausted slave workers from eastern Europe, primarily by lethal injection and neglect. Following Germany's invasion of the Soviet Union on 22 June 1941, Dr Horst Schumann, formerly of Grafeneck, took 575 Soviet prisoners from Auschwitz to Sonnenstein on 28 August that year in order to use them for experiments. All of them subsequently died at his hands.

With its operations more secret than ever, T-4 began to branch out. Erhard Wetzel, Jewish 'expert' for the occupied eastern territories, arranged for Viktor Brack to supply gassing apparatus to the SS in Riga on 25 October 1941. Thus, T-4 became involved directly in the campaign to exterminate Europe's Jews beyond the Reich's borders while continuing the euthanasia programme at home and in areas annexed directly to Germany. In all, 96 'experts', around a quarter of all T-4 personnel, were transferred to the east where they would use their 'skills' in destroying those who suffered from what Hitler considered to be the greatest disability of all – having Jewish blood.

As with T-4, the exterminators of the Holocaust (or Aktion Reinhardt as the Nazis called it, after the recently assassinated Reinhardt Heydrich, Reichsprotektor of Bohemia and Moravia) tried to create an air of calm and normality to ensure the docility and compliance of victims. Killing procedures were well rehearsed and carried out smoothly, swiftly and efficiently, as were the disposal of remains and personal belongings.

Hitler designated Professor Dr Brandt Plenipotentiary for Health and Medical Services on 28 July 1942, allowing his protégé to co-ordinate the needs of military and civilian agencies in the fields of medicine and public health under his direct authority, rather than that of State Secretary for Health, Dr Leonardo Conti, whose influence was on the wane and who was to commit suicide in October 1945.

In early November 1942, Brandt contacted Adolf Eichmann, an SS lieutenant colonel responsible for, among other crimes, the transportation of Jews to death and concentration camps, with a macabre request – he asked to be provided with skulls of 'Jewish-Bolshevik Political Commissars' for research purposes. Eichmann arranged for the 'consignment' of 80 Jewish prisoners to be murdered, pickled in formaldehyde and sent from Auschwitz to Natzweiler concentration camp in Alsace. There Professor Dr August Hirt of Strasbourg University would carry out gruesome anthropological and anatomical studies.

On 17 November 1942, an oral decree, known as the Hungerkost (starvation diet), was implemented to expedite the death of Germany's remaining psychiatric patients. Diets were to completely exclude fats of any kind with a view to inmates dying from famine oedema in three months. Victims of this policy, which was first implemented in Bavaria, were systematically deprived of food to the extent that 90,000 of them starved to death. As wartime stress on Germany's population increased, new patients suffering from stress, depression and breakdown ensured a steady supply of victims for the asylums.

By June 1943 many German psychiatrists had left their posts. While support for the policies of the regime remained strong among the profession, a minority chose to leave rather than participate in the murder of their patients. That month five German professors of psychiatry (De Crinis, Heinze, Nitsche, Rudin and Schneider) wrote to Brandt expressing their concern that 'there has been an exodus of capable doctors from psychiatry to other medical careers'. To Brandt and the Nazi hierarchy this was news to be savoured. Those remaining would be the most committed to Nazi goals and those who left could aid their hard-pressed colleagues at the front and in treating victims of Allied air raids.

January 1943 saw Brandt promoted to Waffen SS Gruppenführer (Major General). The Waffen SS was trained and usually better equipped than other German army formations. Despite his new title, Brandt did not see any action and gained no more departmental responsibilities. What he did obtain was considerably greater authority, particularly when dealing with areas of his remit that were under the control of the German armed forces. He also had the duty of ensuring the provision of emergency beds should any hospitals be destroyed by Allied bombing. To do this, asylums were kept functioning until an air raid increased demand for bed space. Psychiatric patients considered expendable were then transferred to Hadamar and gassed in order to free up their beds in a 'secret' operation known as Aktion Brandt. For example, after the Allies levelled Hamburg in July 1943, killing 44,000 civilians and leaving the city's hospitals in ruins, 349 mentally ill women, some driven mad by the bombing itself, were sent directly to Hadamar for immediate destruction.

A further promotion was bestowed on Brandt in September 1943 when he was made General Commissioner for Health and Sanitation, answerable only to Hitler. This new post gave him control over health and sanitation across the entire Nazi administration, including medical science and research. Brandt's portfolio now bulged with a vast array of posts and responsibilities. One of these was in preparing Germany for chemical warfare.

As their military situation grew increasingly critical, even hotheads in the Nazi leadership who had themselves advocated the use of chemical weapons, now feared that its adversaries might use them against Germany. German intelligence advised that the Soviets possessed more and significantly better quality protective equipment than the Reich, while the Western Allies possessed a new type of poison gas. On 1 March 1944 the ubiquitous Professor Brandt was assigned the task of preparing both civilians and the army for the worst. In carrying out his orders, experiments were conducted on live human subjects in concentration camps resulting in numerous fatalities. At his trial a few years later, witnesses (fellow German doctors) would testify that Brandt knew nothing of such activities. Whether this was from fear of self-incrimination or he genuinely was 'unaware' of such activities on his watch is doubtful, given his involvement in T-4 and instigation of other lethal experiments on humans.

Brandt's final promotion came on 25 August 1944. He now became Reichskommissar fur Sanitaets und Gesundheitswesen (Reich Commissioner for Sanitation and Health). His office was now ranked as the 'highest Reich Authority' allowing the Commissioner to issue instructions to the medical facilities, government, armed forces and NSDAP in the fields of sanitation, health, medical and scientific research. In this capacity he appointed Dr Paul Rostock, a surgeon, to head the Amtschef der Dienstalle Medizinische Wissenschaft und Forschung (Office for Scientific and Medical Research). Despite the gruesome activities that this department oversaw, Rostock was acquitted when tried with Brandt and others after the war. Professor Brandt would not be so lucky.

Crimes committed in the fields of 'science' and 'research' in Nazi Germany were as horrific, if not more so, outside the realm of T-4 and its associated organisations than within. Human beings were recruited directly from concentration camps when experiments were not actually conducted there and for the most part, although not always, Jews and Gypsies were the victims. Soviet prisoners of war and Poles also suffered in large numbers.

Experiments were carried out under an SS foundation known as the Experiments Ahnenerbe (ancestral heritage experiments) by doctors and scientists who were either in the SS itself or honorary members and who wanted to prove the racial superiority of 'Aryans' using scientific, medical, anthropological and archaeological research. Dr Wolfram Sievers, a collector of human skulls and Standartenführer (colonel) in the SS directed its Institut fur Wehrwissenschaftliche Zweckforschung (Institute for Military Research) and was directly responsible for initiating some of the most ghastly medical experiments conducted by the Nazis.

At his trial Karl Brandt would be accused of having had specific accountability for the experiments outlined below, some of which had begun prior to his appointment, while others commenced under his direct authority and at his specific order.

In Auschwitz-Birkenau, amidst a host of experiments conducted by Dr Josef Mengele and others, Drs Carl Clauberg and Horst Schumann worked in Block 30 at the women's hospital to develop cheap mass-sterilisation and castration techniques. Using an assembly line system, Clauberg developed a system for sterilising 1,000 women a day with the help of ten assistants and potent x-rays. Schumann, not to be outdone, castrated up to 90 men a day. The two doctors also tried, pointlessly, to inseminate women with animal semen. All sorts of things were inserted into terrified and helpless women who had caustic substances injected agonisingly into their wombs. Expectant prisoners were injected with formalin, novocaine and progynon to terminate their pregnancies. Not content with torturing his 'patients', Clauberg tormented them too. Those inseminated with animal semen were told that monsters were growing in their wombs. These sterilisation experiments, which commenced in March 1941, continued until the camp was liberated in January 1945.

Auschwitz was a centre for all kinds of cruel and sadistic experiments. Dr

Arnold Dohmen and Professor of Medicine Kurt Gutzeit infected 11 Jewish children with hepatitis and punctured their livers for no discernable scientific reason. Dohmen had previously experimented on animals. Gutzeit goaded him to use people, mocking that he had to be woken from his 'animal experiment lethargy'. Dr Heinrich Berning, Associate Professor at Hamburg University carried out 'famine experiments' on Soviet prisoners in Auschwitz. As they starved, Berning observed their deterioration, measuring loss of weight, libido, their dizziness, nausea, headaches, oedema, abdominal swelling and eventual death, even having the temerity to publish his results after the war.

In the contagious diseases ward, block 20, of Auschwitz, Dr Helmuth Vetter and Dr Helmuth Vetter undertook research into typhus, erysipelas, scarlet fever and typhoid on some 150-250 prisoners between 1942 and 1944, using experimental drugs developed by the Bayer pharmaceutical company. The drugs had modest benefits but did not cure the diseases. In fact that was not the objective – observing the incubation period, bodily reactions and the course of the disease was. Needless to say, almost all of the prisoners used as guinea pigs died.

Dr Kurt Heissmeyer carried out experiments with live tuberculosis bacilli in Auschwitz resulting in the deaths of 200 adult prisoners. As Soviet troops approached the camp he had begun injecting 20 children. To hide the evidence of what he had done all the children were hanged.

In Buchenwald concentration camp Dr Seigfried Handloser, who also held the rank of Generaloberstabsartz (lieutenant general) in the SS, oversaw all 'medical treatment' there. This included live vivisection of prisoners, rubbing poison into the wounds of burned patients, injecting healthy inmates with yellow fever, smallpox, paratyphoid A and B, cholera and tuberculosis. From December 1943 to October 1944, poisons were also placed in the food of prisoners and the outcomes analysed. In September 1944 prisoners were shot with bullets steeped in poison to test how quickly death could thereby be expedited.

At Buchenwald infirmary, Block 61, prisoners were routinely killed by lethal injection. Dr Carl Vaernet, a renegade Dane who was also an SS-Sturmbannführer (major), tried to develop a 'cure' for homosexuality. Fifteen 'patients' were injected in the groin with synthetic hormones to alter their sex drives and sexual preferences. To analyse his patients, all were castrated and all died. Vaernet's findings were utterly useless.

One of the most notorious crimes committed was the provision by Buchenwald doctor and SS-Hauptsturmführer (captain) Waldemar Hoven of skin, tattoos, bones and body parts torn from living and dead prisoners, which his mistress Frau Ilse Koch, the 'Bitch of Buchenwald' and wife of the camp commandant, then had made into book covers, lampshades, gloves and items of furniture.

Dr Hoven and his fellow SS doctors incubated spotted fever (typhus) virus in the bodies of live prisoners in order to create a vaccine. These experiments were carried out from December 1941 until February 1945, at both Buchenwald and Natzweiler concentration camps, where over 90% of those infected, all healthy inmates, died. Vaccines and chemicals were pointlessly injected into approximately 75% of victims. The remaining 25% of prisoners had not even a semblance of protection, being considered the 'control' group.

German scientists and doctors were keen to find a treatment for phosphorous burns. Dr Ding-Schuler carried out experiments in Buchenwald where from November 1943 to January 1944 five prisoners were scorched by phosphorous. As always, pain, injury, disfigurement and often death followed. For the survivors, trauma and disfigurement were their lot.

At Dachau concentration camp trials were conducted between March and August 1942 to simulate the limits of human endurance amidst intense cold at high altitude and at sea using pressure chambers and immersion tanks. The ultimate aim was to save the lives of German pilots who crashed into the sea or lost consciousness due to altitude sickness. The latter seemed rather futile as flight crews used oxygen. The simulated altitude was raised often, to as high as 21,000 metres until the prisoner's eardrums burst or they died in agony. Alternately if they lived, Dr Sigmund Rascher, a Luftwaffe captain, would split open their skulls while they were still conscious to examine them. Of 200 prisoners who took part, around 80-100 died as a direct consequence of these experiments. The survivors were put to death.

Subsequent to their altitude tests, from August 1942 until the following May, Dr Rascher and Dr Erwin Gohrbandt undertook freezing experiments on 300 prisoners at Dachau to discover the most effective way to revive people who had suffered from severe hypothermia. Victims were forced to stand outdoors in severe weather or immersed naked in iced water for up to three hours, many suffering swiftly from rigor and death. Survivors were revived in a variety of ways, which only exacerbated their suffering as the blood flowed back into their chilled veins.

To determine the most effective treatment for patients with malaria, Dr Klaus Schilling, one of the world's most renowned specialists in tropical medicine had over 1,200 prisoners deliberately infected between 1942 and 1945. Most of them were young Polish priests chosen because they were not required to work in Dachau. They were then given a variety of remedies that often proved completely useless, resulting in the direct deaths of 40 and indirect demise of 300-400 others who died after being weakened by the disease. Others had to endure a life of disability. Karl Brandt would be accused of having had specific responsibility for the malaria experiments, continued under his authority.

In July 1944 Dachau was the scene of a bizarre and utterly pointless experiment to see how long a man could survive on a diet of salt water. Dr Oskar

Schroder and Dr Hans Eppinger carried out tests on 42 Gypsy prisoners of which 40 died. Efforts to make the salt water drinkable failed. So dehydrated were the victims that they even licked the mopped floor of the laboratory to obtain fresh moisture.

At Ravensbruck women's concentration camp, from July 1942 until September 1943, the most important antibiotic of its day, sulphanilamide, was given to prisoners intentionally infected with gas gangrene and bacteria by Professor Karl Gebhardt, Chief Surgeon to the SS and President of the German Red Cross. Blood circulation was cut off to simulate battlefield conditions and wood, dirt and glass pushed into the wounds. Sulphanilamide was then applied and its effectiveness measured. Needless to say, many victims died in agony.

Dr Herta Oberheuser, a female paediatrician, injected women and children with oil and evipan and dissected them. She also worked with Gebhardt in his sulphanilamide experiments and from September 1942 to December 1943 on those involving bone, muscle and nerve regeneration and bone transplantation experiments. Ravensbruck prisoners suffered amputation and mutilation as bones, muscles and nerves were excruciatingly removed and transplanted into others.

Dr Hermann Stieve, Director of the Institute of Anatomy at Berlin University, examined the female menstrual cycle under stress. He did this by first telling his Ravensbruck and Plotensee prison patients that they were to be executed.

To speed up killings, experiments mirroring those at Buchenwald to monitor the impact and effect of poison and even poison bullets were conducted on Gypsies at Sachsenhausen concentration camp by Dr Joachim Mrugowsky, the chief doctor at the Hygienic Institute of the Waffen SS in Berlin. He also carried out experiments on contagious jaundice at Brandt's instigation. These were conducted between June 1943 and January 1945. Prisoners were injected with epidemic jaundice and many died, the survivors suffering great pain and were frequently left disabled too.

Mustard (LOST) gas was a major killer in the Great War and fear that it might be used again was the excuse used for gassing prisoners with it and testing a variety of putative treatments on them as they lay suffering from intense pain as a result. 'Studies' were conducted throughout the war at Sachsenhausen, Natzweiler and elsewhere. Professor Dr August Hirt, who carried out these experiments, also prepared cyanide salts to kill inmates in Auschwitz.

Many of the doctors mentioned above conducted numerous other nefarious experiments across the entire concentration camp system. They were assisted by scores of colleagues who often set up their own lethal experiments on vulnerable prisoners towards whom they could behave like malevolent gods. Karl Brandt did nothing whatsoever to ensure that experiments on live subjects were conducted using anaesthetic, had at least nominal scientific value and would not cause unnecessary suffering or loss of life. In effect he allowed a multiplicity of experiments to flourish and medical sadists to have free reign, unimpeded by his office.

The influence of Aktion T-4 also pervaded the mainstream medical and academic establishments. At the Werneck psychiatric hospital, as early as 1940, Nazi party member and Harvard-trained Professor Georg Schaltenbrand injected monkeys with cerebrospinal fluid taken from chronically ill psychiatric patients suffering from multiple sclerosis. He then took the CSF from the monkeys and injected it intra-cisternally into patients who were not suffering from MS to observe if they then displayed symptoms of the disease. He insisted that healthy patients injected in this manner would be unlikely to display symptoms of MS, so the psychiatric patients were utilised instead, without their or their family's consent. Schaltenbrand was the pre-eminent German neurologist of his day with a world-wide reputation, but despite these experiments, which were criticised outside Germany as methodologically and ethically flawed, his reputation survived relatively intact and he continued in his profession and died in 1979. Of the 45 patients who underwent these tests, two died.

While Dr Brandt accumulated increasingly grandiose titles and responsibilities, his position as personal physician to Hitler was being steadily eclipsed. Dr Theodor Morell was a medic notorious for his quack cures and ideas. Fourteen years older than Brandt he had entered Hitler's circle in 1935. That year he used sulphonamide to successfully treat the Führer's photographer, Heinrich Hoffman for a serious infection. Extolling Morell's virtues, Hoffman persuaded Hitler to take him into his circle. As Germany's leader was a hypochondriac who nevertheless suffered from an increasing number of ailments, Morell was in his element. He would inject his patient with a bewildering variety of vitamins, hormones, liquidised bulls testicles and cocktails of up to 28 different drugs. Despite visible side effects such as developing a rash or feeling nauseous, Hitler convinced himself he was in better health with Morell treating him than Brandt, who grew increasingly concerned. As the years passed, Morell became a millionaire, patenting numerous 'miracle cures' on the back of Hitler's patronage. Even the powder used on the Eastern Front to treat lice came from a Morell factory.

In October 1944 Brandt tried to warn Hitler that Morell's pills, potions and constant injections were causing his skin to turn grey, his hands to shake, possibly with the onset of Parkinson's disease and were bringing on the ferocious outbursts of temper that caused him to rage, scream and foam at the mouth. Brandt claimed that the impact of Morell on Hitler was to 'draw on what might call life for years in advance' and that 'every year he aged not a year but four or five years'. Hitler, quite probably syphilitic as well, was fatally dependent on Morell's drugs.

Hitler banned Brandt from criticising Morell and arranged his personal physician's final promotion as a way of removing him. Nevertheless, Brandt was eventually able to persuade Reichsfuhrer SS Heinrich Himmler to remove Morell. From his Hohenlychen clinic where he had been carrying out experiments on live prisoners using gas gangrene, Professor Karl Gebhardt sent his assistant Dr Ludwig Stumpfegger to replace Morell. Stumpfegger stayed with Hitler until the bitter end, while Morell went home to count his millions, dying three years later of natural causes.

As the war drew to a close, Brandt's star fell precipitously following Morell's removal, which the Führer considered he had a hand in. On Sunday 15 April, Eva Braun casually informed him that Brandt had sent his wife and son to Thuringia where they could be captured by the Americans to prevent them falling into the hands of Soviet troops advancing on Berlin. Hitler exploded in fury and he delegated Reichsleiter (realm leader) Martin Bormann to investigate and interview both Braun and Dr Stumpfegger about Brandt's 'betrayal'. The Gestapo arrested Brandt and a court-martialled was hastily contrived, with Reichsjugundführer (realm youth guide) Artur Axmann acting as senior judge. Accused of 'treason, defeatism and cowardice', Brandt was condemned to death on 16 April. Himmler then intervened to delay the execution of his friend and Brandt was transported to Flensburg near the Danish border. At the instigation of Hitler's architect Albert Speer, Brandt was released by order of Grand Admiral Karl Doenitz, Hitler's successor, on 2 May two days after the Fuhrer had committed suicide in his bunker below the Reichstag. Brandt's reprieve was a short one. He was re-arrested only three weeks later by the British.

As for T-4, the killings continued up to and well beyond the fall of the Nazi regime and the dismantling of the T-4 organisation and apparatus. By 1945, the pre-war asylum population of 320,000 had fallen to only 40,000. It is believed that at least 275,000 asylum inmates were murdered. As with the killing of children, adult asylum deaths continued after the conclusion of hostilities for three weeks and actually increased in many places. For example on 28 April 1945, its liberation day, Teupitz asylum in Brandenburg had 600 inmates. By October only 54 remained alive. Of the 887 patients in Altscerbitz 38% died in 1947, higher than in any year under the Nazis. In the Wittenauer-Heilstatten asylum in Berlin, where 4,607 patients were killed during the war, 2500 patients were newly admitted in the year following the end of the conflict. Of these some 1,400, an astonishing 56%, died within a year of entering the facility. Starvation, disease and neglect took the lives of at least 20,000 German psychiatric patients in the immediate postwar years. Karl Brandt and his collaborators had created a machine of death with such momentum that it only ground to a halt after he and other notorious medical murderers had been dealt with.

Later known commonly as the 'doctors' trial', on 9 December 1946, United

States v Karl Brandt et al commenced. Twenty-three doctors and scientists were accused of heinous crimes against Jews, Gypsies, Soviet POWs and civilians. The trial took place in Nuremberg's Palace of Justice under the auspices of the International Military Tribunal that had tried the leading Nazi war criminals only a few weeks previously. The British had intended to try Brandt themselves in an extensive trial they had prepared at which numerous Nazi doctors would appear. However, they handed him over to the Americans who wanted to interrogate him in connection with Nazi preparations for chemical warfare, after which the Americans were unwilling to hand him back. Instead, the Americans carried out their own trial.

The presiding judge, Walter B Beals and his colleagues, Harold L Sebring and Johnson T Crawford were, like the chief counsel for the prosecution, Brigadier General Telford Taylor and his team, all Americans.

Four charges were levelled at each of the accused:

1) Conspiracy to commit war crimes and crimes against humanity.

2) War crimes: the undertaking of medical experiments on prisoners of war and civilians of occupied countries without their consent, as well as the mass murder of concentration camp inmates

3) Crimes against humanity: those described under count 2 also on German nationals.

4) Membership of a criminal organisation, the SS.

Karl Brandt was considered the 'star' defendant in a group described by Telford Taylor as the 'moving spirits and personal participants in murder and torture on a large scale'.

Brandt and the others pleaded that they were 'idealists' who 'did their best for Germany' in the stressful circumstances of war. That they showed not the slightest pity for their own patients, whom they neglected, starved and gassed for careerist, economic or political motives, was evident. The euthanasia programme was exposed and experiments that superficially could be considered to have some validity paled into insignificance compared to those not designed to find 'cures' or 'assist in rescues' but merely to kill.

Brigadier General Taylor appeared to pay tribute to the distinguished careers of many in the dock, describing Dr Brandt as a 'possessor of considerable scientific ability' and 'capacity in medical administration'. He did this not only to show how far Brandt and his coterie of co-defendants had fallen from their professional calling, but also to make it clear that such men were fully able to comprehend the nature of their acts. They were 'exceptionally qualified to form a moral and professional judgement in this respect' yet they were 'responsible for wholesale murder and unspeakably cruel tortures'. The physicians, Taylor remarked 'have in common a callous lack of consideration and human regard for, and an unprincipled willingness to abuse their power over the poor, unfortunate defenceless creatures who had been deprived of their rights by a ruthless and criminal government.' All of the defendants 'violated the Hippocratic commandments which they had solemnly sworn to uphold and abide by, including primum non nocere, the fundamental principle not to do harm.' They and others had turned Germany into an 'infernal combination of lunatic asylum and a charnel house'. Professor Karl Brandt was the only one in the dock who reported personally to Hitler and was a 'moving spirit and personal participant in murder and torture'.

Brandt was directly accused of being the instigator of the contagious jaundice experiments conducted on Gypsies at Sachsenhausen and overseeing countless others. He was involved in 'conspiracy and a common design to commit criminal experiments'. Needless to say, it was pointed out that none of the helpless victims 'volunteered' for experimentation unless the alternative was death or starvation. Even then, it was under duress and the illusion of false promises. Every known standard of medical ethics was departed from and atrocities were imposed simply because the victims were Jewish, Gypsy, Polish or Russian and available.

The experiments conducted at the behest of Brandt and others were, of course, entirely useless, unless one considers that injecting phenol directly into someone's heart will prove fatal in 60 seconds, a discovery. Thousands had died in vain. Free and unrestricted access to people for use as experimental subjects had precluded even basic preparation, thought or investigation. The experiments were not only criminal but constituted a complete scientific failure. No care was given to ensuring that human resources were husbanded or valued. Short cuts, lack of pre-investigation and utter callousness outweighed rational thought, shocking in men and women who were supposedly highly educated and well trained. Results were falsified, yet even then the experiments were shown to be worthless. The infamous Dachau saltwater experiment could have provided answers in a few hours by 'a skilled chemist using a piece of jelly, a semi-permeable membrane and a salt solution'. Thus on 20 May 1944, the day the experiments began, a result would have been forthcoming without detaching much needed doctors from the front or destroying the lives of its 42 Gypsy victims. The Nazi system, considered by many hitherto to be 'scientific' and 'efficient' if 'ruthless', was seen only as utterly incompetent and unscientific. The only significant outcome was the utter degradation and debasing of the German medical profession, the debauching of Germany and the expediting of its defeat.

Ironically, Nazi Germany had given more thought to the rights of animals than people. On 24 November 1933, Hitler, a strict vegetarian, had introduced a law on animal protection. This stated explicitly that sympathy and understanding between man and creature should be woken and developed. Cruelty should be abhorred and animal experiments involving heat, cold, infection, pain or injury prohibited unless under specific and exceptional circumstances. Experimenters were rigorously policed to ensure the use of animals was curtailed in teaching, with experimental surgery on dogs expressly forbidden. It was the 'sacred duty' of German science to reduce painful animal experiments to an absolute minimum.

In total, the trial ran for 133 days and 32 witnesses gave evidence, including asylum directors Dr Friedrich Mennecke and Dr Herman Pfanmuller, who had killed thousands themselves and would both serve prison sentences. Each outlined the T-4 programme, making clear their self-justifying belief in it. Brandt too considered what he did right. In evidence he said: 'I do not feel incriminated ... I can bear responsibility before my conscience ... I was motivated by absolutely humane feelings ... I never had any other belief than that the painful life of these creatures should be shortened ... My only regret is that pain was inflicted on relatives ... I am convinced they have now overcome their sorrow and feel their dead relatives were freed from suffering.' As for his Hippocratic Oath: 'One may hang it on one's office but no one pays any attention to it.'

Judgement was pronounced on 19 August 1947. Karl Brandt was found guilty of war crimes, crimes against humanity and membership of an organisation judged criminal by the judgement of the International Military Tribunal. He was sentenced to death by hanging. Six more of the accused were sentenced to death and hanged at Landsberg Prison on 2 June 1948, the others being Viktor Brack, Dr Rudolf Brandt, Professor Karl Gebhardt, Dr Waldemar Hoven, Dr Joachim Mrugowsky and Dr Wolfram Sievers. Nine of the accused were given life sentences commuted to between 10 and 20 years of which a lot less were actually served. Viktor Brack was executed, still not comprehending the enormity of his crimes. He shouted from the scaffold, 'This is nothing but political revenge. I served my Fatherland as others before me – ' and was hanged before he had finished his declaration. For his part, Brandt considered he too had simply suffered 'victor's justice'.

The trial had a positive outcome for the future as the 'Nuremberg Code' was adopted into international law, making 'murderous and torturous experiments' illegal across the world.

Those who survived the horrors of forced sterilisation, T-4 and concentration camp experiments had to somehow rebuild their lives. People who had been sterilised were the most overlooked after the war. West Germany was reluctant to admit that sterilisations were imposed as part of the Nazis racial agenda. Without their status being legally accepted, victims could not claim compensation. Meanwhile, many psychiatrists who had actively participated in the implementation of T-4 and the forced sterilisation programme not only went back to their practices, continued to be respected and had long, successful careers, but acted as consultants to their former victims seeking compensation. It was a final insult to those who suffered so desperately from the Nazi obsession with creating a racially pure Utopia.

CHAPTER 3
Dr Robert Buchanan: Talked Himself into the Electric Chair

'It's an easy matter for a doctor to get rid of someone if he wants to.'
Dr Robert Buchanan

DR ROBERT WILLIAM Buchanan spent two years on death row, hoping against hope that his frequent appeals for mercy would be heard. They fell on deaf ears. Due to the enormity of the crime he had committed, he was electrocuted on the morning of 2 July 1895.

A Canadian by birth, Buchanan was educated in Edinburgh, in his parents' homeland of Scotland. He had qualified and was already married at the age of 24 when he emigrated from Halifax, Nova Scotia to the United States in 1886 with his attractive, pale-skinned and auburn-haired wife Helen and their daughter.

Setting up home at 267 West Eleventh Street in what is now Greenwich Village, Lower Manhattan, he steadily built up a practice and solid reputation as a hardworking, dedicated and sober young doctor. The Ninth Ward, as the area was known at the time, was not the Bohemian community of today, filled with an eclectic mix of creative, romantic and often gay people. It was a quiet, suburban and rather pedestrian neighbourhood. With patients Buchanan appeared the vision of married, professional respectability but in reality he led a rather sordid double life. At night he lurked around the seedier parts of the city, the worse for drink and in search of sexual adventure. His weakness for the opposite sex apparently extended to his patients and it was rumoured he tried to interest many in becoming his amour.

He soon met some like-minded confederates in a Richard W Macomber, a bar and restaurant owner and William Doria, a retired British army captain. Doria would take Buchanan on tours of sleazy haunts in pursuit of women and strong liquor. One night, Doria and Buchanan found themselves in a brothel in Halsey Street, Newark, run by a Mrs Anna Sutherland. It was well-furnished, prosperous and Buchanan spent a number of weeks amusing himself night after night with the four women who worked there. Doria lived in Newark, a tedious journey from Lower Manhattan and was puzzled as to why Buchanan repeatedly made the journey when plenty of women were available in New York. The young doctor was treating Mrs Sutherland for kidney trouble but also appeared to be deeply involved with her on an intimate level.

Anna Sutherland was a bizarre choice for Buchanan. She was twice his age, fat, repulsive, crude and had been married three times. Buchanan revealed to his friend the main attraction for him was that she was loaded, with a $50,000 fortune. In fact, he boasted to him of his plans to marry her.

Sutherland was besotted with her young lover, despite him being nothing special to look at. Short in stature, weedy and morose looking, even Buchanan's straggly moustache was feeble. Nevertheless, he had a strong sex drive that would have appealed to the debauched brothel keeper. With $1,000 provided by Sutherland he divorced Helen, hypocritically on the grounds of her adultery. For a man once caught by his wife *in flagrante delicto* with a patient and who spent night after night whoring, this was a bit rich. However, his wife was no saint either and when evidence was presented of her infidelity, a divorce was granted on 12 November 1890.

Buchanan now told his friend Macomber that he had a wealthy, childless and infatuated patient who would make him her sole heir. Along with Doria, Macomber was asked to witness the signing of her will on 26 November, in Halsey Street. The will stated that the worldly wealth of Mrs Sutherland would pass in its entirety, barring $50 each to a brother and sister, to whoever was her husband at the time of her death. If unmarried, the entire fortune would pass to her 'beloved friend and physician' Dr Robert Buchanan.

Two days later, Buchanan told Doria he was going to marry Anna Sutherland for her money. His friend was incredulous, given the repellent nature and appearance of the prospective bride. The following day he accompanied the happy couple to the home of Reverend David W Lusk where he witnessed their marriage. The 'blushing bride' gave her age as 41 to an incredulous minister, who nevertheless carried out the ceremony. Buchanan had been divorced for 15 days.

Buchanan bought the home in Greenwich Village he was renting with $9,500 of Anna's money and $500 of his own, installing his mother and daughter soon after. The new Mrs Buchanan settled her affairs in Newark and followed her new husband, replete with a load of garish furniture from Halsey Street. Despite leaving prostitution, she could not contain herself from telling raucous tales of her former life to her husband's female patients and greeted males with, 'What would you like dear, blonde or brunette?' Visiting Macomber's bar, she would curse loudly and coarsely. Understandably, Buchanan appeared embarrassed by his new wife and told all and sundry she was merely his housekeeper.

Wedded bliss did not last long in the Buchanan household. Anna may have had a foul temper but Buchanan's was worse. The young doctor began to beat his wife and she became fed up of his brutality, his spendthrift ways and the boredom of domestic respectability. Eventually, she decided to return to Halsey Street to resume her former profession. Doria warned her that it would ruin Buchanan's reputation if she returned to her former calling. Feeling hurt, neglected and considerably poorer, she did not care a jot. Doria informed Buchanan and the doctor exploded with rage. A scandal could cost him his practice as well as his recently acquired and handsomely paid posts as Police Surgeon and Commissioner in Lunacy.

In spite of this, Buchanan continued with his amorous exploits. Four women were now mistresses of the Nova Scotian: Blanche, Hazel, Maggie and Sadie. Maggie Young was his favourite but he did not tell her that his wife 'did not understand him' but that he was unmarried and the lie, previously repeated to so many, that the former Mrs Sutherland was his housekeeper. Buchanan drank heavily and frequently shot his mouth off about his uncouth wife, for whom he had only contempt. Friends and bar flies at Macomber's frequently heard him boast that 'It's an easy matter for a doctor to kill someone if he wants to.'

In January 1892 another doctor, Carlyle Harris, had been convicted of murder using morphine. Buchanan frequently discussed the case with friends, arrogantly denouncing Harris as an 'amateur and bungler' and claiming that he would know how to hide the symptoms of morphine poisoning, remarks that helped end his life when recounted by his erstwhile 'pals' at his trial.

Dr Carlyle Harris was a recently qualified New York doctor when he became a cause celebre for the murder of his wife Helen in 1891. Helen Potts was the daughter of a poverty-stricken family of New Yorkers. Attractive, she became infatuated with Harris when he was a poor medical student, living off a stipend provided by his grandfather for his living expenses and tuition fees. Chaste and moralistic, Potts refused to submit to her suitor's desires before marriage. Craving her sexually, Harris Carlyle married Helen in secret to overcome her resistance to his advances.

The Harris family was prosperous and would no doubt be concerned that Carlyle had married a woman from an 'inferior' social class. To avoid their disdain, Carlyle persuaded his young bride to not to reveal their union until he qualified and could earn an independent living. Inconveniently, she was soon pregnant and allowed herself to be persuaded into undergoing an abortion at the hands of her new husband. Dr Harris botched the job and his wife was taken ill. The baby was stillborn and, deeply upset, Helen returned to her mother.

Mrs Potts was outraged at the treatment of her daughter and demanded that her son-in-law tell his family of his secret marriage and for the young couple to renew their vows in church. Dr Harris balked at this prospect and took the decision to murder his wife instead.

The ever-persuasive Dr Harris encouraged his wife to enrol as a boarder in a finishing school for young ladies to ensure she had the correct deportment for meeting his parents. Since her attempted abortion, Helen had suffered from continually recurrent headaches. Harris saw his chance. Prescribing capsules of quinine and morphine, he emptied one of the four he gave her and replaced it with pure morphine. After taking the adulterated capsule, Mrs Harris collapsed. Three doctors who examined her immediately diagnosed morphine poisoning from the telltale sign of her pupils contracting to pinpoints. Failing to save her life, the physicians believed that the pharmacist who supplied the capsule had made a grievous error when preparing them.

At the inquest into her death, the marriage was concealed from the Coroner, Dr Louis Schultze, who ordered a postmortem. The verdict was accidental death. There the case may have ended and the tragic fate of Mrs Helen Potts Harris quickly forgotten. It was not to be. Ike White, investigative reporter at the *New York World*, discovered that Harris had been married to Helen. He also found out that Harris was secretary of the notorious Neptune Club, at which orgies allegedly took place in which the female participants were encouraged by giving them soda pop laced with whiskey. White's story provoked outrage and, after a further postmortem, her husband was arrested and tried.

Appearing before judge Recorder Smyth, Harris was doomed by the evidence of Professor Rudolph Witthaus who proved that Harris murdered Helen by tampering with one of the capsules he gave her, having filled it with five grains of morphine sulphate. It was discovered too, that Harris had attended a lecture by Dr Peabody at Columbia only ten days before his wife's death and suspiciously kept himself at a distance at the times she consumed the capsules. Found guilty, Harris was executed in the electric chair. Professor Witthaus was to be instrumental in sending Robert Buchanan to a similar fate.

Again and again, Buchanan moaned and moaned about his wife, 'I wish I'd never married her, I'm going to get rid of her'. Marginally more circumspect, when remembering his deception, he exclaimed he would 'dump that old housekeeper'. Buchanan's intentions towards his spouse were not just expressions provoked by the bottle. He meant it and began to clear a path for her destruction. Firstly, complaining of his wife's vile and coarse language, he moved his mother and daughter out of his home, the latter moving in with the Macombers. He then spread false rumours as to his wife's 'poor health'. Announcing to his drinking buddies that the 'old woman' was 'sure to peg out in less than six months', he reminded friends that he had been treating her for kidney problems for months but now believed she would 'never recover'. He also began to talk of his wife's 'threats' to commit suicide using morphine. 'I wish you would', Dr Buchanan replied to Anna during these imaginary conversations, 'you know where the poisons are kept'.

Around this time, Buchanan began to confide in friends that he feared his wife planned to poison him and that not only had she threatened suicide, she had also threatened to kill him. Buchanan made it be known that he was now 'genuinely afraid' of his spouse.

In March 1892, he told friends he was returning to Scotland to further his medical studies in Edinburgh. They were informed that he had told Anna she could not come with him, her response being to threaten his removal from her will. Dr Buchanan supposedly just shrugged his shoulders, pretending he couldn't care less. A ticket was purchased on 1 April with the ship sailing on the 25th of that month. On 21 April, Dr Buchanan told his cronies that Mrs Buchanan had fallen ill to the extent he could not leave. He arranged for a nurse, Mrs Childs, to look after Anna.

The following day, Buchanan asked for Dr Burnett C MacIntyre to examine his wife. Dr MacIntyre found Mrs Buchanan hysterical, with a constricted throat but not seriously ill. He prescribed a solution of chloral, bromide of sodium, syrup of ginger and water to be taken every two hours. An hour later, Mrs Childs and Mrs Brockway, a prospective house buyer, walked in on Buchanan trying to force his wife to imbibe a spoonful of medicine. Mrs Buchanan balked at the apparently bitter taste and tried to drown it out by eating an orange. Buchanan said he was giving her the medicine prescribed by Dr MacIntyre, even though two hours had not passed and the syrup should have made the taste sweet. Only a few minutes later, Mrs Buchanan fell into a coma. Dr Henry B Watson was called and Buchanan provided him with a medical history of his wife. Dr Watson assumed her nephritic kidneys had caused uraemic poisoning and injected her with digitalis. Dr MacIntyre returned and her urine was tested. No uraemia was found. The doctors now assumed she must have been struck down by an allergy to an ingredient of the medicine, probably the choral, prescribed by Dr MacIntyre earlier.

Mrs Buchanan deteriorated throughout the day, as the baffled doctors tried to treat her, hoping that whatever she had reacted to would pass. Clearly, they concluded, only an allergy or narcotics could induce the type of reaction suffered by the woman before them. Eventually, they had to come to a diagnosis. Buchanan steadfastly countered any thoughts of an allergy, stating that Mrs Buchanan took the choral regularly, frequently prescribed as it was for her by Dr Janeway without adverse effect. That left narcotics as the probable cause of his wife's deteriorating condition. Quietly, Buchanan suggested another possibility – her father had died of a cerebral haemorrhage.

The symptoms of Mrs Buchanan were consistent with a brain haemorrhage and all three doctors accepted it as the cause of her present condition and inevitable death at 3.00pm the following day. At the time of his wife's death, Robert Buchanan was drinking in Macomber's bar. Upon learning of her demise, he returned there, inviting his friends to carry her coffin at the funeral.

Two days later, on 25 April, Anna Buchanan was buried in Greenwood Cemetery, Brooklyn. Not a single soul came to grieve for her save her husband's cronies and pallbearers from Macomber's. After the funeral, at which he had shed no tears, nor betrayed any sense of sorrow, Buchanan expressed relief that 'providence' had removed such a burden. A few drinks later, he was off to visit Mrs Albro, yet another of his numerous lady friends.

Over the next few days, the widower drowned his sorrows, quite merrily it seems. Carousing all over town following the death of his 'sister' as he sometimes put it, Buchanan soon found himself inheriting $18,000, a little less than he had anticipated but still a significant windfall, and the considerable jewellery of his recently, dearly departed wife worth perhaps another $20-30,000. These he boastfully showed off to his drinking buddies.

In Halsey Street Newark, lived James M Smith. An elderly man, he had carried out odd jobs as caretaker of the brothel run by Anna Sutherland. He was unpaid but received money from Mrs Sutherland when required and had hoped to marry her before Buchanan appeared on the scene and destroyed what little hope he retained. In an act of outrageous hypocrisy, the wealthy madame had already turned down Smith, her lover of 11 years, as unsuitable due to his 'living off the immoral earnings of women.' When she left 'the game' Smith was destitute, hating and blaming Buchanan as a gold-digger. Sinking into alcoholism, James Smith would eventually have his revenge.

On hearing of the former madame's demise and familiar with the Carlyle Harris case, James Smith went straight to the coroner, Dr Louis Shultze, accusing Dr Buchanan of murder and demanding an autopsy. The coroner rejected the old hobo's shrill demands and sent him on his way. As luck would have it, Ike White, intrepid investigative reporter of the *New York World*, owned by the distinguished Hungarian, Joseph Pullitzer, did listen and took an interest. Smith told White that the late Mrs Buchanan was not the upright daughter of a Philadelphia banker as she pretended but was a brothel owner who had married a client intent on plundering her wealth.

Excited by tales of money, sex and murder, Ike White spoke to other former employees of the late Mrs Sutherland/Buchanan and began to shadow the doctor, hanging out in Macomber's bar and even interviewed Buchanan himself. Convinced he was onto something, White dug deep. At first, he did not have much luck. The reputable Dr MacIntyre was adamant that poisoning was utterly impossible and refuted even the suggestion. In his professional arrogance, it would have been impossible to pull the wool over his eyes. Dr Watson readily concurred with his esteemed colleague.

The first Mrs Buchanan had long returned to Halifax but before long her former husband stood at the door. Saying nothing of his second marriage, he begged her to forgive him and, for the sake of their daughter, take him back. So it was that only three weeks after the death of his second wife, Dr Robert Buchanan was once again married to his first!

The team of reporters investigating Buchanan were undaunted by the MacIntyre/Watson rebuff, found out about their quarry's re-marriage and continued their pursuit. The new Mrs Buchanan must have found it strange when, upon returning to New York, her husband did not take her home but installed her in a boarding house under the name of Read and then in the Hamilton Hotel, with the pseudonym of Fraser. At the same time, he was denying to friends that he had re-married. Ike White, continually raising the matter of Anna Buchanan's death in his newspaper, may have prompted such unusual behaviour. Buchanan soon appeared to have gone slightly mad. In an effort to lie low, he began to shy away from Macomber's bar and seek a new crowd in different saloons. In doing so he wore a variety of outlandish disguises, even wearing green goggles on occasion. He also stopped strangers in the street and asked if they knew about a doctor who had poisoned his wife. When he eventually slunk back to Macomber's, Buchanan began to question the customers. Did they believe he, their buddy, capable of such a thing?

Nerves fraying, Buchanan consulted his lawyer, Herbert K Knight, to find out which countries did not have extradition treaties with the USA. His lawyer tried to provide reassurance that two doctors had certified that Anna Buchanan had died of a cerebral haemorrhage, not poisoning and so there was nothing to fear. He should pull himself together. Convinced that Smith had plotted his doom, Buchanan fretted that 'Should she be dug up they would find her full of poison'. Knight was told by his client that the dead Mrs Buchanan had been a morphine addict. Despite his proclaimed innocence, Buchanan was convinced he would be tried and found guilty.

Buchanan's paranoia worsened. Believing himself to be stalked, he would visit the presses of the *New York World* early in the morning and snatch a paper to see if he was mentioned. Eventually, wishing he had cremated his former love, he dragged his friend Macomber and a lawyer recommended by Knight, Charles E Davison, to the cemetery to check his wife had not yet risen from the grave. 'My God!' he screeched in terror, when he saw the grave open, 'they have dug her up already!' It was the wrong lair. The correct one remained intact. Despite this, Buchanan was soon employing a man for a dollar a day to check the grave daily. Considering escaping to Michigan and designing a complicated code that would flatter a spy and allow friends to keep him informed, Buchanan drew so much attention to himself that the authorities had to react. Anna Buchanan was exhumed on 22 May and an autopsy carried out by pathologist Dr Henry P Loomis at the Carnegie Institute. Despite being only 32, Loomis had vast experience, having already carried out over 2,000 autopsies. He was highly regarded and, taking 150 brain samples, soon discovered that the alleged cause of Anna

Buchanan's death was not a cerebral haemorrhage. It was obvious too that she had healthy kidneys. Morphine was immediately suspected. However, when Professor Rudolph Witthaus, the famous chemist, was called in and checked the eyes, no pinpointing was observed, appearing to rule out just such a cause. Puzzled, the autopsy was temporarily discontinued.

That night, Ike White sought out Buchanan at Macomber's bar. Originally, he hoped to get him drunk enough to confess but on seeing Buchanan standing wearing thick spectacles that enlarged his eyes, he was reminded of an incident from his school days. A boy in his class had put belladonna drops in his eyes to make the pupils seem bigger. White rushed off to the home of Dr Schultze and easily persuaded him of the merits of seeking belladonna in the body of the late Anna Buchanan.

Belladonna, or deadly nightshade, is a plant that is itself toxic in sufficient quantities. The berries contained atropine, which can be lethal but also has the well-known property of being able to enlarge pupils, leading to widespread use in ophthalmic examinations and soothing the pain caused by light falling on an inflamed eye.

Analysis of Anna Buchanan's cadaver revealed no atropine in the stomach but in the eyeballs. With reports coming in of Buchanan's intended flight, the doctor was arrested on 6 June by inspector Arthur Carey and indicted three days later. He pleaded not guilty on 10 June and was remanded in custody.

The *New York World* had already decided on Buchanan's guilt and ran an enormous amount of copy on the story, denouncing the doctor at every turn. Each detail of the trial was covered and vitriol hurled at Buchanan, exposing his sleazy lifestyle and immoral character.

The trial of Dr Robert Buchanan opened on Monday, 20 March 1893 before Recorder Smyth. The charge was murder in the first degree. The District Attorney, Delancey Nicoll, led for The People, assisted by James Osborne and Francis L Wellman, who had successfully prosecuted Dr Harris. Charles W Brooke and William J O'Sullivan, the latter having been a physician prior to taking up Law, defended Buchanan. Jury selection took a week, with over 200 prospective jurors rejected before the court found 12 good men and true upon whom both sides could agree.

The prosecution case was not strong on hard facts but plenty of circumstantial and anecdotal evidence was presented. Doria and Macomber were among those whose testimony greatly damaged their 'friend'.

Doria recounted the brothel trawling he had carried out with the accused, his avaricious reasons for marrying Anna Sutherland, the violence he then showed towards her and his 'determination' to prevent his amour from returning to her former occupation. Doria relished giving evidence, perhaps because he felt himself duped by the defendant. Buchanan introduced Doria's wife to him and they married three weeks later. Doria was mighty upset to find out she had previously been Buchanan's mistress.

Macomber regaled the court with Buchanan's threats to 'dump, get rid of' and 'do her in'. He had boasted to Macomber that he knew how to disguise the effects of morphine poisoning. 'How?' Macomber had asked. 'Every acid has its neutralising base and every chemical agent its reagent' he replied. As had Doria, Macomber also recounted how Buchanan married the repulsive Anna Sutherland purely and simply for financial gain. Buchanan had also written a letter to Macomber from Canada. It had no direct bearing on the case, was never read out nor its contents noted. Passed from juror to juror it contained such 'filth' that the moral degradation of the defendant was considered beyond doubt, no doubt impacting adversely on Buchanan's chances of acquittal.

James Smith proved a rather forlorn witness, denying he was an inebriate, while admitting he had recently stayed in Essex County Lunatic Asylum where he was treated for alcoholism. His testimony may have had little impact on the case but had it not been for his doggedness, the case would ever have been tried.

Drs MacIntyre and Watson declared their conviction that no morphine had been involved in the death of Mrs Sutherland, but they admitted having failed to consider the possibility that belladonna could have been co-administered with morphine. They agreed that double medicating in such a way could have led to the death of Mrs Sutherland and that it had escaped their attention.

Buchanan's young mistress, Maggie Young, was called to the stand. Pretty, pouting and seemingly naïve, she thrilled and excited the court when admitting 'making love' to Buchanan while Anna Buchanan was supposedly dying elsewhere. Mr Brooke strenuously tried to have her testimony discounted as irrelevant but by the time Mr Smyth ruled it out, the jury had taken on board the kind of man Buchanan was.

More witnesses denounced the beleaguered accused. The jury was already slipping away from Buchanan by the time the forensic evidence was laid before them. He was drab, pathetic, and insignificant. The relationship he had with Anna Sutherland was considered lewd and squalid. The jurors looked at him, contrasting Buchanan with the handsome Dr Harris and the repulsive Anna Sutherland with lovely Helen Potts.

O'Sullivan, using all his medical training, put up a staunch defence on behalf of his client as he cross-examined the witnesses. Professor Witthaus quietly and impressively told the court that he had found one tenth of a grain of morphine in the body of the deceased, from which he calculated a lethal dose of five or six grains had been administered. He then showed the jury the effect of atropine by applying it, then and there, to the eyes of a kitten.

The quietly spoken professor was forced by O'Sullivan to hesitate when asked if liquids formed by putrefaction could cause the same reaction in tests as morphine. He then scored a direct hit by forcing the professor to admit there was no proof that atropine had been found in Anna Buchanan's body. Thus, it could not be shown that atropine had been administered to neutralise the effect of morphine.

Other prosecution witnesses found O'Sullivan feisty, inventive and dogged. After Dr Loomis provided a wax skull to show how he had examined Anna Buchanan's brain, the next witness, Dr T Mitchell Prudden, Professor of Pathology at the College of Physicians and Surgeons, and Director of the Pathological College, refused to accept a brain handed to him by O'Sullivan for demonstration purposes. Denouncing it as a 'caricature of a human brain', Prudden preferred Loomis' demonstration model. Unfortunately for the credibility of his evidence and later his reputation, O'Sullivan's 'model' was actually real.

Dr Arthur W Wolff, next up for the prosecution, provided a fresh brain removed from some poor unfortunate that very morning. Thus the 'battle of the brains' ended in a score draw.

The trial now took a comic, rather bizarre turn. The defence had summoned their own expert, Professor Scheele. A muscular German who had participated in 28 duels and had the sabre scars on his nose and ears to prove it, rather preposterously challenged Mr Wellman to a duel when Mr Wellman suggested he was a mere apothecary. O'Sullivan even had to deny he would turn out as one of Scheele's seconds. Eventually the German dueller was calmed. However, he had not helped Buchanan's case. The next witness was considerably more helpful.

Professor Victor C Vaughan was to blow the forensic evidence of the prosecution out of the water. With permission to turn the court into a mini-laboratory, scientific equipment and white-coated lab technicians arrived to the excitement of the public.

O'Sullivan had sought to prove that alkaloids from corpse putrefaction could produce the same kind of response in reaction to analysis as morphine. The prosecution were adamant they could not. As was known, morphine turned pink when a reagent was added. The experiment was conducted there and then with predictable results. The morphine did indeed turn pink. Using no morphine but only alkaloids from a cadaver, the reagent was added. To gasps from the court, the alkaloids turned a colour of pink indistinguishable from the morphine sample. Journalists frantically hurried to convey the news to their newspapers and soon the findings had reverberated around the world.

It was game, set and match to the defence. Buchanan was sure to walk. Or he would have been had his triumphalist counsel, believing his client almost certain of acquittal, not allowed Buchanan to put himself on the stand.

In England, prior to the Criminal Evidence Act of 1898, the accused could not give evidence. Once the law was changed, convictions increased as self-incrimination led to a higher proportion of accused persons giving evidence being found guilty, than those who chose not to exercise their new right. By contrast, in the USA 'taking the fifth' was seen itself by many as incriminating. If innocent, what would a person have to hide? The recent case of Carlyle Harris, outlined above, was one such instance. By refusing to take the stand, he tilted the public and jury against him and was convicted.

Mr Brooke had taken a back seat throughout most of the trial. He now intervened to dissuade his client from taking the stand. It was to no avail. Buchanan believed that he himself was best suited to secure his own exoneration and demanded the opportunity to have his say. He did and in doing so secured his own destruction.

Buchanan was cut to pieces in the witness box. For Mr Wellman it was like taking candy from a baby. Virtually everything that came out of the mouth of the accused was exposed as a lie. He mumbled, stuttered, stammered, blundered and continually contradicted himself. He even tried to cover his mouth as if trying to stop the words tumbling out.

When it was revealed that the ticket to Scotland, cancelled after his wife had 'taken ill', had in fact been cancelled on 11 April, 10 days before she supposedly became unwell, the extent of Buchanan's pre-meditation was revealed. Truly, Dr Robert Buchanan had not only undone the excellent work of his defence team, he had virtually talked himself into the electric chair.

There was one more bizarre event to come. Buchanan's prison guard, John J Lynch, known as 'Happy Jack' inexplicably decided to take his charge out for a three-hour drinking spree with one of Buchanan's old buddies on the way back from court. 'Happy Jack' was sacked by the prison service.

The Buchanan case was, in the end, not quite 'open and shut'. Notwithstanding Buchanan's mind-numbing stupidity on the stand the jury deliberated for 28 hours and four minutes before returning to court on the morning of Wednesday, 26 April 1893. Their verdict was, 'Guilty of Murder in the First Degree'. Recorder Smyth sentenced the doctor to die in the electric chair. Ike White at the *New York World* was ecstatic and the 'Buchanan is guilty' headline filled the front page of its next edition.

Mrs Helen Buchanan did not take the news quite so well. Despite the contemptuous way she had been treated by her husband, she shrieked with despair on hearing the verdict in an office outside the courtroom. Attempting to throw herself down the stairs, Mrs Buchanan was saved only by the intervention of two men who wrestled her to the floor. Hysterical, she ran onto the street and was bundled by friends into a waiting cab. Despite everything, Helen Buchanan loved her wayward and murderous husband. Had he been so devoted to her, the entire escapade would have been avoided and he would not have so ignominiously met his end.

Buchanan's team appealed twice to the Court of Appeals, once to the United States Supreme Court and even to British Ambassador Lord Pauncefote to intervene, as Buchanan was a British citizen who had never become a naturalised American. The basis of Buchanan's legal appeals was that he had been convicted on the basis of false scientific evidence. In fact, Professor Witthaus was ready for them. He had staked his reputation on proving that Vaughan's methodology was flawed. Impurities were detected in the chemicals Vaughan used and Witthaus was triumphantly vindicated. There were two short stays of execution but ultimately no reprieve for Dr Robert Buchanan.

Dr Buchanan eventually took his seat in the same electric chair occupied by Dr Carlyle Harris just two years earlier. He died a rogue, a murderer and a fool.

CHAPTER 4
Dr Thomas Neill Cream: Transatlantic Killer

'I am Jack the ... '

DR THOMAS NEILL Cream was alleged to have uttered these last dramatic words to his executioner, Mr Billington, as he was hanged on the cold morning of 15 November 1892.

A murderer of at least five London prostitutes, Dr Cream was a man who gained a perverted pleasure from using strychnine to poison his victims and teasing the authorities by accusing well-known figures of his crimes. But he was not that much more famous contemporary murderer of prostitutes. Cream may have wanted to be 'credited' with offences more heinous than his own, but he was in Joliet prison near Chicago when the crimes of Jack the Ripper occurred and his modus operandi was different. Cream was a poisoner, not a frenzied slasher.

An avid attention seeker, had Cream not drawn attention to his own foul deeds, he would have remained obscured from public view and may never have been caught. His methods made it difficult to prove he had actually killed. Only the overwhelming weight of circumstance, showing the number of women who died after an assignation with the bushy-moustached, cross-eyed doctor who gave them a drink or pill, pointed towards his guilt. Cream's counsel tried to refute this, but the judge, Sir Henry 'Hanging' Hawkins, let the evidence from each individual killing be submitted as proof of 'pattern', or 'system'.

Cream's favoured poison was strychnine. From the seeds of an Indian tree, *strychnos nux-vomica*, strychnine was occasionally used to stimulate the nervous system. Its extremely bitter taste was difficult to mask and, crystalline in structure, it did not readily dissolve in water. Strychnine poisoning is an agonising way to die. Sensations of suffocation are followed by twitching, severe convulsions which cause the muscles to go rigid, clenched fingers, spasms that throw the body into an arch, breathing difficulties that turn the face blue, feet arch inwards and eyes stare in terror. All the while the victim is fully conscious and in agony. Such were the horrors afflicted on his prey when Cream murdered using his 'poison of choice'.

Cream's earlier crimes were undoubtedly motivated by greed. His later ones are a matter for speculation. Control, manipulation, sexual obsession or revenge for having been infected with venereal disease by a prostitute are possibilities, as is the theory that he was a sex-obsessed sadist who enjoyed killing and whose grip on sanity rapidly diminished over time.

Cream was born on 27 May 1850 in Glasgow, Scotland, one of eight children to William and Mary Cream. His family were prosperous, respectable and, like tens of thousands of other Scots in 19th-century Britain, they sought a new and better life across the Atlantic. Settling in Quebec, in 1855, William Cream managed a shipbuilding and lumber company and young Thomas at first happily followed in his father's footsteps, albeit with a different firm. At 22 he envisioned a different path, enrolling in the medical faculty at McGill College, Montreal on 12 November 1872.

During his time at McGill, Cream's father lavishly supported him to the extent that he had his own carriage and horses, wore jewellery and only the finest clothes. He also became known as something of a ladies' man.

Cream was also an excellent student and wrote a first-class thesis on the effects of chloroform and in March 1876 he graduated as Doctor of Medicine (MD) and Master of Surgery (CM). Although slightly less exalted qualifications than the equivalent in Cream's native Scotland, they were still good enough to open doors and lead to a solid and remunerative career.

A month after graduating, a fire broke out at his lodgings. Luckily, Cream had insured his possessions for $1,000 two years previously and claimed $978.40. However, the insurance company was suspicious and refused to pay the full claim, forcing Cream to settle for $350.

Around this time he met Miss Flora Eliza Brooks and they were soon engaged. The relationship developed quickly but on 9 September 1876 she fell ill with what was discovered to be the after-effects of an abortion. Her father, a wealthy hotel owner in Waterloo, some 70 miles south of Quebec, was informed of this by Flora's doctor who seemed to have few scruples regarding patient confidentiality. The reaction of Mr Brooks was immediate. He confronted Cream and told him to marry his daughter or be shot. Wisely, Cream chose the former and the couple tied the knot on 11 September in the hotel. A notary prepared a marriage contract and the next day Cream was allowed to leave Canada and his wife to further his studies in London, England. Flora remained at home and died less than a year later, on 12 August 1877, supposedly from 'consumption', although slow poisoning or the lingering effects of the abortion may have played their part. Tuberculosis was possibly given as the cause of death as it was more socially acceptable. The bereaved widower showed the compassionate side of his nature by demanding $1,000 from her family, as was his right under the matrimonial contract. This time he had to accept only $200.

Cream studied at St Thomas' Hospital for two years, where he served as a resident in obstetrics. After his first year he sat and failed the Royal College of Surgeons exams in anatomy and physiology but a year later he sat and passed exams in Edinburgh to qualify with the eminent Royal College of Physicians and Surgeons.

Cream returned to Canada to set up his own practice in London, Ontario. Soon after, on 3 May 1879, the body of a young maid, Kate Hutchinson Gardner, was found dead in the toilet outside his surgery, a bottle of chloroform by her side. An inquest revealed that the dead girl, who Cream alleged named a local man as the father of her unborn child, had sought an abortion. He claimed to know nothing of what had happened to her while the supposed father claimed there was a plot to blackmail him. Experts testified that the girl could not have killed herself using chloroform. In any case, in this instance there was evidence that a pad soaked in chloroform had been pressed against Miss Gardner's face.

Despite strong circumstantial evidence as to the culprit, the verdict of 'death by chloroform administered by a person unknown' was returned. Cream saw the writing on the wall and thought it prudent to cross the border into the United States, where in August 1879 he settled in Chicago, finding his niche as an abortionist. Chicago at that time was reputedly the 'wickedest city in the world' and thousands of women worked as prostitutes, often selling their favours for less than a dollar a trick.

On 20 August 1880, the decomposing body of a patient of Cream, Mrs Mary-Anne Faulkner, was found by police after a tip off from a neighbour in the home of Hattie Mack, an Afro-American midwife who assisted the doctor in abortions. Three days later Cream and Mack, were charged with murder. Cream went on trial on 16 November. Mack turned States evidence and in her statement revealed that Cream had boasted of carrying out upwards of 500 abortions in Canada and America. She claimed Cream had wanted her to burn down the house in order to 'destroy the evidence'.

While the *Chicago Tribune* had called for him to hang, Cream stood in the dock immaculately dressed and appeared every inch the gentleman. Mack by contrast, was unconvincing and refused to confirm her statement in court, claiming she knew 'nuffin' 'bout nuffin'.' His lawyer AS Trude blamed Mack for Faulkner's death claiming that such an experienced physician could not have caused the incompetence that led to Mrs Faulkner's fatality. Years after the all-white, all-male jury had acquitted his client, Trude admitted that Cream had an obsession with 'getting rid' of 'wayward' women.

In December that year another patient died, Miss Ellen Stack, this time from poison. Cream unsuccessfully tried to blackmail Frank Pyatt, the pharmacist who had filled the prescription.

Cream had a fixation with blackmail and 'poison pen' letters. Later in life he paid the ultimate penalty, partially as a result of this obsession. In Chicago he was arrested for trying to blackmail a furrier, Joseph Martin, who was told that unless he gave Cream $20 (allegedly for an unpaid medical bill), he would let it be known that Mr Martin had infected his wife and children with venereal disease. Martin refused to pay and received three venomous postcards in turn. He was arrested on 18 June 1881 and bailed for $1,200 by Mrs Mary McClellan to whose daughter Cream had recently become engaged. His crime did not go unnoticed by the press, who denounced the Scots-Canadian blackmailer and declared: 'Hanging is too good for him!'

Prior to these events, Cream had become involved in the affair which would eventually lead to his downfall. In February 1881, Mrs Julia Stott, the beautiful 33-year-old wife of 61-year-old epileptic stationmaster Daniel Stott of Boone County Illinois, made the first of a series of visits to Chicago to purchase pills that Cream claimed would cure epilepsy. While Mr Stott was provided with the 'remedy' for his illness, Cream gained a mistress. On 11 June 1881, Cream prescribed Mr Stott some medicine and his wife stopped off at the surgery after collecting it from Buck and Rayner's pharmacy. She watched as Cream added some white powder to the mixture. She returned home by train and the next evening, when Daniel Stott sought relief, he died within 15 minutes. His death was considered by the authorities to be the result of an epileptic seizure.

It was not passion that persuaded Cream of the need to kill Stott. It was money. Daniel Stott's life was insured and the beneficiary was Dr Thomas Neill Cream. One would have thought Cream happy with Stott's widow, the insurance money and no one suspicious of Stott's death. Not a bit of it. Emboldened by the ease with which his plan had come to fruition, greed got the better of him. He wrote to the local coroner and alleged that the pharmacists had put too much strychnine in the prescription and demanded an exhumation. At the same time, the grieving widow gave Cream power of attorney to sue the pharmacist for damages. The coroner ignored Cream – the district attorney did not. Stott was exhumed and the corpse was found to contain eight times the lethal dose of strychnine. Cream was still on bail for the Martin case and when the district attorney started putting two and two together Cream decided to jump the border. Caught in Ontario, he returned to Chicago voluntarily and was arrested, as was Julia Stott. Mrs McClellan forfeited her bail money realising also that Cream had returned her kindness by seducing, impregnating, aborting and abandoning her daughter. She would have her revenge.

The trial began on 20 September 1881. Mrs Stott turned state's evidence and she told of how Cream had tampered with her husband's medicine. To show how deadly the concoction was, some had been given to a dog that died in minutes as a result. Then Mrs McClellan had her day in court and stated that Cream had spoken of Stott's death before it had been reported. The insurance policy had settled any doubts and while Julia went free, on 23 September Cream was sentenced to life in prison. He would have been sentenced to death were it not for the fact that he was inexplicably found guilty in the second degree, despite evidence of premeditation.

On 1 November 1881, Cream began his life sentence in Chicago's Joliet prison. Within a decade he was free to kill again. The governor of Joliet considered Cream to be a model prisoner and unilaterally reduced his sentence from life to 17 years on 12 June 1891. It is suspected that political pressure from politicians funded by Cream's family may have contributed to the governor's 'positive view' of Cream. With time off for good behaviour, Dr Cream walked free on 31 July 1891. He returned to Canada where his father had died four years earlier and left his wayward son an estate worth $16,000. Friends noticed a marked change in him and believed him insane. They were therefore greatly relieved when he set sail for England 'for the good of his health.'

Cream arrived in Liverpool on 1 October 1891 and headed straight for London. On 7 October, he found lodgings at 103 Lambeth Palace Road, a squalid and filthy slum inhabited primarily by the destitute and poverty stricken. Prostitution and petty crime were rife, alcoholism endemic and the stench of hopelessness pervaded the air. Cream would fit right in.

Murder was uppermost in Cream's mind from the moment he arrived in Lambeth and he sought out victims straight away. After having sex with a few streetwalkers at their lodgings, he became something of an odd fixture in that volatile community. He had a very bushy moustache, a severe squint that he wore glasses to minimise, was above average height, strongly built, slightly bald and always dressed well. Fond of cigars, gin and chewing gum, Cream had an American accent and a mania for sex. He was always showing 'dirty' photographs to anyone who would look and his conversations were lurid in the extreme. At this time, Cream frequently self-medicated, using a compound of morphine, cocaine and strychnine as an 'aphrodisiac'. All of these drugs could be deadly but Cream knew how to optimise each dose. The euphoria he claimed as a result induced 'greater lucidity, sensitivity, stamina and improved muscle tone'.

It did not take Cream long to kill again. On Tuesday, 13 October, 19-year-old Ellen Donworth, a prostitute living in Duke Street near Westminster Bridge, died from strychnine poisoning. No one knew her assailant but it was known that a man had written to her proposing an appointment between six and seven that evening. At 7.45pm she was seen leaning against a wall in Waterloo Road. Falling over, a Mr James Style helped her up and took her home where she began convulsing. A doctor was called. When able to talk, she said a cross-eyed man with a silk hat and bushy moustache had given her two sips from a bottle of 'white stuff' he carried on his person. Transferred to St Thomas' Hospital, Miss Donworth was dead on arrival.

An inquest from 15-22 October confirmed the death of Ellen Donworth as having been caused by: 'morphine and strychnine administered by a person or persons unknown.' During the course of the inquest, on 19 October, the disordered mind of Dr Cream set down on paper a plan to make money from the death of his penniless young victim. Posing as a 'Detective O'Brien', he wrote to the deputy coroner, Dr Wyatt, promising to bring Ellen Donworth's killer to justice in exchange for a 'substantial reward'. Later that day, he wrote to the next woman he would randomly kill, Matilda Clover.

Matilda Clover was 27, mother of a two-year-old boy and earned a crust through selling her only asset – herself. Receiving a letter from Cream she was told when and where to meet him and to bring the letter and envelope with her. These items Cream would destroy in an attempt to eliminate incriminating evidence. The letter he wrote to Matilda was never found, nor referred to at Cream's trial. Lucy Rose, a friend of Miss Clover, vouched for its existence and the signature on it – 'Fred'.

The evening of 20 October saw Matilda arrive at her lodgings in 27 Lambeth Road with a man she called 'Fred'. He was tall, broad, wore a silk hat and had a bushy moustache. After Cream left, Matilda went out again and returned some time later. At 3.00am her piercing screams woke Lucy Rose from her slumbers. Joined by the landlady, Mrs Vowles, the two women rushed into Matilda's room. The poor woman was screaming and writhing in agony, her head jammed between the bedstead and the wall. 'Fred has given me some pills and they have made me ill', she exclaimed. Her friends thought her a delirious alcoholic and tried to assist her with cups of tea, milk and soda. After 90 minutes, it was clear alcohol was not the cause of Matilda's distress and medical help was sought. It was not until 7.00am that assistance arrived. Doctor's assistant Frank Coppin diagnosed 'epileptic fits and convulsions due to alcoholic poisoning'. She died two hours later.

Dr Graham, a local GP, provided a death certificate for Matilda Clover. He believed she had died of 'delirium tremens, secondary syncope'. In other words, he misdiagnosed strychnine poisoning as death due to heart failure brought on by alcohol poisoning.

Cream now drew suspicion directly on himself. As yet, no one suspected anything unnatural in the death of Matilda Clover. However, Cream made a strange comment to his landlady's daughter, Emily Sleaper, after asking her to take a letter to Lambeth Road: 'I know a girl there I believe has been poisoned', he said, 'and I know who did it'. When pressed who, Cream replied, 'Lord Russell'. At that time, Lord Russell was involved in a divorce trial and Cream appears to have simply picked up on the name from the newspapers. Emily thought it all too strange a request and advised Dr Cream to deliver the letter himself.

Cream now selected the next unfortunate woman to die at his hands. Mrs Louisa Harris, also known as Harvey after her live-in lover, Charles Harvey, spent a night with Cream at a hotel in Berwick Street, adjacent to Oxford Street, on 22 October. The next morning she was none the worse for wear and agreed to meet her client again that night. Before he left, Cream revealed himself a doctor and offered to provide pills to cure some spots he noticed on her forehead. Harvey was suspicious and asked Mr Harvey to follow her. On meeting Cream, she offered to take the pills immediately but Cream suggested she drink some wine first. In a rather macabre gesture, he then bought her a bunch of roses.

After a while, Cream made an excuse about work and suggested they meet later for a further assignation that night. First she was asked to take the pills, or rather capsules. As Louisa pretended to take them, Cream demanded to see her hands were empty. They were, but only because she had thrown them away unseen by her strange customer. Content that another prostitute was scheduled to die in agony that night, Cream left. He never did make the 11.00pm appointment, no doubt because he did not expect Louisa Harvey to either.

Once again, the restless Cream felt compelled to write. This time he wrote to Fred Smith MP, heir to WH Smith the famous stationers. In his letter, he threatened to expose Mr Smith as the murderer of Ellen Donworth unless he, posing as a barrister by the name of 'HM Bayne', was employed as 'counsellor and legal advisor'. Cream suggested that, should Smith wish to accept his kind offer, he could place a few lines to that effect in his shop window, 186 Strand, the following Tuesday. On seeing this, 'Mr Bayne' would pop in for a private interview. Failure to do so would result in Smith's certain conviction.

Smith contacted the police and a stakeout was arranged. The 'barrister' never appeared. Why Cream had therefore taken the trouble of writing the letter is mystifying. Perhaps it was a compulsion, for next he wrote to royal physician Sir William Broadbent.

Posing as detective 'M Malone', Cream demanded £2,500 from Dr Broadbent or he would 'prove' that Broadbent not only poisoned Matilda Clover, whom no one thought had been poisoned, but had also been hired to carry out the evil deed. All Broadbent had to do to 'save himself', was place an advert in the *Daily Chronicle* over the course of the next week, promising to hire M Malone for £2,500. The letter threatened ruin, should Dr Broadbent ignore it. He didn't and went straight to the police. The police placed the advert and waited to pounce outside Broadbent's home should the blackmailer appear. Again, Cream did not show and the letter was put aside as the work of a lunatic. Astonishingly, no effort was made to investigate the death of Matilda Clover.

While Cream was consorting with, and murdering, prostitutes, taking drugs and writing letters, he also found time to become engaged to a Miss Laura Sabbatini, in whose favour he wrote a will that was later to aid greatly in securing his conviction, once the handwriting had been compared to the blackmail letters he had sent.

On 7 January 1892 Cream returned to Canada. He was drunk for most of the trip, trying to wean himself off morphine using alcohol and as a result many passengers avoided him. In Quebec Cream stayed at the Metropole Hotel and met a Mr John Wilson McCulloch and the two became fast friends. McCulloch was wary of Cream however and became even more so when Cream offered to treat him when he became ill. The doctor showed McCulloch his array of medicines including a bottle of white crystal he called 'poison'. When asked what he used the poison for, Cream admitted it was to induce abortions.

McCulloch soon grew tired of Cream and his obvious contempt for women. The doctor had boasted of having three prostitutes in a night, of how they were so desperate for alcohol that he could 'have them' for as little as a shilling a time. Cream also disgusted McCulloch by talking of how he wanted to murder a wealthy American for money and by the doctor's frequent opium-induced stupors. When he later read that Cream was on trial, he wrote of his meetings with the doctor, sailed to England and became a witness for the prosecution.

In Quebec, for reasons possibly unknown even to himself, Cream had 500 leaflets printed and distributed under the name of WH Murray, claiming that the poisoner of Ellen Donworth was resident in the Metropole and the lives of all guests were in danger. On this occasion, he did not even attempt blackmail. Perhaps he simply did it for the thrill, but he was clearly delusional.

Cream stocked up on supplies of strychnine, buying 500 pills for use on the unsuspecting prostitutes of London and on 23 March 1892, he sailed for England via New York on the *Britannic* and disembarked at Liverpool on 1 April. He headed straight for the capital and, after visiting Miss Sabbatini, returned to 103 Lambeth Palace Road on 9 April. Death travelled with him and was soon on the hunt for new victims.

Alice Marsh and Emma Shrivell were aged only 21 and 18 respectively. Up from Brighton, they lived in adjoining rooms at 118 Stamford Street, which runs between Waterloo Road and Blackfriars Road. On the night of 11 April, both women were touting for business when they came across a man Emma later described as a stocky, dark-haired but slightly balding, wearing glasses, a black overcoat and tall silk hat. He introduced himself as 'Fred', told them he was a doctor and they took him home. After a meal with him, Alice and Emma were handed three capsules each. At 11.00pm a man was seen by Constable George Cumley leaving their lodgings. In every way he fitted the description Emma Shrivell was to give of her assailant as she later lay dying.

At 2.30am the landlady at 118 Stamford Street, Mrs Charlotte Vogt, awoke to the sound of screaming and shrieking from Marsh and, minutes later, Emma Shrivell. Both were doubled up in agony and 'twitching', as Mrs Vogt later put it. The police were called for and Constable William Eversfield arrived to be followed soon after by PC Cumley. Both women were conscious and rushed by cab to St Thomas' Hospital where Marsh was pronounced dead on arrival. Shrivell now tried, as she gasped her last, to answer police questions, not realising she was dying. The police were initially mystified as to what exactly caused the two women's death. Their last meal was examined and nothing untoward found. Murder was the only possibility and PC Cumley gave a description to colleagues of the man he saw the night before.

Cream could not resist commenting on the murders. When reading of them in *Lloyds Weekly Newspaper*, he called it 'Cold-blooded murder'. He questioned his landlady, Mrs Sleaper, about Walter Harper, a young medical student who also had rooms in 103 Lambeth Palace Road and announced to her incredulity that he had 'proof' young Harper had slain Marsh and Shrivell. He followed up his announcement by penning a letter in the name of WH Murray to Dr Joseph Harper on 26 April informing him that his son was the murderer. Again, money was demanded in exchange for silence, some £1,500. This time he offered to provide proof before receiving any money. All Dr Harper had to do meantime was place the following notice in the *Daily Chronicle*: 'WHM – will pay for your services – Dr H.'

Throughout the second half of April, Cream continued to assiduously court Sabbatini, visiting her home, accompanying her to church and, to show his 'piety', requesting that a bible be placed in his bedchamber. Whether through stupidity, insanity or misplaced trust, Dr Cream now tried to rope his 'fiancée' into his schemes.

Laura Sabbatini was curious about why Cream wanted her to write letters on 2 and 4 May and even more curious as to the content. Cream gave her no reason. Nevertheless, write the letters she did, the first one being to the foreman of the coroner's Jury in the Marsh/Shrivell inquest. In this letter, Cream indicated that he, or rather his William H Murray alias, would provide proof that young Harper was the poisoner if money was paid 'for his services' to Detective George Clarke, 20 Cockspur Street, Charing Cross, London. The second letter was to Mr Clarke himself and briefly told him that if the coroner, Mr Wyatt, came calling, he was to advise that proof of murder by Harper using strychnine would soon be forthcoming. No such 'George Clarke' existed, although at the same address there was a private detective named Henry John Clark. Mr Clark was devoid of any knowledge of the affair or even why his address and similar name had been used. He knew of no William H Murray.

Many who looked down on their profession, even if on occasion partaking of the services provided, considered the life of a London prostitute in Victorian England worthless. The death of Ellen Donworth had created a brief stir, but the police had other priorities and the furore died down. The case became known locally as the 'Lambeth Mystery'. Now, the death of two prostitutes together caused the police to take action. Prostitutes were questioned across the city, including Lucy Rose. She mentioned the agonising death of Matilda Clover. Exhumed on 6 May, to the embarrassment of Dr Graham who was subsequently accused by the Attorney General of a 'grave dereliction of duty', Miss Clover was found to have died of strychnine poisoning. The authorities were now looking for the killer of at least four women.

On 12 May, PC Cumley spotted Cream, whom he recognised form the time he was seen leaving the apartments occupied by the late Alice Marsh and Emma Shrivell. Cream was pacing up and down outside Canterbury Music Hall in Westminster Bridge Road, a well-known haunt of prostitutes. The police watched him pick up a woman, accompany her home and waited for him to re-emerge, after which they followed the suspect back to 103 Lambeth Palace Road.

In the days that followed, the doctor, who knew he was being followed, decided to confide his thoughts to a loose acquaintance of his, Sergeant Patrick MacIntyre of the CID. Why he took such a suicidal course, who can say? Perhaps Cream considered he could outwit the authorities by trying to re-direct their investigation. At any rate, he informed MacIntyre that a prostitute had been sent to find out his identity, as he was a suspect in the Stamford Street poisonings. MacIntyre listened intently as Cream told him how a detective called Murray had given him a letter in the street addressed to Alice Marsh and Emma Shrivell warning them to be wary of a 'Dr Harper' as he would mete out to each of them the agonising death inflicted on Matilda Clover and Louisa Harvey. The name Clover registered with MacIntyre in connection with the Broadbent blackmail letter, but Louisa Harvey was a new one. Why the imaginary 'Mr Murray' chose to give such a letter to a supposed stranger like Cream seemed to the sergeant decidedly odd. Reporting the incident to his colleagues, the police began to investigate the 'death' of Louisa Harvey and inspector John Tunbridge was assigned to finding the murderer behind the South Lambeth poisonings.

Cream was not yet finished with his campaign of poisonings. On 17 May, he met with a prostitute named Violet Beverley. She was wise to Dr Cream and became suspicious when he gave her a pill to swallow after a drink. Pretending to take it, she threw the pill away, saving her life in the process. Immediately thereafter, Miss Beverley went to the police and gave them a description of the man who had tried to entice her into swallowing the pill. The police now had an opportunity to search Cream's lodgings and they took it. First of all they interviewed Dr Joseph Harper and obtained the letter he received from 'WH Murray'. The letter was compared to others in 103 Lambeth Palace Road and shown to be in Cream's handwriting. His letter to Dr Harper mentioning Matilda Clover, long before she was suspected of having been murdered, damned Dr Cream. Before the inevitable arrest, he tried to book passage to America. He was caught on 3 June before he could escape.

The police proceeded with caution. Cream was not held initially on a charge of murder, but of blackmail. The authorities were intent on holding Cream until further evidence could be secured.

On 22 June, an inquest into the death of Matilda Clover opened at Tooting Vestry Hall. The key witness was Louisa Harvey, who had read of her alleged death in the newspapers and immediately contacted the coroner and chief commissioner of police, offering to come forward. She gave evidence that described exactly the events of 22 and 23 October the previous year. Cream was now asked to give testimony under the name he used in England, Dr Thomas Neill.

His reaction to being asked to explain his actions was outlandish. Not only did he refuse to give evidence, he refused point-blank to say anything at all. He did not give even his name, profession or take the oath. All he would say in response to questions was that, 'I decline to say anything whatever. I have received my instructions'. His solicitor, Mr Waters did not imagine he would go that far and at least expected him to 'swear to tell the truth and nothing but the truth'. His efforts were in vain.

If Cream thought he was doing himself a favour by his obstinacy, he had made a grave misjudgement. On 7 July the jury were out for only 20 minutes when they returned to give the following verdict: 'We are unanimously agreed that Matilda Clover died by strychnine poisoning administered by Thomas Neill with intent to destroy life. We therefore find him guilty of wilful murder'.

On 18 July, Cream was finally charged with murder. A preliminary hearing began at Bow Street Police (now Magistrates) Court on 21 July and lasted until 22 August. The trial itself did not open until Monday 17 October. In the meantime, the cross-eyed ladies' man continued to exercise a form of magnetism over his obviously smitten and naïve fiancée. Writing to Miss Sabbatini, at first in a condemnatory tone for having testified at his hearing that the handwriting on the will he made was his, he then pleaded with her to commit perjury. She was to deny having seen him write anything, burn any of his writings in her possession and say nothing to the police about him if asked.

Larua Sabbatini was either madly in love with her fiancé, deluded or both, for despite the suspicious demands of her 'dear Thomas' she did not for a minute believe him guilty and stuck by him until the end. That the trial revealed him to habitually misuse drugs and frequent prostitutes shook her faith in him not one bit.

The trial opened at the Old Bailey before Justice (later Sir Henry) Hawkins. The Crown displayed some of the most exalted legal talent of the day. The Attorney General, Sir Charles Russell QC, MP (later Lord Russell of Killowen) was ably assisted by the Honourable Bernard Coleridge QC, MP, Messrs Charles Gill and Henry Sutton. Mr Geoghegan, assisted by Messrs Clifford Luxmoore Drew, W Howel Scratton and H Warburton, led the defence.

Although Cream was charged with four murders and one attempted murder, only the Matilda Clover case was proceeded with. Despite what we have read of Cream, the evidence at the Crown's disposal was less than watertight. Both sides in the case knew that evidence from the other murders would have to be introduced to secure a conviction. Mr Geoghegan fought strenuously but in vain to ensure it was not as Judge Hawkins ruled the evidence was admissible. From that moment on, Cream was doomed.

Cream was not allowed to speak in his own defence so Mr Geoghegan had to skilfully cross-examine the prosecution witnesses and rely on his own brilliance to win the day. He had to be, having no defence witnesses to assist his case. Geoghegan reached out to the jury and, in a flowery closing speech, tried to save his client by reminding them that, 'Justice demands that the guilt of the accused shall be brought home as clear as the light of heaven'. To the jury it was very clear indeed. Cream thought differently. As he returned to his cell following his counsel's colourful oration, he sang and danced all the way, so sure he was of an acquittal. The following day brought a reality check. The Attorney General closed for the prosecution, followed by a judge who, in directing the jury, made his own views of Cream's guilt known with little subtlety. The jury were out for only ten minutes before returning with a unanimous guilty verdict. Judge Hawkins pronounced sentence of death on Cream immediately thereafter.

Confident to the last, Cream was overheard saying, 'They will never hang me'. This was perhaps bravado, perhaps a threat that he might kill himself. He was put on suicide watch but hang he did on 15 November 1892 in Newgate Prison while a four- to five-thousand-strong crowd of 'drink-sodden men and repulsive women' loitered in the rain outside, waiting to greet the news that Cream had dropped to his inevitable death. After the hanging, Cream's clothes were sold for £200 to Madame Tussaud's Waxwork Museum in London, where his effigy was displayed for 70 years until replaced by more 'fashionable' killers.

A psychopath, Cream was determined to kill as many prostitutes as possible, probably because one had infected him with venereal disease early in his life. No doubt he would have murdered many more if he had not been caught. Certainly, the suspicion is that many more died at his hands than is recognised, possibly by poisoning or the abortions he induced in so many women, particularly in North America. He was certainly insane and Mr Geoghegan had tried to delay sentence on his client until evidence of that insanity arrived from across the Atlantic. Judge Hawkins had other ideas. In any case the 'McNaughton Rules', introduced in 1843, made it clear that, to be judged criminally insane, a defendant had to be unable to distinguish right from wrong at the time the crime was committed, a tremendously difficult thing to prove in Victorian England. Given the pre-meditated nature of Cream's crimes, the letter writing and his periods of lucidity, under the law of that time, it was a forlorn hope of Geoghegan that a verdict of insanity could be secured.

A curiosity remains. In the late 1870s, Mr Marshall Hall QC, a famous barrister in Victorian England, defended a man accused of bigamy with a host of young women. The defendant claimed to be in a Sydney gaol, Australia, at the time of his supposedly bigamous marriages, an alibi no one believed. True enough when his story was checked out, to everyone's astonishment, the man was telling the truth and acquitted. Years later at the Cream murder trial, Mr Hall was incredulous to see that Cream and the man he had defended were one and the same. He later came to the conclusion that Cream had a criminal doppelganger and the two used each other's prison terms for alibis. It is perhaps rather ludicrous to countenance, but perhaps Cream was 'Jack the ... ' after all!

CHAPTER 5
Dr Hawley Harvey Crippen: Love Me and the World is Mine

I care not for the stars that shine,
I dare not hope to e'er be thine'
I only know I love you.
Love me and the world is mine.

HAWLEY HARVEY CRIPPEN recited this to his young mistress, Ethel Le Neve, during their ill-fated, passionate affair that was ended by the hangman's noose. The case of Dr Crippen is one of the most famous cases in criminal history, made so by the combination of sexual betrayal, a flight from justice, an arrest at sea involving the latest wireless technology and a high-profile trial full of gory details followed by an execution.

The man who was to become one of Britain's most famous murderers was an American, born in Coldwater, Michigan in 1862. An only child, he grew up opinionated and self-centred, keen to follow in the footsteps of his uncle Bradley, the town doctor. Crippen studied medicine at the University of Michigan, and took his MD at the Homeopathic Hospital College in Cleveland, Ohio, in 1884, subsequently endorsed by Philadelphia Medical College. In 1885 Crippen qualified as an ear and throat specialist at the Ophthalmic Hospital in New York. He had previously studied medicine in London for a few months in 1883. When he returned to England in 1897, he was entitled to call himself a doctor but could not practice medicine, homeopathy being considered rather eccentric at the time.

In the years preceding his final move to London, Crippen practiced in a number of towns and cities across America. Trying his hand at dentistry, he eventually found himself in New York. There, while an intern at Hahnemann Hospital Manhattan, he met and married Irish nurse Charlotte Jane Bell in 1887. They soon had a son, Otto Hawley Crippen. Sadly, Charlotte died of apoplexy in January 1892, at Salt Lake City, only a few days before giving birth to another child. Crippen, unable or unwilling to bring up his son alone, sent him to live with his parents in San Jose, California. Back in New York, Crippen met 19-year-old Cora Turner, an erstwhile opera singer, who became his second wife on 1

September that same year. Subsequently, Crippen discovered that Cora's real name was Kunigunde Mackamotski, born into poverty in Brooklyn to a Polish-German family, a deception for which he never forgave her. Crippen later claimed that his young, moderately pretty, coarse and boisterous wife was mistress of a Mr Lincoln, a minor industrialist, when they met, who set her up in a flat and paid for singing lessons. It was only by telling Crippen that Lincoln intended to elope with her that made the infatuated doctor propose. For her part, while Crippen did little to excite her, and she did not love him, he did have 'MD' after his name and a life of diamonds and furs was visualised. She was to be disappointed. The fad for homeopathy was on the wane, with both patients and money in short supply.

Married only a year, the great depression of 1893 forced Crippen to move in with Cora's parents. She then persuaded him to commence employment with Munyon's Homeopathic Remedies, a company dealing in patent medicines, in 1894. 'Professor' Horace Munyon, owner of the company, had supposedly found a cure for piles and his advertisement, featuring a picture of himself with upraised finger, was the cause of many bawdy jokes. Munyon took a shine to Crippen, making him general manager of his central office in Philadelphia within a year. He was then placed in charge of the Canada office before being offered promotion overseas in early 1897, at the guaranteed and almost unheard of salary of $10,000 a year. Prosperous at last, Crippen and his young wife settled unhappily in London. For although Cora had the furs and jewellery she wanted, she was less than enamoured with the husband who had paid for them. Initially, Cora did not sail with Crippen to England, preferring a dalliance in America with former Chicago prizefighter turned showman, Bruce Miller, before rejoining her spouse in August 1897.

Cora's ambition was to be an opera star but she was prevented by her modest talent and her dumpy figure, at a time when the svelte, sophisticated 'Gibson Girl', created by American artist Charles Dana Gibson, was in vogue. Reluctantly, Cora became a music-hall entertainer instead, having dabbled in vaudeville back in the States. Unfortunately, in November 1899, Horace Munyon came across a full-page advert Crippen had placed declaring himself her business manager, thereby discovering that Cora Crippen and music-hall singer Belle Ellmore were one and the same person. Believing Crippen to be less than committed to his company, Munyon sacked him.

Crippen then tried a number of independent ventures before finding a job with a less salubrious employer in December 1901, Drouet's Institute for the Deaf, on Regent's Road, as an ear specialist, purveyor of outlandish potions and general manager. Drouet's was basically a mail-order establishment offering quack remedies for ear infections. Crippen's duties included 'diagnosing' ailments from correspondence and suggesting remedies from the Drouet's inventory. His salary was substantially less than that he had enjoyed at Munyon's. It was at this difficult time he also found love letters from Bruce Miller to Cora, signed off with 'love and kisses to brown eyes"

In 1902 Crippen was recalled to America for six months. Cora did not follow and continued her numerous affairs with a number of lovers, primarily from the world of the stage.

Mrs Crippen was no retiring Victorian Lady – with her profession she never could be. She was boisterous and big hearted, embarrassingly frank and popular with her London audience, especially men, who pursued her ardently. It was not that she was merely extrovert but her incessant bullying of her mild-mannered husband and open contempt for him that probably drove him into the sympathetic arms of another. Cora was domineering, with dreams of stardom that outweighed all other considerations, demanding that Crippen pay for her to train as a singer on the music-hall stage, despite his repugnance at her choice of career. Prone to histrionics, Cora often had screaming tantrums during which she belittled and threatened to leave her unexciting little husband whom she only just towered over. Hating the name Hawley, she called him 'Peter' instead. To keep her in the style to which she was acquainted, like many people of the day, the Crippens took in lodgers, and not a few of whom ended up in bed with the lascivious Cora. Crippen and Cora never had children together. He blamed a 'miscarriage' she supposedly had years earlier while cavorting with Mr Lincoln that resulted in the removal of her ovaries.

A small man, Crippen was only 1.6m tall (5'3') and had metallic grey eyes, hidden behind the thick lenses of gold-rimmed spectacles, a bushy moustache and light sandy-coloured hair. He walked with his shoulders tensely bunched and truly seemed a man most unlikely to stimulate amorous thoughts in a much younger woman. Crippen was also prone to dress outlandishly for an ostensibly quiet and unassuming man, wearing loud shirts, a yellow bow tie and huge diamond stickpin. He also developed a reputation for meanness, offering to buy a round of drinks only to 'discover' he had no money on him. To Cora's friends he was 'the half-crown king', as he was always borrowing that amount. Crippen himself neither drank nor smoked.

Drouet's went bankrupt when the firm was found guilty of gross negligence following the death by infection of a customer. Crippen went into business as a dentist with a Dr Gilbert Rylance, opening as the Yale Tooth Specialists in Oxford Street in the same building as Munyon's Homeopathic Remedies. He employed as a bookkeeper a woman he had met at Drouet's when she was an 18-year-old typist working in the same building as him.

Ethel Clara Le Neve, Crippen's mistress and some 20 years his junior, would inflame passions in Crippen that eventually led to the hangman's noose. Ethel's real name was Neave, although Crippen was not as perturbed by this 'deception' as he had been by Cora's name change. Born in Diss, Norfolk, Ethel was a moaning, chronic hypochondriac and known to all by the nickname of 'not very well thank you'. Miserable as a child because she was jealous of her vivacious, younger sister Nina, Ethel had a hang-up about a supposed deformed 'frog foot' and hated her father for correctly informing her it could be 'cured' by simply walking normally.

Crippen liked to play the gentleman with Ethel and from summer 1903, he took her to fine restaurants, behaved impeccably and always walked her home in the evenings. For his part, Crippen was enchanted by her pretty face, sensuous mouth, and apparently sweet, reserved and ladylike countenance. A pathological liar, who some speculated was not just the inspiration but the instigator of Mrs Crippen's murder, Ethel loved Crippen but only agreed to surrender herself to him after he caught Cora in bed with their German lodger, Richard Ehrlich and she realised his marriage was a sham. That very day, 6 December 1906, Ethel Le Neve became Dr Crippen's lover. The two would always refer to it as their 'wedding day'. She lived with her parents and so the lovers met for trysts in cheap hotels.

The Crippens lived well, despite the occasional failure of some business ventures and the slow progress of his dental practice. From September 1905, they rented a three-storey house in Holloway, 39 Hilldrop Crescent, decorated tastelessly throughout in Cora's favourite colour, pink. It was always dirty and shockingly untidy. Crippen tolerated his wife's numerous infidelities before and after he began his affair with Ethel and it appears that both women dominated him. Certainly, he seemed in no hurry to extricate himself from the marriage and met his mistress in the afternoon, always returning home at night. Even when Ethel became pregnant, Crippen hesitated to leave Cora. Ethel set up home in Hampstead and fruitlessly awaited her lover. Cora, by now aware of the affair between her husband and Ethel Le Neve thanks to local gossip, told her friends who considered Crippen a 'sponger', that Ethel did not even know who the father of her baby was. This incensed Crippen, even more so when Ethel miscarried.

Forgetting her own behaviour, Cora called Ethel a 'whore, trollop and home-wrecker' whom she mocked as 'the little typewriter'. By January 1910, Crippen was told that if he did not give up Ethel, Cora would leave him and take their joint savings of £600, a lot of money at a time when his business was struggling. The bank was advised on the 15th that a withdrawal could soon be expected from the Crippens joint bank account.

Crippen snapped. He could not give up the woman with whom he was passionately in love. A divorce would bring scandal but, more importantly, Cora would have taken his modest life savings long before he could get her into court. Murder was on his mind.

On Monday, 31 January 1910, Dr Crippen and his wife hosted a dinner party at home for a couple of close friends; the retired mime artiste Paul Martinetti and his wife Clara. The evening progressed well, with both couples enjoying dinner, followed by cards. It was not to last. Mr Martinetti felt unwell and needed to go to the bathroom. Dr Crippen assumed that he could find his way without difficulty. When he got lost, Mrs Crippen yelled at her husband for being a poor host, incapable of looking after his guests properly. At 1.30am the Martinettis departed, hearing Cora screaming abuse at her husband as soon as the front door of number 39 closed, as she repeated her threats to leave him.

The following day, Crippen arrived at his work at 9.00am as normal and treated some patients before stepping out to pawn Cora's diamond ring and earrings. To allay suspicions, the doctor travelled to the Martinetti home in Shaftsbury Avenue, arriving around noon. He was concerned at his friend's discomfort from the previous night and wanted to check if Paul was feeling better. Mr Martinetti was in bed but Clara spoke to Crippen and asked after Cora, who the doctor cheerfully replied, was in good health and spirits. In fact, the very opposite was true! That night, for the first time, Ethel would sleep in the Crippen home.

Dr Crippen had poisoned his wife with a lethal dose of hyoscine hydrobromide, purchased on 17 January from Lewis and Burrows, the chemist he frequented throughout his profession. Crippen had witnessed it being used to quieten alcoholics and the violently insane at the Bedlam Institute in London's Royal Bethlehem Hospital. It is an alkaloid derived from the plant henbane and also found in the leaves and roots of deadly nightshade; it was also used to sedate patients undergoing anaesthesia and as a sexual depressant. He brought the poison home on 19 January and probably administered it via a glass of stout Cora habitually drunk before retiring, as an aid to sleep.

To dispose of Cora's body, Crippen dissected it, removed the bones and buried the remains in his cellar. It is likely this was carried out, at least in part, before he nonchanantly called on the Martinettis.

At his place of employment, Crippen permitted his wife to hold meetings of the Music Hall Ladies' Guild, of which she was honorary treasurer and an enthusiastic and popular member. The guild was an organisation dedicated to raising money for destitute former 'artistes'. On 2 February at their next gathering, the normally dedicated attendee, Cora Crippen, failed to show. Upon commencement of proceedings, Ethel Le Neve handed two typed letters to secretary Miss May. These appeared to bear the signature of Belle Ellmore, Cora Crippen's stage name. They explained the reason for Mrs Crippen's absence. She had been urgently recalled to the United States due to a sudden family illness. This was a surprise to the ladies but they assumed that it must be something very grave and Cora herself only very recently informed.

On 20 February, the Music Hall Ladies' Guild held a dinner and ball. The attendees were astonished when Dr Crippen appeared with Miss Le Neve not only on his arm but wearing Cora Crippen's jewellery and clothes. Gossip spread like wildfire and suspicions were aroused. Friends checked with shipping lines and discovered that no woman with the name Cora Crippen/Turner or Belle Ellmore had travelled to America in February. She could, of course, have travelled under Kunigunde Mackamotski, a name unknown to her London friends, but it was highly unlikely.

Lil Hawthorne, a music-hall friend of Cora, made enquiries in New York where she was touring, to no avail. Crippen's excuses for his wife's absence grew increasingly feeble and when Ethel Le Neve moved into the Crippen home on 12 March, after insisting her lover first dispose of his wife's stage costumes, foul play was suspected. This was compounded when Crippen spun a tale that his wife was taken ill while in California visiting her sick relative. He soon added that she had died in Los Angeles. The Martinettis received a telegram from Victoria Station, not as one might expect directly from Crippen or the United States, informing them that Cora was dead. Dr Crippen tried to show his distress by going into mourning, having memorial cards printed and an obituary notice published in show business newspaper *The Era* using Cora's Belle Ellmore stage name on 26 March. Few people were fooled and Dr Crippen must have believed the game was up. He gave three-months' notice to his landlord. Taking fright, the lovers fled to Dieppe.

On the cross-channel ferry, Dr Crippen was observed to carry a large bag, which was missing when he disembarked. Did it contain the head, bones and other dismembered remains of the late Mrs Crippen?

In France Crippen awaited news. Nothing untoward happened and the lovers soon returned to London. As April and May passed uneventfully, he advised the landlord that he would stay longer in Hilldrop Crescent than previously anticipated. Unfortunately for Crippen, he was not yet out of the woods. Two old acquaintances of Cora, Mr and Mrs Nash (Lil Hawthorne), arrived on his doorstep out of the blue to tell Cora of their recent adventures touring the music halls of America. When a flustered Crippen tried to explain his wife's demise, failing to answer questions in specific detail, the Nashes became concerned. A close friend of theirs just happened to be Detective Superintendent Froest, the head of Scotland Yard's homicide investigations. The Nashes told him of their concerns on 30 June and he too thought the explanations of Dr Crippen to be both furtive and unconvincing. He agreed to have the matter fully investigated.

Meanwhile, Crippen wrote to Otto, his estranged son in California with whom Cora had supposedly stayed. He told him she had died of pneumonia in San Francisco. Otto Crippen did not cover for his father. When Melinda May of the Ladies' Guild asked him about it, he truthfully admitted no knowledge of Cora's whereabouts.

Although the murder of Cora Crippen later appeared to have been premeditated, with not a single bloodstain ever found, for example, it is extraordinary how little thought the murderer gave to how he would explain her disappearance. By making up stories 'on the hoof', he sealed his doom.

After speaking to members of the Music Hall Ladies' Guild and other friends of Cora Crippen, the police began to take a serious interest in her disappearance. On Friday 8 July, Detective Chief Inspector Walter C Dew and Detective Sergeant Mitchell arrived at Hilldrop Crescent. Crippen was apparently not at home but Ethel Le Neve was. In plain view she wore a brooch previously described by ladies of the guild as belonging to their friend and colleague, Cora Crippen. Shocked at the police appearing at 'her' home, Miss Le Neve disappeared upstairs returning with Dr Crippen himself.

Explaining the reason for his visit was the unsatisfactory explanations Dr Crippen had given for the death of his wife, Detective Chief Inspector Dew asked for an explanation directly from the man himself. Crippen, without emotion, agreed to provide a statement. He outlined not only his wife's death, but also how they met in the first place and the condition of their marriage up until her disappearance. It was not a happy picture. The couple had long ago stopped sleeping together and occupied separate rooms. While in the United States on business, he believed his wife had embarked on an affair with Bruce Miller. It was his embarrassment and humiliation at being allegedly cuckolded by Mr Miller, whom Crippen believed had now eloped with his wife that persuaded him to lie and inform all and sundry that his wife was dead.

It seemed on the surface a plausible enough story but for experienced detectives like Dew and Mitchell it simply did not ring true. Why had no one else heard of this 'elopement', not even her closest friends? More pertinently, if Cora Crippen had left her little husband, why leave her clothes and jewellery behind? Crippen stuck doggedly by his flawed story, continually elaborating. He clearly hated his wife, as he recounted Cora taunting him with tales of Miller's presents, love letters and wealth. How, as a music hall artiste himself, Miller could more easily empathise with her thwarted ambitions while being in a position to help realise them. The detectives were shown letters from Miller, whom Crippen now explained was probably with Cora in Chicago. Trying to appear co-operative, Crippen eventually agreed to circulate an advert in America, seeking the whereabouts of Cora Crippen/Belle Ellmore. Leaving Hilldrop Crescent, the police were almost persuaded by the doctor's story. Had he kept his nerve, he may even have escaped justice.

The police released a missing person's description of Mrs Crippen and tried to check the doctor's story. Returning to 39 Hilldrop Crescent the following Monday to seek further information, it was discovered that the lovers had flown the nest on 9 July, having terminated their maid's employment. Now thoroughly suspicious, the police obtained a warrant to search the house. It was a house no one would ever sleep in again. Derelict for 30 years after the Crippen trial, 39 Hilldrop Crescent was bombed by the Luftwaffe in 1940.

The police found nothing in their search of the Crippen home. A second rummage around the following day also revealed nothing but Dew had a hunch that the house would eventually yield something. The coal cellar in particular had drawn his attention, he knew not why. On 14 July Dew searched again. At first, as on the two previous searches, nothing seemed unusual. He stared at the brick floor. Using a poker, Dew prodded the plaster between the cellar floor bricks. The plaster was soft. The bricks lifted easily. One by one the bricks were removed. With a spade, Dew dug and dug, deeper and deeper until eventually, buried in slaked lime, he came upon human remains.

Dr Marshall, the police surgeon, assisted Dew in digging out the remains, after which pathologist Dr Augustus Pepper examined them. Curiously, not a single bone was discovered. The body had been eviscerated and the entire skeleton removed. What was left were the flesh and organs of the unfortunate victim. No doubt it was anticipated that these would swiftly decompose in the soil, mixed with the lime to further expedite the process. Unknown to Crippen, unlike quicklime, slaked lime actually preserves decaying tissue. Why Crippen did not dispose of Cora's soft tissue with the bones and skull which were never found, is a mystery.

Brown hair, wrapped around a Hinde clasp, a handkerchief, woman's chemise and a labelled man's pyjama jacket were also found. The expert removal of flesh from bone indicated the employment of an experienced and skilful, professional hand – a doctor perhaps?

What of the lovers?

Spooked by the police visit on 8 July, Crippen and Le Neve once again fled across the channel. After spending a few days in Brussels and Rotterdam, the couple arrived in Antwerp, with the intention of boarding a ship for New York. As it happens, a White Star liner, the SS *Montrose*, a cargo vessel converted to transporting passengers was in harbour and on 20 July set sail, not for New York but Quebec, Canada. It would have to do. Among with 280 passengers, travelling second class, were Mr John Philo Robinson and his 16-year-old son, also called John. Mr Robinson was a short, clean-shaven middle-aged man in grey hat, brown suit with white canvas shoes. His 'son' was a slim youth wearing trousers split at the back and held together only by a safety pin. To Captain Henry Kendall, the Robinsons appeared quite odd, particularly their habit of holding and squeezing each other's hands, something one does not see often between father and teenage son.

As the voyage progressed, Captain Kendall kept a watchful eye on the Robinsons. Young John spoke rarely and had a high-pitched English, feminine voice. The 'father' had an educated American accent and would inform other passengers and crew that Master Robinson was in poor health. They were bound for California, where the climate would be more to his liking.

A warrant was issued for the arrest of both Crippen and Le Neve. Handbills were given out at ports and posters displayed, describing and featuring the couple under the heading, in block capitals: WANTED FOR MURDER AND MUTILATION. A £250 reward was offered for information leading to capture of the fugitives. The press were alerted and Captain Kendall soon read in the *Daily Mail* of the third and successful search of the Crippen home and the furore surrounding the disappearance of Dr Crippen and his mistress on suspicion of murder. The newspaper carried a picture of the wanted 'cellar murderer' and Kendall was convinced Robinson was he. Crippen himself remained blissfully unaware of the intense publicity he engendered. Kendall tried to keep it that way, asking his crew to hide any current newspapers that might mention the case from 'Mr Robinson's' view. Using the new Marconi radio, for which the case would become even more famous, Captain Kendall made history by sending the first ever wireless telegraph resulting in the apprehension of a fugitive. Sent from 120 miles west of Cornwall, England, it read:

> *Have strong suspicion that Crippen London Cellar Murderer and accomplice are among saloon passengers. Moustache taken off growing Beard. Accomplice dressed as boy. Voice manner and build undoubtedly a girl. Both travelling as Mr and Master Robinson.* Kendall.

Received at the offices of the White Star Line in Liverpool, the cable was immediately forwarded to Scotland Yard. On 22 July, Detective Chief Inspector Dew read the telegraph from the *Montrose* and immediately set off with Sergeant Mitchell for Liverpool. Accompanying them were two wardresses, Miss Foster and Miss Stone, who would handle Miss Le Neve, post-arrest. On 23 July they boarded the SS *Laurentic* bound for Quebec, a much faster ship than Captain Kendall's vessel.

Blissfully unaware the net was closing Crippen and Le Neve enjoyed their last few days together, dreaming of a new life in the New World. No news reached them of their notoriety back in England, the *Montrose* being devoid of newspapers. For their part, the police hoped against hope that they were not on some wild goose chase. After all, others had already been arrested in England on suspicion of being Crippen, one of them on two occasions. They need not have worried. They would soon have their prey.

The *Laurentic* passed the *Montrose* on 27 of July at dead of night and reached its destination on 30 July, 24 hours before the vessel carrying Crippin and Le Neve. As the *Montrose* approached Quebec Harbour, Crippen realised his plans had come to naught. A ship's quartermaster had already tipped him off that he would be arrested on arrival. Hoping desperately to escape his fate, Crippen later alleged that he tried to bribe the quartermaster into saying he had fallen overboard, even writing a suicide note to cover his tracks. Perhaps he thought better of it, the quartermaster could not be bribed or, possibly, it was a figment of his imagination.

When the police approached him, Crippen was shocked to find the same two officers who had called at his home only a few short weeks previously. By way of a re-introduction, Dew said, 'Good morning Dr Crippen. I am Inspector Dew. I am here to arrest you for the murder of your wife, Cora Crippen, in London on or about second February last.' Crippen was crestfallen. He knew the likely outcome of a trial. Turning to Captain Kendall, he shouted: 'You shall pay for this treachery sir!' Curiously enough, disaster did later strike Kendall. While Captain of the passenger liner *Empress of Ireland* his ship collided with a Norwegian coal freighter, the *Storstad*, while on a voyage from Quebec to Liverpool on 29 May 1914. Of 1,477 passengers and crew on board, all but 465 drowned. Kendall did not fall victim to what the press called 'Crippen's curse'. Declining to go down with all hands, he lived to the ripe old age of 91.

Extradition proceedings against Crippen and Le Neve commenced swiftly and on 20 August, Dew and his prisoners were aboard the SS *Megantic*, bound from Montreal to Liverpool. Miss Le Neve was handcuffed to Miss Stone and Crippen to Sergeant Mitchell. Only once did the lovers meet, although no words were spoken.

On 28 August, to great commotion, the prisoners and their escorts arrived in Liverpool. The case had caught the attention of the world's press. Again, when alighting the Euston train, curious and boisterous crowds surrounded the man accused of the abominable murder and dismemberment of his wife. Deputy Chief Inspector Dew was the hero of the hour. He did not feel like it and was to retire three weeks after the Crippen trial concluded, aged only 47. Perhaps the sympathy he felt for Crippen was too much to let him become involved in such a case again. Certainly his memoirs, *I Caught Crippen*, published in 1938, strongly gave that impression.

To entertain a fascinated public, music-hall ditties were written, such as 'Miss Le Neve'.

> *Oh Miss Le Neve, oh Miss Le Neve,*
> *Is it true that you are sittin'*
> *On the lap of Dr Crippen*
> *In your boy's clothes,*
> *On the Montrose, Miss Le Neve?*

Even 51 years after the trial, Crippen's fame was such that a musical Belle, or the Ballad of Dr Crippen opened in London's West End, none too successfully, however.

While Crippen lay incarcerated in Pentonville, his case gripped the imagination of an enthralled public, as gruesome details of the victim's demise were revealed daily in the newspapers and more and more detail of the convoluted lives of the accused became known. He was even called a latter-day 'Jack the Ripper'. Articles appeared with fabricated quotes in the name of inspector Dew, in which he supposedly heard the 'confession' of Crippen in every detail. So incensed was Dew by this assault on his reputation that he sued nine newspapers for libel, winning damages from all, including the *Montreal Star*, *Evening Standard* and *Daily Chronicle*. In the meantime the public, probably the jury too, were convinced of Crippen's guilt.

Crippen's solicitor, Arthur John Edward Newton did him no favours, seeing him not as a man on trial for his life, but a source of money and publicity. Newton cobbled together a group of fraudsters and swindlers who agreed to fund the defence in exchange for exclusive rights to Crippen's story.

The greatest barrister of the day, Sir Edward Marshall Hall, KC, who actually believed in Crippen's innocence, was sought to defend him. However, he insisted on a fee up front and Newton would not pay. As a result, Crippen was defended by a KC with much less talent and no belief in the innocence of his client.

As the day of the trial dawned, over 1,000 curious citizens of all social classes, a horde of pressmen and their photographers lined the streets, held back by scores of police officers. Three hundred people packed into court, including 50 reporters.

* * *

The trial of Dr Hawley Harvey Crippen opened to a packed and bustling Court Number One at the Old Bailey on Tuesday, 18 October 1910. Mr RD Muir assisted by Mr Travers Humphreys and Mr Ingleby Oddie represented the Crown; Mr Alfred A Tobin KC, assisted by Messrs Roome and Huntley Jenkins, defended Crippen. The Lord Chief Justice of England, the Right Honourable Lord Alverstone, presided. Asked to plead, the defendant replied, 'Not guilty my Lord.'

Packed by the press corps and members of an intrigued public throughout, the trial of Crippen lasted five days. Mr Muir for the prosecution opened by presenting a series of key witnesses, including not only the Martinettis but also, arriving recently from America, Bruce Miller, the man Crippen had implied had eloped with his wife. Miller was adamant that no 'illicit relationship' with Mrs Crippen had ever existed, dismissing the defendant's claims as preposterous. The correspondence between Mr Miller and Cora was innocuous and the defence could not unsettle the witness.

On the second day of the trial, Detective Chief Inspector Dew and Dr Pepper provided damning evidence against the defendant. Dew produced Crippen's statement, offered when first they met and informed the court of a pyjama jacket found in the coal cellar and three pairs of pyjamas in the house, one of which had a missing jacket. After detailing further the gruesome discovery in the Crippen coal cellar and the transatlantic pursuit of Dr Crippen, Dew was easily able to deal with any points raised by Crippen's defence.

Dr Pepper explained that the missing pyjama jacket matched the one found in the coal cellar. No bones or reproductive organs had been found to indicate the sex of the remains. From the flesh and organs found, only a piece of skin, with what looked like the scar from an operation, appeared to offer a clue as to the victim's identity. Tellingly, the Martinettis in their evidence had testified that Cora Crippen had such a scar, from removal of her ovaries years before. Pepper also stated that the person (or persons) placing the remains in the cellar must have had knowledge, skill and experience of human anatomy. The hair from the Hinde clasp matched Mrs Crippen's from her home and, Dr Pepper added, the remains could have been buried not more than eight months prior to discovery. Dr Crippen's team disputed the findings of Dr Pepper but made little headway.

As the trial reached its midpoint, the renowned pathologist Dr Bernard Spilsbury (soon to be knighted) gave his expert opinion on the evidence, in this the first of many important trials at which he would appear. He said that, without a doubt, the piece of flesh under dispute contained the remnant of an operational scar. Gruesomely, the jury asked to see the flesh itself and it was duly passed round on a soup plate. Grandstanding by the defence failed to have much impact on the young pathologist and two more doctors, William Willcox and Arthur Luff, who followed him into the witness box.

Dr Willcox had examined the viscera and found evidence of hyoscine in the organs. Dr Luff supported the findings of his colleague. Mr Charles Hetherington, a pharmacist, then testified that Dr Crippen had purchased five grains of hyoscine hydrobromide on 17 or 18 January that year, only a fortnight or so before Cora Crippen disappeared. A therapeutic dose was only one hundredth of a grain. A fatal dose was a quarter of a grain and Willcox and Luff proved that at least twice that amount was present in the body of Mrs Crippen and had been ingested orally. The defence called a Dr Blyth to refute that hyoscine was even in the remains. He could not.

The prosecution rested, confident it had exposed Crippen as an adulterous, cold-blooded murderer who planned the poisoning of his wife well in advance, attempted to destroy the evidence in a brutal, ghastly way, concocted a tissue of lies to explain her disappearance and then fled from capture with his mistress.

Opening for the defence, Mr Tobin tried to paint a picture of his client as a rather sad and pathetic figure; a man much maligned and misunderstood. Dr

Crippen, as witness in his own defence, agreed with this assessment, adding that in his professional capacity he had not the necessary skill, training or experience to eviscerate a corpse. With regards to Mr Miller, Crippen stressed that a relationship did exist and that is why his wife left him. As for the hyoscine, he needed it to carry out his job.

With the trial nearing its zenith, more and more people tried to gain entry to the public gallery, as the entire country remained enthralled by the case. Members of the public had to write in requesting a seat in court. Only a few who did so were lucky enough to be chosen to view the drama unfolding.

After adjourning for the evening, cross-examination began early next morning with Mr Muir immediately on the attack. He was cold, calm, polite and relentless. Crippen buckled beneath a barrage of questions that slowly but steadily revealed the truth about the events of late January/early February 1910 in the Crippen home.

Seemingly innocuous questions were designed to catch out the suspected murderer. 'When had he last seen her? Did she eat breakfast? What did she have? What did she say? Did he give her money? Why did she leave her clothes and jewellery? Why did he pawn it/give it to Miss Le Neve? When did his mistress move into number 39 Hilldrop Crescent?' Mr Muir then quizzed Crippen about letters concocted by him concerning Cora's supposed death in America, the telegram to the Martinettis and his trip to Dieppe with Ethel.

After expanding on previous questions to further expose Crippen's deceptions, Muir moved onto the remains in the cellar. The courtroom hushed as the matter of the pyjamas was addressed. Muir asked when the three pairs of pyjamas were purchased. Crippen responded vaguely, insisting that the pair in question were bought separately in 1905. Muir proved they were manufactured from the same batch of cloth and purchased together. A Mr Chilvers was called. An employee of Jones Brothers, from whom Crippen confirmed he bought the pyjamas, he had a record of their sale. Mr Chilvers added that the label on the pyjamas bore the words 'Jones Brothers Holloway Limited', adding that the company had existed only since 1906, a year after Crippen claimed he purchased them. It was now clear in the minds of the jurors that the pyjamas found in the coal cellar must have belonged to the Crippens and could only have been buried there by the man standing before them in the dock.

Moving onto the defendant's flight from justice, Mr Muir comprehensively dismantled Crippen's feeble responses to questions now asked in short staccato bursts.

The defence had one last card to play before closing speeches – Dr Turnbull, Director of the Pathological Institute, was called to identify the incriminating piece of flesh marked with a scar. Arthur Newton, Crippen's solicitor, had promised he would not have to testify and Turnbull was both aghast and ill-prepared.

He tried to identify the skin as being from a thigh and said the scar was a 'fold'. Spilsbury calmly showed that the skin was attached to a rectus muscle, using forceps to clearly show Dr Turnbull's mistake. Dr Wall, called to back up Dr Turnbull, admitted they were wrong. Mr Muir, Scottish-born with a hankering for the stage in his youth, had shaken the usually placid Dr Crippen and turned the testimony of defence witnesses to his advantage. Few now doubted the outcome.

After closing speeches and the summing up, the jury retired at 2.15pm, Saturday 22 October. Returning a mere 37 minutes later, they gave their verdict: guilty. As Lord Alverstone placed the black cap solemnly on his head, Crippen blurted out, 'I still protest my innocence'. Facing the now convicted murderer, the judge read out the sentence of death.

Crippen had been badly advised by his defence counsel and Mr Newton, who was jailed and disbarred three years later for forging Crippen's 'confession'. Crippen should also never have placed himself in the witness stand. Once he did, his conviction was guaranteed. Possibly he no longer really cared. Had Crippen pleaded guilty to killing Cora in a fit of passion, revealing the way she had humiliated and laughed at him, he could have possibly saved himself, but at the price of years, possibly life, in prison for manslaughter without his beloved Ethel. He would also have had to divulge Ethel's pregnancy, miscarriage and the whole sordid tale. In fact, throughout his own case he seemed distracted, more concerned for his mistress than himself and he constantly asked after her.

On Tuesday 25 October it was the turn of Ethel Le Neve to face trial, as an 'accessory after the fact' in the murder of Cora Crippen.

The prosecution case, led by the same team that secured the conviction of Crippen, presented their evidence in a similar vein, denouncing Miss Le Neve as a woman who profited from the death of her rival in love and well aware of that woman's fate when she moved into the Crippen home. Her decision to flee twice with her lover implied, to the Crown at least, full knowledge of Dr Crippen's crime.

Defended by England's youngest King's Counsel, Frederick Edwin Smith, no evidence was submitted on behalf of Miss Le Neve, who wisely did not give evidence. Mr Smith made an impassioned and emotional speech on behalf of his client instead, telling the jury she was merely the love-struck dupe of an older, cunning and wicked man. She had known nothing of the murder of Cora Crippen/Belle Ellmore. Her only crime, he added, was to love and trust in Dr Crippen so unreservedly. Finally, he asked the jury to find Miss Le Neve guilty only if they believed she had actively participated in the murder itself and its immediate aftermath by assisting in the disposal of the body.

Following a sympathetic summing up from Lord Alverstone, in less than 20 minutes the jury found Ethel Le Neve not guilty. She had been tried and acquitted in less than a day.

Crippen's spirits rose briefly following the exoneration of his mistress. He appealed. The appellate jury dismissed it. Only Home Secretary Winston Churchill could offer any reprieve now. He did not and so Crippen sought to cheat justice by cutting his wrists, using his spectacles as a razor. It was to no avail. He was quickly discovered and saved for execution.

While awaiting his fate, Crippen wrote constantly to his beloved Ethel, who now visited him daily. Eleven of these letters are still extant. He told her how kind prison governor Major Mytton-Davies was in breaking the news that, finally, he was to die. Ethel refrained from telling him the governor had nonchalantly chased her from his door when she went to plead for her lover's life. A letter followed each visit. Crippen's always had a poignant heading such as, 'Not even death can come between us ... ' and 'I first kissed your face ... '. All displayed heartfelt love, devotion and concern for the love of his life. In Ethel's letters we can only assume similar sentiments were expressed. It was Crippen's last wish that Ethel's letters and photograph go to the grave with him. Prison staff, by now quite fond of their infamous, polite and well-mannered inmate, honoured his request. Crippen in anguish romantically and tearfully declared to Ethel, 'How am I to endure to take my last look at your dear face; what agony must I go through when you disappear forever from my eyes?' His final words to her were, 'We shall meet again!'

By now the press and public who had howled for Crippen's head a few short weeks earlier were muted. The murder, dismemberment and burial of Cora Crippen was not forgotten but people were touched by the obvious love Crippen and Le Neve had for one another. On 20 November *Lloyds Weekly* printed his 'Farewell letter to the World', in which he took great pains to declare the innocence of his amour, while hinting at his own.

Executioner John Ellis carried out the sentence of hanging at 9.00am on the morning of Wednesday, 23 November 1910, in Pentonville prison.

The irony in this case is that Crippen possibly did not kill his wife with poison after all. Dr Ingleby Oddie, who had served on the prosecution team, speculated that poisoning was the plan. The hyocine would give the appearance of a heart attack and a death certificate soon follow – the murder would never be detected. Unfortunately for Crippen, Oddie postulated, hyocine does not always sedate. The shouting and hysterical screaming neighbours heard in the early hours of 1 February could have been the death throes of Cora. Such cries might have panicked Crippen who, fearing an inquest and discovery of the poison, shot her instead and then disposed of the body as best he could. Dr Crippen had possessed a gun, ammunition and at least one neighbour said a loud bang 'like a pistol shot' was indeed heard. Inspector Dew did find a gun in his first search of the Crippen house. No bloodstains were found either, even though a bloody dismemberment had taken place. Only in the enamel bath could dissection have been carried out with minimal evidence remaining. One thing is certain; no one will ever know the truth.

On the very day her former lover was hanged, Ethel, calling herself 'Miss Allen', boarded the SS *Majestic* bound for Canada. There she worked as a secretary and wrote her memoirs, returning to England in 1916. She changed her name again, to Nelson, met an accountant, Stanley Smith, married and had a son and a daughter. The Smiths settled in Bournemouth and opened a teashop. They were very happy together and Mr Smith was apparently the spitting image of Crippen. No one, including her husband until his death, was aware that she was Ethel Le Neve.

In 1954 an author, Ursula Bloom, who wanted to write a book telling the story from the lovers' perspective, visited Ethel. By now 71, and 13 years from her own death on 6 August 1967, she would not co-operate and the book was never written. Frustrated, Ms Bloom asked Ethel whether, if Crippen were alive today would she marry him? Staring at her intently, Ethel replied, 'Yes I would.'

*   *   *

Postscript

It seems that there our story ends. Or does it? A hundred years after Dr Crippen was hanged scientists at Michigan State University led by forensic biologist Dr David Foran carried out DNA tests on the remains found at Hilldrop Crescent. It was concluded they were not the remains of Cora Crippen.

Using one of Dr Spilsbury's histological slides secured from the Royal London Hospital Archives and Museum, DNA from the remains was compared to mitochondrial DNA (mtDNA), which is inherited through the maternal line only, from three of Mrs Crippen's living female relatives. They found no match. Further DNA testing proved that the tissue was in fact that of a male.

The findings were published in the *Journal of Forensic Science* in January 2011 and co-authored by poisoning expert John Trestrail III of the Centre for the Study of Criminal Poisoning in Los Lunas, New Mexico, who pursued the sampling of tissues from the case.

Scotland Yard still retains a lock of hair trapped in a curler that was found with the remains. That hair sample intrigued Mr Trestrail, who kicked off an effort to sample tissues from the case that culminated in the study.

The study authors argue that there was no contamination from latter-day handlers of the slide that would have delivered the wrong conclusion in terms of the sex to which the flesh belonged. If they are correct, then the genealogical and DNA investigation proves that that the remains did not come from Cora Crippen.

Professor Allan Jamieson of the Forensic Institute in Glasgow, agrees that the study provides powerful evidence that the body did not belong to Cora, while genetics professor Mark Jobling of the University of Leicester is more cautious, fearing that contamination of the slide still might explain the results. Like the study authors and Professor Jamieson, he believes it is unfortunate that the lock of hair found with the remains was not made available for testing and comparison with the tissue to provide important corroboration – or not as the case may be – and reduce the risk of a false result.

But if the researchers are right, one can only speculate about who the remains belonged to, how they got there and what happened to Cora. Is it possible that Crippen murdered someone else and those were the remains discovered? Or could the evidence have been planted? Could Ethel have known the true identity of the remains foiund in the garden?

Crippen's relatives now hope to secure an official pardon but the authorities in London have refused such requests as they are not related closely enough to raise legal questions about the case.

It seems that the case of Dr Hawley Harvey Crippen will remain a fascinating and tantalising one, for many years to come.

CHAPTER 6
Dr Philip Cross: No Fool Like an Old Fool

DR PHILIP CROSS was a happily married retired army surgeon, 62-years-old, when she walked into his life. A young woman of only 20, Evelyn Skinner, known as Effie, was not particularly beautiful. Pretty, she radiated softness, vulnerability and possessed an ethereal quality that impacted immediately upon the aged doctor, who recounted to his prison warder, 'It was as if I was struck by a thunderbolt.' He had not been looking for love, but it certainly found him and Mrs Cross was to suffer the tragic consequences.

* * *

Dr Philip Henry Eustace Cross and his wife Mary, known by her middle name of Laura, enjoyed 18 years of married life together. They met in the summer of 1869 when Dr Cross was in Ireland on leave from army service in India. Laura was from an Irish family of good social standing and, after a whirlwind courtship, the couple married in August of that year at St James' Church, Piccadilly in London. The match did not amuse Laura's parents, the Marriotts. Cross was 22-years older than his new wife, with only his modest army pay on which to survive.

The wedding was rushed as Dr Cross had to embark for Montreal, Canada, to rejoin his regiment. Mrs Cross was soon bored with army life and went home. Having served the Crown on five continents as an army surgeon and reaching the rank of major, Cross felt much the same as his wife and successfully sought an honourable discharge.

Retiring to Ireland on a pension of £250 a year, Dr Cross became financially secure when his wife inherited a small legacy and dutifully handed it over to her husband. A property was bought and the doctor began a fairly comfortable life of hunting, shooting and fishing, while his wife concentrated on raising their growing family.

There were ups and downs as in any relationship, but no strains were evident to outsiders. Mrs Cross bore five children, three girls and two boys. The children proved a handful, two of them suffering from epilepsy. The family home, Shandy Hall, in the hamlet of Dripsey, near Coachford village, County Cork was fine, if rambling and everyone appeared content with their lot. The doctor seemed settled and relaxed in his retirement. And so he was until Effie caught his eye.

For the first time, Dr Cross realised his life was only satisfactory. He wanted bliss. Burning with desire for Effie, he was convinced she could give him the joy he now desperately sought. The lass that had entered his life became a secret obsession and he watched her keenly, waiting only for the opportunity to prove his masculinity and capture her sweet young heart.

Effie had joined the Cross household in October 1886 as the children's governess. A neighbour, Mrs Caulfield, who knew Miss Skinner to be 'modest and gentle', recommended her. As the new governess settled in, Dr Cross quickly let his infatuation show. Her youth and sparkle enraptured him. The other servants, and soon the neighbours, began to notice. One day, as Effie chatted to him about the children, he bent over and kissed her, half expecting her to repel him, run away or tell his wife. Effie did nothing of the sort. She remained at Shandy Hall, perhaps due to straitened circumstances or because of a growing affection for her ageing suitor. Possibly her motives were more mercenary. Believing he now had a chance to win Effie's love Dr Cross pursued Miss Skinner ardently. The young woman responded positively.

It took Mrs Cross only a few days to discern the faraway look in the eyes of her lovesick husband and the growing intimacy between him and the young governess. Laura Cross knew she could not compete with Effie on looks or youth. Fearing Dr Cross might make an fool of himself, her or their family she took pre-emptive action and sacked her employee. At first her husband seemed to concur. 'Perhaps it would be a good thing, if that's how you feel about it. I'll give Miss Skinner a cheque in lieu of notice and say she must leave at once,' he told his wife. Inwardly he was bereft and Effie shattered. She packed her bags and left for Carlow. Had Mrs Cross believed that she had nipped any shenanigans in the bud she was completely mistaken.

On a pretext of attending the races, Mrs Cross' husband trailed lustily after the woman of his dreams having arranged to tryst with her, not in Carlow but in a Dublin hotel the very next day. Effie registered as 'Mrs Osborne' and was soon joined by 'Mr Osborne' who insisted on a double bed for him and his 'wife'. His luggage was labelled 'P. X.' but the hotel manager, Mr William Poole, thought lit-tle of it at the time. After all, it was none of his business.

In Dublin, Effie gave herself to her elderly amour and the lovers shared five days and nights together. Dr Cross felt ecstatic, but it was not enough and could never be enough. Effie Skinner was his world now and he would stop at nothing until he could not only possess her sexually, but also make her his wife. He thus plotted the death of his devoted, innocent and loving spouse.

As Effie headed across the sea to England, her lover returned home. A friend of his wife, Miss Margaret Jefferson, who informed him that his wife was taken ill on the very day Effie Skinner departed, met him.

Laura Cross had always enjoyed rude health. It was therefore a surprise to all who knew her when she began to suffer from severe vomiting on Friday, 26 May

1887. Her husband attended and diagnosed weakness of the heart, insisting he would treat it himself. Miss Jefferson suggested a second opinion from another doctor but the squire of Shandy Hall would hear none of it, refusing even to seek the aid of a nurse.

Over the next few days, the patient deteriorated. The medicine given to Laura seemed only to make her increasingly ill. She had frequent spasms and could not move her hands or feet. Despite the obvious decline of Mrs Cross, friends and neighbours who enquired of her were cheerily informed that her condition was improving. They were not allowed to see her in person as she supposedly had an 'infectious fever'. Even her brother-in-law, a clergyman, was turned away. Eventually a Dr Thomas Godfrey was able to examine Mrs Cross. His opinion was that the patient was suffering from a bilious attack and recommended nothing more than a strong purgative. Dr Thomas never returned. When asked about this at his colleague's trial, Godfrey simply responded that, 'She was not my patient'. His lack of interest was criticised after the trial of Dr Cross by no less than the *Lancet*, which not only berated Godfrey's indifference and incompetence but also expressed concern that within the noble profession of medicine lurked 'criminals of the deepest hue'.

Mrs Cross died at 1.00am on the morning of 2 June. 'My poor Laura has just passed away. It's a happy release,' Dr Cross told Mrs Jefferson, coldly. The servants were ushered in, unemotionally given the bad news and told to wash the corpse before dressing it in a nightshirt. A funeral was swiftly arranged for the following day and the body placed unceremoniously in a coffin to await its final journey to the graveyard

Mrs Jefferson urged Dr Cross to contact Laura's brother. The doctor argued indignantly that it would be pointless to write to his former brother-in-law, Sir William Marriott, Tory MP for Brighton, as the gentleman was in England and therefore unable to reach Dripsey in time for the funeral. Dr Cross signed the death certificate, recording his wife's death as due to 'typhoid fever'. In the excitement he did not forgot her alleged heart condition and another neighbour was told that 'angina pectoris' had caused Laura's death.

The late Mrs Cross was buried with unseemly haste the following day, rather furtively at 6.30 in the morning, attended by around 20 friends and family members. Laura's brother was informed that his sister was not interred in the family vault at Carrigrohan, as it was 'full up'. Rather, she was laid to rest in Magourney Cemetery in nearby Coachford.

Dr Philip Cross made no effort to even appear to mourn the late mother of his children, despite their apparently many happy years together. Soon he sped away from Shandy Hall, boarding a ship on the pretext of breaking the news to his children who were at school in England and as yet unaware that their mother had passed away. It was a pretext. A mere 10 days after the death of his wife,

Cross married Effie Skinner. To add further affront the marriage took place in the same church, St James, where he had married Laura two decades before.

They say love is blind. Not so blind that Cross was unaware of what the gossips would say if he returned to Ireland with a wife young enough to be his granddaughter, a couple of weeks after Laura's death. He decided their marriage should remain secret for the time being. Effie would be re-employed as governess, he would be seen to court her and eventually she would emerge from her cocoon to all and sundry as the new Mrs Cross. By the time Dr Cross reached Shandy Hall, his plans were dashed. Wagging tongues had spread the news before him. Seeing that his new marriage had been rumbled, Dr Cross thought it pointless to keep Effie in London. Who cared if people talked? He and Mrs Effie Cross were in love and that was all that mattered. Any scandal would be short-lived, possibly even a blessing in disguise. He and Effie would live openly as man and wife sooner than anticipated. In fact, the married life of Philip and Effie Cross was to be anything but a long and happy one.

Rumours abounded in County Cork as to the real cause of the 'illness' that claimed the life of the first Mrs Cross. The police were neither immune nor inured to such tittle-tattle. They had encountered the somewhat irascible Dr Cross before. In 1885 Dr Cross was prosecuted and convicted of assaulting a farmer, Mr Phil Connell, who objected to Cross hunting on his land. An affray occurred and Dr Cross sliced off Connell's ear with a whip before riding off. Mr Connell was awarded £200 in damages.

An anonymous letter was sent to the authorities accusing the doctor of the dastardly deed of poisoning his first wife. After some weeks, pressure mounted to exhume the body of Laura Cross from Magourney graveyard. Sir William Marriott wrote to Dr Cross asking for an explanation as to the circumstances surrounding his sister's death. Cross informed his former brother-in-law that, as Laura had died on a Friday and Sunday was the day for 'Popish' funerals, she was buried on the Saturday to avoid decomposition in the summer heat, a certainty had he waited until Monday. Such a reply proved unsatisfactory and Marriott demanded that the Royal Irish Constabulary disinter his sister's body.

District Police Inspector Tyacke decided upon action, despite concerns that members of Dr Cross' social class were against any proceedings. The coroner, James Horgan, a prominent nationalist solicitor, asked Professor Charles Pearson, of Queen's College, Cork, to attend and Laura Cross was unceremoniously exhumed from her cold, lonely burial place.

Professor Pearson and his colleague, Dr Crowley, analysed the corpse and found strychnine and 3.2 grains of arsenic in her body. There was no trace of heart disease or typhoid fever. There was, however, evidence that she had been polished off with a pillow. The police soon located the chemist nearby from whom Dr Cross had bought the poison. He was immediately arrested.

Following his arrest, Cross was taken before the local police court and resident magistrate, Mr Gardiner, who asked inspector Tyacke if the accused had said anything upon his arrest. Gardiner then carried out a preliminary investigation. The accused, somewhat shocked, declared 'there is a god above me who will see the villainy of such a charge'.

Inspector Tyacke explained how he had discovered two bottles of poison in a bedside drawer in Shandy Hall where he also found the diary of Dr Cross in which he stated, matter-of-factly, on June 2 that, 'Mary Laura Cross departed this life. May she go to heaven is my prayer. Expense of funeral etc., five guineas.' Hardly the comments of a man grieving or even particularly bothered, by the death of his dear wife. The diary mentioned the failure of Laura's weak heart from 'exhaustion' and how 'typhoid fever debilitated the poor dear'.

The magistrate had heard enough and explained that 'in view of what we heard, I must commit you to trial.' In response, Dr Cross declared himself 'As innocent as any man in this room,' to which Mr Gardiner replied, 'That is something for another tribunal to consider.'

The trial of Dr Cross before the Munster Assizes in Cork town was a sensation. Crimes of passion were not supposed to happen in rural 19th-century Ireland and the public clamoured daily for news of the thrilling revelations revealed in court. Sex and murder is a glorious mixture to a salacious gossip-hungry public.

Dr Cross had been arrested in August and his trial opened on 13 December. The able and tireless Judge Murphy presided, the Attorney General, John Gibson QC, conducted the prosecution and John (later Lord) Atkinson QC defended. Ireland was a restless nation yet for once Home Rule, the Land League and the proclivities of Charles Stewart Parnell, the Irish Nationalist leader, paled into insignificance compared to the goings on at Munster Assizes.

The press were sympathetic to the accused, describing him as 'upright, of martial bearing, no ordinary man' and 'the very embodiment of composure'. Dr Cross pleaded not guilty.

The prosecution opened up with a withering attack from the Attorney General, whose preliminary address to the jury lasted several hours. He pointed out that there was 'positive evidence that this lady did not die, as he alleges, from either heart disease or fever'. Moving on, Gibson declared the sole motivation of the accused as being the need to gratify his own lust for a young woman he heartlessly seduced. Desire for Miss Skinner drove him to kill Mrs Cross, 'in order to fly back to his paramour and to elevate her to the position of the wife he had poisoned'. Gibson concluded his opening by declaring the alleged felony 'exceeded in wickedness, callousness and cowardice, any of the crimes yet dealt with in a court of justice, one of the most horrible that ever disgraced our common humanity', adding finally that 'it is for you, gentlemen of the jury, to say whether this wicked intrigue had its origin under the very roof that sheltered his ailing spouse, the mother of his children'.

Having taken up the entire first day with the Crown's opening address, the first prosecution witnesses were not heard until the following day. Mr William Poole confirmed that Dr Cross and Miss Skinner had stayed in his hotel prior to the death of Mrs Cross as 'Mr and Mrs Osborne'. Inspector Tyacke testified that he had found the Dublin hotel bill in the doctor's pocket-book and informed the court of where and when he had found two bottles containing strychnine and arsenic respectively, the bottles being labelled 'strychnine' and 'dog poison'. The contents of Cross' diary at the time of his wife's death were also revealed.

Under cross-examination, inspector Tyacke revealed that he had asked the doctor what the arsenic was for, to be told, 'sheep dipping'. Warily, Tyacke agreed with Mr Atkinson when pressed if that was indeed an occasional use of that drug. The chemist who sold the arsenic to Dr Cross then took the stand and confirmed that the doctor had purchased it just prior to the deceased's 'illness'.

Professor Pearson was probably the key witness in the trial and in his evidence made it clear that poisoning alone caused the death of Mrs Cross. Pearson went on to state that the strychnine and arsenic discovered in her viscera was toxic and there was nothing else found that could have caused death naturally. Judge and jury were given a thorough explanation of the analysis undertaken and shown bottles containing the poison extracted from the victim. The defence cross-examined.

Unflappable, Pearson refused to rise to the bait when Mr Atkinson tried first to trap him into withdrawing statements and then tried to goad the witness into losing his temper. It was Atkinson who broke first, shouting, 'Do you really know anything you have been talking about?' Calmly, Pearson responded to this attack on his professionalism by declaring, 'I happen to know a great deal about it.' The prosecution case rested after the jury heard of the strange behaviour and goings on at Shandy Hall during the last few days on earth of the late Mrs Cross.

The defence tried its best. Accomplished though he was, Atkinson faced an uphill struggle. His address on behalf of his client was 'so beautifully delivered, felicitously phrased and closely reasoned throughout,' that he met with thunderous applause on finishing. Wonderful phraseology is not enough. Hard facts are more important and Atkinson could produce little to discomfit the hard forensic evidence of the prosecution.

Atkinson clutched at straws. He argued that a guilty man would have destroyed or concealed the poisons found at Shandy Hall, which, in any case, could have been brought into the Cross home by anyone. The evidence against his client was 'purely circumstantial' and, as a medical man, Dr Cross had access to drugs that would leave no trace. While this argument gained ground for the defendant, Atkinson was deemed preposterous in his insistence that the doctor had no motive, when everyone knew exactly that he had a very strong motive: Effie.

Realising he had gone too far, Mr Atkinson urged the jury to discount the 'immoral behaviour' of his client but stretched incredulity when calling for it to be ignored as extraneous to the case before them. He also urged the disregarding of Professor Pearson's expert testimony, again claiming that it was somehow irrelevant.

Henrietta Cross, sister of the accused, was called to support Atkinson's view of the Cross marriage as being, if not exactly idyllic, then at least happy until the very end. Henrietta did what she could to support her sibling, but proved to be of little help, confirming that Mrs Cross was unaware of her husband's infidelity with Effie in Dublin.

On behalf of his client, counsel claimed that Laura Cross had taken arsenic to 'improve her complexion'. This could not explain her consumption of strychnine. The jury found it hard to believe she would have taken such a lethal poison readily. Of course she could have and may even have done so enraged at her beloved husband's blatant and obvious infidelity with what his wife saw as a mere slip of a girl. The balance of probability suggested otherwise. How would Mrs Cross have accessed strychnine and why would she want to suffer such a slow, agonising and un-Christian death? Was it an accident? If Laura had taken arsenic in toxic doses by mistake, should her experienced doctor husband not have recognised the symptoms and advised her to stop? Clearly, Dr Cross had motive, means and opportunity to kill his wife. No one else had an incentive to see Laura Cross dead, nor access to deadly poison or indeed the lady herself. The prosecution made sure the jury were continuously apprised of this obvious scenario.

Despite the circumstantial evidence against his patron, counsel for the accused argued his client's innocence vehemently. For his part, Dr Cross sat impassively in the dock, sometimes arrogantly, not for a minute believing he would be convicted. Prior to hearing the verdict, Dr Cross sent urgently for his solicitor, who thought his client had some vital information to impart at this late stage. Said the doctor, 'After yesterday's proceedings my dinner was cold, and I should feel obliged if you would take care that today it will be kept hot!' Only minutes later he would hear of his gloomy fate.

Having exhausted their modest list of witnesses, the defence rested and, after a week-long trial, on 18 December 1887, Mr Justice Murphy proceeded to the summing up. He reminded the jury that they must ignore the defendant's 'immorality' and 'callous indifference to the proper decencies of domestic conduct'. They must focus exclusively on whether or not the death of Mrs Laura Cross was 'due to the deliberate action of her husband'. Justice Murphy advised the jury that a crime had been committed and that they must consider who had motive, means and opportunity. In doing so, attention was drawn to the cold way in which the servants at Shandy Hall were informed of their mistress's death, the 'foul adultery' committed by Dr Cross and young Effie, proven by both witnesses and letters. The jury were then asked to decide whether exhaustion of the heart had carried off the victim and, if so, what caused it. The jury were reminded that, after Laura's death, Cross 'hurried with callous and wicked speed to replace the wife not yet cold in her grave'. Finally, the jury were told that if they believed the accused's first wife had been 'done to death' after being poisoned by her husband, then they must find him guilty.

With the words of Mr Justice Murphy still ringing in their ears, it did not take long for the jury to reach the same conclusion he obviously had. After only an hour, the 12 good men and true returned to give their unanimous verdict – 'Guilty!'

The convicted murderer in the dock was asked if he had anything to say before sentence was pronounced. He had a lot to say. For some 40 minutes he addressed the court, expressing his complete innocence. The only wrong the retired army surgeon had committed was 'to Miss Skinner'. The speech was so full of denial and self-pity the court grew restless and so he was unsubtly hurried along.

Dr Philip Cross had been convicted of 'wilful murder'. Only one sentence was possible and the court fell into a deep hush as the judge tremulously placed a black cloth atop his judicial wig. Mr Murphy informed the court that he agreed with the verdict and had to dispense his solemn duty under the law. As Cross listened unflinchingly, sentence of death by hanging was announced.

Dr Cross' social peers, who had hung around the court for days like a bad smell, had agitated for acquittal. Dr Cross was, after all, one of them. They were acutely embarrassed to see a member of their class convicted of murder. For his part, Dr Cross refused to accept he was doomed and began to petition all and sundry, anyone who would support a reprieve. Several hundred signatures were gathered, mostly from opponents of the death penalty, rather than from those who thought the old doctor innocent and thus unjustly convicted. The Viceroy of Ireland, Lord Londonderry was contacted and asked to show mercy. The petition was returned marked, 'No grounds'.

In vain, the siblings and offspring of the condemned man tried to avert the inevitable. The Chief Secretary of Ireland agreed to meet them at his office in Dublin Castle. He was sympathetic but could do nothing. Although Philip Cross had been convicted purely on circumstance, few doubted his guilt. To reprieve him would be seen as the 'toffs' looking after one of their own. Public opinion strongly supported carrying out the sentence handed down. Justice must therefore be served.

Innocent of any involvement, Effie was devastated to have been the catalyst for so dastardly a deed and refused to visit her murderous husband rotting in his condemned cell. She left Ireland and vanished. Heartbroken at being spurned by his young love, the hair of Dr Cross turned chalk-white overnight as he now accepted the inevitable and steeled himself. He told his warders he feared not death, having faced it many times before on the battlefield. The Dublin press remained sympathetic and would later eulogise that the retired army surgeon 'faced death with the courage he showed before the trenches at Sebastopol' more than 30 years earlier. The night before the execution, even Judge Murphy needed consoling, as he confided to his friend Sir Denis Henry (later Lord Chief Justice, Belfast).

A professional hangman, Mr James Berry, veteran of over 120 judicial killings was brought over from England, courtesy of the Home Office. The press, much to their consternation, were banned from witnessing further events unfold. Indignant, they later berated officials who had barred them, accusing them of 'acting improperly in thus declining to gratify the natural curiosity of the public'. Having missed the enactment of capital punishment, journalists were left to invent flowery and dramatic descriptions of how Dr Philip Henry Eustace Cross met his end.

Still grieving for his lost love Effie, the old murderer was executed on 10 January 1888 and buried in a limed coffin in the grounds of Cork Prison.

CHAPTER 7
Dr Francois Duvalier: Papa Doc

THE FUTURE DICTATOR of Haiti first came to prominence as a specialist in tropical medicine. After becoming Director General of the National Health Service and Minister for Health and Labour, he was popularly elected as the first-ever president of the Caribbean nation of Haiti to win power through universal adult suffrage. While ballot rigging was undoubtedly in play, Duvalier was genuinely well-liked and admired. By the time of his death 14 years later, he was universally feared and reviled as one of the worst murderers, torturers and kleptomaniacs ever to hold power.

*　*　*

A small nation of only 27,750 square kilometres, teeming with over ten million inhabitants, Haiti occupies the western third of the island of Hispaniola. Once it must have seemed like a paradise, for Haiti was blanketed by tropical rain forest, with palm-lined beaches and colourful exotic flowers. By the mid-20th century, most of the forest cover had been hacked or burned down, fertile pastureland over-grazed and beaches that, elsewhere would have thronged with visitors enticed by a burgeoning tourist industry, lay deserted.

The first Europeans to visit the Caribbean were under the command of Christopher Columbus, who reached the island Spaniards later named Hispaniola during his first exploratory voyage in 1492. The island was occupied by Ciboney Indians from 5000BC and Arawaks from around 1000BC. Both Native American Indian cultures, together with a more sophisticated Taino Arawak culture that arrived from Mexico in 200AD, were peaceful. The natives grew maize, built temples and worshipped human and animal spirits. The name they gave their island was 'Hayti,' meaning 'mountainous land'.

In 1496 the Spaniards founded the town of Santo Domingo and began to colonise the island in search of gold. The half million or so natives were enslaved, ruthlessly exploited and forced to work in mines and agricultural estates established by the colonists. Disease, to which the natives had no resistance, overwork, despair and Spanish brutality almost exterminated them within decades. From 1520 slaves were brought from Africa primarily to work on sugar plantations, as there was more wealth to be wrought from 'white gold' than mining for the real stuff, which existed in only tiny quantities on the island.

After the conquest of Mexico, Spanish interest in Hispaniola waned and many colonists and 'conquistadors' moved to 'New Spain' as their new possession was then called. French pirates began to use the western part of Hispaniola, particularly the small island of La Tortue, as a base to attack and loot Spanish shipping. The pirates were encouraged by an expansionist France to settle on Hispaniola itself and soon flourishing French sugar and coffee industries developed, all built on slavery. Eventually, at the treaty of Ryswick in 1697, Spain acknowledged their rivals' claims to western Hispaniola and it became a formal French colony with the name of Saint Domingue. By the end of the 18th century some half-a-million black slaves, two thirds of them African-born, toiled for around 40,000 whites, most of whom wanted independence from France with themselves in control. There were also 28,000 mixed race 'mulattos,' the offspring of slaves and their white masters. Often free, the mulattos also exploited the slaves, treating them with open contempt. Some 30,000 blacks were also emancipated, frequently wealthy and slave-owning. Strongly pro-slavery, their slaves were badly treated, as their masters strived to be more European than the French themselves, drenching themselves in French clothing, language and culture, denigrating Creole and their own African roots. Devout Catholics, they despised African beliefs and tried to show themselves as distinct from the slaves. Despite their efforts to become French, the whites scorned them.

The life of a slave in Saint Domingue was hard in what was the richest, most desired colony not only in the West Indies, but the entire world. Often cruelly worked to death on a meagre diet, the death rate of slaves exceeded the birth rate seven-fold. To replenish numbers, tens of thousands of fresh slaves were imported from Africa annually. Seething with hate and resentment, the slaves saw little of the wealth from the sugar, cotton, coffee, cocoa, sisal, fruit and vegetables exported to France.

African-born field slaves would form the backbone of the forthcoming slave revolt. They also retained much of their native languages and traditions, which would later fuse with French to produce a unique Creole cultural, linguistic and religious hybrid. The latter, combining African and Catholic beliefs would ensure a cult known as 'voodoo' survived and flourished.

Following the 1789 French revolution, the whites, mulattos and free blacks bickered among themselves. Seeing their oppressors weaken, the slaves of Saint Domingue rebelled against their colonial masters, on 21 August 1791, led by Francois Toussaint L'Ouverture, born a slave in 1743 but freed in 1777. The spark was a Petwo voodoo service on 14 August at which a woman named Boukman claimed to be possessed by Ougoun Feraille, the voodoo warrior spirit. In his voice she called for all slaves to rise up and slaughter the whites.

Thousands of whites and mulattos, men women and children, were massacred and the country set ablaze. With British and Spanish help, the rebels built up a sizeable guerrilla army, aided by maroons; runaway slaves who lived deep in the mountains.

For years black slaves, free blacks, poor whites, rich whites and mulattos fought against and between each other. The French National Assembly dispatched a three-man commission led by Leger Felicite Sonthronax to take charge. Eventually, in order to retain French control, Sonthronax took the momentous step of freeing the slaves in exchange for their help in resisting British and Spanish incursions. The declaration, made on 29 August 1793 and ratified in Paris on 4 February the following year, brought freedom to the slaves but internecine warfare continued.

Military expeditions sent by France to reclaim its most prosperous colony were decimated by yellow fever as Haiti was engulfed in a savage war of unbelievable horror perpetrated by all sides. Rape, torture and murder of non-combatants of every age and both sexes were de rigueur. Heads were mounted on spikes along roadsides and on pikes erected on stockade walls. Dogs were used to tear apart prisoners and eyes were gouged out. After a hard-fought and bloody struggle, independence was declared on 1 January 1804. Almost a third of the pre-war black population was dead, the plantations looted and burned to the ground and the countryside utterly devastated in the preceding orgy of destruction. The new nation was named 'Haiti' and Saint Domingue confined to history.

Toussaint L'Ouverture had died in a French prison on 2 November 1802, and the first ruler was his former general Jean Jaques Dessalines, an illiterate ex-slave who declared himself emperor, tearing the white from the French tricolour to create Haiti's new flag. His first act was to order the entire slaughter – man, woman and child – of the remaining white population, thousands having already been killed or fled. Members of the Catholic clergy were not spared, resulting in the breaking of ties between Haiti and the Vatican.

Dessalines launched a vicious wave of terror against the ex-slaves and introduced forced labour, restricting them to their former plantations. Slavery was formally abolished 'for all time' although his subjects barely noticed as they toiled under barely different conditions, minus the whip. The Haitian constitution, promulgated in 1804, prohibited the ownership of property by whites and confiscated all that they previously owned. Assassinated by mulatto officers in 1806, Dessalines' 'empire' soon split into a northern kingdom, ruled by Henri Christophe, and a republic in the south and west, ruled by a mulatto, Alexandre Petion.

Petion broke up some of the estates to raise money and pay his soldiers, creating a class of smallholding peasants who subsisted on the bounty of their land. Gone were the sugar plantations of before. Yams, corn and bananas were the new staples of a nation the Europeans and United States refused to trade with, for fear of encouraging revolt among their own slaves.

French language and culture, even in the absence of any Frenchmen, remained attractive to Haiti's new rulers. It allowed them to distinguish themselves from the illiterate masses. Even amongst the Creole-speaking majority, French mores proliferated. Curiously, everyone in Haiti had, or soon took, French Christian and surnames, even those born in Africa who had perhaps been enslaved only briefly.

Haiti re-united in 1820 when Christophe shot himself with a silver bullet and two years later the Haitian army, under its new ruler, General Jean-Pierre Boyer, conquered the rest of Hispaniola. In 1826, Boyer introduced a labour law restricting peasants to their farms. This repressive law also banned travel without an overseer or landowner's approval, prevented workers' associations buying plantations and insisted on labourer respect for the new, usually mulatto, elite, all on pain of imprisonment.

In 1844 the Haitians were driven out of eastern Hispaniola. Throughout the rest of the 19th century and into the 20th, Haiti lurched from dictatorship to murderous dictatorship, ravaged by coups, foreign invasion and civil wars, often between the predominantly black and the powerful minority mulatto population, who continued to own considerable territory, the land distribution 'reforms' of Petion having impacted only modestly, even in south and west Haiti.

During the early years of independence, voodoo came out of the shadows after decades during which the French had banned it. Voodoo had originally taken many forms, developing from 1730-1790 until the Benin form was ascendant. Benin, West Africa, is the only country today in which voodoo is an official religion. From 1790 to 1800 it became cohesive and spread rapidly. Toussaint, Dessalines and Cristophe suppressed voodoo, but after the latter's death it became publicly acceptable. Almost all voodoo worshippers considered themselves Catholic too and the two religions merged in a strange amalgam of Christianity and African spirit worship.

From 1860, when the Vatican re-established relations with Haiti, until 1945, voodoo was again persecuted at the behest of the Roman Catholic Church, an all-out campaign to eradicate it peaking in the early 1940s. At that time, shrines were burned, voodoo priests killed and the religion shunned. After the failure of these efforts, Catholics gave up trying to destroy voodoo and almost legitimised it by accepting voodoo drums and melodies into church services. The main enemy of voodoo during the Duvalier years and since has been the rapid growth of Protestant evangelism. Evangelists currently own seven of the country's 11 radio stations and frequently denounce voodoo as devil worship. Some 15% of Haitians are now Protestant and hold no truck with the religion promoted by Papa Doc. Ironically, since 1975 there has been a voodoo revival in connection with the peasant movement towards progressive reform in Haiti.

By 1915, anarchic Haiti had suffered 22 heads of state in only 71 years, almost all of whom died violently or were forced to seek exile in France or Jamaica. The last of these, President Jean Vilbrun Gullaume Sam, was impaled on the spiked fence of the French Embassy. He had hidden in the toilet, fearing for his life after murdering one of his predecessors, the mulatto President Oreste Zamor, in prison along with 167 of his supporters. Sam was then dragged off and torn limb from limb by his mulatto subjects seeking revenge. This was too much for the Americans and on 28 July 1915 the US occupied Haiti. The pretext was that it feared German encroachment, although a garrison remained until 1934, long after any German threat had vanished.

The Americans restored order, installed a telephone system, the rule of law and built roads, schools and hospitals, but were never welcome. A guerrilla movement, the Cacos, harried them until their leader Charlemagne Peraulte was assassinated by a marine. When President Franklin Delano Roosevelt withdrew the marines, a seething, resentful population quickly evicted from office the puppet government left behind. The President, Stenio Vincent, was allowed to limp on to avoid an American return. Vincent retired in 1941. Stability soon evaporated as, in the years preceding Duvalier, a dozen 'strongmen' ruled Haiti in turn before their overthrow and replacement by yet another populist dictator from either the army 'Military Council' or political elite.

The world's first independent black republic, Haiti suffered from chronic instability, endemic poverty, illiteracy and low life expectancy. Corruption was the norm. Resentment of the wealthy, usually mulatto minority was strong, and would be fully exploited by future President Dr Francois Duvalier. When Duvalier assumed the presidency, on 22 October 1957, Haitians rejoiced, believing a new day of democracy and prosperity had dawned.

Duvalier was born on 14 April 1907, in the capital, Port-au-Prince, during the military dictatorship of Nord Alexis. He was one-year-old when General Antoine Simon overthrew Alexis, four when revolution overthrew Simon, five when Simon's successor, President Cincinnatus Leconte, was blown to pieces following the dynamiting of the old, wooden Palais Nationale and six when President Tancrede Auguste was poisoned. At the funeral of Auguste, two generals squabbled over the succession, Michel Oreste succeeding, to be followed in the next two years by Oreste Zamor and Joseph Davilmar Theodore respectively. It was little wonder perhaps that, when he himself became president, retaining power was Duvalier's one overriding priority.

The man who later became 'Papa Doc' was the scion of a prosperous middle-class black family. His father, Duval Duvalier, was a respected journalist and justice of the peace, his mother, Uritia Abraham, a bakery worker. Education was revered in the Duvalier household and young Francois attended the prestigious

Lycée Petion and was taught by his political mentor and future President Dumarsais Estime, at a time when only 9% of Haitians of his generation obtained any schooling at all.

Leaving high school, Duvalier hoped to follow in his father's footsteps as a journalist and gained employment on the *Action Nationale* newspaper using the pseudonym 'Abderrahman', the first Iberian caliph, who founded a medical school in Cordoba, Spain.

Duvalier soon realised that journalism was not his forte and enrolled at the University of Haiti to study medicine, graduating in 1934. He did his internship at Hospice Saint Francois de Sales. There he met a pale skinned, half-black, half-mulatto woman, Simone Ovide Faine. She was illegitimate, socially beneath him, yet very beautiful.

By 1938, Duvalier helped found *Les Griots* (poets, storytellers in Guinean), a publication dedicated to 'Negritude' (black pride), with Lorimer Denis. The following year he and Simone were married at St Pierre's church, Petionville on 27 December 1939 and subsequently had three daughters, Marie-Denise, Simone and Nicole, followed by Jean-Claude, eventual successor to his father as dictator and known to posterity as 'Baby Doc'.

The Second World War saw Duvalier employed as an assistant to the US Army Medical Mission from 1943-46 and afterwards he studied at the University of Michigan, Ann Arbor, taking two semesters in public health. He did not want to settle in the United States and when his studies were completed he returned home to Haiti.

In Haiti, Duvalier gained popularity by exaggerating his role in a US government-sponsored campaign to eliminate yaws, a severe and infectious bacterial disease easily treated with penicillin. Soon people came to believe Duvalier had eliminated the disease almost single-handedly.

Describing himself as a 'quiet country doctor', Duvalier built up support and became increasingly involved in the Negritude movement, led by Dr Jean Price Mars. At this time, Duvalier began an ethnological study of voodoo that stood him in good stead when he eventually became 'President for Life'. In many ways it was natural for a Haitian doctor to be interested in voodoo. After all, 60% of voodoo, and much of its popularity, stems from its focus on healing, whether with herbs, spirits or modern medicine. It was, of course, not for this, but the more unsavoury aspects of voodoo that Papa Doc's regime became infamous.

Enjoying his popularity among the public and image as a 'fatherly' doctor, Duvalier gave himself the epithet by which he would universally be known – 'Papa Doc'. Certainly he was much loved at this time, spending every available minute tending to the sick and poor, steadfastly building himself a bedrock constituency among Haiti's most poverty-stricken blacks. An astute observer and judge of character, Duvalier was familiar with their daily lives, beliefs, hopes, fears and what would be needed to cow and control them. He also realised their predisposition to paternalistic and brutal authority.

Over the next few years and during his rule, the sombre-suited, enigmatic Duvalier presented an image of quiet authority and undoubted intelligence. He joined the Worker-Peasant Movement (MOP) led by Daniel Fignole in 1946, becoming almost at once the party's secretary general. The party rejected Marxism, believing whites overseas and mulattos at home to be the architects of Haiti's woes. This racism would later evolve into a form of 'black fascism' under Duvalier.

In late 1946, a military coup against mulatto President Elie Lescot led to the Military Council installing the black Dumarsais Estime in power. His protégé, Duvalier, was promptly made Director General of the National Public Health Service and Secretary of Labour. Two years later, Estime gave him the combined post of Minister of Public Health and Labour. Duvalier used this platform to build a coalition of interest with the armed forces.

Post-war prosperity in the United States reached Haiti and a period of artistic creativity later known as the 'Haitian Renaissance' began. The new government encouraged this and black access to state jobs widened. Laws were passed raising the minimum wage, reforming health, banning non-Haitians from teaching the nation's history and foreign investment increased. Corruption mounted as well and the old elite felt shut out from the largesse swirling around Estime's regime.

Remaining loyal when another black, Paul Eugene Magliore, overthrew Estime on 10 May 1950, Duvalier returned to work for the American Medical Mission where he organised against the military regime, eventually being forced in 1954 to go into hiding. Re-emerging in August 1956, Duvalier decided to challenge Magliore, who, fast losing support following his inept response to the devastation of Hurricane Hazel that struck Haiti on 5 October 1954, decided to stand down in December following a general strike. A general political amnesty was then granted. Over the next nine months, five governments formed and fell. An election was called in 1957 to replace Magliore and Duvalier made his move. Seemingly humble, gentle and passive, he was endorsed by both the army and the desperately impoverished black masses. His rivals each had a strong constituency. Senator Louis Dejoie, a wealthy mulatto businessman and descendant of former President Fabre-Nicholas Geffrard, had the support of mulatto officers, the Catholic church, business and the elite. Daniel Fignole, former MOP leader, was a handsome rabble-rouser adored by the troops, some officers and poor of the capital. Clement Jumelle had the backing of the public administration and professional classes.

On 25 May, Dejoie supporters attempted a bloody coup, leading to over a hundred deaths. That day, Fignole declared himself president only to be arrested and shipped overseas 19 days later by machine-gun wielding troops after doubling soldiers' pay and being subsequently accused of trying to bribe the army. When the Port-au-Prince mob heard two days later, on 16 June, that their hero was in exile, they erupted in fury across the city in an orgy of looting that plunged the city into darkness. The army was ordered by chief of staff General Antonio Thrasybule Kebreau to 'restore order'. Thousands were slaughtered by gunfire, run over by tanks or bayoneted while taking refuge. Jumelle, seeing Duvalier controlled the army, temporarily fled abroad.

In the election, Dejoie won in the capital but lost the countryside, polling only 463 votes from the armed forces to Duvalier's 18,841. Ballot-rigging was widespread and Dejoie supporters denounced the result as fraudulent. Along with the other defeated candidates, he would plot for years against the regime, like Fignole first from America, later from Cuba. Meanwhile, they were deprived of citizenship and their property confiscated.

The new president was elected on 22 September 1957 for a non-renewable six years and took office one month later. His supporters won 23 of 37 seats in the Chamber of Deputies and every seat in the Senate. Duvalier immediately promised to install a benevolent 'Noirist' regime, that is one that favoured the poor masses of black, Creole-speaking, voodoo-worshipping poor to the detriment of the pale-skinned, upper-class, wealthy, French-speaking, Catholic mulattos, who had either ruled directly themselves or through stooges, for much of Haiti's unhappy history. The poor would gain their rightful share of the nation's wealth, access to education, jobs and health care, through the efforts of a president who was really 'one of them', who heeded and understood their plight, for had he not often come among them?

From independence onwards descendents of the 'free blacks' and mulattos of the colonial era formed themselves into a class which was openly contemptuous of the Haitian peasantry. Disdaining Creole, they spoke only French and saw themselves as having no part of the 'African' culture around them. The privileged minority saw no need for a change in relative status between themselves and the descendants of those who were slaves in 1791. True, they employed Creole servants and peasants worked their land, but culturally they remained distinct, ignoring their obviously African genetic heritage.

The peasants loathed their Francophone compatriots, the 'aristocracy of the yellow skin' as they were known, who lived in comfort while the majority toiled in a once rich land despoiled by overpopulation, cultivating exhausted fields, ever less fertile through overuse. Plots of land traditionally divided between sons, became progressively smaller, accelerating migration to the squalid slums of Port-au-Prince.

Insecurity played a part in peasant alienation, as few could read documents presented to them, or understand the French language of court and government, leaving them bewildered and defenceless when confronted by the activities of the state or the elite and their friends in government. As a result, land titles could not be proven and small farms were gobbled up by the powerful landed gentry.

In advancing his political career, Duvalier was intent on utilising the endemic inferiority complex many blacks suffered as a result of what they perceived to be US economic exploitation and Francophone cultural dominance. Cynically, the ideology of respect for African traditions and influence was prostituted to impose a parasitic caste of rogues upon the Haitian people. Anti-mulatto rhetoric and racism was designed more to keep the historic ruling class in its place, than create a spirit of equality or promote prosperity. Blacks who sided with, or were part of, the Europeanised elite, were 'collaborators' and treated as such. A new black middle class, it was intended, would emerge and become permanently entrenched in power. By dividing, Duvalier would rule.

The image of a compassionate ruler swiftly proved a façade. Duvalier showed himself almost at once to be vicious, ruthless and cruel. The mild-mannered, conscientious doctor became the worst kind of despot. The first steps Duvalier took on gaining power were to ensure he stayed there. Within a year, Duvalier, or 'Papa Doc', as he now preferred to be known, suspended the constitution. His much-vaunted humanitarianism disappeared as he used voodoo to hold sway over his superstitious people, organising purges and executions of those who had supported rivals or predecessors. Intimidation was widespread. A gang of thugs who devoted themselves to him in the election campaign by planting bombs and murdering opponents, were transformed and expanded into a secret police force of hired voodoo killers known as the Tontons Macoute (Haitian Creole for 'bogeyman'), who took people in the dead of night and made them disappear forever.

The army was seen as a potential threat to Duvalier's power. Its leading officers, most of them mulattos, were sacked and replaced by Duvalier cronies who were young, black and loyal to the president personally. Kebreau, who thought himself Duvalier's master, was replaced and fled across the border. Some officers more reluctant to depart simply disappeared at the hands of the Tontons Macoute.

Soon after assuming power, Duvalier began to woo his fellow Caribbean dictators through sycophancy and by promising to clamp down on communism in Haiti, a policy that warmed the hearts of American politicians too. President Rafael Trujillo Molinas of the Dominican Republic, with which Haiti shared Hispaniola, was originally hostile but soon realised that both dictators had a vested interest in watching each other's back. President Fulgencio Batista of Cuba was flattered by the award of Haiti's highest medal of honour in exchange for a 'loan' of $4 million that Duvalier pocketed. When, in January 1959, Fidel Castro came to power in Cuba, Duvalier simply fawned over him instead.

It soon dawned on US diplomats what kind of man the new president was. They felt muted in their criticism because Papa Doc played the 'race card' when chided. As America maintained a close relationship with Trujillo, Duvalier denounced the US for neglecting Haiti as little more than a 'poor Negro republic', more than happy to seek aid elsewhere if not forthcoming from the US. In so doing, he kept aid flowing, at least initially. When Washington grew tired of this tactic, he switched again to anti-communism, particularly during the Cuban Missile Crisis of 1962. After this he switched support back to Castro, while letting it be known to US officials that more aid would again place Haiti in the American camp. Time and again Duvalier acted in this, eventually fairly predictable, way. Time and again the US stumped up aid money that never reached beyond Duvalier and a few close associates. Occasionally, aghast at the nature of Duvalier's regime, America demanded a change in his policies. At such times, Haiti indignantly renounced aid with conditions attached as a flagrant violation of the nation's sovereignty. Gradually, the US decided to tolerate Duvalier while looking forward to the day his regime would crumble.

Coup attempts flourished throughout Duvalier's misrule. In February 1958, Duvalier persuaded the legislature to declare a state of siege and after only nine months the first of many coups was attempted. One of the most bizarre was an endeavour by eight men to overthrow the regime by invading Haiti, rallying dissidents to their side and assassinating the president. Led by Captain Ails Pasquet, a mulatto officer and Arthur Payne, a former deputy sheriff from Miami, the group comprised two other deputy sheriffs from Buffalo and New York, accompanied by two American mercenaries and two more mulatto officers.

The would-be adventurers sailed from the Florida Keys on the *Mollie* and landed near Montrouis on 28 June 1958, 60 kilometres north of Port-au-Prince. The group killed a local police chief who stumbled upon them as they unloaded their weapons. Commandeering his jeep, they flagged down a 'tap-tap', a kind of Haitian taxi-bus and hijacked it. Driving straight into the heart of Dessalines barracks, the rebels surprised the sleeping garrison and took 50 soldiers hostage. The rebels had few weapons, having expected to find more at the barracks. In fact, the weapons had been removed and were stored at the presidential palace. Duvalier was badly shaken and prepared to flee Haiti via the Columbian embassy. At dawn, the rebels allowed a mulatto officer they held hostage to buy cigarettes. He quickly informed his superiors that the 'invasion force' consisted of only eight lightly armed men. Duvalier, wearing military apparel, ordered the barracks stormed. Six of the rebels were killed in the ensuing assault. A mob tore the other two to pieces, paraded their remains through the streets and triumphantly took them to the palace. For their part, the US was embarrassed at the involvement of its citizens in the escapade and, denying any responsibility, the State Department offered a grovelling apology, grudgingly accepted by Papa Doc.

Haitians demanded the repatriation of former President Paul Magliore and Louis Dejoie, who were blamed by Duvalier for funding the invasion and picketed the American embassy in Port-au-Prince. Realising the fate that would await the enemies of Duvalier if repatriated, the State Department politely declined the request. The mini-invasion prompted the Haitian legislature to give Duvalier emergency powers and he began ruling by decree.

After the failure of the eight-man invasion and what the dictator saw as its 'complicity', the army was dramatically slimmed down and the military academy closed. In the old days of the US occupation, the Guarde d'Haiti (Haitian Guard) had been formed. Supposedly impartial, they acted in an almost 'Praetorian' manner, often choosing who did and did not rule, post-1934. In exchange for personal privilege, their new master expected their loyalty to be to him alone and so he strengthened the guard, making it several hundred strong. Political parties were banned and curfews introduced. Meanwhile, Duvalier sought to portray himself as the defender of Haitian independence in the face of a rapacious and imperialist US.

Duvalier was convinced that he must strike at all real and potential opponents before they could seriously threaten his regime. One such 'threat' was his former rival for the presidency, Clement Jumelle. Searching for him, the Tontons Macoute located his two brothers in the town of Bois Verna, exactly one month after the eight-man invasion, shot them in cold blood and then photographed their corpses holding guns. Clement Jumelle now fled in fear for his life. As he went into hiding, it was announced that he and his brothers were behind the Petionville and Mahotieres bomb explosions of 30 April and 29 June earlier that year, the former of which was originally blamed on Dejoie. In the search for the surviving Jumelle brother, Jean-Jaques Monfiston, owner of the house in which Charles and Ducasse were discovered, was taken to the gloomy US-built Fort Dimanche and hideously tortured to death. He revealed nothing. Clement Jumelle was never caught, dying soon after of uraemia. Macoutes hijacked Jumelle's funeral cortege and he was secretly buried in his hometown of Saint-Marc.

The political opposition such as it was, was fractured, corrupt and inept. Papa Doc had them swept up and sent to Fort Dimanche where they could be leisurely tortured to death by his Tontons Macoute, officially known as the Voluntaires de la Securite Nationale (Volunteers for National Security or VSN), who grew to eventually number up to 15,000 men, twice the size of the shrunken, emasculated regular army, The nation's press and radio barons, truculent newspaper editors and journalists of newspapers such as the *L'Independent* and *Miroir*, were rounded up and jailed on trumped-up charges of sedition and their offices bombed. Not only was Duvalier here to stay, he wanted everyone to know it!

Tontons Macoute were recruited from Duvalier supporters he met when in hiding and knew as Negritude followers. As volunteers, they received no salary, were lightly armed with antiquated firearms and dressed casually in denim, wearing the ubiquitous sunglasses and a red neckerchief representing Ougoun, a voodoo demon. Tontons Macoute owed their loyalty to Papa Doc alone. To make ends meet, they terrorised, pillaged and extorted from the people. Those who resisted were killed or mutilated. During Duvalier's despotism, babies would be burned to death, whole families extirpated and brutality legitimised. Invoking the powers of voodoo, the Tontons Macoute patrolled the cities, towns and countryside killing, raping and stealing as they wished. They behaved almost like a religious cult and were feared as one. The superstitious populace, cowed by dread of physical violence, also had to contend with the horror that the Tontons Macoute could summon evil spirits against anyone who defied them.

In Duvalier's Haiti, venturing out during the hours of darkness could be a life-threatening venture. The rigorously enforced curfew might bring down prowling Tontons Macoute who would, at the very least, 'shake down' the miscreant and dole out a severe beating.

The twenty-ninth of June was 'Macoute Day', in memory of the Pasquet invasion and Tontons Macoute swarmed into the Palais Nationale to hear words of wisdom from Papa Doc. They supported him utterly, revelling in power for the first time and believing it would be torn from them if their patron fell. Soon they were everywhere, establishing a huge network of informers. People would be terrified of them. Some Tontons Macoute were women. Madame Max, one of the most notorious and sadistic, was reputed to enjoy mutilating and tearing off the genitals of male victims. Duvalierist minister Luckner Cambronne announced that a good Tontons Macoute 'stands ready to kill his children, children to kill their parents'.

Haiti soon became a 'kleptocracy', with industrialists, landowners, shopkeepers and anyone else with a modicum of wealth stripped of it. This 'redistribution' was not from the wealthy to the poor but from the people upwards through every echelon of society right to their president, who soon amassed vast riches. Ideologically, the regime was bankrupt. The Noirism espoused by Duvalier was merely a sop that delivered no tangible gains whatsoever for his core constituency; save the ranks of those Tontons Macoute recruited from it and their families. Power and loot were Papa Doc's primary motivations. Voodoo gave him the power to manipulate and harness for himself the ignorance of the population.

As the educated and wealthy minority grew to fear Papa Doc, the illiterate peasants began to see him as a monster, a demon of the night. It was rumoured that Dr Duvalier was a houngan (voodoo priest), who acted as a mediator between the iwa (spirit) and human worlds through trance. Mrs Duvalier was considered a mambo, the female equivalent. Revelling in his reputation, Papa Doc masqueraded as evil voodoo divinity 'Baron Samedi', who could put the living in touch with the dead. Many were struck by their president's physical resemblance to the deity, especially when Duvalier dressed in the supernatural being's attire of black top hat, tails and sunglasses. To emphasise that he and Samedi were one and the same, Duvalier had posters of himself displayed in the guise of the evil one. Topping this, posters also showed Christ leaning on Duvalier's shoulders proclaiming: 'I have chosen him!'

Rumours abounded that black magic ceremonies were held in the Palais Nationale at which goats entrails were studied, bocors (sorcerers) and zombies (the living dead) were called upon and live babies bloodily sacrificed. To absorb the power of Haiti's first despot, Duvalier occasionally slept on the gravestone of General Dessalines.

On 12 August 1959, another attempt was made to oust Duvalier. This group of 30 or so was led by Henri d'Anton and consisted of Cuban guerrillas and Haitian exiles. They landed at Haiti's most southern point, Les Irois. Once again when faced with overthrow, Duvalier panicked. He did not need to. The Haitian army, ignominiously bolstered by US Marines – the US Government being fearful of a Cuban 'domino effect' in the Caribbean – crushed the rebels. By 22 August all but five Cubans were killed. The rest were captured and after being paraded in the capital, repatriated to Cuba.

Like many a dictator before him, Papa Doc needed to believe himself adored by 'his' people. At the same time he was paranoid about potential enemies, believing friends and allies were out to usurp him. Any found to be ambitious or a potential threat were murdered, including, with some poetic justice, the head of the Tontons Macoute itself, Papa Doc's closest friend, Clement Barbot.

Barbot became the island's effective ruler when Papa Doc was felled on 24 May 1959 by a massive heart attack and plunged into a coma. With the best cardiologists available flown in from the US, Duvalier made a slow but steady recovery. In the interim, Barbot effectively held the reins of power. Duvalier could not reconcile himself to this and, on 14 July 1960, when Barbot questioned Duvalier's sanity and refused to share extorted money with him, his own Tontons Macoute arrested him on charges of corruption. Dragged off to Fort Dimanche, now nicknamed Fort Mort (Death), Barbot was tortured for 18 months before being finally released.

While Barbot was incarcerated, Duvalier sought to legitimise his rule and secure an extension of his presidency until 1967. On 8 April 1961, the bicameral parliament was abolished. On 30 April an 'election' was held. Incredibly, 100% of votes cast were for the president, as he won by 1,320,478 to nil.

As international criticism of Duvalier increased, the doctor turned Haiti into a one-party state, appointing all 58 of the congressional seats in his new legislature to Duvalierists. The Americans, having aided Haiti to prevent 'another Cuba' on its doorstep, suspended assistance in 1961, which that year constituted almost half of its budget. The Americans believed, rightly, that most of their largesse was ending up in the dictator's bank accounts. Suspension of US aid gave Duvalier the opportunity to again appear defiant and independent of America, which was denounced as a 'bully' to the Haitian masses. On 15 September 1961, 'parliament' responded by voting Duvalier full economic powers. By now taxes were sky-high, half the national budget was going to the presidential guard or the Macoute and monopolies were being sold for kickbacks. Meanwhile the Haitian infrastructure crumbled.

No one was safe from Duvalier and Barbot realised he was living on borrowed time unless he struck first. Apparently reconciled to Duvalier, Barbot swore revenge. On 26 April 1963, he botched an attempt to kill the president's children. Two bodyguards were killed and an enraged Duvalier ordered the liquidation of Barbot and his associates. For weeks, Tontons Macoute hunted down Barbot allies, army officers and anyone with whom they had personal grievances. Hundreds were dragged off to Fort Dimanche. Bizarrely, Duvalier believed his bodyguards were killed by army crack shot Lieutenant Francois Benoit, who at the time was hiding in the embassy of the Dominican Republic. Benoit's house was stormed and his parents, servants, dogs and a passing neighbour machine-gunned. The house was razed to the ground and with it Benoit's infant son. The already crippled economy, reeling from the depredations of Duvalierist gangsters, ground to a halt as roadblocks were established across the island, traffic grid-locked and 'dubious' persons arrested, never to be seen again.

Papa Doc believed Dominican Republic President, Juan Bosch Gavino, to be behind the plot. The two presidents were at loggerheads and Bosch was harbouring Haitian exiles known to be plotting against Duvalier. Papa Doc ordered the Haitian presidential guard to occupy the Dominican chancery in Petionville. Gavino was outraged, ordered his troops to the border and threatened to invade. An invasion would result in the fall of Papa Doc. However, the Dominican army was unenthusiastic and the crisis petered out.

As corpses littered the streets of the capital, Duvalier insanely ordered a carnival to be held. Peasants were bussed into town and free rum distributed as dancers entertained a crowd exhorted by their president: 'I am the personification of the Haitian fatherland ... bullets and machine guns cannot harm me ... I am already an immaterial being!'

Meanwhile, Barbot and his brother Harry were organising their forces. They planned to take over the country by first seizing Information Minister Georges Figaro and using him to slip two carloads of ten men into the palace. There, the Barbot's expected to be joined by 20 Tontons Macoute still supposedly loyal to their former chief. After killing Duvalier, the regime would fall. The day of the operation, 14 July, the plan was aborted. A peasant reported to the authorities that he had been shot at. Duvalier immediately dispatched troops to the area. The Barbots and their associates were cornered in a sugar-cane field. It was set alight and the rebels gunned down while trying to escape the smoke and flames. Despite the failure of Barbot, another group headed by Hector Riobe, whose father had been stripped of his wealth and murdered in the street by Duvalier's henchmen, launched an attack originally meant to dovetail with Barbot's. Armed with a flame-thrower and possessing an armoured car, Riobe and his comrades attempted to move against Petionville police station. After a shoot out, Riobe fled to the hills, taking Kenscoff barracks. Tontons Macoute who responded to the attack were ambushed and slaughtered.

Riobe and his supporters retreated to a well-provisioned cave in the mountains with only one entrance but was soon discovered by the Duvalierists, who laid siege to it for days. As the battle raged, fatalities grew. Finally, Papa Doc brought Hector Riobe's mother, who appealed to her son to surrender. His reply was a single gunshot. The last surviving insurgent, he had taken his own life.

The attempts to overthrow Duvalier by Barbot and Riobe galvanised a third group of rebels into action. Based in Santa Domingo, exiled Haitian general Leon Cantave was permitted by the Dominican Army to train a contingent of 70 exiled Haitian peasants, who were drilled and taught how to shoot. When Gavino learned of their presence, Cantave's 'army' were ordered to leave. On 2 August 1963, they crossed into Haiti, clad in the boots and uniforms of the Dominican Army. On 5 August, they entered the small town of Derac, killing two militiamen and six Tontons Macoute. The invaders then marched on the Ouanaminthe army barracks; Cantave believed the garrison would come over to him. In fact, Papa Doc had known of Cantave's plans and the army commander was under guard. He would later be executed.

Cantave switched his attack to Fort Liberté. Calling on the fort to surrender, the Duvalierist commander shouted back, 'Take the fort if you can'. After a feeble attack, Cantave scurried back across the border with his troops but minus much of their equipment. Undeterred, he sent a column back to Haiti on 15 August, where after some modest success they were driven out. By now the CIA were financing Cantave and, after yet another cross-border raid, he again invaded Haiti, this time on 22 September, with 210 men equipped by the Americans with bazookas, machine guns and assault rifles. The attempt was a dismal failure, as a forewarned Duvalier marshalled his troops and repelled Cantave. A government did fall however. Rising tensions between Haiti and the Dominican Republic were used as an excuse to topple Gavino. Cantave went into exile in New York and his army was dissipated.

During the numerous coup attempts, the reaction of the regime soon formed a familiar pattern. Sirens blared, a curfew was imposed and roadblocks established at which drivers were routinely fleeced. Anyone looking 'suspicious' was beaten, arrested and/or murdered. Families of invaders were routinely massacred, their bodies left to rot in the streets and ultimately denied burial.

On 4 October 1963, a hurricane struck Haiti and, on 10 November, a landslide. Together these disasters killed 5,500 Haitians, bringing further misery to the country. Such environmental disasters were bound to happen. Only 30% of the country was arable although today 40% is cultivated. The search for land to farm and charcoal to burn has almost completely destroyed the forest cover and topsoil continues to wash into the sea by the thousand tonne. Haiti is becoming a desert, a transformation expedited by the desperate impoverishment of the Duvalier years.

When President Kennedy was assassinated, Papa Doc let it be known that his death was brought about by an ouanga, a voodoo charm he used against a man he considered behind the frequent attempts to overthrow him. The masses were impressed. If a man as great as President Kennedy could succumb to their all-powerful sorcerer-president, what chance would an ordinary Haitian have if offering resistance?

Although they were ostensibly Catholic, the majority of poor Haitians believed in voodoo. Those who did not, the educated Catholic elites, who fought against voodoo in the 19th century and mid 20th, were the least disposed to the new order. Courting notoriety, the populist president took on the church, three-quarters of whose priests were foreign, mostly French and Canadian, from the start of his presidency. Macoutes invaded Port-au-Prince Cathedral during Mass and mercilessly beat up both worshippers and clergy. Duvalier further emphasised his 'nationalist' credentials by expelling priests almost all foreign bishops, including two archbishops and leaving the remainder fearful and wary of offending him.

For this and numerous other transgressions, the Papal Nuncio was recalled and Papa Doc formally excommunicated in 1964 from a church he was only nominally a member of. Astonishingly, Pope Paul VI reinstated him in 1966 and even allowed Duvalier to appoint and discipline bishops. It was not long before a number of Tontons Macoute found themselves members of the Haitian Catholic hierarchy. Duvalier's reputed practice of black magic and sorcery and his subjugation of Catholicism gave him an almost respectable, if feared, persona among those at the bottom of Haitian society and even provided him a modicum of popular support.

By 1964 Haiti was on its knees. Per capita income had plummeted to a woeful $80 a year. As this included the huge wealth of the Duvaliers and their supporters, the poor were even more destitute than the figure suggests. There was widespread malnutrition, fuel shortages and power cuts. Infant mortality from easily preventable diseases was shockingly high and life expectancy only around

45 years. The small, educated, pre-Duvalier middle class had had enough and 'voted with their feet', fleeing to the US in their thousands. A few were 'co-opted' by the regime and participated in its system of rule by patronage. Soon Haiti was bereft of its intellectuals, specialists and even basic social services, as some 80% sought new lives elsewhere. Teachers, engineers and doctors could barely subsist on salaries that were often stolen by Tontons Macoute thugs. Many of the peasants, to whom the regime supposedly dedicated itself, lost their tiny land holdings, which were expropriated and handed over to gangsters. Sharecroppers could not buy fertiliser or pipe water to their eroded and overworked plots. Left homeless, destitute and abandoned by government, rural migrants were driven to seek work for a pittance in the sweatshop factories of Port-au-Prince.

In the capital's sprawling slums, such as Site Soley and Kiton, the deprived were effectively abandoned to their fate, aspiring to eke out a meagre existence in Duvalier's brave, new Haiti. A few chose to build rafts and attempted to float in the direction of America and, they hoped, a better life. Thousands drowned, thousands of others were returned to face Papa Doc's wrath, while many more sought escape over the border, finding employment for poverty wages in the sugar-cane fields of the Dominican Republic, working in conditions little better than those under which their slave ancestors toiled and died. The economic and social impact of losing so many skilled professionals and hard-working peasants on the fabric of Haiti is incalculable.

Duvalier was defiant. Unabashedly, in April 1964, he changed the constitution and appointed himself 'President for Life'. The idea was not his, he insisted. He was merely 'bowing to popular demand'. It was not an original idea; seven previous heads of state in Haiti had done likewise. Simultaneously, Duvalier announced a new red and black flag, supposedly representing L'Union fait la force (the union of blacks and mulattos). The black represented Africa and, Duvalier hoped, would resonate with his poorer subjects. Those journalists still alive and in post, printed eulogies to this new state of affairs:

> *Duvalier is the professor of energy ... an electrifier of souls ... one of the greatest leaders of modern times ... the renovator of the Haitian fatherland ... synthesises all there is of courage, bravery, genius, diplomacy, patriotism and tact in the titans of ancient and modern times.*

This kind of propaganda spin washed over some but was taken in by many. To indoctrinate Haitian children in support of their megalomaniac president, schools were ordered to recite a Duvalier version of the Lord's Prayer, known as the Catechisme de la revolution:

Our Doc, who art in the National Palace for life, hallowed be
Thy name by present and future generations.
Thy will be done in Port-au-Prince as it is in the provinces.
Give us this day our new Haiti and forgive not the trespasses of
those anti-patriots who daily spit upon our country.
Let them succumb to temptation and under the weight of their
venom, deliver them not from any evil …

The madness and ego-centrism continued, with the dictator insisting he was the re-incarnation of five famous forebears combined. When children were asked who Dessalines, Toussaint, Christophe, Petion and Estime were, the correct answer was:

'Dessalines, Toussaint, Christophe, Petion and Estime are five
distinct Chiefs of State who are substantiated in and form only
one and the same President in the person of Dr Francois
Duvalier.'

As the number of Haitian exiles multiplied, so did stories of the horrors inflicted on the Haitian people. Yvan Laraque, a political foe of Duvalier who tried to stage a coup at Jeremie Airport, was murdered in northern Haiti. As an example to others, his body was taken to the capital, stripped down to its underwear and propped up under a coca-cola sign between Grand Rue and Somoza Avenue that read, 'Welcome to Haiti'. As it decomposed and stank in the sun, Tontons Macoute murdered those who supported Laraque, along with their families. Men, women and children were tortured to death at Fort Dimanche while Duvalier allegedly watched approvingly through peepholes in the walls.

On occasion, children were hacked to death in front of their parents, infants in their mother arms, before they too were gruesomely despatched. For sport, and as an example to others who might contemplate rebellion, in 1964 the Sansaricq, Drouin and Villedrouin mulatto families were ordered to walk through the streets of Jeremie stark naked, whereupon the adults were shot dead after the children were first knifed, in full view of the citizenry. These families, once the most powerful, cultured and educated in their locale, were completely wiped out and their houses pillaged and burned.

As well as murdering known and suspected opponents of the regime, it was postulated that the Tontons Macoutes randomly killed 300 people a year, merely to maintain a state of terror. In all, some 20-60,000 people were murdered during Papa Doc's bloody reign.

Despite the grinding poverty that immersed Haiti, Duvalier decided to construct a new town in his name. 'Duvalierville' provided an excuse to further milk the populace and the dwindling number of foreigners with financial interests in Haiti. The town, now known as Cabaret, was brimful of monuments to Duvalier's 'greatness' and neon signs proclaimed 'I am the best thing that ever happened to you' and 'I have no enemies save the enemies of Haiti'.

Coup attempts continued and by the time Marcel Numa and Louis Drouin were shot to death by firing squad on 12 November 1964, an astonishing 11 had already failed. On this occasion, the execution was shown live on television – huge crowds were encouraged to attend the bloody spectacle and given leaflets informing them that 'their' Papa Doc would always protect them from such traitors.

Eventually, fear of communist Cuba made the US re-think its Haiti policy. Food and medical supplies were provided along with financial assistance, most of which Duvalier and his aides inevitably stole. However, Duvalier still earned grudging respect from some. His austere, eccentric appearance belied a quick, devious mind and he was certainly considered wily and shrewd. 'He was tough, very tough, but he cares for the people,' was the belief of many. Papa Doc would visit a market, gravely declare the prices too high and, after he left, prices would fall, endearing him to the poor.

By 1967 innumerable attempts had been made on the life of Papa Doc yet still he survived. 'God and the people are the source of my power. I have twice been given the power. I have taken it and damn it, I will keep it,' Duvalier frequently said. God and the people were thus credited, in Duvalier's eyes, with providing his right to rule, terrorise and exploit. That year, bombs exploded in the Palais Nationale. Tontons Macoute dragged off 19 presidential guards, along with the alleged leader of the plot, Duvalier's son-in-law Colonel Max Dominique, who was married to Marie-Denise Duvalier. Among the guards arrested was Major Jose Borges, head of radio station Voice of the Duvalierist Revolution. Like the others arrested, with the exception of Dominique, he was tortured, murdered and disposed of in Fort Dimanche. Dominique was permitted to assist in shooting his colleagues before being sent overseas as Haiti's new ambassador to Spain. The president spoke to the nation: 'I am an arm of steel, hitting inexorably, hitting inexorably, hitting inexorably. I have shot these officers to protect the revolution and those who serve it. I align myself with great leaders of peoples such as Kemal Ataturk, Lenin, Kwame Nkrumah, Patrice Lumumba, Azikwe and Mao Zedong.'

As in most developing countries in those days and with Cuba less than a hundred kilometres away, Haiti had a Communist Party looking to one day seize power. In June 1969, Duvalier liquidated it, catching almost its entire Central Committee in an attack on a 'safe house' in Avenue Martin Luther King. All were murdered. Nelson Rockefeller, Governor of New York, visited the island and Papa Doc emphasised his virulent anti-communism. The two were photographed together waving from the balcony of the presidential palace to crowds of Haitians bussed in for the occasion. America and Duvalier's Haiti were seen by the world to be friends once more.

As the years slowly passed, other coups failed. In April 1970 even the Coast Guard made an attempt, all five boats shelling the Palais Nationale. Once again it failed. After a two-day stalemate, the coup ended with the fleet sailing to the US naval base at Guantanamo Bay, Cuba, to seek political asylum.

At the end of the 60s it seemed Duvalier would go on forever. True, he had diabetes and a heart condition, had been ill for many years and was, if frail, obviously still in command. The army was quiescent, the opposition hopelessly divided and bickering among itself, planning more for the day Dr Duvalier died rather than working for his removal. Cabinet ministers were frequently re-shuffled, sacked, demoted, arrested, occasionally brought back into favour and sometimes disappeared. Papa Doc was more securely in power than ever. The church, now packed with voodoo-worshipping Macoute priests, was reconciled. The peasants and urban poor were docile, although the 'Duvalierist Revolution' delivered nothing. Their lot did not improve. For the privileged few that worked with the regime, gains were spectacular. The 30 or so clans who ran Haiti for the preceding one-and-a-half centuries, expanded to around 200 wealthy families, almost all black, mostly drawn from the bourgeoisie, all dollar millionaires and fervent Duvalierists. The banning of strikes, poverty wages, government contracts and private monopoly eventually reconciled the business class to the administration they loathed, realising that stability and continuity might be the lesser of many evils and that having Papa Doc's son succeed his father as president could be to their advantage.

At the beginning of his rule no one thought Duvalier would last. He showed them all. Politicians, generals, priests and plotters had come and gone. Many had been destroyed, obliterated while Papa Doc ruled supreme, feared and without serious challenge. It seemed to the simple folk that Duvalier was indeed Baron Samedi, evil, all-powerful and immortal. Actually, their Papa Doc had not long to live. On 21 April 1971, Duvalier finally succumbed to heart disease. The nation 'mourned'.

Exploiting black nationalism in his almost exclusively black nation assisted Papa Doc's maintenance of power throughout the 14 years of his rule. While a minority supported him to the end, social and economic progress were non-existent during the Duvalier years and when the dictator died more than 90% of Haitians were uneducated, over one-sixth had fled abroad and there were more Haitian doctors in Paris, Montreal or New York than in their homeland.

Of course, the regime of Papa Doc did not really end with his death. Duvalier named his fat, dim-witted 19-year-old son Jean-Claude, soon to be known as 'Baby Doc', as his successor. Said the president to his people: 'Caesar

Augustus was 19 when he took into his hands Rome's destinies and his reign remains the "century of Augustus".'

Only two months before Papa Doc passed away, a referendum had been held to reduce eligibility for the presidency from 40 to 18 and ratify his son's succession. A resounding 2,391,916 in favour, with none against, approved it.

Born on 3 July 1951, the vacuous Baby Doc, also nicknamed 'Tête-Panier' (basket head) became the world's youngest president, ruling Haiti for a further 14 years before being toppled on 7 February 1986. Inevitably, his obvious incompetence, corruption and acute unpopularity, due mainly to the ostentatious living of his hated mulatto wife Michele Bennett, while he presided over Haiti's decline to becoming the poorest nation in the Americas, forced him to seek a life of luxurious exile in France.

On 25 March 2004, the anti-corruption body Transparency International placed Baby Doc sixth on its list of most corrupt dictators of the previous two decades, accusing him of looting between $300 and $800 million during his presidency. The amount stolen by his father remains unknown as dies its whereabouts.

To this day, the legacy of a country pillaged by the Duvaliers remains political instability, economic stagnation, desperate poverty, superstition, illiteracy and disease. HIV/AIDS possibly had its genesis in Haiti, where it is now rife. Said one opponent of Papa Doc's rule, 'He has performed an economic miracle. He taught us to live without money, eat without food and live without life'.

And of the end of Papa Doc? After a funeral lasting almost seven hours over two days at which 101 cannonades were fired, church bells pealed and a sycophantic song entitled, 'Francoise, we thank you for loving us, your star will be shining in the night' was sung, Papa Doc Duvalier was finally buried, among thronging, weeping, hysterical crowds, if not exactly 'laid to rest'. A sudden gust of wind rose up and the crowd were gripped by panic, believing that the soul of their former chief was leaving his body. Houngan that he was, many feared that the old monster would not stay dead!

On the very day Baby Doc fell, an angry mob invaded the National Cemetery, extinguished the 'eternal flame', and with their bare hands tore down and smashed to pieces his father's grandiose mausoleum. Bashing in the roof and ripping open the vault, the frenzied horde was stunned into silence. The tomb was empty! Almost 15 years after he died, Papa Doc had the last laugh. The mob dispersed, frightened and confused. Papa Doc had once again returned to haunt their waking hours and dreams ... just as he had done when he was alive.

CHAPTER 8
Dr Henry Howard Holmes: The Monster of 63rd Street

'Like the man-eating tigers of the tropical jungle, whose appetites for blood have once been aroused, I roamed about this world seeking whom I could destroy.'

Dr Henry Howard Holmes

DR HENRY HOWARD Holmes was not only one of the most vicious and sadistic killers in American history; he was also that country's first documented serial killer. Although never as infamous as London's Jack the Ripper in terms of savagery, Holmes' crimes matched and probably exceeded those of his infamous counterpart. In terms of sheer scale, Holmes misdeeds dwarfed them.

* * *

Born Herman Webster Mudgett on 16 May 1860, in Gilmantown, New Hampshire into a devout Methodist family, Holmes was cruelly and frequently beaten by his postmaster father. Thin and reedy, he was also the target of neighbourhood bullies. He had few friends and was considered too studious and solitary.

Like many latter-day serial killers, young Mudgett had a fascination for torturing and dismembering small animals. He loved performing 'operations and experiments' on creatures ranging from frogs and salamanders to rabbits, cats and dogs, revelling in their pain and taking care to ensure they stayed alive, helpless and in distress for as long as possible. To do this, Mudgett developed a technique he later used on his human victims, involving the stretching of their bodies and the cutting of ligaments. Although agonising, no major arteries or veins were severed. Mudgett became a bully too and was brutal towards other children, if they were smaller or weaker than him. He was constantly in trouble but his parents took solace in Herman's excellent school grades and expected him to simply 'grow out' of his bad behaviour.

One incident from his childhood that Mudgett recalled in later years was when two older schoolboys dragged him into the empty surgery of a local physician and put him face to face with a skeleton. Herman was only five years old at the time and terrified, believing that it would seize him. The event, if it ever truly happened, supposedly spurred Mudgett forward into a medical career, his curiosity being further aroused by his continuing 'experiments'. Like Dr Marcel Petiot decades later, Herman Mudgett convinced himself that, as a boy, he had invented among sundry other creations, a perpetual motion machine.

Herman was bright enough to further his education and upon leaving school at 16 he worked as a teacher in both Gilmanton and nearby Alton. After three years Mudgett entered medical school at the University of Vermont in Burlington.

Women were important to Herman throughout his life and he had already eloped and married Clara Lovering, the daughter of a prosperous farmer from Loudon, in his home state, in 1878. Clara soon gave birth to a son. Luckily for her husband, she inherited a small legacy that was made available to pay his university tuition fees.

After a year in Burlington, Mudgett transferred to the more prestigious medical school at the University of Michigan in Ann Arbor, enrolling on 21 September 1882. He had already dropped the name of Mudgett, preferring to call himself 'Henry Howard Holmes', the name under which he was admitted by the university. He enjoyed undergraduate life and began a lifelong career as a swindler by working during his first summer break as a book salesman and cheating his employer of the entire sum he garnered.

The young undergraduate was fascinated by anatomy, even taking a baby's body home from class to dissect during the holidays. Soon Holmes was stealing corpses from the university's hospital and local graveyards, disfiguring them with acid and claiming on life insurance policies previously taken out under fictitious names, pretending they were members of his family. Holmes graduated in June 1884 and after swindling an insurance company out of $12,500 in conjunction with an accomplice, later to become a famous New York doctor, Holmes abandoned his wife and baby son. His reputation sank after he was accused of a variety of petty crimes and even defrauding his own in-laws. To escape his bad name, Mudgett now changed it formally to 'Dr Henry Howard Holmes.' It would be many years before his wife and child ever saw him again.

Holmes was of slim build, average height and had brown, sandy hair and blue eyes. Considered handsome, for most of his adult life he sported a large, bushy moustache. He was a smooth talker and women found his soft-spoken polite manner, obvious intelligence, charm, elegance and immaculate clothing very attractive.

The career of Holmes was to prove peripatetic at best. He took a number of jobs in teaching and medicine in small towns in New York State that proved to be financially unrewarding. In Norristown, Pennsylvania, Holmes found employment as the director of an asylum. A wealthy patient offered the doctor $5,000 to help him escape. Soon after, the patient was found drowned in a pond on the asylum's grounds with his money gone. Holmes moved on. Working as a pharmacist in Philadelphia, he left after poisoning a customer. In due course, after a couple of restless years during which he had moved from Philadelphia to New York to Minneapolis, Holmes settled in the booming city of Chicago in July 1886.

In Chicago, Holmes would make his mark. He was initially employed as a chemist in a busy pharmacy located on the corner of 63rd and Wallace streets in the prosperous and rapidly growing suburb of Englewood, despite a lack of references and being completely unknown in the district. The owner, Mr ES Holton, died of prostate cancer a month after Holmes arrived. His widow became increasingly reliant on her new employee who had proved successful, particularly with the ladies, on whom he used his charms incessantly and he was promoted to manager. After a few months Mrs Holton was persuaded to sell Holmes her business in instalments, provided she could continue to live above the shop with her daughter. Holmes soon fell behind with his payments and Mrs Holton took him to court. Before the case could be resolved she vanished, along with her daughter. Holmes told customers he had settled his differences with the Holtons and they had left the district bound for a new life in California. Whether she did or not, neither hide nor hair of Mrs Holton and her daughter were ever seen again.

In January 1887 Holmes bigamously married Miss Myrtle Z Belknap, a woman unaware of his previous marriage. Without the surname of 'Mudgett' as a millstone round his neck, he did not bother with the tedious process of divorcing Clara. Blonde, buxom, brown-eyed and capable, Myrtle worked with her husband in his pharmacy and soon she was pregnant. Despite this, within a year she was again living with her parents in Wilmette, Illinois. Her father was convinced his new son-in-law was slowly poisoning him and wanted his daughter to have nothing to do with Dr Henry Howard Holmes. The couple separated. Holmes must have retained some residual affection for her because he provided for her and his daughter Lucy until his death and she eventually inherited Holmes' wealth after his execution.

Holmes' pharmacy prospered, but he was greedy. He did not want to just be prosperous; the possession of real wealth was his ambition and he began creating his own quack 'cure-all' medicines, including a fake treatment for alcoholism, and sold them by mail order. Adjacent plots of land were vacant across the road from his existing premises and he procured their lease in 1888 by a Byzantine series of frauds, loans and unfulfilled promises. Deeds were drawn up in the name of imaginary people and switched to and from them in such bewildering fashion that a decade later litigation had still failed to resolve ownership. Meanwhile, Holmes instructed the construction of a two-storey turreted building, again funded by illegal and convoluted methods. It was to be a hotel with a difference, as a lot more people were to check-in than ever check-out. Holmes was a bloodthirsty sadist who enjoyed the appalling fear and agony he was to put his 'guests' through. He designed the hotel as a deathtrap for the unwary, primarily as a way of killing, raping and robbing unsuspecting young women and disposing of their remains.

Myriad contractors were hired by Holmes to build what he called, and would soon be commonly known as, his 'castle'. They were rarely paid and usually fired after a few days, Holmes often citing 'inferior workmanship'. If they sued him, he simply obtained continuances until the plaintiff gave up in frustration. In this way, not only did Holmes save money, he was able to hide the true nature of his creation. Each of the companies employed had no idea as to the final plan Holmes was working to and he kept it that way.

Holmes was a charmer with an avaricious bent to say the least. He had an unquenchable thirst for money and would do anything and everything to make or steal a buck. To furnish his new pride and joy, Holmes bought on credit and promptly sold the next day for cash, often to several different people. Creditors were never paid and the furniture seldom reached its new owners. One supplier, the Tobey Furniture Company, sent someone to investigate. Nothing was found until one of Holmes' employees was given a $50 inducement. The investigator was led into an empty room. The employee felt along the wall until he came to a hidden door, concealed under the wallpaper. Behind it was a secret room containing most of the missing furniture and a huge quantity of goods from other companies. The merchandise had been delivered there by way of a service elevator that stopped between two floors. By removing a few wooden planks, access to the room was obtained.

Holmes was not the most discreet of people. Years later, when his crimes came to light, Mr George Bowman, a bricklayer who had worked on Holmes' building, told police how, after only two days on the site and without ever having exchanged a word with him, Holmes approached with a murderous proposal. Asking Bowman if he wanted to make some 'easy money', Holmes pointed to a man working in the basement and told him it was his brother-in-law, 'who has no love for me, nor I for him'. Bowman was then offered $50 to drop a stone on the man's head. He declined and left the building site soon after. Who was the man? Bowman never knew. It was unlikely to have been Holmes' brother-in-law. Most likely it was some random individual Holmes wanted killed either for his own amusement, because he had insured the prospective victim, or both.

Holmes purchased and installed a huge safe directly into the fabric of his building. When the manufacturers came looking for payment, Holmes told them he had no money. The safe, which resembled a huge vault, could be reclaimed providing the building encasing it remained undamaged. When this proved impossible, the safe was left in situ.

The building Holmes erected was placed in the names of Hiram S Campbell and AS Yates and two of Holmes employees, Henry Owens, his porter and Miss

Minnie Williams, his secretary and future victim. It was in the name of the 'Campbell-Yates Manufacturing Company' that orders for goods and services were made by company agent, Howard H Holmes. Vast quantities of materials arrived. Only a small proportion was used to construct Holmes' edifice. Usually, as soon as contracted items arrived they were sold on for cash. Companies looking for recompense were directed to Mr Wharton Plummer, the 'company's' lawyer, who advised that the mythical Mr Campbell was a real estate owner of considerable wealth. Further enquirers at the site itself were advised that Mr Campbell had 'just stepped out'.

Holmes began wheeling and dealing in property. He bought a restaurant, barber's shop and sundry other businesses. Fitting them out with furnishings bought with credit, Holmes would sell them on just before the creditors arrived and took back their furnishings. He even sold the former Houston pharmacy. The new owner bought on a Friday but when he arrived to open the following Monday his stock and fittings had all been removed and sold on. Some days later an ornamental fountain was taken worth $1,500. Meanwhile Holmes maintained his own pharmacy business by simply moving it across the road to his new building.

Incredibly, Holmes somehow avoided being prosecuted, beaten up or worse. His crimes however, were only just beginning. It took two years to construct the hotel, the elaborate design and his frequent hiring and firing of workmen hampering and delaying completion. The two storeys and turrets gave the building a European feel. Although Holmes called it his castle, it would soon be known by a number of epithets – 'Bluebeard's Castle', 'Nightmare Castle' and 'Murder Castle'. The ground floor consisted of businesses and the top floor Holmes' private apartments and office. In between was a nightmarish maze of six hallways, 51 doors and 35 rooms, some apparently normal, others windowless and unlockable from the inside. There was a dissecting room and stairways that ended blindly, secret passages and closets, false floors, trapdoors, and greased human-sized chutes that led to a torture chamber, dissecting table and mortuary in the basement.

All the rooms in Holmes' establishment were sound-proof, escape-proof and had peepholes in the walls where he could spy on his prey. Gas vents, with fake cut-off valves but operable only from a cupboard in Holmes' bedroom, were fitted to enable him to asphyxiate his 'guests' at will. At least one room was asbestos-lined so that the murderer could gleefully torch the occupants. The safe, which resembled a huge vault, also had gas pipes fitted. Of course, Holmes often did not bother gassing those who found themselves within, gaining as he did much more satisfaction from their much slower death through oxygen starvation. Attempts at escaping from any room activated a buzzer, alerting Holmes. There was an elevator without a shaft and a shaft without an elevator. It was all to impress on victims an air of hopelessness if contemplating escape from the labyrinth he had created. Holmes had thought of everything and he even ensured that an escape chute was installed leading out behind the building should immediate flight be necessary.

Holmes' torture chamber contained some elaborate pieces of equipment. One was what he called an 'elasticity determinator', which he later claimed could stretch his unfortunate victims to twice their length while subjecting them to unimaginable suffering. It was, to all intents and purposes, a medieval rack, although Holmes on occasion convinced himself he was merely 'experimenting' how best to create a race of giants! Sometimes if the occasion demanded or he was in the mood for some 'amusement', he would bring victims to the chamber and torture them until they revealed any riches he may not yet have discovered. On other occasions torments were inflicted just to excite Holmes sexually. Victims' agonies ended only when they died or he killed them. Many of the 'operations' Holmes carried out were identical to those he had first tried out on animals as a child. He admitted that while money was his primary motivation, it was not his only one and later admitted that he would have murdered for the sheer thrill of it alone. Referring in his later confession to the murder of Emeline Cigrand, 'I committed this and other crimes for the pleasure of killing my fellow beings to hear their cries for mercy'.

To dispose of the evidence of his crimes, Holmes had a large lime pit dug below the earthen floor of his basement, with a huge furnace installed that could burn flesh and bone to ashes. Vats of acid were kept on the premises to dissolve corpses and belongings Holmes could not sell. Often, the bodies were not destroyed at all. Holmes would practice his surgical skills on the corpses, remove organs to be kept as 'trophies' or for further 'experimentation' and sell the skeletons, if they had 'sentimental' value, of the newly deceased to medical schools for anatomical research.

To outsiders, Holmes had built an elegant façade. In fact, the entire structure was jerry-built, 125 by 50 feet in dimension, with an admittedly impressive exterior. The pharmacy entrance on the ground floor had a beautifully designed Catherine wheel that dazzled anyone who studied it. Inside were pastel-coloured walls in frescoed stucco. The floors were inlaid with black and white diamond tiles and the stairway was enclosed in what seemed to be a grand oriole window. Although all five of the commercial outlets were impressive, when later inspected by the Commissioner for Buildings Joseph Downey, he condemned the building, describing the rooms as 'uninhabitable' and the sanitation as 'horrible'.

Holmes' hotel of death opened for business in 1890. Before embarking on the slaughter, Holmes' petty greed intervened and tapped into the city water supply beneath his building. The diverted supply was mixed with vanilla and herbs and sold as an elixir known as Linden Grove Mineral Water, for five cents a glass. He also hacked into the gas main and not only stole gas from the gas supplier, but by throwing some old bits of metal in a tank over the gas tap he persuaded a Canadian to buy the patent to his 'invention' for $2,000. The Canadian was so distraught at being swindled he reputedly died of a broken heart.

In 1893 the World's Fair came to Chicago, the Columbian Exposition, celebrating Christopher Columbus' discovery of America, opened only a few hundred yards from 63rd Street and the doctor eyed rich pickings. Thousands of people needing accommodation flocked to the city from all over America. People who would soon disappear before anyone knew they had even arrived. He placed adverts in newspapers offering both employment and, in different sections, lucrative marriage opportunities. With Holmes' good looks and charm, women flocked to his hotel. Most were naïve, some were gullible and all were innocent. Few ever emerged from Holmes' clutches alive.

It is impossible to begin an accurate assessment of who exactly died at the hands of Holmes in his horrible edifice. When he was later in jail for murdering his associate, Benjamin F Pitezel, Holmes 'confessed' to some 27 killings. It is believed he did carry out most of those murders, yet it could only tell part of the story.

Mrs Julia S Conner and her eight-year-old daughter Pearl are believed to be the first to die. Mr Icilius T 'Ned' Conner, husband of Julia, had been conned by Holmes into buying the Holmes' pharmacy only to find it stripped of fittings. Bizarrely, he forgave his swindler and soon Julie, his 18-year-old sister Gertrude and he himself were all working for Holmes. Both Gertrude and Julia were extremely attractive, the latter standing almost six feet tall. Holmes proposed to Gertrude, who refused him and returned home. She died a month later from poisoned medicine Holmes supplied before she left. Holmes then began an affair with Julia who told Ned her lover was 'handsome, caring, intelligent and he loves me'. The couple soon divorced and Julia, taking Pearl with her, moved fatefully into Holmes hotel. Ned Conner found another job but kept in touch, even with Holmes. As for the doctor, he complained frequently that Julia was possessive to the point that she became enraged when he spoke to another woman. Eventually, after catching Holmes in bed with another woman, Julia spurned him and started a relationship with another man. She returned to Holmes claiming to be pregnant. He agreed to marry her, declaring Julia the 'love of his life', providing she would first undergo a termination that he, as a qualified doctor, would perform. Soon both Julia and Pearl disappeared, leaving their possessions and an unfinished meal. They had moved to California Holmes told his janitor, Mr Pat Quinlan. To Ned he said she had moved to Idaho. The last time either was seen alive was on Christmas Eve 1891.

In January 1892, Holmes asked one of his employees, Mr Charles M Chappell, who apparently knew how to mount skeletons, to articulate one for him. He was shown the corpse of a tall young woman in the dissecting room. Half the flesh had already been torn off 'like a jackrabbit skinned by splitting the skin down the face and rolling it back off the entire body', as Mr Chappell later told police. Why he did not report what he saw at the time? Chappell could not answer. Perhaps he considered the woman to have died naturally, otherwise why would Holmes have approached him so boldly? Chappell did agree to strip the skeleton completely for $36. Holmes later sold it to Hahnemann Medical College, Philadelphia, for $200.

Emeline G Cigrand was a very beautiful woman of 20. Ben Pitezel spotted her while he was taking a cure for alcoholism in the town of Dwight, Illinois. Emeline worked as a secretary in Keeley's institute, a sanatorium where alcoholics were treated by giving them the quack 'gold cure' – injections of bichloride of gold, a mixture of gold, salts and vegetables. When Pitezel excitedly told Holmes of her charms, Holmes offered her a lucrative job as his secretary if she would work for him. Emeline obliged and entered his employment in May 1892. She wrote home to friends in Dwight of how kind her new boss was, of how he brought her flowers, bought her gifts and promised to take her travelling across Europe. Her amour was the son of an English Lord, she told her sister Philomina. Emeline was clearly taken with Holmes and the two became lovers. It did not last. Excitedly she told friends and family that she would marry on 7 December before sailing to a new life in Europe. The correspondence between Emeline and her friends would cease on 6 December 1892. Holmes had murdered her, telling friends that she had 'left to get married'. Emeline's intended was a Mr Robert E Phelps. In reality, this was the pseudonym used by Ben Pitezel when he first met her, a name subsequently used by Holmes himself.

Minnie and Nannie Williams were sisters. Born in Mississippi, they were separated after being orphaned at an early age. Minnie was raised by an uncle in Dallas and educated in Boston. She was plain, short, fleshy and heir to $40,000 ($52,500 Holmes would later claim). Nannie was brought up in Jackson, Mississippi and New Orleans, Louisiana by another uncle. While in Boston, Minnie fell in love with the dashing Mr Harry Gordon, moving in March 1893 to his home in Chicago. 'Harry Gordon' was none other than Dr HH Holmes. Nannie was invited to join the happy couple and see the World's Fair. On 4 July, Nannie wrote to an aunt explaining how much she had enjoyed the exposition and was looking forward to visiting Europe with Minnie and 'brother Harry'. It was the last anyone ever heard from either sister.

Holmes would later arrive in Texas to lay claim to the property he had 'inherited' from his most recent 'wife', Minnie. He immediately began building an expensive home on the property, using the alias HM Pratt, secured a $20,000 mortgage on it and fled the state, making his escape on a stolen horse. When arrested for fraud in November 1894, Holmes claimed that Minnie had clubbed her sister to death with a stool, jealous at an infatuation Nannie allegedly had for Holmes, and had then fled abroad. In reality, the sisters disappeared together some time in the afternoon of 5 July 1893. Holmes had murdered Minnie for her property and Nannie was next in line to inherit. Nannie had been lured to Chicago to ensure she was unable to claim what Holmes considered 'his'.

While a resident of Englewood, Holmes reputedly hired at least 100 young women in succession to serve as his secretary. As a requirement of their employment, each had to sign a life insurance policy for $5,000 with Dr Holmes as their beneficiary. This ultimately proved to be their death warrant. Many, if not the majority of them, succumbed to Holmes' worldly charms and became his mistress. If they did not fall for him willingly, once in their boss' power force could be used, rape being one of Holmes many specialities. How many of these young women vanished into the depths of Holmes' castle is anyone's guess. Almost all it is believed. They were placed in one of his 'special' bedrooms, gassed or rendered unconscious and taken to Holmes' underground 'laboratory'. In addition at least 50 people, mostly single females whom Holmes first wined and dined, officially known to be missing, were traced to 63rd Street. There the trail ran cold and it is now assumed that all of them met their death at Holmes' bloody hands. Miss Jennifer Thompson, a blonde, blue-eyed, innocent girl of the kind most favoured by Holmes, was only 17 when he employed her. From the small town of El Dorado, Illinois, she was dazzled by the hustle and bustle of Chicago and overjoyed to have found such a well-paid and respectable position. She confided to Holmes that her family believed her to be in New York, as that was her intended destination when she left home. As yet Jennifer had not found the time to tell her folks of her whereabouts and good fortune. Knowing that Jennifer would not be found, Holmes chloroformed, raped, tortured and murdered her before selling on her skeleton.

Mrs Pansy Lee was a widowed guest from New Orleans. Holmes discovered that she had with her a trunk containing $4,000, which he asked if he could place in his vault for safekeeping. Mrs Lee politely refused. Holmes gassed her, took the money and incinerated her lifeless corpse.

In the majority of cases, the precise details of how Holmes' victims met their deaths are a matter of conjecture. He did formally confess later to 27 murders and provided some details. Other information was elicited from snippets he told the few people he trusted 'off the record'. However, the equipment he kept in the basement told its own story. From Holmes' confession and forensic evidence, it is certain that his prey all died in abominable circumstances. He used his elasticity determinator to full effect. A young woman might wake from a chloroform-induced stupor to find herself tied to the strange mediaeval-looking contraption. She may have been sexually assaulted. Holmes would be staring intently, frighteningly at her; he would turn the crank handle and she would feel her arms and legs tighten and stretch. Holmes would turn the handle more and more as the woman screamed in agony, fear and bewilderment. As limbs were torn from their sockets, Holmes would cut the ligaments in sexual frenzy. As pain consumed his victim, now bleeding profusely and probably losing consciousness, Holmes would do everything he could to prolong her ordeal. Eventually he would be sexually satisfied. She could then die. Perhaps he would strangle her with a noose, dissect her alive or, if feeling generous or bored, stuff a cyanide capsule in her mouth. Dead at last, the poor woman could be incinerated, dissolved in acid, buried or stripped of flesh and her skeleton articulated.

Holmes was psychotic and mercy was alien to him. His victims had to be completely stripped of their dignity and utterly degraded before they could die. As always fianacial gain motivated Holmes, who enjoyed the spoils of his wickedness. He always sought potential victims to insure before murdering them. Mrs Strowers, Holmes' washerwoman stated that Holmes had once offered her $6,000 in cash to take out a $10,000 policy. After some consideration she wisely declined. Had she accepted, her death would have soon followed. It is probable that some unfortunates did accept Holmes' offer and paid with their lives.

In the autumn of 1893, Holmes tried a fire insurance scam. His house had been recently insured for $21,000. Somehow the roof caught alight, in several places simultaneously, causing damage estimated at $5,500. As the insurance was in the name of HS Campbell the insurers would pay out to no one else. Holmes was enraged as Campbell did not exist and so Holmes never saw a cent.

Holmes' numerous creditors, emboldened by the failure of the insurance claim, began to press for debts to be repaid. On 22 November 1893, Holmes abruptly left Chicago with his associate, Benjamin Freelon Pitezel. Pitezel was over six-feet tall, weighed nearly 14 stone, had thick dark hair and sported a trim moustache on a once handsome face now worn by the ravages of alcohol. Addicted to drink, Pitezel had spent his life in a number of casual jobs and had served time on numerous occasions for crimes ranging from theft and fraud to horse stealing. Bar-room brawls and serving as Holmes' 'muscle' from November 1889 had deprived Pitezel of his front teeth. Undoubtedly he knew more about Holmes' crimes than anyone alive. This made him, especially as he was rarely sober, a liability to Holmes.

Pitezel had married Carrie Canning in 1877 and the couple had four children living in 1893, Jeanette (Dessie), Etta Alice, Howard and Nellie. On 9 November 1893, Holmes took out a $10,000 insurance policy on Pitezel with Fidelity Mutual Life of Philadelphia. His associate was in on the deal. The plan was for Pitezel to lie low, Holmes would substitute a disfigured corpse for him and the two would meet up later and share the proceeds. Carrie did not trust Holmes, whom she suspected of swindling her husband out of monies supposedly divided from previous scams. Holmes had 'invested' money for his none-too-bright associate he said, but Carrie had her doubts.

While preparing for the Pitezel plan to bear fruit, Holmes was still active on the romantic front. On 9 January 1894, he bigamously married 24-year-old blonde sales clerk Georgina Yoke of Franklin, Indiana in Denver, Colorado. She was pretty with sparkling blue eyes, a vivacious personality and captivating smile. Like so many before her, Holmes had seduced Georgina with his looks, charm and generosity. He told her that he was an orphan. To secure an inheritance from an uncle who did not actually exist, he was changing his name to Henry Mansfield Howard and married her under that name, a wise precaution for a bigamist.

The 'Howards' or rather 'Pratts' as Holmes changed his name yet again, travelled to St Louis, Missouri and met up with Pitezel. On 15 June Holmes bought a pharmacy with a small deposit, stocked it on credit and sold on the merchandise. The shop was then sold to Pitezel and creditors referred to him. The scam failed. The Merrill Drug Company had Holmes arrested on 19 July for fraud and he was thrown into gaol.

In prison Holmes shared a cell with Mr Marion C Hedgepath, a train robber, gunslinger and murderer known as the 'Handsome Bandit'. Holmes told him of his planned swindle involving Pitezel's fake death and offered Hedgepath $500 in exchange for the name and address of a crooked lawyer, whose services he might one day require. Hedgepath suggested Mr Jeptha D Howe. Holmes was released on 28 July. Rearrested the following day, Georgina bailed him out two days later and he fled first to New York and then Philadelphia, where he met up with Georgina on 5 August. She was apparently unable to even consider her husband capable of any wrongdoing at this juncture, believing him the victim of jealous and unscrupulous business rivals.

Pitezel followed Holmes to Philadelphia on 9 August and rented a small house at 1316 Callowhill Street in the name of BF Perry, buyer and seller of patents. The property was adjacent to what would become his next home, the city morgue.

Pitezel spent most of his waking hours drinking in local saloons. On Sunday 2 September while he lay in a state of drunken unconsciousness, Holmes sneaked into his house, bound Pitezel and poisoned his erstwhile friend with chloroform, after first gleefully and mercilessly torturing him by burning his face and upper body with lighted benzene. Two days later, Mr Eugene Smith, who had designed a set of saws he wanted 'Perry' to patent or invest in, found Pitezel's body. After waiting for 15 minutes and seeing Perry's coat and hat hanging up, Smith looked round. He could smell the partly decomposed body even before he saw it. Decay had set in swiftly, as the body had been placed where the sun could shine on the body during the hottest part of the day. The police were convinced that an accidental explosion of chloroform had killed the man. A broken bottle and burned match were found near the corpse. Dr William J Scott, who examined Pitezel's body, did not believe that death was the result of some drunken mishap. An autopsy was carried out by Dr William K Mattern and cause of death declared as, 'congestion of the lungs, caused by inhalation of flame or chloroform'. After 11 days, no one claimed Perry's body, which was then buried in Potter's Field, the local cemetery.

A letter was received at the offices of Fidelity Mutual Life from Mrs Pitezel's new solicitor, Jeptha Howe, claiming that BF Perry was in fact BF Pitezel. The company were suspicious, as the latest premium, $157.50, was received on the very last day possible, by wire, 9 August 1894 and Pitezel was using an assumed name. They attempted to seek out anyone who might know the deceased. Inevitably, Holmes appeared on the scene.

On 22 September, Holmes and Pitezel's 15-year-old daughter, Alice, identified Perry's body, exhumed for the occasion. Before identifying the fetid remains, Holmes raped Alice and was to do so repeatedly in the coming months before murdering her and two of her siblings.

Alice was chosen by Holmes to identify her father because her mother would realise it really was Pitezel, whereas a young impressionable girl could be persuaded it was not. Alice was understandably distraught at both Holmes' treatment of her and seeing the putrid body, even if she thought it someone other than her father. As instructed earlier by Holmes, Alice indicated that the body was Benjamin Pitezel's and was spared having to watch further indignities. She waited out of sight while a more detailed examination of the body was carried out.

In the presence of Jeptha Howe, the coroner, Dr Mattern and a representative of Fidelity Mutual Life, Dr Holmes, in a mood of exasperation, donned a pair of surgical gloves, cut away the deceased's clothes and searched for identifying marks after Mattern failed to find any. There were four; a bruised thumb nail, wart on the back of the neck, a leg cut and Pitezel's missing front teeth. Holmes soon found the distinguishing features and pointed them out.

The next day, Holmes, on behalf of Mrs Carrie Pitezel, was given a cheque for $9,175.85. Mrs Pitezel was charged $2,500 by the shady Jeptha Howe and Holmes swindled her out of all but $500 of the rest. Hedgepath was paid nothing. Furious, he wrote to the police, telling them all he knew about the scam Holmes had discussed with him. In Philadelphia a warrant was issued for Holmes' arrest on fraud charges. Fidelity Mutual Life, who believed Pitezel to be still alive and BF Perry to be someone else, appointed Pinkerton Detective Frank P Geyer, a man with 20 years experience on the police force, and their own investigator, inspector William E Gary, to search for Holmes.

On the run, Holmes criss-crossed America and Canada, accompanied by Georgina and the entire Pitezel family whom he separated, so that they did not know where each other was. Mrs Pitezel was told that Ben was still alive, living in a city just beyond their reach. She travelled with her baby boy and daughter Dessie. Holmes had informed Mrs Pitezel that he had found a home for Alice,

Nellie and Howard. In fact they all travelled on the same train and were lodged close to each other. Georgina Yoke was completely unaware of the Pitezels as Holmes juggled their itineraries. After several weeks, Holmes resolved to murder Mrs Pitezel and her family. Suspicious, after reaching Burlington she would go no further. Holmes was thwarted. He determined to kill the other children as planned, murdering Howard on 10 October and the girls 15 days later.

Meanwhile, he visited his legal wife, Clara, his now 13-year-old son and his parents. All had thought him dead. Actually, Holmes told them, he had been attacked, robbed, hit on the head and suffered amnesia for all the years he had been gone. Only now, said the inveterate liar, had his memory returned. They believed him.

On 17 November 1894, Pinkerton agent John Cornish finally caught Holmes in Boston after a tip-off from Geyer. Fearing he would be sent to face charges in Texas, Holmes pleaded guilty to fraud in Pennsylvania, knowing the maximum sentence was only two years imprisonment. He also pleaded guilty only to buying a cadaver and pretending it was Perry/Pitezel. The real Pitezel's whereabouts was unknown to him but he had seen him 'recently' in Cincinnati and Detroit. And what of the three missing Pitezel children? They were with their father, probably en route to South America. Trying to curry favour, Holmes implicated Mrs Pitezel in his scam. She was arrested, held until 19 June 1895 and released into a life of poverty thereafter.

As Holmes festered in jail, he realised that his tale of Pitezel heading into the Latin American sunset had fooled no one. On 27 December, he admitted seeing Pitezel in Callowhill Street on the day of his death. Holmes had arrived at 10.30am but could not find his associate. Instead he found a suicide note in Pitezel's hand, saying he could be found on the top floor of the house. Finding Pitezel dead from chloroform poisoning, Holmes decided to move the body and make the death look accidental, to ensure the insurance company would pay up, as they did not in cases of suicide.

No one believed Holmes story and murder was now considered a distinct possibility. An indictment was drawn up that left scope for Pitezel to have died by suicide, murder or accident, as Holmes, Hedgepath and Howe were charged with conspiracy to cheat the insurance company by claiming that Pitezel had died as the result of an accident.

On 3 June 1895 Holmes was tried and pleaded guilty a day later. The judge delayed sentence to a later date. Holmes was happy but it gave the authorities an opportunity to investigate his other crimes.

Where were Alice, Nellie and Howard? The police suspected that they had been slain by Holmes who was questioned but appeared shocked that anyone could possibly think him capable of killing 'three innocent children' for which he had 'no motive'. Holmes possessed at the time of his arrest a small tin box containing letters the Pitezel children had written to their mother that he did not post. This gave detectives a clue to where the children and Holmes had stayed.

Detective Geyer knew that Holmes was in the habit of renting houses or hotels wherever he stayed. Real estate agents and hotel registers were laboriously and meticulously checked to no avail. Holmes had used many aliases and homes were often rented privately. The press were told of Geyer's investigations and people came forward readily with information. All leads were fruitlessly checked. Eventually, in Toronto a Scot, Mr Thomas W Ryves, report to the police that he had positively identified Alice Pitezel as having stayed for a week at 16 St Vincent Street, the house next to his, the previous October. A man, possibly Holmes, had borrowed a spade from him. After speaking to Mt Ryves on 15 July 1895, Geyer hurried to the house and informed the owner of his suspicions. Using the same shovel previously loaned to Holmes, Geyer dug into the soft earth of the dark, dank cellar below 16 St Vincent Street until a terrible smell, the stench of decomposition, engulfed him. He had found Alice and Nellie Pitezel.

The bodies were informally identified through toys and pieces of partially burned clothing. An autopsy revealed the cause of death to be by suffocation. Mrs Pitezel was notified. Utterly devastated, she formally identified her daughters after their bodies had been carefully cleaned and washed by the authorities.

Geyer, accompanied by insurance inspector William E Gary, commenced a determined search for Howard Pitezel, whom he was now convinced Holmes had murdered. Leads were followed in Illinois, Michigan and Ohio. In Irvington, Indiana, a real estate agent, Mr Brown, identified Holmes from a photograph. Elated, Geyer visited the house. Its owner, a Dr Thompson, was happy to allow a search. A large bloodstained stove was found in a barn although digging deeply in the floor of the barn revealed nothing. Disconsolately, Geyer and Gary left. Some days later, the editor of the Indianapolis *Evening News* called Geyer. Dr Thompson had something to show him. Back at the Irvington house two boys, Walter Jenny and Oscar Kettenbach had continued the search. A chimney led from the basement to the roof of the house. A pipe hole three-and-a-half feet from the ground protruded from the chimney. Young Walter had put his hand in and found a skull and femur which Dr Thompson identified as belonging to a boy of eight to twelve years old.

Geyer dismantled the chimney and found a child's internal organs that had been baked hard. Walter and Oscar told how both of them had helped Holmes and Howard set up the stove. Holmes told them he would heat it using corncobs. Asked by the boys why he did not use natural gas, Holmes replied that it was 'too unhealthy for children'.

Mrs Pitezel was once more called on to carry out the gruesome identification of her child. Clothes, toys and other artefacts belonging to her son were found in the house and among the charred remains. The hope she had held out that

Howard was still alive was finally shattered. Inquests held into the deaths of the Pitezel children gave verdicts that Dr Henry Howard Holmes had killed all three unlawfully.

After the bodies of Alice and Nellie Pitezel were discovered, the Chicago police decided to investigate Holmes' now derelict building on 63rd Street. On 20 July 1895, sergeants Fitzpatrick and Norton entered the eerily silent building, with the pretext of searching for evidence regarding the disappearance of Minnie and Nannie Williams. The police were astonished to find the maze of passageways and dead ends within. It soon became obvious that the purpose of the building was murder, a view strengthened when a huge stove in Holmes' office three feet in diameter and eight feet high was found to contain clothing and human bones, while the chimney revealed some traces of hair. Next to it was a First National Bank deposit book in the name of a Miss Lucy Burbank, which recorded significant payments into the account of up to $300 a day. Who Miss Burbank was, no one ever found out.

The vault contained a human footprint, seemingly made by someone frantically trying to get out. Holmes would later confess it was that of Nannie Williams. In a first-floor bedroom, bloodstained overalls and an undershirt were found. Dried blood was discovered throughout the room. In the bathroom was a secret trapdoor with steps leading to the basement. In an adjacent room a little girl's dress, shirt and shoes were located, wedged into the plasterwork.

The basement provided the most gruesome discoveries; the ribs and pelvis of a child aged 8-14 buried in quicklime; a barrel of acid and box of surgical knives; a bloody noose and bloodstained dissecting table under which lay a jumble of female skeletons. Beneath the floor were two large brick cellars full of quicklime containing bones of women and children. The elasticity determinator was found too. Continuing to explore, the police opened a breach in a hollow wall. Immediately the air was filled with a foul stench. A plumber was sent for. Striking a match, a huge explosion rocked the building and scorched the basement. Only the plumber remained uninjured. Subsequent investigations revealed that behind the wall, Holmes had installed an oil tank to fuel a crematorium that could reach temperatures of 3,000 degrees Celsius. Gas had escaped from it and this, when lit, had caused the explosion.

The composition of the oil remained undetermined. Police were shocked to discover that mixing it with benzene produced a vapour that paralysed and then killed in seconds. It was surmised that this gas killed many of the victims. That some were chosen for a more agonising death was clear from Holmes' purchasing of up to ten bottles of chloroform a week when the World's Fair was in town. Undoubtedly he wanted to keep some victims alive while he amused himself by torturing them.

It is ironic, given the scale and ferocity of his crimes, that Holmes was finally undone, not by revelations of what took place in Chicago, but because of what he did to his associate in crime, Benjamin Pitezel. Other jurisdictions, from Toronto to Texas wanted to try Holmes. Philadelphia held him however and believed that their evidence was strong and easier to prove.

Before the police could conclude their investigations into 63rd Street, expose more of its macabre secrets and hold Holmes held to account, on 19 August 1895, the building mysteriously burned to the ground.

On 23 September 1895, Holmes was arraigned in Philadelphia's Court of Oyer and Terminer for the murder of Benjamin Pitezel. He was pensive, gaunt and devoid of the self-assurance he normally displayed. Seemingly lost in thought, Holmes did not appear to take much cognisance of his surroundings, emerging from his trance only to quietly reply, 'I'm not guilty sir', to the question of whether or not he was guilty or not guilty of murdering Benjamin F Pitezel. Asked how he wished to be tried, he gave the standard answer, 'By God and my countrymen'. Trial was set for for 28 October. He returned to his cell and received a letter from his mother. It read, 'Herman, tell the truth whatever it may be. Remember the teachings of your mother and the influences that surrounded you when you were a boy.' Had he done so, perhaps he would not have gone on trial for his life. Then again, was it not those very influences that had helped make him the monster he now was?

The trial of Dr Henry Howard Holmes commenced at 10.00am on Monday, 28 October 1895 before Judge Michael Arnold. The public were barred from attending, with only lawyers, prospective jurors, journalists and lawyers permitted. There were chaotic scenes, as Holmes' lawyers, Samuel P Rotan and William A Shoemaker demanded a two-month continuance that was immediately rejected by Judge Arnold. In a fit of pique, Rotan and Shoemaker announced their immediate withdrawal from the case. Furious at this attempt to derail proceedings, the two were threatened with disbarment. Despite such threats, the lawyers walked out. Holmes discharged his legal representatives, but Arnold would allow no further delay to employ replacements. The defendant therefore agreed to conduct his own defence.

A jury had to be empanelled and Holmes took the opportunity to question prospective jurors. In a murder trial, up to 20 peremptory challenges could be made, as well as objecting to those for good cause. Holmes took up this opportunity 18 times. The judge informed him that he could not reject a juror just because the individual concerned had formed opinions about the case from newspapers, 'unless that opinion is so fixed as to be immovable'. By lunchtime a jury was sworn in and District Attorney George S Graham opened for 'the People'.

Mr Graham spoke for an hour and 40 minutes, outlining in detail the prosecution case. Holmes was calm and impassive. As the day draw to a close, he sought a list of prosecution witnesses. Graham refused. Holmes then requested an interview with his 'wife' to which Graham retorted sarcastically, 'Which one?' Emotional, Holmes tearfully replied, 'You know which one, the one you term Miss Yoke'. Graham made it clear that she had refused to see the accused. Nevertheless, Arnold said, Holmes could write her a letter.

On day two of the trial, the public were admitted, packing out the gallery. Some 500 people thronged to hear details of the accused's scurrilous past. Holmes now had a desk covered with stationery and the paraphernalia of a bona fide attorney. He was in his element.

The first prosecution witness was Dessie Pitezel, the oldest child of that family, who identified a crayoned portrait of her deceased father. Mr Eugene Smith told of how he discovered Benjamin Pitezel's tortured body. Holmes was contemptuous of an illiterate man he considered too stupid to remember any significant detail. He was wrong. Smith remembered the time that Holmes visited the murdered man's house on the day the killing took place. On this, Holmes' cross-examination could not shake him.

Dr William J Scott testified that he had examined the corpse of Pitezel and found chloroform in the lungs and stomach. It was this that had swiftly killed the man. The burns on Pitezel's face, made by Holmes to make it look as if an accidental chloroform explosion had killed him, were superficial and made while the victim still lived, no doubt inflicting deliberate agony upon him. Accidental ingestion of the chloroform was deemed impossible, as Pitezel would have vomited.

After Dr Scott left the stand, Dr William K Mattern, like his colleague a general practitioner, took his place and confirmed the medical points already made. The third and last medical witness was Dr Henry Leffman, professor of toxicology at Pennsylvania Women's College, one of America's foremost analytical chemists. He added his weight to that of his fellow medical professionals. Murder was now proved.

On Wednesday 30 October, Mrs Carrie Alice Pitezel testified. She was a broken woman in every way, having lost a husband, son and three children to the psychopath once considered a friend of the family. Now, she had to face the prospect of him cross-examining her in court.

Fragile, dressed completely in black and speaking so quietly that a clerk had to repeat her every word, Mrs Pitezel fought back tears as she described the duplicitousness of her late husband's former partner in crime, who not only killed her nearest and dearest, but then swindled her out of the insurance money thus generated. She had trusted Holmes with young Alice and her other children, Howard and Nellie. All the while he had led her a merry dance across much of the northeastern states and Canada, pretending she would meet her husband, yet always

Ben was 'one step ahead', according to Holmes. If she arrived in Toronto, Ben was supposedly in Montreal, if Montreal then Burlington, Vermont. Eventually, exhausted by the farce, Mrs Pitezel called Holmes a liar and demanded to see her husband. Holmes then left and wrote to her from Boston and asked if she could go to Lowell, fetch a bottle of nitro-glycerine he judged safe from the cellar and carry it up three flights of stairs to the attic. She was not taken in and had refused.

Holmes had meantime re-instated his legal representatives and Mr Rotan cross-examined. In doing so, he did not help his client. Rotan attempted to make Holmes appear generous towards the Pitezels. The witness disputed this, recounting frequent arguments and drunken threats her husband had made to 'lay out' Holmes, for trying to con him out of his share of their ill-gotten gains. The jury was thus given motive as to why Holmes killed Benjamin Pitezel – he knew he was being conned, was prepared to use violence and, a drunk, could blab about Holmes' innumerable criminal activities.

The following day 'Miss' Georgina Yoke appeared as a witness for the prosecution. Rotan and Shoemaker protested that a wife could not testify against her husband. The district attorney provided plenty of evidence that Holmes was already married and so Miss Yoke testified.

As the tall, slender and graceful woman who had once believed herself to be his 'wife' spoke, her soft words impacted immediately on Holmes who sobbed into his hands. No one took the defendant's misery seriously, as he frequently recovered at salient points to take down notes.

Miss Yoke testified that her 'husband' had been gone from around 10.30 in the morning until three or four in the afternoon of the day Pitezel was murdered, arriving home 'hurried and somewhat worried', insisting on leaving for Indianapolis that night. Their landlady was told by Holmes that Harrisburg was their destination, telling Miss Yoke that this was to prevent creditors he had in St Louis from picking up his trail. She recounted numerous frauds and charades, even that he had given his name to her as Henry M Howard when they met in St Louis. She recalled that it was under this name they had married in Denver.

Miss Yoke had damned Holmes as a bigamous fraudster. Holmes now sought to cross-examine. Nothing of consequence was added, as she replied in whispers, her eyes cast down in dignified contempt.

That afternoon, Holmes successfully objected to the district attorney's attempt to introduce witnesses relating to his alleged murder of Alice, Howard and Nellie Pitezel. Judge Arnold agreed that only Benjamin Pitezel's murder was being tried and a relieved Holmes won a minor victory. Thirty witnesses, who were ready to testify, having been fed and housed at public expense for six weeks, were sent home. Of course, should the accused be acquitted of murdering Benjamin Pitezel, other jurisdictions would then be free to try him for the murder of the Pitezel children or his many other alleged crimes.

On Friday, 1 November, Mr Graham concluded the case for the prosecution by wrapping up some loose ends. The defence was convinced that proof of Holmes' guilt had not been forthcoming. Citing poverty, Holmes' team brought in no witnesses and so would present their case on argument alone.

On Saturday, 2 November, concluding arguments were heard. Mr Graham had the easier task, relying on solid fact and detailed evidence from witnesses. He reviewed the public gallery, filled as it was with society ladies who would not normally attend trials of this nature. Curiosity regarding the murderous lothario, Holmes, had perhaps got the better of many respectable women, who normally would have found attending such a trial rather vulgar.

Graham recounted a total of 35 witnesses who had testified against the accused. A 'complete chain' of evidence had been detailed, outlining how the defendant had maliciously murdered a man deemed a threat to him by burning and then killing him with chloroform. That Holmes alone had motive, means and opportunity and stood to gain by a death that he chose suspiciously to flee from immediately thereafter, only served to confirm his guilt.

On Saturday afternoon, Mr Rotan closed for the defence, his colleague, Mr Shoemaker suffering from 'nervous exhaustion'. Aggressively and confidently, Rotan conceded that his client had contrived an insurance scam with the deceased, was present at 1316 Callowhill Street on the day Pitezel died and that no chloroform explosion had occurred. Nevertheless, in presenting no defence witnesses, Rotan argued that reasonable doubt should be enough to acquit his client. Judge Arnold now took centre stage.

He charged the jury at 4.30pm, defining the crimes of manslaughter and the degrees of murder, emphasising that, if the prosecution proved that murder had been committed and that it was deliberate and premeditated, then a verdict of murder in the first degree should be returned. Yes, he indicated, the evidence presented had been only circumstantial, however, this could be enough if it was 'overwhelming'. After little more than an hour, the jury retired to consider its verdict.

At 8.40pm on 2 November 1895, the jury returned after some three hours of deliberation. The court was engulfed in a deathly silence. Judge Arnold took his seat and addressed the jury. 'Jurors, look upon the prisoner. How say you? Do you find the accused, Hermann Webster Mudgett, alias Henry Howard Holmes guilty or not guilty of murdering Benjamin F Pitezel?' The foreman responded, 'Guilty of murder in the first degree'. Holmes stood to attention, unmoved. Sentence of death was delivered. The trial, a fairly mundane event in reality, was described in the press as, 'The most extraordinary case in the annals of the American courts'.

As he languished in gaol, Holmes had plenty of time to reflect on his depraved and murderous existence. In so doing, he decided to confess his 'sins'. On 9 April 1896, Holmes attested to a statement describing in shocking detail the murder of 27 people and the attempted murder of a further six. Such was the greed of a man with only a few short weeks to live that he sold his confession for $10,000 to newspaper magnate William Randolph Hearst who reputedly insisted that Holmes omit none of the gory details. For Holmes, confessing appeared to relieve a great responsibility. He became a Catholic and apparently chose to unburden himself to 'smooth a path' to the afterlife.

In fact, Holmes had confused names, dates and his motives. It is certain that he also grossly underestimated the true number of his victims. The first murder he committed, claimed Holmes, was of Dr Robert Leacock in 1886, slain for $40,000 in life insurance. The next was a tenant of his Chicago 'castle', Dr Russell, bludgeoned to death with a chair. Dr Russell was also the first whose skeleton was sold to Chicago Medical College, for $25.

Mrs Julia Conner and her daughter Pearl were supposedly poisoned, Holmes claiming an unnamed man and anonymous woman assisted him. The motive was obscure – Julia's rumoured pregnancy perhaps? More likely, Holmes had simply tired of her possessiveness. As for her death, Holmes was a little coy. He later hinted that she was not killed by poison at all but rather she had been taken alive into his basement torture chamber where he 'operated' on her and Pearl while they were still alive and fully conscious. Afterwards, Pearl's body was completely destroyed, Julia's, as we have already seen, was stripped of its flesh and her skeleton articulated.

A Mr Rodgers of West Morgantown, Virginia, was victim number five. He was struck on the head by an oar during a fishing trip with Holmes after the latter discovered he was carrying a few dollars.

An unknown associate assisted Holmes in crushing the skull of businessman Mr Charles Cole. Alone, Holmes gassed a servant named Lizzie in his Chicago castle vault as his janitor, Pat Quinlan, had become 'too attached' to her.

Victims eight, nine and ten were Mrs Sarah Cook, the unborn child she carried and her niece, Sarah Haracamp. Mrs Cook, who worked for Holmes, had chanced upon the murderer while he was preparing Lizzie's skeleton for shipment to Chicago Medical College. Paralysed by fear of what they had seen, they were easily forced into the vault and asphyxiated.

Miss Emeline Cigrand was employed, like so many others, as Holmes' secretary. He seduced her. In his confession he claimed to be jealous that she was to marry another whereas in fact Emeline thought she was marrying him! Holmes asked her to fetch an envelope from the vault-like safe and then pushed her in on the very day their wedding was to take place. The door was slammed shut and Emeline suffered, in Holmes own words, 'a slow and lingering death' from asphyxiation while he repeatedly masturbated into his handkerchief outside. In fact it was solely this sexual gratification that motivated him to kill Miss Cigrand. Holmes excited himself listening to her desperate cries for help and sensing her forlorn battering at the inside door of the vault, pressed his groin against it to catch the vibrations. The greater Emeline's terror, the more thrilling Holmes found her slow, inevitable destruction. As he did with other women, Emeline's body was not incinerated or dissolved in acid but stripped of flesh and the skeleton mounted and sold.

Holmes now admitted to failure. To obtain a mere $90 by selling their skeletons, he tried to kill three women employed in his restaurant. They overpowered him as he tried to chloroform them and escaped. Why they did not go to the police is anyone's guess.

Another employee, Rosine Van Jasand, was the next victim Holmes confessed to killing. She first became his mistress before being slain using cyanide. Her remains were buried in the basement.

Janitor Robert Latimer had got wind of Holmes' schemes. Attempting to blackmail the doctor he was persuaded to enter the vault. Here, Holmes planned to starve him to death. At length he finished him off by means unknown after realising the vault was needed for his next victim. Miss Anna Betts and Miss Gertrude Conner were slowly poisoned. An unknown woman was victim 16. The murderer sold her some property, invited her into his vault, ended her life and took back the cash, butchering and burning her body. Holmes next killed Mr Warner, owner of Warner Glass Bending, whose company had built the brick kiln in the basement of Holmes' Chicago property. To test it, Holmes pushed Warner inside. In less than a minute an oil jet produced a white-hot flame that reduced even Mr Warner's bones to ashes. Another confederate, an Englishman attested Holmes, assisted Holmes to destroy victim 18. A Mr Rogers, a wealthy banker, who was locked in a castle room, starved and nauseated with gas until he wrote cheques to the tune of $70,000. Rogers was then killed with chloroform and his skeleton sold. He killed victim 19 with chloroform too. A wealthy woman, her name he had long forgotten.

For the first time, Holmes showed some remorse as he recalled the murders of Minnie and Nannie Williams. The former he killed for $52,500 in cash and real estate, the latter for 'all she possessed'. Minnie was poisoned, Nannie died in the vault. Number 22 was an unknown man Holmes wanted to introduce into his criminal schemes. Realising that the man did not have the 'abilities' he sought; the prospective 'partner' was killed by means unknown. Finding out that Minnie and Nannie Williams had a brother who was the beneficiary of an insurance policy they held, Holmes travelled to meet him in Leadville, Colorado and shot him dead. Three further prospective victims escaped Holmes. He declined to say whom, when or how.

Holmes last four admitted victims were Ben Pitezel and three of his five children. The doctor admitted that from the first moment he met Mr Pitezel he planned to kill him. First Holmes would gain his confidence, then strike when least expected. Sadism was an undoubted incentive to kill the Pitezel family, Holmes admitting that he, 'Expected to experience sufficient satisfaction in witnessing their deaths to repay me for even the physical exertion put forth on their behalf over seven long years'. Indeed he did enjoy their demise, clearly relishing the retelling in his confession.

Holmes told how he bound a drunken Ben Pitezel hand and foot while he was in a stupor, doused his face and clothing with benzene and burned him slowly and agonisingly to death, while ignoring his victim's 'cries for mercy, prayers and plea for a speedy end'.

After Pitezel's slow and painfully cruel death, Holmes removed the bindings, poured one-and-a-half ounces of chloroform down his gullet and anticipated a postmortem finding of 'accidental death'. But the chloroform masked the alcohol completely; the authorities suspected murder and Holmes was doomed.

With glee, Holmes described the death of the Pitezel children. Young Howard was poisoned at around 6.00pm on the 10 October 1894 in Irvington, Indiana, dismembered and fed into a gas stove. His sisters had been told that Howard was staying with a cousin. In fact, a house had been rented for the sole purpose of murdering the boy.

On 25 October in Toronto, Alice and Nellie Pitezel were told to climb into a large trunk at around 5.00pm Holmes locked them in, met their mother at a nearby hotel and returned to his hotel for dinner. He then saw Mrs Pitezel off at the railway station as she boarded a train to Ogdensburg, New York on yet another fruitless search for her husband. After waving Mrs Pitezel farewell, the killer returned again to his hotel, connected a hosepipe from the gas main to a small hole in the trunk and gassed the children. After the murders, Holmes stripped the blackened corpses of the girls and buried them in the basement with, he said, 'fiendish delight!'. He added, alluding to Alice's rape that, 'her death was the least of the wrongs suffered at my hands.'

Having completed his confession, Holmes judged himself to have become 'a moral idiot, a degenerate'. He claimed that he suffered from recently acquired physical defects attributable to his advanced criminal degeneracy, such as, 'a marked deficiency of an ear, an eye and my nose; one arm and one leg being shorter than the other and deep lines of criminality displaying obvious guilt on my face'. All were figments of his twisted imagination and Holmes now believed he was morphing into the devil. Fear began to ravage the soul of Holmes and he asserted that feelings of guilt at his heinous life were finally beginning to trouble him, haunting both the restless nights and anxious days leading to his execution. The Holmes confession was a mixture of truths, half-truths and complete fabrications. Subsequent investigations revealed that Messrs Warner and Latimer were still alive and another 'victim' had died in a train crash. Possibly, Holmes deliberately included them to make his entire story seem preposterous, leading to a reprieve or declaration of insanity. Perhaps he simply could not remember. Holmes jumbled up events because he could not recall specific details. He was undoubtedly a compulsive liar, telling Rotan that 133 people had died at his hands. While all the evidence shows this figure to be nearer the mark than the 27 admitted, it is unlikely to be the precise figure. Was it even close or one just conjured out of thin air? The truth was probably beyond Holmes.

The night before his execution, Holmes was mired in self-pity. A coward, he feared death and what could be beyond it. Two Catholic priests, Fathers Dailey and McPake, tried to comfort him and a crucifix was placed above his bed.

At 6.00am on 7 May 1896, Holmes was wakened only with difficulty from a deep sleep by keepers George Weaver and John Henry. 'Good morning!' said a rather cheery Holmes, 'is it six o'clock already?' After hearing that it was, Holmes announced he felt, 'First rate. I never slept better in my life.'

The condemned man shaved, dressed meticulously and ate a hearty break-fast, behaving as if it was just another day. He then began to finish the writing of several letters he was addressing to relatives, women in his life and even the fam-ilies of some victims.

Mr Rotan arrived and told his client that he had evicted from his office the previous day a man who had offered $5,000 for Holmes' corpse. Holmes had no intention of his skeleton becoming a curiosity, like those of some of his victims. He left instructions for his lifeless body to be completely encased in a ton of cement.

Outside Pennsylvania's Moyamensing Prison a large crowd had assembled, their morbid curiosity aroused. They would not be permitted to see the last moments of the mass murderer. Sheriff Clement, charged with the arrangements, admitted only 51 invited guests, including the 12 men of the sheriff's jury who legally had to witness Pennsylvanian executions. One of them, Mr Samuel Wood, had also served on the jury that convicted Holmes. All of the guests arrived early and so the execution proceeded without delay. At 10.00am the murderer, accom-panied by Rotan, Assistant Superintendent Richardson and Holmes' priests, dressed in white robes and chanting the Miserere, walked the 13 steps from his cell to the scaffold, erected in the corridor. Amidst hushed silence, Holmes addressed the expectant gathering that stood before the gallows, 'Gentlemen, I have very few words to say. In fact I would make no remarks at all, were it not that if I did not speak it would imply I acquiesced in my own execution. I am guilty only of taking the lives of two women. I am not guilty of killing any member of the Pitezel family. I have never committed murder.'

The witnesses were unmoved by such a ridiculous recantation at this late stage in proceedings. What purpose could it serve? If anything, it was believed Holmes had killed many more people than he had ever admitted to. All the mur-derer had done was to ensure he entered the hereafter without first clearing his conscience. This only damned him further. As for the two women he referred to, who were they? How, when and why had they been killed and why were their deaths not murder?

Holmes kneeled in silent prayer, a crucifix clasped tightly in his hand. Looking nervously at his executioner Mr Richardson, he stood up saying, 'Take your time about it. I am in no hurry.'

Handcuffed, hooded and with the noose around his neck, when the lever was pulled Holmes plunged through the trapdoor below his feet, swung violently from side to side, twitched and repeatedly clenched and unclenched his fingers as his life was draining away. It was a dreadful scene and two spectators fainted. After 15 minutes Holmes was cut down and pronounced dead.

When the hood was removed, Holmes face was seen to be horribly contorted. The noose had bitten deep into his flesh and was only with difficulty cut away. According to Holmes' last wish his body was not autopsied. It took 13 strong men to carry Holmes' coffin to its final resting place, Holy Cross Cemetery, Delaware County. There, Holmes' coffin was placed in a ten-foot deep hole and embedded in cement, a further two feet of which were poured onto the lid of the coffin, locking him in for eternity. In death, Holmes corpse was given a consideration denied to any of his victims.

Did Holmes numerous victims get justice? Countless people were undoubtedly murdered in the most bestial ways imaginable, yet their murderer never had to answer for it in open court. Remarkably for such an evil man, many had a good word to say about Holmes. His 'wives', obviously had much to complain about. Yet Miss Yoke described the man who killed, tortured and mutilated as being 'without blemish' in terms of how he behaved towards her. Said Miss Belknap of Holmes, 'He was so kind, so gentle and thoughtful that we forgot our cares and worries', adding that, 'He was never vexed or irritable but always happy and free from care.' Apparently he was loving and affectionate to their daughter and 'would take crying babies from their mothers, play and romp with them and soon have them sound asleep.' Holmes was a psychopath, despite any positive traits he sometimes showed. He was truly a 'Jekyll and Hyde' character.

Henry Howard Holmes was undoubtedly one of the most evil killers in history and his crimes impacted on the conscience of many Americans in that vibrant and still youthful nation. Word soon spread that the murderous doctor had the 'evil eye', or an 'astral quality'. Reports circulated that a horoscope drawn up during his trial implied death and misfortune for those with a hand in his conviction and execution, and that Holmes' restless and malignant spirit would seek revenge. It was not long after the burial of Holmes that those connected to his demise began to die in mysterious circumstances.

Dr William K Mattern, coroner's physician and witness against Holmes at his trial died of blood poisoning. Coroner Ashbridge who held the inquest into

Ben Pitezel's death fell seriously ill of causes unknown. He recovered slowly. Judge Arnold also became sick and hovered on the brink of death. The superintendent of Moyamensing Prison, where Holmes was incarcerated, committed suicide. Peter Cigrand, father of Emeline, was hideously burned just before setting off to witness Holmes' execution. But it was the demise of Father McPake that really set tongues wagging. His bloodstained, robbed and battered body was discovered in a churchyard. Surprisingly 'uraemia', was diagnosed as the cause of death.

A fire gutted the office of Mr O LeForrest Perry of Fidelity Mutual Life, whose detectives had been influential in securing Holmes' arrest. Linford L Biles, foreman of the jury that convicted the serial killer, died in a freak accident. He was electrocuted on the roof of his house by a loose telegraph wire that had started a fire. Biles had tried to douse the flames when the wire struck and instantly killed him.

The 'curse of Holmes' was superstitious nonsense of course. Nothing ever happened to District Attorney Graham, Frank Geyer and countless others who ensured Holmes was tried, convicted and the judicial sentence carried out. Nevertheless, it added further to the nefarious legend of the man dubbed 'America's first serial killer'.

CHAPTER 9
Dr Jean-Paul Marat: Friend of the People

JEAN-PAUL MARAT was one of the most extreme of the French revolutionaries who seized power in Paris in 1789. He was renowned for his ferocious, relentless and uncompromising hostility to anyone he considered to be an opponent of the French Revolution. A leader of the Club des Cordeliers, Marat became a key figure. To him, the Revolution could never go far enough.

Marat never personally killed anyone; yet he inspired and encouraged the Paris mob to denounce its perceived enemies and helped encourage and inspire a spiral of increasing political violence that threatened to engulf the very Revolution itself.

✱   ✱   ✱

Born on 24 May 1743, in Boudry, in the Prussian principality of Neuchâtel, Marat was the second son of nine children born to Louise Cabrol, a French Huguenot refugee from Castres in Languedoc and Giovanni Mara, a Sardinian from Cagliari. By the age of 16 Marat had reached his full adult height of precisely five feet and he was slight of build to boot. Jean-Paul had a nose like the beak of a hawk, was cross-eyed, had a mouth to match his nose and a shock of red hair that would make him instantly recognisable in the years ahead.

Marat left home and found employment as a private tutor to the wealthy Nairac family in Bordeaux. After two years he moved on to Paris and studied medicine, moving to London in 1765. Although he had no formal qualifications from his time in Paris, Marat worked as a doctor. He soon became a fixture of the émigré Italian and French intelligentsia and began to write about philosophy.

By 1770, Marat had moved to Newcastle upon Tyne, and found work as a veterinarian. His first published work was *Chains of Slavery* in 1773. Marat recalled, somewhat improbably, that he lived on black coffee for three months while writing, sleeping only two hours a night after which he claimed to have slept for 13 consecutive days thereafter. The rather cumbersome subtitle, *A work in which the clandestine and villainous attempts of Princes to ruin Liberty are pointed out, and the dreadful scenes of Despotism disclosed* showed Marat's radicalism and gained him honorary membership of the patriotic societies of Newcastle, Berwick and Carlisle. In 1773 he also wrote the *Philosophical Essay on Man*, attacking the view of the philosopher Helvetius that science was unnecessary for a philosopher.

An essay on curing a friend of gonorrhea helped him secure an honorary medical degree from St Andrews University in June 1775. On his return to London, he further enhanced his reputation with the publication of an *Enquiry into the Nature, Cause, and Cure of a Singular Disease of the Eyes*.

In 1776, Marat returned to Paris where his growing medical reputation and the patronage of the Marquis de l'Aubespine, the husband of a patient, secured his appointment, in 1777, as physician to the bodyguard of the Comte d'Artois, youngest brother of King Louis XVI's and the future King Charles X.

Marat was soon in great demand as a court doctor and he used his new-found wealth to set up a laboratory in the Marquise de l'Aubespine's house. He began a series of scientific experiments and explorations into heat, fire, light and electricity, becoming increasingly famous in academic circles. However, his frequent applications to join the *Académie des Sciences* were rejected. Members were horrified by his disagreements with tghe revered Sir Isaac Newton. Goethe described his rejection by the academy as a blatant example of scientific despotism.

In 1780, Marat published the *Plan de législation criminelle* in which he argued for the necessity of 12-man juries to ensure fair trials and a common death penalty for all without heed to social class. In April 1786, Marat resigned his court appointment and devoted his energies full-time to scientific research, publishing a translation of Newton's *Opticks* a year later. His inquisitive mind later led to a collection of experimental essays including one on the impact of light on soap bubbles. However, most of his work came to naught and he sank into despair, even composing his last will and testament, believing he could not go on.

As the French Revolution approached, Marat put his medical and scientific career aside and focused almost exclusively on radical politics. In 1788, the Parlement of Paris and other Notables advised the assembly of the Estates-General for the first time in 175 years. When they met a year later in July he published *La Constitution* and on 16 September 1789, Marat began his own paper, *L'Ami du Peuple* (Friend of the People) where he showed his suspicion of those in power, and declared them 'enemies of the people'. Although he never actually joined a faction during the French Revolution, he criticised several groups, denouncing their alleged disloyalties until he was proven wrong or they were proven guilty.

Throughout the summer of 1789, Marat, unkindly nicknamed by some the 'terrible dwarf' would be seen standing on a barrel in Paris haranguing crowds with his impassioned oratory. Often dirty and unkempt, he was very theatrical and would cross his arms with seemingly simmering resentment when he had nothing more to say. While some people laughed or were disgusted by his appearance and rhetoric, many others listened and became convinced by the quality and conviction in Marat's ferocious arguments.

In pre-revolutionary France the clergy made up the first estate, noblemen the second and the masses the third. It was this last group that Marat appealed to. On 8 October his calls for insurrection did not amuse the authorities and they forced him into hiding. Marat did not hesitate to attack and lambast even the most influential and powerful groups in Paris, including the Constituent Assembly, Ministers, and the Cour du Châtelet. In January 1790, he joined the radical Club des Cordeliers, then under the leadership of the lawyer Danton and was nearly arrested for lambasting Gilbert du Motier, the Marquis de la Fayette.

On 22 January the tribunal of the Châtelet issued a warrant for Marat's arrest and despite the support of the Cordeliers' district which was in uproar in support of him. He fled once more to England and while in London penned the *Dénonciation contre Necker*, an attack on Jacques Necker who was Louis XVI's finance minister. In May, he returned to Paris to continue the publication of *L'Ami du Peuple*, and continued his attacks on many of France's most powerful citizens. Fearing reprisal, Marat went into hiding in the Paris sewers, where he almost certainly aggravated a debilitating chronic skin disease, dermatitis herpetiformis.

During this period, Marat made regular attacks on the more conservative revolutionary leaders. In a pamphlet from 26 July 1790, entitled *C'en est fait de nous*, he wrote:

> *Five or six hundred heads would have guaranteed your freedom and happiness but a false humanity restrained your arms and stopped your blows. If you don't strike now, millions of your brothers will die, your enemies will triumph and your blood will flood the streets. They'll slit your throats without mercy and disembowel your wives. And their bloody hands will rip out your children's entrails to erase your love of liberty forever.*

This led to Assembly Deputy for Riom, Pierre Victor Malouet to urge Marat's arrest for 'having incited the fury of the people'. As a precaution, Marat left for England once again.

Despite being exiled, Marat still fulminated from afar against what he considered to be perceived injustice and the exploitation of the masses by a parasitic aristocracy and on 22 August 1790 called for a purging of the army's aristocratic officers. Even after returning from exile, for much of the period from 1790 to 1792, Marat frequently had to go into hiding.

On 7 March Marat denounced Queen Marie Antoinette for scheming with her brother, the Emperor of Austria, when she called for him to invade France and overthrow the Revolution. Marat heightened the public frenzy by warning of aristocratic plots to murder the republicans and all true citizens in their beds. He demanded that: '20,000 heads should be cut off to ensure public order'. The hysteria provoked and stoked by Marat led to massacres in which thousands of innocent people ranging from members of aristocratic families to occupants of hospitals, asylums and jails were indiscriminately slaughtered.

On New Year's Day 1791 Marat became engaged to Simonne Evrard, the 26-year-old sister-in-law of his typographer, Jean-Antoine Corne, who had in the past financially supported him and given him shelter on a number of occasions. They were married in April of the following year.

Marat only emerged publicly on the day of the 10th of August insurrection, when the Tuileries Palace was attacked by the mob and the royal family forced to shelter within the Legislative Assembly. The spark for this uprising was Karl Wilhelm Ferdinand, Duke of Brunswick-Luneburg's proclamation from Coblenz, calling for the crushing of the Revolution. This helped inflame popular outrage in Paris among the sans-culottes (those without silk knee-breeches) the radical lower-class revolutionaries comprised mostly of urban labourers who were the hard core of the revolutionary left.

As Marat called for 'people's justice', a euphemism for summary execution, the mob slaughtered 24 priests being transported to the revolutionary prison, the Abbey of Saint-Germain-des-Prés, then mutilated the bodies, 'with circumstances of barbarity too shocking to describe' according to the British diplomatic dispatch. On 2 September 150 priests in the convent of Carmelites were massacred, mostly by sans-culottes and in the following five days mobs broke into other Paris prisons and murdered more prisoners, whom they believed to be counter-revolutionaries. Summary trials took place in all the Paris prisons and almost 1,400 prisoners were executed, including more than 200 priests, almost 100 Swiss guards and many political prisoners and aristocrats. The crowds butchered the Princesse de Lamballe, a friend of Marie Antoinette and the Duc d'Orleans' sister-in-law, mutilating her body. Her head was then mounted on a pike in full view of the terrified queen.

Marat's goal was to eliminate all the people closely related to the king. He talked about his wish to see a new dictatorship installed where the true values of the Revolution would be implemented. His extremist ideas led to him being accused of having been directly involved in the massacres.

Arousing passion, particularly envy, fear and loathing of his enemies and the utopian society the Revolution was supposed to create, Marat became the darling of the masses and his biting, defiant and always provocative oratory could work them into frenzied hysteria. He was called 'Friend of the People' a title he enjoyed. Carrying a dagger, to the mob he was their advocate, doctor and inspiration.

Marat was elected to the National Convention in September 1792 as one of 26 Paris deputies. He sat with the Montagnards (mountain men) so called because they sat on the highest benches in the assembly. This group was distinguished mostly by hatred of the Girondins, so named because their leading figures, Jaques Brissot, Étienne Clavierre and Jean-Marie Roland emanated from that region. The 100 or so Montagnards tended to be men of action and strident defenders of the lower classes. When France declared itself a republic on 22 September, Marat promptly renamed his *L'Ami du Peuple* as *Le Journal de la République Française*. His stance during the trial of the deposed King Louis XVI was a surprising one as he expressed the view that the king should not be accused of having broken any laws prior to his agreement to accept the French Constitution of 1791. Nevertheless, he fully supported the king's execution in January 1793.

Marat's allies, the Jacobins, were named after a former Jacobin Dominican convent in which they gathered for meetings. Their policies were extreme but well-prepared, printed and circulated. By 1792 Maximilien Robespierre was in control of them with Marat one of his keenest supporters and collaborators.

Once elected, Marat began to mastermind the defeat of the Girondin faction who were more moderate than the Jacobins and took power in the Convention, the republican assembly that governed France from September 1792. The Girondins had embroiled France in a series of costly and unpopular wars that had gone badly for France. To Marat, no one was above suspicion in his hunt for enemies of the Revolution. Despite the Revolution being saved by a great victory over the Prussians on 20 September, on 16 October Marat denounced Colonel Charles Dumuriez as a traitor for demanding the punishment of volunteers who had executed French émigré prisoners. Marat was ignored and Dumouriez backed by the Convention.

Marat was himself denounced by Baron Jean Cloots who called him a 'dangerous anarchist' and demanded the guillotine for Danton, Marat and Robespierre – a fate that eventually befell Cloots on 24 March 1794.

Marat showed that he was not afraid to take unpopular decisions, even when completely isolated politically. For example, opposing 'conquest' on 27 November 1792 he was the only deputy of the Convention to vote against the annexation of Savoy by France.

On 21 January 1793, Louis XVI was guillotined four days after a vote carried by a majority of 53, causing massive political upheaval. Marat had been one of those who voted for the king's execution for 'conspiring against the liberty of the nation and the security of the state.'

From January to May, Marat fought bitterly with the Girondins whom he believed to be covert enemies of the republic, 'disguised royalists' as he put it.

In April a Committee of Public Safety was established with the task of protecting the newly established republic against foreign attacks and internal rebellion. Marat was elected President of the Jacobins Club, demanding the arrest of 'suspects' and 'counter-revolutionaries' while urging the expulsion of Girondist deputies from the Convention. The Girondins won the first round when the Convention ordered that Marat should be tried before the Revolutionary Tribunal. Their plans were wrecked when Marat was acquitted and with much popular support he was carried back to the Convention in triumph with a greatly enhanced public profile.

After Marat called for an uprising against the Girondists on 26 May, the mob finally lost patience with the Girondins and expelled them from power on 2 June. The fall of the Girondins was one of Marat's last achievements. Forced to retire from the Convention as a result of his worsening skin disease, he continued to work from home where he was almost continually immersed in a copper-lined bath containing medicinal waters. Now that the Montagnards no longer needed Marat's support in the struggle against the Girondins, Robespierre and other leading Montagnards began to separate themselves from him while the Convention largely ignored his letters.

Taking power, the Jacobins then launched 'The Terror', in which 20 former Girondin ministers were guillotined. Marat soon became jealous of another revolutionary, Jacques Roux, a renegade priest who led a group called the *Enragés* dedicated to ending social inequality. Marat, who in February had incited the Paris mob to sack shops in a frenzied attack on 'hoarders and speculators', now denounced Roux for opposing this and encouraging price fixing. To Marat, with the Jacobins in power, Roux was a 'false patriot, leading good citizens astray with irresponsible acts that encouraged counter revolution.' Changed days! Marat was more likely annoyed that Roux was even more radical than he was.

On 9 July 1793, Charlotte Corday d'Armont, an impoverished 25-year-old noblewoman with Girondist sympathies travelled to Paris from Caen to assassinate Marat. She failed to track him down at the National Assembly and on 13 July arrived at his home in Rue des Cordeliers claiming to have knowledge of a Girondist plot in Caen but was not allowed to see him. She came back in the evening and Marat agreed to interview her, despite his wife's protests. The interview lasted around 15 minutes. She read out the list of Girondist Deputies who she claimed were involved in the plot which he wrote down having a board across his bath as a makeshift desk. After he had finished writing, Corday rose from her chair and suddenly drew from her bodice a six-inch kitchen knife and brought the blade down hard into Marat's chest, where it pierced the carotid artery close to his heart. He bled to death in a few moments, crying out to his wife, 'Aidez-moi, ma chère amie!' Miss Corday was found standing impassively at the bathroom window, satisfied that the deed was done.

At her trial, Corday claimed that he told her in reference to enemies unnamed that, 'Their heads will fall within a fortnight', a statement she altered later to, 'Soon I shall have them all guillotined in Paris.' This was improbable, for although Marat incited people, he did not have the authority to have anyone guillotined. Corday first declared that she had originally planned to kill Marat on 14 July, the fourth anniversary of the storming of the Bastille prison which had sparked the Revolution on the Camps de Mars to make the killing more symbolic. Only when the festivities were cancelled did she determine to go to Marat's home. Having then tried to plead insanity, her plea was rejected and she was executed on 17 July 1793. During her four-day trial, she testified that she had carried out the assassination alone, saying 'I killed one man to save one hundred thousand.'

Marat's killing contributed to the mounting suspicion which fed the growing terror now engulfing France; a terror in which thousands of the Jacobins' adversaries – both real and imagined, royalists and Girondins – were executed for treason. After the assassination the painter Jacques-Louis David, a member of the Committee of General Security, was asked to organise the funeral. He immortalised Marat in his famous painting The Death of Marat, showing him slumped over the side of his bath with flawless skin that in reality was discoloured and scabbed from his chronic skin disease, in an attempt to show the 50-year-old in rude health at the time of his death.

The entire National Convention attended Marat's elaborate state funeral and he was buried under a weeping willow in the garden of the former Club des Cordeliers. On his tomb, a plaque bore the inscription: 'Unité, Indivisibilité de la République, Liberté, Égalité, Fraternité ou la mort' with the phrase 'Here sleeps Marat, the friend of the people who was killed by the enemies of the people on July 13th, 1793'. His heart was embalmed separately and placed in an urn in an altar erected to his memory at the Cordeliers.

All Paris went into mourning for Marat. Public buildings were draped with black and his portrait was displayed in the Panthéon. A pension for life was bestowed upon his widow and lavish resolutions of gratitude were laid at her feet in loving token for all she had done to support a hero of the Revolution.

He was declared an 'Immortel' and his remains were transferred to the Panthéon on 25 November 1793 and his central role in the French Revolution was confirmed with the fulsome elegy, 'Like Jesus, Marat loved ardently the people, and only them. Like Jesus Marat hated kings, nobles, priests, rogues and like Jesus he never stopped fighting against these plagues of the people.' The eulogy was given by the Marquis de Sade, delegate of the Section Piques, the Place Vendôme sans-culottes who took their name from their favourite weapon, the pike and an ally of Marat's in the National Convention, although there is a suggestion that Marat had fallen out with de Sade and was arranging for him to be arrested. De Sade was increasingly appalled with the excesses of the Reign of Terror and was removed from office and imprisoned for 'moderatism' on the fifth of December.

On 19 November 1793, the port city of Le Havre-de-Grâce changed its name to Le Havre-de-Marat and subsequently Le Havre-Marat. When the Jacobins started their de-christianisation campaign to set up the Cult of Reason of Hébert and Chaumette and Cult of the Supreme Being of Robespierre, Marat was made a quasi-saint and his bust sometimes replaced crucifixes in the churches of Paris, now devoid of priests following the anti-clerical violence of the Revolution. However, by early 1795, Marat's memory had become tarnished and on 13 January 1795, Le Havre-Marat became simply Le Havre, the name it bears today. In February, his coffin was removed from the Panthéon and his busts and sculptures destroyed. His final resting place was the cemetery of the church of Saint-Étienne-du-Mont.

Described during his time as a man 'short in stature, deformed in person, and hideous in face', Marat was never considered attractive to behold. His unusual skin disease led to constant inflammation and blistering. He was sick for the three years prior to his assassination, bathing often to help ease the pain caused by his debilitating disease. The bandana that is seen wrapped around his head at his time of death in the David painting was soaked in vinegar to ease his suffering.

Later generations of radicals revered Marat and in the Soviet Union, streets were given his name. The Russian tennis player Marat Safin is named after him. The Marquis de Sade wrote an admiring eulogy for Marat. Plays, songs, films and even the Opera Il Piccolo Marat by Pietro Mascagni and Giovacchino Forzano were written in his honour. Marat/Sade, a 1963 play by Peter Weiss, first performed in German was recently revived in London's West End.

Marat may never have personally killed anyone. The ferocity of his oratory in setting aflame the mob and his constant haranguing and denounciation of opponents both in public and in print raised the stakes and the temperature of the mob, leading to frenzied outbreaks of violence looting and murder. In Marat's case his pen and speech inspired the sword, which is why he is cast among our rogues gallery of 'killer doctors'.

CHAPTER 10
Dr Josef Mengele: The Angel of Death

'Here the Jews enter through the door and leave through the chimney'.

Dr Josef Mengele

THE SMALL RESORT of Bertioga lies some 25 miles south of São Paolo, Brazil. There, on the local beach around 4.30pm on the afternoon of 7 February 1979, Dr Josef Mengele cheated justice for eternity. Suffering a stroke, the Auschwitz 'Angel of Death' was no more.

* * *

Josef Mengele was born in the small Bavarian town of Günzburg on 16 March 1911, the eldest of three brothers, to factory owner Karl Mengele and his wife Walpurga. The First World War ensured lucrative contracts as the Mengele factory, previously a producer of farm equipment, began to manufacture hardware for the armed forces. After the war the factory once again manufactured agricultural machinery and the family prospered.

The Mengeles were a well-respected, close-knit and religious family. Walpurga, obese and dowdy, doted on her boys; having suffered a miscarriage three years before Josef was born, she was particularly close to him. Known for her volatile temper, gargantuan gluttony and stern appearance, the Josef alone appeared to make her smile and was closer to Walpurga than his father, who seemed continually absorbed in the factory.

At home, Josef always gave the impression of being happy, a little quiet and eager to please. At school he was a mediocre pupil, struggling to keep up with his peers. Matters deteriorated further when, at 15, he suffered from the severe bone marrow disease osteomyelitis, an illness that often proved fatal in those days. A systemic infection and nephritis, an inflammation of the kidneys, followed and he remained ill and off school for six months. Indeed, it looked as if he would always struggle academically. Nevertheless, Josef had self-discipline, was well-behaved and very popular with teachers and pupils alike. Gradually he began to do better and grew into a handsome, confident, charming and well-groomed young man.

Josef Mengele passed his Abitur, (high school exams) in April 1930 with good, although not excellent grades, and was accepted into the medical and philosophy faculties at Munich University six months later.

The ladies soon began to notice the dapper Josef Mengele, who stood out from the other bright young things in Günzburg, always dressing impeccably in only the finest suits and wearing only the most expensive fabrics. Always the perfect gentleman, Josef was known for his dancing skills at the numerous balls he attended and as a man who respected women like a gentleman of old. His looks generated even more admirers. Of medium height and build, Josef Mengele had an enigmatic smile, with a distinctive gap in his upper front teeth, large vari-coloured eyes and classic features. Acutely aware of his physical attributes, he seemed a young man destined for the finer things in life, not the horrors he would immerse himself in only a few short years later.

While Mengele spent much of his time cultivating an image at once carefree and at the same time virtuous and serious, he also involved himself in politics, joining the Stalhelm (steel helmets) party in March 1931 while studying in Munich. A nationalist volkish (people's) party that like so many in Germany of the time hearkened back to a bygone age, the Stahlhelm would prove a bridge into the Nazi Party.

Günzburg would always be too small for the ferociously ambitious Mengele. Deciding to make it on his own, he chose to study medicine rather than inherit the family business, knowing that he would face an uphill struggle to excel, give his mediocrity at school. Undoubtedly hard work and dedication paid dividends and perhaps Josef surprised even himself because he not only graduated, but found time to enjoy classical music concerts, fine dining and museums.

Whilst Mengele pursued his studies, Germany was changing. The Nazis were growing stronger and their demand for 'racial purity' found an audience not only in the streets and beer cellars, but also in the lofty academic world of Munich University. Mengele responded to the Nazi call and, absorbing himself in theories of eugenics and 'Social Darwinism', began to see himself as a racial scientist. The followers of eugenics and Social Darwinism held similar beliefs – the former that populations could improve through selective breeding of those with 'desirable' characteristics, the latter agreed with this but were prepared to take more extreme methods to achieve their desired 'results'.

In Sweden, the UK and USA as well as Germany, eugenics had many followers across the political spectrum. Democratic, as well as demagogic politicians advocated the implementation of eugenics as the best way to 'improve' humanity and 'weed out' undesirable traits. Such advocates considered themselves idealists, believing it their duty to shape the destiny of mankind towards a better future; one freed from poverty, physical and mental handicap. Eugenicists believed that criminality, alcoholism, insanity, laziness and other traits could simply be bred out over time. Social Darwinists of the Nazi creed believed there was no time to waste and that the blood of blue-eyed, blonde-haired 'Aryans' was being contaminated by that of 'races' they considered 'inferior'. Such races included those intertwined with Germans for millennia, Slavs and Jews among them. The Nazis were convinced that both Slavs and Jews were *untermensch* (subhuman), while the German/Nordic races were *ubermensch* (supermen). Nazis believed the Slavs were 'stupid' the Jews 'devious, cunning, resourceful' and 'evil personified'. It was such warped beliefs, enthusiastically held by Mengele until his death, which put him on the road to Auschwitz.

In 1935 Mengele was awarded a PhD in Anthropology for his thesis entitled: *Racial Morphological Research on the Lower Jaw Section of Four Racial Groups*. The paper was meticulously researched and devoid of racism or anti-Semitism. By this time, the Nazis had held power in Germany for two years and were tightening their grip on academic life and work in Germany. The Nuremberg Laws were introduced, removing Jews entirely from academic life and forbidding all sexual relations between them and those of German blood.

Mengele graduated in medicine in the summer of 1936 and began a four-month stint at Leipzig's university clinic that was necessary to obtain his full medical degree. With a history of educational achievement by the age of 25, Mengele soon became a disciple of Professor Otmar Freiherr Von Verschuer, Germany's leading racial 'expert', joining his staff on 1 January 1937. Von Verschuer had built up the grandiose sounding 'Institute for Hereditary, Biology and Racial Purity' at the University of Frankfurt. At this lofty institution, Mengele helped his new colleagues decide who was and who was not a Jew, when those suspected of breaking the Nuremberg Laws were tried. Thousands of dossiers were compiled, which would become invaluable in future years as the Nazis sought out Jews for deportation and extermination.

In May 1937, Mengele finally joined the Nazi Party, as member number 5,574,974. The Stahlhelm had been co-opted into the Sturmabteilung (storm troopers) at Hitler's express instruction in January 1934. Membership of the Nazi party had been forbidden by the Führer for four years after his accession to power to prevent 'opportunists, careerists and liberals' from swamping the 'true believers'. In the years before the war, Mengele worked diligently at perfecting his vocation as a racial scientist, joining both the Arztebund (Nazi Doctors' Association) and in May 1938 – with profound implications for the future – the SS.

In the late thirties, the SS was still rather obscure. Formed as Hitler's Schutz Staffeln (protection squad), it had expanded into running concentration camps and its leader, the pompously titled Reichsführer SS, Heinrich Himmler, had pretensions of making the still tiny SS a rival to the army itself. In the meantime, the SS was seen as an elite organisation that recruited only the finest specimens of racially pure German manhood and was pitiless to enemies of the Nazi regime.

In the summer of 1938, the University of Frankfurt awarded Mengele his medical degree. He also became engaged to the tall, blonde and beautiful Irene Schoenbein, the daughter of a university professor and six years his junior. They were married in July 1939 but not without some difficulties. While Mengele could show documentation to prove he was of 'pure' Aryan descent, Irene could not provide sufficient evidence that her grandfather was legitimate. As this could mean her family was 'possibly infected' by Jewish ancestry, the marriage was in doubt. Mengele's family influence (Hitler had twice visited the Mengele factory) and Irene's 'obvious' Nordic ancestry won the day and the couple were married. However, their names were omitted from the Sippenbuch (Kinship Book) for SS men and their wives who could prove their ancestry back to 1750. This meant that the Mengeles would be deprived of the coveted 'swords and spoons' award-ed to SS men on the birth of each child. Perhaps this slur impacted on Mengele to such an extent that his hatred of Jews, until then barely evident, would boil over into bestial cruelty some years later.

In October 1938 Mengele was called up for three-months service in the army. An expert hiker and skier, Mengele revelled in his posting to a Tyrolean mountain regiment. Hatred of his commanding officer, leading to a fight between them, caused Mengele to turn his back on the army. With the coming of war, Mengele was at first prevented from serving due to a kidney infection that he had as a child. In June 1940 he was called up at last, achieving a posting to the Waffen SS as an Untersturmführer (second lieutenant). Mengele saw no combat initially, being employed by the Genealogical Section of the Race and Resettlement Office to examine the racial suitability of those who would colonise the conquered lands and reviewed the citizenship applications of Volksdeutsch, those of German ethnic origin who lived outside Germany's borders, using racial criteria.

In June 1941 Mengele participated in Operation Barbarossa, the Nazi inva-sion of the Soviet Union. There, he was awarded the Iron Cross, second class, for heroics under fire. In January 1942 he transferred to the predominantly Scandinavian Viking SS division to serve as a field doctor. Again he proved him-self something of a hero, winning the Iron Cross, first class, for pulling two wounded men from a burning tank. Mengele was intensely proud of his medals and displayed them prominently on his uniform for the rest of the war.

Conditions at the front were appalling and medical supplies rarely kept up with mounting casualties. Often Mengele had to take decisions as to which German soldiers would live or die. While Mengele loathed this task, which could only have helped inure him to suffering, he was to have no such scruples in 'selecting' those who would live from those who would die in Auschwitz.

By the end of 1942, a wounded second lieutenant Josef Mengele had been invalided out of the front and would serve there no more. Instead, he went back to the Race and Resettlement Office at Verschuer's insistence. After a few months working in Berlin Mengele, now promoted to Hauptsturmführer (captain), was given the 'practical' research post he craved. His old boss Verschuer helped him obtain a posting to Auschwitz-Birkenau, where the latest crackpot eugenics theories could be indulged, using living human subjects of almost limitless variety and number.

The Hippocratic Oath meant nothing to Nazi doctors as far as those they considered racially inferior were concerned, with Jews occupying the lowest rung of the ladder. To the anti-Semitic Mengele, they provided merely the canvas on which to carry out experiments of the most fiendish design. Of course, he was no pioneer. In Buchenwald and Dachau concentration camps, Jews were injected with virulent strains of virus and bacteria, exposed to cholera, diphtheria, typhoid, influenza and yellow fever. Prisoners were struck on the head repeatedly with rifle butts to see how many hits it would take before they suffered irreversible brain damage. Jews were fed on a diet of salt water to observe how long they could survive, injected with gas gangrene, exposed to low atmospheric pressure to simulate high altitude and placed in tanks of freezing water to simulate the effect of freezing conditions on downed aircrew.

In Auschwitz, Dr Horst Schumann, who on one occasion castrated 90 men in a single day, had been conducting sterilisation experiments by exposing men, women and children to massive doses of X-ray radiation. Professor Karl Clauberg, a gynaecologist of renown, had developed over a period of a year, a system for sterilising 1,000 women in a day using one doctor and ten assistants. In Auschwitz, Mengele would go beyond all that had gone before with his own experiments. In that hell-on-earth, Mengele also had another task to perform – selecting his victims.

The Nazis had a whole plethora of slave-labour camps and seven extermination centres where the destruction of Europe's Jews could be carried out in utmost secrecy: Auschwitz, Belzec, Chelmno, Maijdanek, Maly Trostenets, Sobibor and Treblinka. With the exception of Maly Trostenets, all were located in Poland. Auschwitz, in Upper Silesia, was actually two camps that combined the role of extermination centre and the largest slave labour camp in occupied Europe with, at its peak, 140,000 slave workers: Auschwitz-Birkenau. The former was where the stronger, fitter inmates were 'exterminated through labour', being worked to death, starved, exposed to the elements and regularly beaten, shot or 'selected' for the gas chamber, while forced to aid the German war effort. Birkenau, two miles from Auschwitz itself, was where the gas chambers and crematoria were located and where the majority of new arrivals were murdered on arrival. Here the ovens were stoked 24 hours a day. More people would be killed there than anywhere else under Nazi rule. It was also in Birkenau that Mengele conducted his vile and inhuman experiments.

A dank, miserable place even before the war, Auschwitz was chosen for its quiet location and a railway junction interconnected with the railway networks of all of Europe, making the task of bringing in victims logistically easier for the Nazis.

In the towns and villages of occupied Europe, the Endlosung (Final Solution), to what the Nazis perceived to be the 'Jewish Problem' was gathering pace. Entire communities of Jews, regardless of age and infirmity, were uprooted and herded into ghettos where starvation and disease took an inexorable toll. Thus corralled, it was relatively easy to force the weakened survivors onto cattle trucks when the time came for their deportation to the death camps. Packed in like sardines and locked in without heating, food, water or sanitation, the deportees began a nightmare train journey often lasting days in freezing cold or sweltering heat, amidst increasingly squalid conditions. Terrified, exhausted, jostling, shouting, dying, many went insane or tried to kill themselves. Mothers, anticipating an even bleaker future, occasionally tried to throw very young children from the train in the hope that others would find and look after them.

As the 'transports' of Jews approached Auschwitz their horrified passengers' nostrils were filled with the ominous and vile stench of burning flesh and scorched hair. A pall of smoke, which could be seen for 50 kilometres, rose high above the death camp and flames rose from the red brick chimneys of the crematoria.

When the transports eventually reached their destination, the bedraggled, bewildered survivors heard the doors of their cattle trucks open and the shouts of SS guards yelling for them to get off the train. 'Raus! Raus!' ('Quickly! Quickly!') the guards would scream as they clubbed or whipped those who were too slow, setting their vicious guard dogs on any who hinted at resistance or defiance. Often arriving at dead of night beneath searchlights, the disoriented prisoners struggled to stay together in family groups.

One Nazi in particular is remembered by the few who survived their first day in Auschwitz. Dr Josef Mengele's other role was as the man prisoners called 'the selector', a job in which he revelled. Arriving on 24 May 1943, Mengele took part in his first selection the following day with the arrival of a transport of 2,862 Dutch Jews. On 25th he sent 1035 Gypsies he suspected of having typhus, after a perfunctory examination of their barracks to be gassed.

Chain-smoking and always dressed immaculately in his beautifully tailored white SS medical uniform with white gloves and polished boots, the handsome Dr Mengele greeted the arrival of a transport with an air of nonchalance and grace. He then chose, in an instant, which prisoners were to live beyond that day and who would be sent immediately to the gas chambers. He rarely smiled or showed emotion and merely flicked his gloved hand to the right, for life or the left, for death. Occasionally he would whistle a cheery tune – The Blue Danube Waltz, or an aria from Tosca. At one selection a beautiful girl caught his eye. Asking her if she was educated and knew the tune he whistled, she answered: 'I'm not sure. Tannenhauser?' to which Mengele replied 'Sorry. It's Lohengrin.' For her mistake she was directed to the left.

Sometimes Mengele would wink knowingly to a family selected for annihilation. Reassured, they would walk assuredly to their doom. Mockingly, he would stop to chat to one of the new arrivals, feigning concern while revelling in their tales of horror regarding their journey and mistreatment. After such a conversation the prisoners would usually be sent to their destruction. When a cattle truck of rabbis from Hungary arrived, Mengele greeted them with more energy than usual forcing them to dance and sing the Kol Nidre, the anguished prayer that ushers in Yom Kippur, the Day of Atonement, as he cracked his whip. Tiring of their humiliation, the rabbis stood tall and marched off to their deaths singing the prayer Shema Yisrael, Adonai eloheinu, Adonai echad (Hear O Israel, the Lord our God, the Lord is one).

On occasion, entire transports would arrive in such a terrible state that all those who spilled from the trucks were immediately gassed without any selection process whatever. Usually, 15-20% were deemed fit enough to be worked to death in Auschwitz itself. All children under 14, the elderly, sick, infirm or middle-aged were gassed on arrival. Only a few exceptions were made. In all, Mengele carried out selections on at least 74 transports, possibly hundreds more. He had a saying: 'Here the Jews enter through the door and leave through the chimney'.

As a 'racial scientist', Mengele immersed himself in research from the moment he arrived at the vast arena that was Auschwitz. For his experiments, Mengele could choose any 'specimen' he wished. Those who were unusual: deformed, lame, giants, midgets or dwarfs were sought out by the guards as the trains spewed out their human cargo. One other group caught the eye of the Herr Doktor: twins.

Mengele was fascinated, almost obsessed by twins, identical and fraternal, of any age. Here he thought lay the secret of genetics. So keen was he to ensure no sets of twins were missed that he volunteered to attend transport selections 'day and night', in the words of one prisoner. Some 1500 pairs of twins were selected over a period of some 18 months. Of these, perhaps less than 200 individuals were to survive.

In the confusion at the Auschwitz arrival 'ramp' many parents tried to hide their twins. Prisoners, who helped the SS empty the trains, would shout, 'twins good' or 'twins will live' in many languages. The terrified new arrivals had to make instant decisions. A mother who was selected for labour would often ask to keep her child company in the group she did not know was destined for destruction. Asking Dr Mengele if she could join her child, he was always more than happy to comply. Within an hour, mother and child would be gassed, their bodies violently torn in a search for valuables, burned and reduced to ash and fragments of bone.

Occasionally, twins would be hauled out of the line marching to the crema-toria. Sometimes, if only infants or babies, their mother would be spared in order to look after them. The rest of their family would be enslaved or exterminated. In the late spring and summer of 1944, with Hitler clearly losing the war, some 437,403 Hungarian Jews arrived between 15 May and 8 July. Few of these were chosen for anything other than immediate destruction as the Nazis hastened to annihilate European Jewry before being overrun by advancing Soviet troops. More than 10,000 Jews a day were being burned after gassing, as not only Hungarians but the surviving Jewish populations of Austria, Belgium, Czechoslovakia, France, Greece, Italy, Netherlands and Romania also arrived. In all, at least 1,100,000 people would perish in Auschwitz, 90% of them Jews.

Once chosen, the twins and other 'specimens' would be taken to their living quarters, not in Auschwitz but near the Birkenau gas chambers. Most were in shock, having been informed that their mothers, fathers, sisters and brothers so cruelly taken from them were now dead. Their new 'home' was a nightmare world of heaps of rotting corpses ,with the nauseating, all-pervading stench of burning flesh in the air and overwhelming heat from the furnaces.

While slave labourers in Auschwitz had their heads shaved and were forced to wear prison garb, the mostly child specimens of Mengele did not. Their bar-racks, nicknamed 'the zoo', were cleaner and their food slightly better, though all remained hungry. The boys' quarters were sited almost immediately opposite the crematoria.

Once his 'patients' had arrived, Mengele, the 'Devil's Doctor', could begin his 'work' which he carried out with gusto, gaining a reputation as a fanatical workaholic among his SS comrades and those prisoner-doctors forced to work for him. So what kind of research did Mengele carry out and to what purpose?

First, victims had to complete an extensive questionnaire. Young children were assisted in this. He or she would be asked to give their age, specify physical traits such as weight, height, eye and hair colour, any health problems, social, geo-graphic and ethnic background. Mengele would then personally interview his prospective victims and take further notes. All completed reports would be for-warded to Berlin. By taking such steps, Mengele wanted his research to be con-sidered valid and tried to show it had been undertaken in a scientific way.

In Birkenau each morning, thoroughly dedicated to his gruesome task, Mengele had his victims prepared for experimentation. They were bathed, cleaned and carried in trucks emblazoned with the Red Cross to one of his many laboratories. In one, blood tests and X-rays were carried out. These were frequent, painful and undertaken almost daily, usually by one of the many Jewish medical specialists press-ganged into working for the Nazis on pain of death. Mengele often took part himself, occasionally scolding a prisoner-doctor who had inflict-ed pain on a child unnecessarily, as he saw it. As part of his twisted personality he enacted a fatherly bedside manner, even giving the children sweets. As a result, the children nicknamed him 'The Good Uncle'. At the same time Mengele was simultaneously planning and implementing the most barbarous experiments imaginable. Blood had almost a mystical significance for the Nazis and Mengele was no exception, believing it held the key to the mysteries of life and genetic inheritance. Large quantities were shipped to the German Research Association for further study. In focusing on twins, Mengele hoped to achieve a scientific breakthrough that would allow for a reduced gestation period and the multiple births the Nazi hierarchy hoped would help replace Germany's catastrophic wartime casualties and provide the raw material for future wars of conquest.

One group who suffered most grievously from the frequent blood tests were the midgets, who were given double rations when bled. Often they would volunteer to bleed more often for the luxury of extra rations. They eventually bled to death.

Other laboratories were even more horrific. Thousands of experiments were performed and anaesthetic was never used, resulting in agony for the victims. During experiments, victims were always naked. A pair of twins might be sewn together until they died, as happened with two boys, Tito and Nono, one of whom was a hunchback. One identical twin had his brother taken from him one day. An operation was performed on him, leaving him paralysed. Subsequently, the same boy had his sex organs removed. A short time later he disappeared. He was 12 years old.

If one twin died of natural causes, his sibling was killed to provide comparative data. Only in Auschwitz-Birkenau did twins die at the same time, making them available for immediate autopsy.

Surgical experiments frequently included the removal of organs or limbs, partial or entire, immersion in water to correlate loss of temperature and consciousness, lumbar punctures, transplantation of blood and organs between twins, the injection of various painful and toxic methylene dyes into the eyes to attempt a permanent colour change, children were m,ade to stand on their heads to see how long it took for blood to drain from their organs, female victims were sterilised, boys castrated, sex changes attempted (always unsuccessfully), and injections of typhus and tuberculosis were carried out to see how long the disease took to incubate. Wounds were deliberately infected with gangrene to see how each twin would react. Bone marrow transplants were carried out that caused extreme agony for the victims, causing death or leading to amputation and a trip to the gas chamber soon after.

On occasion 'endurance' tests were carried out in both Birkenau and the nearby synthetic rubber plant at Monowitz, whereby groups of eight or more women would be given increasing electrical voltages until they died, fell unconscious or into a coma.

A wall of Mengele's laboratory was lined with human eyes, pinned up like specimen butterflies and classified by colour. Three pairs of Jewish twins under 10 years of age with 'heterochromic' (ie varicoloured) eyes were gassed and their eyes and organs shipped to Verschuer in Berlin along with those from a pair of Gypsy twins, for whose eyes Mengele had their entire family murdered and dissected. The shipment was marked 'War Materials – Urgent'. When a complaint was received that eight records had arrived but only seven sets of eyes, an unrelated child was killed and his eyes forwarded as an alleged twin. Mengele was thus only too happy to corrupt the results of his own warped experiments.

So many and varied were the hideous experiments that no proper studies could be carried out, even if they had any scientific merit, which they did not. It appeared to the prisoner-doctors forced to assist that some were carried out for reasons of pure sadism alone. After the war, the head of a Gypsy that Mengele had sent to Berlin for analysis was found in a box along with photographs of four other Gypsies he had castrated. Photographs of Mengele himself were rare, as if he knew he would be held to account after the war.

Near the crematoria was the conveniently situated pathology unit. Here autopsies were carried out on the bodies of those who had died and the results meticulously recorded. If a prisoner seemed to Mengele to be particularly fascinating, he or she would be despatched by an injection of phenol, evipal or chloroform straight into the heart and dissected while still warm. Prisoners were also executed by a shot to the back of the neck. On one such occasion 80 corpses were pickled in formaldehyde and shipped to Natzweiler Concentration Camp in France for 'further study'.

Mengele had many other duties. Even in Auschwitz, babies were born. To their mothers no mercy was shown. Any woman showing signs of pregnancy was gassed. For those women near full-term, Mengele would deliver the child himself, often meticulously careful in his delicate work. Usually, mother and child were sent immediately afterwards to be gassed. Sometimes Mengele would let the baby live but tape the mother breasts; he would amuse himself by watching the mother's anguish as he let the baby starve to death. On another occasion Mengele dissected a one-year-old child while the baby was alive.

Some Jewish doctors performed abortions surreptitiously to save the lives of mothers before their pregnancy showed. If the confinement was advanced, they tried to reduce the mother's torment by telling them their baby was stillborn. Mengele himself became a father on 11 March 1944 when his only son Rolf was born. It was an occasion he mentioned to no one in Auschwitz-Birkenau and one that mellowed him not the slightest.

Jewish doctors, who worked with Mengele under duress, such as Miklos Nyiszli, Gisela Perl and Olga Lengyel and survived the war, testified to Dr Mengele's zeal, vicious temper and cruelty. He beat one poor girl to a bloody pulp for simply avoiding gas chamber selection six times, all the while calling her a 'dirty Jew'. He was totally unpredictable, raging at his underlings for surreptitiously eating stolen food one minute, whistling a tune the next. Mengele threw a Russian prisoner's baby onto a pile of corpses, shot a prisoner dead in a fit of temper and in a fury, smashed open the skull of an old man who wanted to join his son's work detail.

One of worst atrocities Mengele committed was the burning alive of 300 children on an open fire. Witnessed by a number of Jewish and Russian prisoners, Mengele had a pit dug and a fire lit in the yard at Birkenau. Ten trucks containing Ukrainian children from a nursery in the town of Dnepropetrovsk backed up to the fire and dumped the screaming children directly onto the flames. None of the children was more than five years old.

To fellow SS members, Mengele was the most fanatical of Nazis. Unlike his medical colleagues who dreaded selections and usually had to be drunk to carry them out, Mengele was enthusiastic and always sober. SS Dr Hans Munch, who was acquitted of indulging in criminal activities at Auschwitz after the war, implausibly because he 'knew nothing' of Mengele's barbarous experiments, described his colleague as being 'driven by ambition'. To him, Mengele wanted to be a star in Germany's post-war academic firmament and saw his vile experimental research as a way to achieve it. This, combined with limitless power within the camp and the 'insane' atmosphere of the place, turned Dr Josef Mengele into a monster. The lives of *untermenschen* were worth nothing; they simply provided him with material, a human canvas on which to work.

Mengele's responsibilities included ensuring that Auschwitz remained free of epidemic. He caught both malaria and typhus in the camp. To 'quarantine' a camp population suspected of harbouring typhus Mengele simply despatched the barracks where the disease was suspected straight to the gas chambers. Such was the fate of the camp's Gypsies. In the summer of 1944, some 4,000 Gypsies lived in appalling conditions in Auschwitz. Considered 'parasites' by the Nazis, spreaders of syphilis and racially inferior, they were nevertheless considered marginally superior to Jews. As a result, the Gypsies were not separated by sex and allowed to reside in a family enclosure with their children, where, despite starvation and poor sanitation, their community survived. Children played, their parents told stories, danced and sang songs. Violin music and traditional laments filled the air nightly. Resembling a Gypsy himself in physical appearance, Mengele enjoyed visiting the camp and was always pursued by youngsters eager for the sweets and chocolates he carried with him. Mengele would indulge the Gypsy children and occasionally some were taken to add to his experimental work. Others would sing for him and dance jigs. One four-year-old boy took to Mengele's liking and became his mascot, accompanying him round the camp dressed always in white.

The conditions in the Gypsy camp deteriorated on a daily basis and disease

took hold. On 2 August 1944, the order came to seal the Gypsy camp and liqui-
date its inhabitants. The Gypsies knew their fate and wailed all night. The following day, 2,987 were exterminated and 1,408 sent to Buchenwald concentration
camp in Germany. One four-year-old girl who told Mengele she did not want to
leave was grabbed by a German prisoner and, on Mengele's orders, 'flung against
the wheel of a lorry where her skull was shattered'. The Gypsies used in
Mengele's experiments were not spared. They were not sent west but died in
Birkenau with their people. Thoughtfully, Mengele ordered their bodies marked
with an 'X'. They would thereafter be dissected rather than incinerated like the
rest. As for his 'mascot', Mengele took him to the gas chamber by hand, shoved
the trusting little boy inside and left him to his fate.

The dutiful doctor also carried out selections from amongst those prisoners
who had survived their initial arrival, on at least 31 occasions. Often accompanying Mengele was the 'Blonde Angel', SS Guard Irma Grese, whose penchant for
sadism matched that of Mengele himself. This physically attractive couple provoked fear, hatred and even grudging admiration, particularly from the female
prisoners. Mengele himself was not unaware of the sexual allure he held for
women prisoners and always maintained his impeccable dress sense. As they were
forced to parade naked in front of him, he would speak quietly and softly.
Mengele then sought their trust. Women would often confide they were feeling
unwell or exhausted. Such faith would be rewarded with a trip to what Mengele
called the 'bakery' (gas chamber) or lethal injection. Such was the anti-Semitism
of Mengele that, at the 1944 Festival of Yom Kippur, he 'celebrated' by ordering
the gassing of 1,000 Jewish boys and girls. He 'greeted' the Jewish New Year in
1944 by selecting a further 328 Jewish children for the gas chambers.

Although Mengele may have appeared attractive to female prisoners, he was
not immune to the beauty of a woman in his charge, regardless of being shorn of
her hair, the rags she wore and lack of make up. Arousal in such circumstances
stirred even greater malice within Mengele than usual. One such woman was a
tall, blonde, statuesque 15-year-old Jewess from Transylvania. When he saw her
naked, Mengele found himself overwhelmed by lust. His assistants and other prisoners noticed it. He acted it on it soon after, not by taking the girl as a lover, but
by subjecting her to twisted gynaecological experiments. Soon she was unrecognisable, old beyond her years, sick-looking and bloated from the surgery inflicted
upon her. Attractive no longer, Mengele had dealt with his shameful feelings of
desire for her. After all, she was a Jew and he was an Aryan so such an attraction
to her was an abomination.

Occasionally, Mengele would 'adopt' a child, like the little Gypsy boy.
Typically, the child would be male, three or four years old and ideally be a mirror
image of Mengele himself. Mengele would cuddle the boy, dress him smartly,
hand him sweets, chocolates and toys. He would also play with the child and talk

to him, laugh and joke too. Eventually, after a few weeks Mengele would tire of his pet and nonchalantly walk 'his' child hand-in-hand to the gas chamber.

As 1944 drew to a close, some 70 elderly women were 'spared' by Mengele from immediate gassing upon arrival. 'God bless you for your goodness!' the women wailed in gratitude. 'Why bless me when you do not know me?' Mengele replied, who then ordered them to be killed immediately by phenol injection.

Mengele enjoyed managing the death camp's 'hospital'. Here, prisoners who could still be worked to death were, on occasion, brought to recuperate from their debilitating conditions. Prisoner-doctors were asked to assess the prisoners' ailments and when they would be 'fit' to return to their backbreaking toil. The doctors were in the difficult situation of trying to second guess their capricious master. If the prisoners' recovery time was too long, the trek to the gas chamber was the inevitable result. If too short, death by exhaustion was certain following a return to the barracks.

To his Nazi superiors, Mengele was an 'exemplary officer'. On 19 August 1944, a report on Mengele by Commandant Rudolf Hoess, who had been convicted of murder in Weimar days, described Mengele's mental state as 'outstanding'. The doctor 'carried out all tasks given to him, often under very difficult conditions, to the complete satisfaction of his superiors ... often using his little off-duty time to utilise the scientific material at his disposal to make a valuable contribution to anthropological science.' The report added: 'Mengele shows the impeccable demeanour of an SS officer. He is just, strict when required, popular and respected by colleagues and subordinates.'

Irene Mengele left her son Rolf with his grandparents and visited her husband in autumn 1944, staying for three weeks. She was aware of the exterminations but probably not the nature of Josef's 'research'. She described in her diary their time spent together in Auschwitz as 'idyllic'. The couple bathed in the nearby River Sola, picked blackberries, listened to music played by the camp orchestra and enjoyed the lavish food and hospitality available to the families of SS offices. She acknowledged the camp's 'sweet stench' and was proud of her 'charming, funny and sociable' husband.

After contracting diphtheria, Irene Mengele spent more than a month in hospital before returning to the camp for a 'second honeymoon'. As the gassing of Jews reached a climax, the Mengeles took a week's leave in Günzburg, Josef returned alone on 6 November.

Mengele was at the height of his powers but it would all soon end. The Russians approached with each passing day. The SS grew ever fearful of retribution and Mengele became increasingly despondent about the future. By early 1945, the crematoria had already been blown up on Himmler's orders. Able-bodied prisoners were force-marched through winter snows to new destinations in Germany and documents were shredded. Warehouses full of goods stolen from victims were shipped west. Carrying out his experiments until almost the last moment, Mengele had his equipment, samples and reports sent off to Berlin, Frankfurt, Günzburg and other 'safe' locations. He could not bear for such 'valuable' work to fall into the hands of the hated Bolsheviks. When one prisoner accidentally spilled grease on one of his files, Mengele disapprovingly asked: 'How can you be so careless with these files, which I have compiled with so much love?'

From the very start, Mengele believed bizarrely that his work had real scientific merit but there was to be no Utopia, no promised land, no blueprint for a race of new superhumans. Dreams of winning the Nobel Prize would remain a fantasy in the twisted mind of Mengele.

On 17 January 1945, Mengele simply disappeared. The camp was set on fire and, on 27 January, the encroaching Soviet troops finally arrived. A few thousand sick prisoners remained in the wreckage of the camp. The survivors of Mengele's experiments were also found – cold, ill, hungry, frightened and exhausted. Almost all were children – the twins. A few others who survived the death marches also survived. Despite the best efforts of their liberators, many died as a result of what they had suffered. The rest would bear the physical and mental scars for the rest of their lives.

And Mengele? For a few weeks he found himself employed as a physician in Gross-Rosen concentration camp, 300 kilometres from Auschwitz. Although bacteriological experiments had been carried out on Soviet prisoners of war for three years, Mengele had no experiments or selections to carry out and on 18 February, as Soviet troops closed in, he de-camped to Mauthausen in Austria. This was the last concentration camp to be liberated and thereafter Mengele was on the run. He was smart enough to shed his SS uniform but was soon afterwards captured, in the guise of a Wehrmacht officer, having joined a *kriegslazarett* (war hospital) unit on 2 May. There he met a friend Dr Hans Otto Kahler. Despite Kahler's grandfather being half-Jewish, Verschuer had employed him in Frankfurt before the war.

On 3 May 1945, Irene Mengele heard an Allied radio broadcast detailing some of her husband's actions and declaring him wanted for 'mass murder and other crimes'. She was apparently relieved that he was still alive.

Mengele became anxious and depressed as a prisoner. Working initially in the field hospital, he was stuck in an area between the Russian and American lines while the allies discussed jurisdiction. The identity of the Wehrmacht soldier he acquired was constantly changed but he daily feared exposure as a member of the SS. He also had an affair with a nurse and entrusted her with some of his files. The Allies were combing all camps for SS, Gestapo and Nazi Party functionaries. Soon, 50,000 were identified with a view to screening out and prosecuting the war criminals among them. SS men were particularly easy to find as all had a blood group tattoo under their left arm. Mengele was lucky; he abhorred tattoos and had adamantly refused to have one when he joined the SS. As a result, having recently made a successful break for the American sector, the former Auschwitz doctor was not suspected of SS membership, even when he reverted to his own name. US troops assumed responsibility for Mengele and his colleagues on 15 June and he was released on 18 August 1945. Mengele was now 34 years old. Little did he know this was the number of years he was to spend 'on the run'.

* * *

In hiding, Mengele was despondent, cautious and doubted his luck would hold. He returned to Günzburg and his family, but did not live with them, preferring to hide in the woods. Soon, fearing detection, he moved again. Dr Kahler introduced Mengele to a neurologist, Dr Fritz Ullmann, whom he had met in captivity. Ullmann became Mengele's confidant and to him he admitted his heinous crimes. Ullmann provided Mengele with another false identity, that of himself. While staying with a childhood friend, Dr Albert Miller, American troops arrested Miller for his Nazi connections. A fearful Mengele hid in a back room.

After a fruitful but highly dangerous three-week journey into Soviet occupied East Germany to find the nurse who held the notes he treasured, Mengele returned to Bavaria. At first he stayed with a pharmacist friend in Munich who had served with him in the Viking SS Division. Mengele next contacted and obtained the assistance of Ullmann's brother-in-law, yet another doctor, who found a farm for Mengele to live and work on. In the Bavarian hamlet of Mangolding, the war criminal worked for a farmer, George Fischer, as Fritz Hollmann, ironically selecting potatoes into those fit or unfit for human consumption.

For the best part of three years, Mengele laboured on the small Alpine farm, with occasional forays home. He worked hard, ate well, played and laughed with the Fischer children and read prodigiously. The family guessed their employee was a wanted Nazi. His soft hands, educated accent and obvious intelligence gave him away. They never enquired of 'Hollmann's' past and, satisfied with his work, discipline and temperament, helped register him in his new name.

Elsewhere in Germany, poverty, starvation and uncertainty plagued the ravaged country. Younger brother Alois was in Yugoslavian captivity, the Americans detained his father for his Nazi sympathies, his mother died in early 1946 and his wife and son Rolf lived with Mengeles' in-laws in Günzburg. The name of Mengele, hitherto unknown, was becoming more and more familiar to the Americans. With his murderous role in Auschwitz recounted by numerous survivors, Mengele became a wanted man. This intensified even more so after the Belsen trials.

Held at the end of 1945 on Luneburg Heath at the site of the Bergen-Belsen concentration camp, at this trial some of Mengele's old cronies were brought to justice, including Irma Grese and the former commandant of Auschwitz and Belsen, Dr Josef Kramer. Both were hanged but not before Grese admitted to the cruelties she was accused of and named Mengele as the man who ordered her to act so viciously. To add insult to injury, his old mentor Verschuer retained his professorship and accused Mengele of carrying out experiments without his knowledge. Verschuer claimed to know nothing of the gassings, experiments without anaesthetic or the source of the blood, tissue and skeletal samples Mengele forwarded to him during the war. Colleagues supported Verschuer in claiming that Mengele was an aberration, a person for whom they had only con-tempt. Verschuer temporarily fell into disfavour, losing his post at the Kaiser Wilhelm Institute. In 1949 he was judged fit to resume his career by a commit-tee of fellow professors and was appointed Professor of Genetics at Munster University until his death in 1969.

In 1946, Manfred Wolfson of the US War Crimes Council in Berlin was asked to look into the cases of both Verschuer and Mengele. The former was exposed as a rampant racial Nazi, the latter as a mass murderer. After taking evi-dence and investigating Mengele's wartime activities, Wolfson produced a report recommending that: 'Former SS Hauptsturmfuhrer Dr Josef Mengele be placed on the wanted list and indicted for war crimes.' That autumn, 23 Nazi doctors went on trial for war crimes, in which some 200 were believed to have participat-ed. Astonishingly, Mengele, the most notorious of all, was not even indicted. The report on him had been 'lost' somehow. Yet even the worst of those tried, such as Dr Waldemar Hoven of Buchenwald, who had carried out hideous experi-ments, had not undertaken selections. Others had selected but not experiment-ed. Even the prosecution did not mention Mengele, who had experimented and selected on a monumental scale, in the trial. Such was the scale of medical crimes that the horrors of Auschwitz were inadvertently ignored.

Such trials, and a further judgement of Auschwitz personnel in Poland in 1947, persuaded Mengele that he must flee. He left Mangolding for a while and returned to live first with friends and relatives in Günzburg and then, fearing detection or betrayal, in the woods outside the town before finally returning to the Fischers' farm.

The attitude in Günzburg to Mengele was that he was unjustly accused. Those who knew Josef did not believe one iota of the 'nonsense' the Allies were spreading about him. At the same time the town was itself being 'de-Nazified', having expelled all 309 of its Jewish inhabitants after Hitler had taken power, Günzburgers had little sympathy for tales of anti-Semitic atrocities.

American troops had called on both Irene Mengele and her father-in-law, Karl. Irene simply said she had no idea where her husband was, probably dead. Karl said much the same thing. Apparently, that was enough for the somewhat disinterested investigators. The family were bothered no further and concentrated on rebuilding the family firm. With West Germany in the midst of massive reconstruction, the Mengeles produced vast numbers of wheelbarrows as well as their customary farm machinery and their post-war prosperity was soon assured.

While in hiding, something remarkable happened to Mengele – he was pronounced dead! The Nuremberg war crimes investigators concluded that Mengele had died in October 1946, despite not having a shred of evidence to support their decision. Hearing of this, the Mengele family used it as an opportunity to 'close the book' on the doctor and held a funeral in Günzburg at which his brothers, father and wife tearfully said farewell, knowing all the while that the war criminal was still alive nearby. Irene Mengele took to wearing widow's weeds and prayed in church for the soul of her 'dear departed husband'. All the time, she visited him twice-monthly for trysts by the Sinnsee. In spite of her support, the deeply insecure Mengele became insanely jealous, continually accusing her of seeing other men. The couple became progressively estranged and their marriage was never to recover.

Meanwhile, in the United States, Dr Gisela Perl, a Jewish doctor who was one of Mengele's assistants, published a graphic account of the nightmare that was Auschwitz. The crimes of Mengele took centre stage. Dr Perl also wrote to the US War Crimes Council in Washington, pleading to be allowed to speak as a prosecution witness at what she supposed would be Mengele's forthcoming trial in Nuremberg. Her letter received not even the courtesy of a reply. Her book was also ignored and when she wrote to Washington again, she was informed, on 12 February 1948, that Mengele was dead. Thus, no trial was forthcoming and Mengele was not even condemned in absentia. In fact, prosecutors at first thought the war criminal was in custody, then that he was a prisoner of the Poles and finally that the Poles had tried, sentenced and executed him. Such incompetence took the heat off Mengele and he was soon to make a clean getaway.

After a fruitless attempt to obtain forged documents, Mengele took a train to Innsbruck and walked over the Alps, crossing into Italy on Easter Sunday, 17 April 1949. Paid guides, ignorant of who he was, helped him every step of the way. Heading for the South Tyrol, whose inhabitants were stateless because of an unresolved border dispute between Austria and Italy, Mengele easily obtained an International Red Cross ID card in the name of 'Helmut Gregor' that he subsequently used to obtain a Swiss passport.

Moving to Genoa, with a view to escaping Europe altogether, Mengele was met by his boyhood friend Karl Sedlmeier, who, acting on behalf of Mengele's wealthy father, gave the doctor not only a large sum of money but a box of slides he had sent from Auschwitz to his home for safe keeping. Mengele was overjoyed and intended to resume his experiments once he reached his new homeland of Argentina. First, he needed a medical examination and inoculations. He was contemptuous of the Croat doctor who examined him without bothering to sterilise the instruments from his previous patient. Clearly, Mengele considered this doctor unprofessional, yet failed to see the irony of his indignation, considering his own experiments. Taking a bribe to backdate Mengele's inoculations, the Croat doctor announced him fit and healthy.

After several setbacks, including a three-week spell in prison for trying to bribe an official from whom he sought an exit visa, Mengele was ready to set sail, departing on the *North King* in the summer of 1949 to begin a new life. Arriving in Buenos Aires on 26 August 1949, Mengele felt safe at last. He now lived in the domain of Juan Peron, dictator and President of Argentina and husband of Eva Duarte or 'Evita' as she was often known. Peron had long admired both Mussolini and Hitler and believed Germany would return to the Nazi fold within a decade. He had provided 10,000 blank Argentine passports and identities to facilitate the emigration to Argentina of Nazi fugitives. Six German U-boats had delivered more than 20 tonnes of gold (much of it dental gold stolen from the mouths of Jews in death camps), 100 kilos of platinum, 4,638 carats of diamonds and precious works of art. Four Germans in charge of overseeing the booty, paid into the personal accounts of Juan Peron and Eva Duarte, would meet violent ends over the next few years. The loot would never return to Germany or the families from whom it was stolen.

Thousands of Jews and Nazis alike had left Europe in the previous decade seeking a new life. Both communities prospered side-by-side with no conflict between them. The Nazis sought to blend into a German community that had been in Argentina for more than a century and was significant to the extent that three of Buenos Aires 18 daily newspapers were published in German. Although nostalgic for the 'old days and old ways' of Hitler's Reich, apart from forming a few organisations proclaiming loyalty to their Nazi creed, they caused no trouble. Mengele had to start afresh. His first home was a cramped room in a cheap hotel he shared with two others in the suburb of Vicente Lopez. He could not practise as a doctor and found work as a carpenter. He was good enough at it to make ends meet and when money arrived from his family, he was able to establish a business selling farm equipment like his family did, half-a-world away. Gradually he prospered.

In a matter of months, through securing the assistance of Federico Haase, a famous architect with family connections to politicians in Paraguay and social contacts with senior Nazis in both Paraguay and Argentina, Mengele became a fixture on the local Nazi social scene. His past was known and respected by many. The fact that he was wanted as a war criminal mattered little in such circles and, if anything, gave him more credibility. In 1953 he even had an article published in one of their publications, the virulently anti-Semitic *Der Weg* (The Way), on a subject close to his heart: genetics, under the pseudonym 'G Helmuth'.

By the mid-1950s Mengele was homesick and it was later alleged by Sedlmeier that he made a brief journey home to West Germany. He missed his family and Irene divorced him on 25 March 1954, an event not precluded by his supposed 'death' in 1946. A beautiful woman, Irene Mengele grew tired of living in Günzburg and being married to a fugitive whom she never saw. Mengele remained jealous of her after arriving in Argentina and continued to accuse her of infidelity. He was arrogant and haughty in his letters, expecting her and his son to follow him into exile. She had no intention of doing so, even though she did not believe Mengele guilty of the crimes attributed to him. Once divorced, the former Mrs Mengele married businessman Alfons Hackenjos in her hometown of Freiburg. Remarkably, not only did Mengele remarry too, he married the widow of his brother Karl.

Karl Mengele junior had died in 1949. In March 1956 his beautiful widow Martha met the still handsome, dashing Josef Mengele again on a family skiing holiday to Engelberg, Switzerland. There he not only charmed her but also her son, Karl Heinz, and his own teenage offspring Rolf, who knew his father only as 'Uncle Fritz', with exciting stories of the Russian front, pocket money, his apparent warmth and sense of humour. Rolf stayed with his mother, but that year Martha and Karl Heinz moved to Argentina to be with her new amour. They married in Uruguay in July 1958. Although many were shocked in Günzburg at the Josef-Martha union, the Mengele family backed the marriage as a way of ensuring the family firm stayed in Mengele hands.

Life for the war criminal in the 1950s was good, even after Peron's regime was ousted in a 1955 coup. Backed by his father's money, Mengele's business grew steadily. In 1954 his father visited him in Buenos Aires and gave his son a million marks to buy half of a pharmaceutical company, Fadro Farm. Gradually, Mengele moved into larger and more elegant homes, and eventually settled into a villa at 970 Virray Vertiz, in the luxurious suburb of Olivos, near Peron's old estate. The mortgage was in the name of 'Karl Mengele & Sons'. Many Jews and other wealthy Germans lived nearby. At work he would often whistle a cheery tune, just as he had done as a boy, just as he had done in Auschwitz. Once again his clothing was beautifully tailored. He bought himself a sports car, dined and socialised with the elite of Argentine society.

Living almost openly, Mengele's confidence and feelings of security were such that in 1956 he decided to change his name from Helmut Gregor back to Josef Mengele. Astonishingly, although this meant confessing when he requested a West German passport from their embassy to having lived under a false name since arriving in Argentina, their staff did not bat an eyelid. Mengele gave the West Germans his birth certificate, addresses in Günzburg and Buenos Aires and details of his divorce from Irene. Despite Mengele's application having supposedly been checked with Bonn, no wanted lists were perused. That the West German ambassador to Argentina, Werner Junkers, was himself a former Nazi was perhaps more than a coincidence, although he later denied any knowledge of the former Auschwitz doctor.

The Mengele idyll did not last. Shortly after his marriage Mengele was arrested for practising medicine without a licence, specifically as an abortionist. Charges were not pursued after a $500 bribe was paid. Soon after, Mengele's father died and it is believed he went to the funeral to pay his final respects. Returning to Argentina, Mengele realised he was once again a wanted man. Yet how had he been able to live so openly for so long?

In the immediate postwar years there was a genuine effort to catch, try and punish Nazi war criminals. The task was enormous and in the chaos it was inevitable that many would escape justice, sometimes for a few years, often permanently. Eventually, after the surviving Nazi 'bigwigs' were tried and sentenced, the public became weary of the daily horrors exposed by the trials, particularly in Germany itself. At the same time, the Iron Curtain had descended on Europe and in both the Soviet and Western spheres of Germany, capturing the hearts and minds of the German people took precedence. Both sides used people guilty of war crimes to undermine their former allies. Those who were tried and found guilty of war crimes in the late 1940s and early 1950s were often given remarkably light sentences. For example, Otto Bradfish, who murdered 15,000 Jews as part of an *Einsatzgruppen* (special action group) death squad received only 10 years hard labour. Israel was pre-occupied in the decade after its foundation primarily with survival and the integration of hundreds of thousands of refugees, many of them Holocaust survivors. Hunting Nazis was a luxury it could not afford. Thus, Mengele and his cohort had years of respite before they would again fear retribution.

In 1959, the West Germans were at long last persuaded to look for Mengele. Auschwitz survivors wanted justice and began their own investigations. One such survivor, Vienna based Hermann Langbein, remembered a man now known as 'The Angel of Death'. It is not known exactly how Mengele acquired his nickname, one much more resonant of his crimes than 'The Selector'. It seemed to have emerged after the war, perhaps from the evil spirit the ancient Hebrews called the *Malach Hamavet*. In any case, the nickname added drama to the search for Mengele. Langbein had long been frustrated that such a monster had eluded the hangman and resolved to find him. The divorce papers of Irene and Josef Mengele provided the first clue, revealing that his quarry was alive and living in Buenos Aires.

Preparing a file on Mengele with the assistance of other Holocaust survivors Langbein demanded that the West German government take action. Some 14 years after the war, there was no interest. Eventually, Langbein found a prosecutor in Freiburg, Judge Robert Muller, who agreed to pursue the matter and

Germany finally issued its first arrest warrant for Mengele on 7 June 1959. There were 17 counts of premeditated murder. The charges accused Mengele of:

> *Killing numerous prisoners with phenol, benzene and/or air injections and in the gas chamber; killing a 14 year old girl by splitting her head with a dagger; injecting dyes into the eyes of women and children which killed them; killing several pairs of Gypsy twins with his own hands or by poisoning for the purpose of undertaking medical studies on their bodies during autopsy; and ordering prisoners to be shot for refusing to write to relatives saying they were being well treated.*

The warrant was passed to the West German Foreign Ministry, which now sought Mengele's extradition from Argentina. The press soon heard about it and the World Jewish Congress appealed to Auschwitz survivors to provide Langbein with evidence of what they witnessed Mengele do or their ill-treatment at his hands.

Mengele soon got word that the game was up in Argentina. Helped by Colonel Hans Ulrich Rudel, a Nazi war hero and alleged 'Fuhrer of the Fourth Reich', he fled to Paraguay, where a large, influential and sympathetic Nazi community awaited him. Alfredo Stroessner, dictator of Paraguay, was himself of Bavarian origin and Mengele became a Paraguayan citizen, under his own name, on 27 November 1959 after Werner Jung, head of the local Nazi Party during the war and White Russian Captain, Alejandro von Eckstein, vouched that he was a resident of six years standing. This was despite the Paraguayans being fully aware that he was wanted in West Germany for war crimes. He lived for a while under his own name in south-east Paraguay, a place where tens of thousands of Germans had settled in the half-century before the war. Pro-Nazi during the Hitler era, the area was known as Nueva Bavaria.

Mengele still had assets in Argentina and made several trips to Buenos Aires to sell his villa, pharmaceutical shares and equipment business. The Argentines thus had numerous opportunities to arrest him but were not so much sluggish as obstructive. In fact, they denied he had ever entered their country – despite his listing in the Buenos Aires telephone book under his own name. The Germans too were lackadaisical and took six months to point out this fact. They did not even hand the extradition warrant to the Argentine consul general in Munich, Alberto Malddonni, until 11 March 1960. Previously, on 27 October 1959, Argentina had indicated that no extradition treaty existed between their country and West Germany and that the Mengele case would be submitted to their solicitor general for a 'recommendation' once the warrant was in their hands. Eventually the warrant arrived in Buenos Aires on 30 June 1960, over a year after it was issued. For reasons known only to themselves and to their lasting shame, the government of Argentina said that, as Dr Mengele's crimes were 'political', they would take no action at all. The Argentines had contrived to let the mass-murderer escape.

While staying in Paraguay at the home of his friend Alban Krug with Martha and Karl Heinz, Mengele pondered his next move. In the meantime, his world was rocked by a world-famous event that had recently taken place on the streets of the Argentine capital. In May 1960, agents of Mossad, Israel's intelligence service, kidnapped Adolf Eichmann, one of the most important war criminals still at large and flew him to Israel. Eichmann had dedicated himself to the pursuit of the 'Final Solution' by rounding up Europe's Jews for deportation and extermination. He had met the death-camp doctor on a number of occasions but the two did not get on. Perhaps wary of Mengele's reputation, the cash-strapped Eichmann politely declined when Dr Mengele offered to look after his medical needs free of charge. Mossad had hoped to capture Mengele too but he had already vanished and they did not have the agents on the ground to mount a pursuit.

For Mengele, it appeared only a matter of time before he too was hunted down, caught and taken for trial in Israel. He felt that he had to go deeper into hiding and move to Brazil but Martha thought differently; she had no intention of living a life looking over her shoulder in an impoverished Latin-American backwater. She left her husband and took Karl Heinz back to West Germany.

For Nazi hunters, there was a new lease of life. Langbein and Simon Wiesenthal, another Holocaust survivor working out of Vienna, persuaded a West Germany embarrassed by its Nazi past to do more to bring war criminals to justice. Soon, Richard Baer, a former commandant of Auschwitz, SS General Karl Wolff and a number of Eichmann's former cronies were arrested. It was clear to Mengele that the days of skiing holidays in Europe and hobnobbing with the Argentine elite were now over.

The West German government placed a reward of 20,000 deutschmarks for information leading to the capture of Mengele, the first time it had offered a reward for the capture of a war criminal. The Argentines were now keen to catch Mengele, as they believed this would provide them with considerable international prestige and set up a nationwide manhunt. It was too late, the Auschwitz doctor had vanished again.

Mengele remained at large for so long because he never seemed to have troubling obtaining help. In Paraguay, Rudel put him in touch with a fanatical Austrian Nazi, Wolfgang Gerhard. Gerhard, whose son was called Adolf and whose Brazilian wife Ruth once gave her landlady a present of two bars of soap made from Auschwitz victims, helped Mengele move on to Brazil in November 1960, where the death-camp doctor hoped to stay one step ahead of his pursuers.

In May 1962, Eichmann was executed. Two years earlier, Argentina had protested not only to Israel, but also to the United Nations, that Israel had violated its sovereignty by kidnapping Eichmann. A rise in anti-Semitism in South America and rebukes for Israel for violating international law brought fear of Nazi revenge for Eichmann's death. Synagogues were vandalised, Jews assaulted and a Jewish girl, Merta Penjerek, was murdered. Although Israel had sent a tough group of agents to find Mengele in the wake of the Eichmann success and they discovered he had stayed with the Krugs, they were nowhere near catching him. Reluctantly, Israel decided to call off its hunt for Mengele, despite considering him a much greater prize than Eichmann. With Nazi scientists now employed in the rocket programme of Egyptian dictator Gamal Abdel Nasser, Israel believed that its agents were much better employed addressing that threat.

Mengele was vain enough to believe that he would be the focus of all Israeli attempts to seek out Nazis in South America and remained convinced for the rest of his life that an active search team was on permanent lookout for him. Although he had friends and assistance in hiding, the myth later perpetrated that a powerful postwar Nazi organisation, such as ODESSA (Organisation der ehemaligen SS-Angehörigen), and the Paraguayan government protected him is false.

Tales soon spread that the war criminal controlled a vast web of agents, paid with looted Nazi gold. Norit Eldad, an Israeli woman, was killed in a climbing accident in the Andean resort of Bariloche. To the press, she was a Mossad agent who was hurled to her death by Mengele's agents or possibly the monster himself. Nazi-hunter Simon Wiesenthal in his book *The Murderers Among Us* claimed that Eldad was an Auschwitz survivor sterilised by Mengele and was murdered by him when he recognised her camp tattoo. It was all nonsense.

Throughout his time in hiding, Mengele maintained regular contact with his family in Bavaria. His son Rolf discovered in 1960 that Josef Mengele was his father and would remain loyal to him, despite being appraised fully of his monstrous crimes. Hans Sedlmeier continued to send funds and one might consider that, had Mengele's mail to his former home simply been monitored, his exact location could have been easily pinpointed.

Unknown to Mengele, in the early 1960s regular sightings of him and action by both the Brazilian and Argentine police led to the arrest of a number of Germans suspected of being him. Ironically, one of them was the blind German Jew Lothar Hermann, the man who had originally notified the Israelis of Eichmann's whereabouts after his daughter had dated Eichmann's son.

Mengele remained an unrepentant Nazi throughout, showing not a shred of remorse for his wartime activities, fervently believing all the while that he was the real victim. When not wallowing in self-pity, Mengele would write in his diary of his continuing loyalty to the Fuhrer's long defunct regime, recalling with fondness 'the incredible zest for life of the German nation under Hitler'.

In Brazil Mengele lived at first on the Gerhard farm at Itapeceria, 70 kilometres from São Paulo. Gerhard then found a Hungarian couple, Geza and Gitta Stammer, to look after Mengele and in 1961 the doctor went to live on their small farm at Nova Europa, 300 kilometres from São Paulo and bought with Mengele family money. The Stammers were fascists who were initially unaware of their guest's true identity, presented to them as he was as Herr Hochbichler, a Swiss exile. Mengele managed the farm for no salary as part of the deal. For long hours, he would scan the horizon from a six-metre high watchtower. He seldom left the the place.

Now middle-aged, Mengele hated multi-racial, vibrant and youthful Brazil. He was getting older, increasingly bad-tempered, was missing his comforts and suffered from hypochondria. The man who had gassed thousands for the mildest complaint, daily moaned of his own minor afflictions. He looked down on his hosts as socially, intellectually and racially inferior and became increasingly bored and morose. He attempted to write a 'novel' obviously based on his own life with himself as the 'hero'. Mengele also wrote in his diary describing the flora and fauna of his surroundings and commenting on his imaginary illnesses. He was terrified of being discovered and constantly wore a bush hat, even in the most inappropriate of circumstances. Years earlier, Mengele had briefly considered plastic surgery. A scar was left on his forehead that he believed could somehow identify him. His features were otherwise unchanged as, having been given only a local anaesthetic Mengele had second thoughts and terminated the operation almost before it had begun.

In his Brazilian exile Mengele proclaimed an undying love of Germany, yet felt ever more the scapegoat for its past. He was comforted by German music and philosophy which he absorbed avidly.

In mid-1962 Mengele reluctantly moved again. The Stammers bought a 45-hectare farm at Serra Negra, 150 kilometres north of São Paulo in which the Mengele family took a half share. The climate was better and the verdant soil more suitable for growing coffee. The cooler climate also suited cattle much better. As had happened on their previous farms, Mengele's relationship with his hosts and the farm workers was a difficult one. He shouted at the workers, was arrogant, opinionated and intolerant. He bullied the Stammers and even tried to interfere in the way they raised their children. Gradually, their relationship soured as they rejected his domineering ways. Only money kept them in his life and, after 1963 when they guessed the war criminal's true identity, he was effectively in their power, making him fearful and suspicious, but without altering his abusive treatment of them. When the Stammers mentioned to Gerhard that they were considering informing the authorities, he responded that 'Something might happen to their children, if they did.

It is alleged that Mengele and Mrs Stammer were lovers. Geza Stammer often worked away from home as a surveyor for several weeks at a time, and his wife soon became very close to her host. Her own children believed an affair had occurred and later commented, as did farm labourers, that they would hold hands and spend time together alone in his bedroom. Mengele even wrote a love poem dedicated to 'beautiful Gitta' found later in his diary. The romance fizzled out eventually, due to Mengele's insufferable high-handedness, tedious intellectual snobbery and his oft-stated view that as a German he was racially superior to the non-Aryan Stammers who were merely 'Finno-Ugric'.

In 1963 Konrad Adenauer, Chancellor of West Germany, offered Paraguay's President Stroessner $2.5 million if he would extradite Mengele. The offer was declined, leading many to believe that the war criminal was not only still in Paraguay but influential within leading political circles.

In 1964, a major war-crimes trial began in West Germany. Franz Stangl, former commandant of Treblinka and recently extradited from Brazil, was one of the 'star' defendants. In absentia, detailed evidence was given regarding the scale of Mengele's crimes and he became an object of loathing for the German public. What later hurt Mengele the most was that the trial made clear the utter worthlessness of the degrading and inhuman experiments he had undertaken. It had all been for nothing.

Convinced that the Angel of Death was living in Paraguay, West German ambassador Eckart Briest asked President Stroessner to hand him over. Furious, Stroessner insisted that Mengele was either in 'Brazil or Peru' and had the diplomat deported, creating a breach with West Germany. The West Germans now raised the reward for his capture to 50,000 deutschemarks.

In the wake of the Frankfurt trial, Hermann Langbein managed to persuade both the universities of Frankfurt and Munich to rescind Mengele's medical and doctoral degrees. Backed by Mengele's money, Martha, the war criminal's estranged wife, fought in the courts unsuccessfully to prevent it. Frankfurt University accused Mengele of violating his Hippocratic Oath and invited him to come and defend himself, an offer that Mengele unsurprisingly did not respond to.

The situation between the Stammers and Mengele had now deteriorated to such an extent that he sought new accommodation and new friends. On behalf of the Mengele family, Hans Sedlmeier smoothed things over financially with the Stammers, while Wolfgang Gerhard introduced Dr Mengele to new 'minders'; Wolfram and Liselotte Bossert. Both dedicated Nazis. Wolfram had been a Hitler Youth leader in the war and actually admired Mengele, despite, or rather because of, the horrors associated with his name. Their children 'doted' on Mengele, who was as charming as ever where children were concerned, and even called him titio (little uncle), just as many of his Jewish and Gypsy victims once had. The Bosserts, warped by ideology, even considered the man who had experimented on thousands of young and innocent children and sent vast numbers to their deaths a 'good influence' on their family. The Bosserts looked after Mengele, who still lived with the Stammers, revelling in his company and conversation.

Early in 1969, the Stammers and their unwelcome guest moved again to facilitate Geza's surveying work, most of which was in São Paolo. A four-bedroom house in one hectare of land was bought just 40 kilometres from the city at Caieiras. Mengele tried to bicker less with the Stammers, spending much of his time planting lemon trees and shrubs. The Bosserts persuaded him to go out a little more and not to continually draw attention to himself by suspiciously covering his face with his hat or hands whenever anyone glanced in his direction.

By the early 1970s, almost a decade had passed since West Germany had initiated the Frankfurt trials. The Germans had made no effort in pursuit of war criminals since. One investigating judge, Horst von Glasenapp, was not prepared to let things lie and, fearing key witnesses might pass away, travelled across Europe, to Israel and North America. He devoted six years to building up testimony that could be used to convict Mengele, if and when he was apprehended. Karl Sedlmeier was interviewed and admitted he had met Mengele but lied that he had not seen him for 10 years, saying he did not know where the war criminal was. Sedlmeier's house was searched but the police had tipped him off. Nothing was found.

The Israelis continued to have other priorities. While they were convinced that Mengele was in Brazil, more immediate crises confronted them. The murder of 11 Israeli athletes at the 1972 Olympic Games in Munich by the Palestinians of Black September, an attack of which Mengele 'disapproved', as the 'wrong way' to kill Jews, ensured that avenging their athletes would occupy Mossad more than the hunt for men like Josef Mengele.

Alois Mengele, younger brother, died of cancer in 1974. Of all the Mengele clan he had been most disturbed by what he had heard about the brother he once idolised. Prior to his death, Alois had been estranged from the fugitive, having discovered to his horror that the stories of his brother's cruelty and sadism were all too true. The loss of his Alois' affection was a bitter blow for Mengele.

In 1975, Wolfgang Gerhard left Brazil and returned to Austria. As his wife and son were dying of cancer, he believed they would receive better treatment there. Before leaving, Gerhard gave Mengele his identity papers.

With Gerhard gone, the Stammers felt their position strengthen. Frequently they threatened to expose the old murderer and so Mengele was obliged to find a new home. The Stammers sold their house in Caieiras and found him a small, rather decrepit bungalow at 5555 Alvarenga Road in the poor São Paolo neighbourhood of El Dorado and left him to fend for himself. The old doctor became depressed and, on occasion, suicidal. His relationship with the Bosserts and frequent correspondence to and from Günzburg kept him going.

Suffering a stroke in 1976, Mengele recovered only slowly. He felt increasingly helpless and isolated. He continued to write incessantly to relatives in Bavaria offering, advice, criticism and even rebukes to his son when he believed the occasion demanded it. He even insisted on seeing Rolf one last time. Keen to find out more about the father reviled as a monster, Rolf Mengele travelled to Brazil on a false passport and met his father in October 1977. During their meeting, Auschwitz was discussed. Dr Mengele swore he had never 'personally' killed anyone, that he had even tried to save lives and was forced to work their under pain of death, a somewhat unlikely tale given his SS rank and status as a winner of the Iron Cross. Tellingly, Mengele showed no remorse for his activities in Auschwitz-Birkenau.

The departure of his son left Mengele alone again. Then, remarkably, he fell in love. The woman in question, Elsa Gulpian de Oliviera, was his Brazilian housekeeper, some 40 years his junior. She wanted marriage. Mengele was still married to Martha, and although he considered Elsa racially and socially beneath him, he courted her in the 'proper manner' before asking her to move in with him. However, after a year Elsa married another and Mengele became even more aggressive and domineering towards his friends, the Bosserts. Suffering now from constant insomnia, Mengele was fading fast. He completed a memoir, complaining that the values of his youth: 'Race, nation, class and social status', had disappeared. Unrepentant to the end, he remained wistful for the Nazi era.

In February 1979, Mengele accepted an invitation to the Bossert cottage at Bertioga beach. Constantly complaining about his aches and pains, his miserable life and homesickness, Mengele went for a swim at around 4.30pm to obtain relief from the burning Brazilian sun. Mengele was suddenly gripped by paralysis. He struggled desperately for the shore, trying to swim one-armed. Wolfram Bossert saw his friend's distress and tried to save him, an effort that led to him being hospitalised. Bosserts efforts were in vain. Mengele had suffered a stroke, gave up the fight, drowned, and was dragged ashore with difficulty . The Angel of Death was not yet 68 years old.

Even in death, mystery continued to surround Mengele. Quickly buried to avoid decomposition, his friends notified Günzburg and ensured that no one outside his close circle was aware he had died, just as they had kept secret his life and true identity. If they thought the memory of his crimes would fade away, a minor footnote in history, it did not quite work out that way.

Rolf Mengele travelled to Brazil, dealt with his father's estate and divided it among the Bosserts and Stammers as a thank you for helping his father.

Ironically, interest in Mengele then mounted. Oscar-winning actor Gregory Peck played him in the movie, The Boys From Brazil that brought his name to the attention of millions. 'Sightings' of him, apparently unchanged from his Auschwitz days, occurred across Argentina, Brazil and Paraguay with increasing frequency, as Nazi hunters, Holocaust survivors and members of the US Congress all demanded action. In Paraguay, US Ambassador Robert White insisted that the Stroessner regime hand him over, despite their repeated denials as to knowledge of Mengele's whereabouts. Under pressure, the Paraguayan Government eventually revoked Mengele's citizenship, granted 20 years earlier.

The Nazi hunter Simon Wiesenthal, portrayed in The Boys from Brazil by Sir Lawrence Olivier, who ironically had played a dentist based very loosely on Mengele in the film Marathon Man, produced regular reports on Mengele. The fugitive was 'spotted' dining with Klaus Barbie, the 'butcher of Lyons', shopping in the Paraguayan capital of Asuncion, working on a Mennonite farm in the Paraguayan jungle and relaxing with Martin Bormann, now known to have died in Berlin at the end of the war. It was even alleged by Professor Richard Arens of Temple University Philadelphia that on a recent visit to Paraguay he was informed by Paraguayan officials that Mengele was employed by the Stroessner regime to advise on methods of torture. Supposedly, Mengele was even carrying out medical experiments, this time on Ache Indians in Paraguay's remote Gran Chaco. The whole sordid and entirely fictional tale was published by Time magazine.

As Mengele hysteria mounted, US Secretary of State Cyrus Vance even issued an arrest warrant for Mengele when the FBI was informed of a certain flight he was arriving on in Miami under his own name. Such nonsense at least kept the now dead doctor in the headlines and ensured his crimes would not be forgotten.

By 1985, the West German and Israeli governments, California-based Simon Wiesenthal Centre, the Washington Post and others had together placed a reward for the capture of the deceased doctor totalling $3.3 million. Journalists and bounty hunters searched the more remote corners of South America for their long-extinct prey. Unfortunately, there was little to go on. No reliable photographs of their elusive quarry existed and no definitive sightings had occurred for a generation. The 'Günzburg connection' was not explored and time wasted following speculative rumours. Eventually, it finally dawned on the authorities that the extended Mengele clan, including friends and employees past and present, held the key.

Hans Sedlmeier, who in the 1970s admitted to journalists and von Glassenapp to helping Mengele in previous years, had his home searched in the spring of 1985. This time he was not tipped off and a notebook and letters detailing the names and addresses of the Stammers and Bosserts were found. Quickly interviewed, Liselotte Bossert told investigators that their search was over. Mengele was dead, buried in an untended grave in Embu under the name of

Wolfgang Gerhard. Rolf Mengele confirmed that he was aware of his father's death and burial in Embu, but had stayed silent out of respect for the many who had helped him escape justice over the years. Expressing 'profound sympathy' for his father's victims and relatives earned Rolf a rebuke from the rest of the Mengele clan, who no longer acknowledge him.

Hundreds of journalists and television crews waited excitedly nearby when the crumpled remains buried in Embu were unearthed. With undue haste, forensic scientists attested in only three days and with 'scientific certainty', that the bones, teeth and hair found were those of Dr Josef Mengele. Not everyone was convinced. It appeared far too neat, too easy, especially when the Bosserts began to change their version of Mengele's death. Perhaps the anti-climax of finding a dead and rotting Mengele ruined the chase. Nevertheless, there were more compelling reasons for doubting the evidence available.

The osteomylitis that Mengele suffered as a child should have been clearly visible on the Embu skeleton, yet mysteriously not a trace of the disease was found on the bones. Tantalisingly, the skull of Mengele was supposedly 57cm long, yet the Embu skull was only 50.5 cm in length. The US team of forensic scientists swore before congress that the skeleton was Mengele's. Despite this, doubts remained. The Mengele family offered to provide medical records but never did. X-rays from Mengele's youth were not forthcoming from West Germany and it took a year for his alleged dental records to appear, although these confirmed the skeleton to be Mengele's. In 1986, the Justice Department had the skeleton examined again by an expert from the Smithsonian Institute, focusing on the osteomylitis. No evidence of the disease was found. Only Dr Lowell Levine, who examined the dental evidence was willing, of all the scientific investigators, to put his findings on paper. It was never published because the case was never closed.

Israeli Auschwitz survivor, police colonel and Nazi hunter Menachem Russek carried out his own investigations in Brazil and Germany. He concluded that the death of Mengele was rather too convenient. At his insistence, Israel kept the case open, obliging West Germany and the US to do likewise. As a result, the findings of these governments were never published. Russek himself was cajoled into retirement by Israel and prevented from publishing his conclusions.

Finally, to settle the matter, in 1992 a team of British scientists led by Dr Alex Jeffreys of Leicester University, carried out a DNA test comparing samples from a reluctant Rolf Mengele and the Embu skeleton, proving with '99.97% certainty' that the Embu remains were indeed Josef Mengele. Finally the Angel of Death was no more.

CHAPTER 11
Dr William Palmer: 'What's Your Poison?'

'I am a murdered man.'

DR WILLIAM PALMER was one of the most ruthless poisoners of the mid-19th century. Addicted to women, gambling and alcohol, for years he rode his luck, seemingly above suspicion. Palmer was to ride his luck too hard, too far for too long and die at the end of a rope – a murderer, fraud, forger and debtor. His effigy stood, reviled, in Madame Tussaud's waxwork Chamber of Horrors for 127 years. The phrase 'What's your poison?' supposedly emanates from the Palmer case.

*　*　*

Something of a rake while training to be a doctor, Palmer practised as an abortionist and fathered at least 14 illegitimate children. Another illegitimate son, born many years after Palmer qualified, died suddenly and in great agony after a visit to his father while just a few months old. At the time, it was believed the child died of natural causes. A few years previously, when in 1846 Mr George Abley, a 27-year-old plumber and glazier friend of Dr Palmer, died in Staffordshire Infirmary immediately after drinking brandy with him in the Lamb and Flag Inn, Little Haywood, it was put down to being 'one of those things'. The coroner, Mr William Ward, recorded the death on 30 November as being due to 'exhaustion'. Mr Abley was thin, weak and possibly consumptive. The foreman of the inquest jury, Edward Jenkinson, thought otherwise and declared that Palmer had a fancy for Abley's shapely wife whom he had treated as an outpatient at Stafford Infirmary. He alleged that Palmer was refused by the faithful Mrs Abley but determined to have her anyway. Thus, he plied Mr Abley with the drink from which he died. Jenkinson's view was ignored and put down to personal jealousy of Dr Palmer. In fact, Palmer had poisoned Mr Abley with strychnine to 'see how it worked'.

The pursuit of cash thrilled Dr Palmer and he spent his life in its embrace. He never had enough and was submerged in debt on a semi-permanent basis. Maintaining his status and lifestyle was his overwhelming goal. Only 'fortuitous' legacies kept his head above water. There were quite a few of those.

Born on 21 October 1824, in the pretty little market town of Rugeley in rural

Staffordshire, Palmer was the son of a wealthy family of five boys and two girls. His father, Joseph, was almost uneducated. Originally a sawyer, Joseph became a timber dealer, somehow amassing a fortune of £75,000 by the time he died, supposedly from illegally cutting timber on the estates of the unsuspecting Marquis of Anglesey.

When Palmer's father died suddenly in 1837, young William was 12 and attending the prestigious Rugeley Free Grammar School, which dated back to Elizabethan times. Leaving school at 17, he was apprenticed to Evans & Evans, a wholesale chemist in Liverpool and soon embarked upon a life of crime. Monies that should have arrived by post repeatedly vanished. Eventually, young Palmer was identified as the culprit and sacked for stealing. His mother, Sarah, was entreated to pay back the money to avoid her son going to prison, which she did. Palmer's employment at the chemist's was not wasted. There he began to learn the properties of the many drugs he later became better acquainted with and put to profitable use.

Mrs Palmer considered her son bright if 'high spirited'. He had apparently stolen for 'romantic' reasons. He had an older girlfriend, Jane Widnall, who enjoyed the finer, more expensive things in life. She wanted to marry William Palmer but ditched him on realising he could not inherit from his father before his 21st birthday.

To enable him to make something of himself, Palmer became a trainee to Dr Edward Tylecote, a local physician. Dr Tylecote found his new charge to be dishonest, unreliable and sexually voracious. After Palmer once more got himself mixed up with Miss Widnall, the couple eloped with Tylecote's money. Again, Palmer was forced to return home and the money was paid back by his mother.

Undeterred, Mrs Palmer secured her son's admission to Stafford Infirmary as a 'walking pupil'. Paying five guineas, he registered on 24 May 1844. Palmer took a keen interest in poisons and often borrowed books on the subject. The hospital authorities did not let him take any drugs home. After the unfortunate 'Abley incident' Palmer crept away from a Stafford that was suspicious of him and he endeavoured to complete his studies at St Bartholomew's Hospital, London. There Palmer continued his womanising, drinking and gambling for which he had become infamous in Stafford. Sarah Palmer was alerted that her son had virtually no chance of graduating as a result. Determined he would become a doctor, she hired a Dr Steagal to provide William with private tuition. If he passed, Steagal would receive £100. Working hard, William Palmer did pass but his tutor then had to sue Mrs Palmer to get the money due to him.

Palmer qualified in August 1846 and become a member of the Royal College of Physicians and Surgeons. Finishing a five-year medical training that included his time with Tylecote, Stafford and in London, Palmer returned to Rugeley that year and opened a practice opposite the Talbot Arms Inn in Market Street, in a house he rented for £25 a year from Lord Lichfield.

Palmer's medical practice soon grew and he prospered for a time. An assistant, Ben Thirley, was hired to cope with demand. It did not take long before Palmer had virtually abandoned his practice to Thirley as he spent most of his time at the racecourse.

Regardless of having inherited £7,000 in 1845 when he reached his majority, Palmer was soon broke, thanks to his obsession with gambling which was popular in Rugeley, famous for its annual horse fair and with its own racecourse at Etching Hill, now long since gone. Palmer though, was not interested in a harmless flutter, spending a few shillings or pounds. He was intent on making his fortune at the track and soon had a stable of 15 horses on the outskirts of town. Thinking nothing of placing bets of hundreds, even thousands of pounds, Palmer quickly fell into debt and was banned from running his horses or selling them through Tattersall's, the leading European bloodstock auctioneers.

In October 1847, Palmer married Anne Thornton, known as Annie, the illegitimate daughter of an Indian army officer, Lieutenant Colonel William Brookes, who killed himself in 1834 with a shot to the head. The colonel was one of five brothers, all but one of whom committed suicide. No doubt the colonel's death was at least partly to escape Annie's mother, Mary, a foul-mouthed alcoholic brawler who had been Brookes' former housekeeper and mistress and never stopped cursing him for refusing to marry her. As a result of her behaviour, Annie had been made a ward in chancery and brought up by a guardian, Mr Charles Dawson.

Palmer had known Annie for some years. Dr Tylecote was often called to Miss Bond's school in Haywood, where Annie was a pupil and there she met Palmer. The two corresponded for some years and Annie at least, fell in love. She was a 'clever, amiable, accomplished and lovable girl'. As a ward, Annie had money held by trustees during her spinsterhood amounting to £250 a year. Upon marriage this money automatically transferred to her spouse.

Despite the hostility of Charles Dawson, who disliked Palmer, William and Annie were married at St Nicholas Church, Abbots Bromley, Staffordshire, on 7 October 1847. She was 20, he not quite 23. Sadly, Palmer found his new wife to be not as rich as he thought or hoped, although a gift from his new mother-in-law of £700 did not go amiss. For her part, Annie was grateful that a man of Palmer's standing wanted to marry someone with the lowly status of a bastard. Annie bore him five children. Tragically, only one child survived infancy, the others all dying mysteriously and agonisingly of 'convulsions'. Palmer had often muttered how expensive children were.

Mrs Matilda Bradshaw was the Palmer's cleaning lady. When, on 27 January 1854, Palmer's four-day-old son John died, she ran into the Bell public house next door, shouting that Palmer had 'done away' with another baby. Asked what had happened, she recounted that while caring for John, Palmer came in and said he would take charge of his son. Having gone downstairs, she heard the baby scream and ran upstairs only to find the baby dead. Distressed, Mrs Bradshaw said Palmer had dipped his finger in poison and then in honey to make the baby suck his finger. Asked if she had actually seen this, she replied: 'No, but I know it in my heart to be true.'

Mary Thornton lived in a house behind St Mary's church in Stafford. She had no servants, ate little, drank copiously and kept her house full of cats. She hated Palmer, accusing him of poisoning her cats and swore at him whenever they met. To her he was a blatant fortune-hunter and nothing more. Palmer's mother-in-law nevertheless had the wealth he believed was due to him and, on 6 January 1849, she was found delirious with drink and invited to stay with the Palmers. She was suddenly taken seriously ill and died 12 days later, aged 50. Almost immediately, Dr Bamford, an elderly and almost blind colleague of Palmer, certified the death as being due to 'apoplexy' and she was buried on 22 January. Following this calamity, Palmer's wife Annie inherited her wealth. It was not as much as the doctor hoped. Mary Thornton had not inherited the nine houses that Colonel Brookes left in his will as he had thought. A Mr Shawcross had. Palmer apparently did not know this. He was not a happy man.

In May of the following year, Mr Leonard Bladen, a 49-year-old bookmaker to whom Dr Palmer owed substantial debts, was taken ill suddenly, again after staying with the Palmers. After attending Chester races, Bladen wrote to his wife explaining that he would be home in a couple of days £1,000 richer. Hearing of her husband's illness, Mrs Bladen rushed to be with him. On arrival in Rugeley she was just in time to see her husband die painfully in a state of delirium on 10 May. Checking his belongings, she was surprised to find only £15 in his possession. Mysteriously, the book outlining who owed the bookmaker money had disappeared. As for the large sum of money Palmer supposedly owed, the doctor said that Bladen had already gambled it away at Chester races. Bladen was then quickly and unceremoniously buried, courtesy of Palmer, who made all the funeral arrangements.

'Where will it all end?' Annie Palmer was heard to declare at Bladen's death. Not with her, that was for sure. She was to die in haste a further three years down the line, in the intervening years others were to meet a similar fate. Uncle Joseph 'Beau' Bentley fell unconscious from a chair and died three days after engaging in a drinking contest with Palmer, on 27 October 1852. His distressed widow refused to take some pills Palmer offered 'to calm her nerves' and threw them out the window. The next morning several chickens were found dead in the garden. By now Palmer's practice had all but evaporated. He remained a sexual predator – no young woman was safe from his amorous intentions. An illegitimate son, neither the first nor last, was born to one of Palmer's mistresses, Elizabeth

Mumford, just 18 months after his wedding. At the same time, Palmer still managed to appear respectable and attended Holy Communion where he was considered by fellow churchgoers as the most sincere of Christians. In the meantime his reckless lifestyle soon aged him and he began to look at least a decade older than his years. He was a snappy dresser, of ruddy complexion, average height, stockily built, slightly 'padded' in the face, with a high forehead, brown hair brushed over a balding head and 'modest' features. He was neither handsome nor ugly, although observers of the time described his appearance as 'common and mean'. Palmer's most remarked-upon features were his soft, feminine hands in which he took much pride with frequently manicuring, taking care to keep them gloved and out of the sunlight.

A somewhat inept and unlucky 'punter', Palmer was soon in hock to moneylenders, paying huge amounts of interest; he was always desperate for cash. A reputation for attempts at race-fixing and horse-doping followed him and Palmer was also known to welsh on bets. In his trial, the Attorney General was rumoured to be keen to convict Palmer in part because, some years earlier, the doctor was reputed to have nobbled his horse.

One of the more obscure deaths attributed to Palmer, one where the facts, if there were any, appear thin on the ground, concerned the mysterious case of a creditor named Bly, to whom £800 was allegedly owed. Mr Bly lived in Beccles, Norfolk, and often accompanied Dr Palmer to the races. Bly usually won, Palmer lost. When Bly was taken suddenly ill, curled up in agony, Palmer offered to treat his friend, who was forced to take to his bed in a country inn. Hearing of her husband's plight, Mrs Bly tried to see him. At first, Palmer tried to prevent her. Eventually she reached her husband's bedside. Bly repented over a misspent life, said he was dying and informed his wife that Palmer owed him £800. After Mr Bly's death, his widow mentioned the money to Palmer. The doctor sorrowfully told her that Bly was delusional and that Palmer had been owed the £800. In respect of her feelings he would not have mentioned it, but seeing as she had raised the issue, when could he be paid?

The Bly murder, like one rumoured to have taken place in the Isle of Man, was avidly reported in the press before Palmer was tried. However, there is no evidence that such a crime was ever committed, something that could not be said of his next dastardly murder.

In 1854, Mrs Palmer met a swift death, according to her husband, from 'apoplexy'. Earlier that year, he lost £10,000 on a horse at a major race meeting. Palmer insured his wife in April, paying an enormous first premium of £760. She took ill on 19 September, vomiting soon after her husband served her breakfast. Mrs Palmer grew steadily worse, dying eight days later, according to Dr Bamford, of 'English Cholera'. She was 27 years old. Most likely, Palmer departed from strychnine to kill his wife slowly with antimony, a metallic poison, usually known as tartar emetic after its chief property. Only 250-1000mg is required to kill, through blocking the enzymes needed for heart muscle, liver and kidneys to function. £13,000 was the sum Dr Palmer received for his wife's demise. The insurance company was at first suspicious, but eventually coughed up without launching an investigation, a fact that only emboldened the murderous Dr Palmer further.

During his marriage, Palmer continued having trysts with a whole host of women. One relationship was with Elizabeth Tharme, his 18-year-old maidservant. She gave birth to a son, Alfred, nine months to the day Mrs Palmer died. Neither Palmer nor anyone else was named as the child's father on the birth certificate. Palmer did take an interest in Alfred. The baby had been left with a 'nurse' in nearby Armitage to be cared for. Palmer sent for the boy. Alfred was soon seized with convulsions and died on 17 November 1855, just four days before the death of the man for whom Palmer would hang.

The death of Mrs Palmer was sufficient to stave off her husband's bankruptcy. It was not enough to satisfy Palmer's greed. Within three months, he owed thousands more to a couple of unscrupulous moneylenders, Messrs Pratt and Padwick. Each was in possession of a stack of IOU's, apparently countersigned by Palmer's mother. Of course her signature was a fake. Had she known anything of her son's forgeries, he would have been disowned and in trouble with the authorities. Palmer had to find more money before his mother was asked to pay his debts.

He desperately looked for someone else to insure and murder. The perfect victim was his own brother, Walter. Only this time he would not go for a trifling amount like the £13,000 paid out on his wife. He would try for the then colossal sum of £82,000 but no company would take on a policy that might pay out that much. Walter Palmer was an alcoholic and a great risk at the best of times and, like his younger brother William, had squandered his inheritance, being declared bankrupt in 1849. He needed money and accepted £400 William offered him if he would let his brother insure his life. Mr Pratt was then recruited to help Palmer spread the sum insured over several unsuspecting companies. A Mr Tom Walkenden was hired to keep Walter sober long enough to fill in the forms and persuade the insurance company doctors that he was fit and well. The insurers were wary. Only the Prince of Wales Insurance Company accepted Palmer's premiums and £13,000 was the most that Walter's life could be insured for, not nearly enough to cover Palmers debts. It would have to do. Walter was pronounced 'healthy, robust and temperate', by Mr Waddell, a Stafford surgeon. On 5 April, the first premium of £710.67 was paid and the policy put in place. Dr Palmer never did give his brother the £400 he promised. William was handed only £60 and provided with unlimited credit at a local inn.

On 16 August 1855, right on cue, Walter Palmer died after a fortuitous (for

William Palmer) drinking binge. Within an hour of being informed of his brother's demise, Dr Palmer was enquiring excitedly of that day's racing results. To kill his brother, the poison most probably used was prussic acid (cyanide), a powerful antiseptic that kills swiftly through inhibiting respiration, leading to convulsions, cardiac arrhythmia, coma and a quick death. When later exhumed, Walter's body was too decomposed for cyanide poisoning to be confirmed.

Palmer showed his true colours once again, when informing his sister-in-law, Agnes, of Walter's death. In telling her of his brother's demise and subsequent burial, he sought payment of £325 Walter allegedly owed him. Palmer also sent his solicitor, Mr Jeremiah Smith, to persuade Agnes to give up any claim to her husband's insurance policy. She refused and in turn demanded £500 Walter had told her William owed him.

The wrangle over who would benefit from Walter's death soon proved academic. To Palmer's annoyance, this time the insurance company refused to pay up. Palmer was outraged and cursed their obstinacy. After threatening legal action he backed off, knowing that if his bluff was called an investigation could ruin him. Apparently undeterred by the setback, Palmer simply tried to insure someone else, George Bates, a 'friend'. Jeremiah Smith acted as a 'go-between' with the insurance industry in exchange for 5% commission on the expected pay out. Mr Bates did not die in the familiar way though. The Midland Insurance Company refused to accept a premium that would put a price of £10,000 on Mr Bates' head. Two detectives, Inspectors Field and Simpson, were hired. As part of their investigations, they interviewed a shoeshine boy, Tom Myatt, at the Grand Junction Hotel, Stafford, as he often overheard conversations involving Palmer. On hearing of this discussion, Dr Palmer invited the shoeshine boy out for a drink, at the end of which the boy fell severely ill, although thankfully he survived.

After these frustrations, Palmer tried a different tack, dispensing with insurance for his next crime. By late 1855, Palmer was once again in dire financial straits and Jane Bergin, a former mistress, was blackmailing him. Palmer had allegedly performed an abortion on her and then broke his promise that they would marry. Palmer wrote 34 letters to Miss Bergin, who demanded £100 not to show them to all and sundry. In one of the letters, Palmer tried to persuade her to undergo dental treatment at the hands of a 'friend' who would carry out an extraction 'as silent as death'. No doubt he would have. Miss Bergin declined Palmer's kind offer and, on 15 November 1855, he felt obliged to send her £40. Moneylenders stalked Palmer daily, demanding the return of loans, occasionally secured for crippling rates of interest regularly exceeding 60%. He also feared having to face imminent fraud charges for forging his mother's signature on another loan guarantee. Two thoroughbreds had been bought for 2,000 guineas each and he hoped that wins at the track would pay off the debts before anyone was the wiser. Like so many of his gambles, this one did not pay off. By October 1855, Palmer owed £15,000 with a further £11,500 accruing in November. He needed cash, lots of it, and fast.

On 13 November 1855 Palmer and a friend, the weak and pasty-faced John Parsons Cook, watched Cook's horse, Polestar, ride to victory at the Shrewsbury Handicap. Previously almost broke, having squandered a £12,000 inheritance at the track, Cook's last hope was a win for his horse. When it did win he was almost £3,000 richer, money Palmer eyed enviously. To celebrate, Cook went to the nearby Raven Hotel where he threw a party. Palmer returned to Rugeley but came back the following day to dine that evening with his friend. They began drinking brandy. Immediately, Cook sprang to his feet exclaiming, 'Good, god, there's something in that that burned my throat.' Calmly, Palmer replied: 'Nonsense' and continued to quaff the brandy. Within hours Cook felt very ill. Next morning, Cook and Palmer travelled to Rugeley with Cook taking up residence in room 10 of the Talbot Inn just opposite Palmer's house.

Over the next few days, Palmer 'looked after' Cook and gave him several pills. Possibly Cook was suspicious of Palmer because he blamed something 'that damned Palmer' had given him for making him sick, which was undoubtedly why he refused to stay in Palmer's home. At the Talbot Arms, Cook's illness worsened after a maid brought him a cup of coffee Palmer had prepared. Palmer called on Cook regularly at the inn and asked his colleague, Dr Bamford, to look in on him too.

At the nearby Albion Inn, a friend of Palmer's was staying, Mrs Ann Rowley, whom he asked to prepare broth for his friend on 18 November. Palmer later took the broth, placed it in a basin and returned it to Mrs Rowley who was then requested to take it to Mr Cook, saying it was a gift from a Rugeley solicitor, Mr Jeremiah Smith. Why not make and take the broth himself? Maybe Palmer wished to allay gossip about the misgivings his friend now held. Convoluted Palmer's plan may have been, but it worked. Cook took only a spoonful of the broth and was immediately violently sick. A maid, Elizabeth Mills, who innocently attempted to finish it off, later suffered likewise.

Cook was obstinately still alive. Palmer now departed briefly for London to meet with a bookmaker, Mr Herring, from whom he collected £1,000 of Polestar winnings on behalf of Cook. Returning to Rugeley next morning, Dr Palmer met an assistant chemist, Mr Charles Newton and procured three grains of strychnine from him. By now it was noticed by the staff and guests of the Talbot Inn that Cook's health had improved somewhat in his friend's absence. That night, after Palmer called, Cook screamed in agony at the pain of his recurrent illness. The following morning, 19 November, he seemed much better.

On Tuesday 20 November Dr William Henry Jones, Cook's own doctor, appeared on the scene, summoned by Palmer on the 18 November. Also Dr

Bamford re-appeared. Bamford, Jones and Palmer agreed that all three would jointly draw up a prescription to soothe the patient's internal irritation. Dr Bamford formulated the prescription in his surgery and Palmer collected it. Speculation is that he then switched it for something considerably more potent. Certainly, as would be revealed at the trial, Palmer found time to make another deadly purchase of poison. Despite his doctors imploring him, it was after 11.00pm before Mr Cook could be persuaded to take his medicine.

Despite (or more so because of) the tender care his friend Dr William Palmer gave him, after taking a few pills, Cook's body went into convulsions with such violence that the back of his head jerked back to touch his heels, a sure sign of strychnine poisoning, although curiously none was later found in his body. Within a couple of hours, Palmer's friend was dead. He was 28 years old. The ancient Dr Bamford, now well into his eighties, was again called on to sign the death certificate of a Palmer victim.

The stepfather of Cook, Mr William Stevens, was suspicious at the sudden, tragic death of his stepson. He was even more alarmed to find that Palmer had already made funeral arrangements with a Rugeley undertaker. His concerns increased on finding that the ledger Cook kept of his betting transactions had disappeared. On discovering Palmer to be a beneficiary in John Cook's death to the tune of £4,000 that Palmer had allegedly loaned Cook, Stevens demanded an autopsy and appointed a solicitor to look into Palmer's financial affairs. Palmer brazenly attended the autopsy to almost comic effect.

The postmortem was carried out on 26 November, under the guidance of Dr John Harland, an acquaintance of Palmer who was one of the doctors who had previously declared the late Walter Palmer fit and healthy enough to be insured. The actual autopsy itself, was undertaken by Mr Charles Devonshire, a medical student and Mr Charles Newton, assistant chemist, who was conducting his first postmortem and had to be given a couple of brandies (by Palmer) to steady his nerves.

The autopsy was a farce. The stomach was inadvertently turned inside out and, after jostling the 'surgeons', not only did Palmer ensure some of the contents spilled on the floor, he was also able to take it out of the room before being noticed. When retrieved, the contents were not intact. Nevertheless, they were forwarded to Alfred Swaine Taylor, Professor of Medical Jurisprudence at Guy's Hospital London and England's most eminent toxicologist, who examined the samples and then had Mr Devonshire carry out a second postmortem on Mr Cook on 29 November.

Two incisions were made in the stomach and a non-fatal dose of antimony found within. Antimony is a naturally occurring metal. Physicians used tartrate of potassium antimony occasionally as a treatment for tropical diseases such as kala-azar, bilharzia and schistosomiasis. More often antimony was used as an emetic or for relief of bronchitis. In large doses it is highly toxic. As a poison, Palmer probably favoured antimony as it could be administered to drinks in powdered form.

Despite his findings, Taylor was convinced that strychnine had been the main cause of Cook's death. Stating his findings in a letter, Taylor sent them to the authorities at Rugeley. Amazingly, Palmer, who had been neither arrested nor charged, was able to intercept the letter by having his friend and Rugeley postmaster, Samuel Cheshire, steal it, a crime for which Cheshire subsequently served two years imprisonment.

The inquest was held on 12 December at Rugeley Borough Court in the Town Hall. Dr Taylor made the most telling contribution and the jurors pronounced Palmer 'Guilty of wilful murder'. The following day, delivering a gift of fish and game later interpreted as an attempted bribe, Dr Palmer contacted the coroner, Mr William Webb Ward, and pointed out the non-fatal dose of antimony and that no strychnine or arsenic had been found in Cook. He enclosed a £10 note.

Dr Palmer thought he was in the clear. However, when it was proven that Cook's signature on a cheque for £350 he had cashed as his friend lay dying was a forgery, the good doctor was duly arrested on 15 December 1856 and charged with murder. In fact he was already under house arrest for debt, a warrant having been issued by the moneylender Mr Padwick against his mother for fraud. Padwick believed Mrs Sarah Palmer had acquiesced in the forgery of her signature by her son.

Palmer was feeling ill. The newspapers reported the story and a crowd gathered outside Palmer's home, hoping to catch sight of the notorious doctor. As soon as he was well enough he was taken to Stafford Gaol. On arrival Palmer refused to change into prison garb. He was still unwell and demanded to retain his own clothes. Suspecting his new inmate might have poison about his person and be planning suicide, prison governor Captain William Fulford confiscated the clothing and ordered a meticulous search of Palmer and his attire. As nothing was found, the garments were returned a fortnight later.

Palmer remained in his prison bed refusing to eat and taking only sips of water. It was not clear if he intended to starve himself to death to avoid the ordeal of a trial and conviction or was simply protesting at his arrest. In any case, after six days Captain Fulford tired of Palmer's antics and informed him he would be force fed by the turnkeys, who would shove a rubber tube down his throat and pump soup directly into his stomach. Meekly, knowing how horrible this would be, Palmer relented and began eating normally.

While Palmer was holding his hunger strike, the authorities, looking for further evidence against him, exhumed the bodies of his late wife and brother on 22 December. The cadavers were then taken to be 'viewed' at the Talbot Arms Inn.

Mrs Palmer had been dead for 15 months, but her body was in good condition. The body of Walter Palmer, only four months dead, was in a state of advanced gangrenous putrefaction. When a hole was punched in the lid of his coffin the noxious gases were so overwhelming that all present were violently sick. It took four days for the smell to subside enough for the body to be examined. The stench of death was so vile that it seemed to soak into the walls of the inn and trade dropped off soon after, never to recover, as customers complained of the smell months, even years, later.

Annie Palmer's body was discovered to contain a lethal dose of antimony and at an inquest, on 12 January 1856, the jury recorded the cause of her death as murder. At the inquest into the death of Walter Palmer on 23 January, no evidence of poisoning was found in his cadaver. Dr Taylor believed this might have been because in this case cyanide was used. Cyanide leaves virtually no permanent trace, degrading after time into gases that gradually vacate a decomposing body. The jury again returned a verdict of wilful murder. In the case of Mr Cook, the circumstantial evidence for strychnine poisoning seemed superficially overwhelming. Why then had no strychnine been found in his body?

Professor Taylor used a method of analysis pioneered by Belgian chemist Jean Servais Stas. This, the 'Stas method' was developed from the fact that all alkaloids are soluble in organic solvents and, as bases, combine with acids to form water-soluble crystalline salts. Body components dissolve either in water, alcohol or are insoluble in both. If an organ containing an alkaloid is pulped, stirred in alcohol and acid and then filtered, the alkaloid will dissolve out of the pulp as the alcoholic filtrate. Repeating the process eventually leads to the extraction of pure alkaloid. This can be crystallised through evaporation or isolated in solution in an organic solvent such as ether. Tests could then be carried out. Taylor's tests failed to find strychnine because he took too small a sample for the reagents then in use to work. Loss of the stomach contents and testing of the viscera some time after death also made the task of testing for strychnine difficult. Ironically, soon after the Palmer trial concluded, a new, more accurate method involving a live frog would be developed.

On 20 January 1856 Palmer was taken to appear at the Lord Chancellor's court, Westminster, as a witness in an action brought against his mother. Mr Padwick, the moneylender, was attempting to recover £2,000 loaned to Palmer on 3 July 1854 and secured on Sarah Palmer's signature. Palmer testified that the moniker on the original document was not that of his mother and claimed to have persuaded his late wife to forge his mother's signature. The case against Sarah Palmer was dropped and Palmer was returned to Stafford Gaol to await his murder trial.

The day after he appeared in London, Palmer's horses, 17 in total, were auctioned by Tattersall's to raise money to pay his debts. The sale fetched £3,906, considerably less than Palmer had paid for them. On 4 May 1856, in preparation for his trial, William Palmer set off for London on the 6.26am train accompanied by the deputy governor of Stafford Gaol, Mr Mountford, and a prison warder.

* * *

The trial of Dr William Palmer began on 14 May 1856. Legislation had to be enacted by parliament to move the trial from Staffordshire to London, as it was believed the doctor would not receive a fair trial in that county. This act, The Trial of Offences Act 1856, was given royal assent on 11 April 1856 and was henceforth known as 'The Palmer Act'. A consequent act would make it impossible for someone to insure the life of a stranger, or even distant relative, unless it was clear that the death of the stranger or relative would involve the policyholder in some financial loss.

The 'Trial of the Century', as the press excitedly called it, unfolded before Lord Chief Justice Campbell. Few trials have created such avid interest not just in the UK, but also throughout the world. After all, this was a murder involving not the feckless poor or aristocratic toffs but a middle-class professional doctor who could be an acquaintance of anyone. His youth, wild reputation and the quality of legal talent brought to the bar to argue the case only added to the interest.

Such was the curiosity generated by the trial that the Lord Mayor of London, Chief Lord of the Admiralty Sir John Parkington, the dukes of Wellington and Cambridge, the Prince of Saxe-Weimar, the Marquess of Anglesey, prime ministers past and present William Gladstone and Lord Derby and umpteen other sundry members of the aristocracy turned out to enjoy the spectacle.

The Attorney General, Sir Alexander Cockburn, England's principal law officer for the Crown and Head of the English Bar, led for the prosecution. About to become a judge, Cockburn was keenly aware of the public mood against Palmer and the notoriety of a man now pilloried daily in newsprint as journalists garnered more and more information on Palmer's allegedly numerous misdeeds and crimes. Reputed to be one of the finest orators of his generation, he wanted Palmer's head badly. Assisting him were Mr Edwin James QC, Sir William Bodkin, Prosecuting Counsel, Mr Serjeant Huddlestone and Mr Welshby.

Palmer's solicitor, Mr 'Honest John' Smith, marshalled the defence. He hired Mr Serjeant Wilkins, who had studied medicine before law and was therefore deemed perfect for the case. Unfortunately for Palmer, Wilkins withdrew in late April citing 'ill health'. In fact, he was heavily in debt and had fled to France to avoid arrest himself. Mr Serjeant Shee QC, an able Irish Barrister and MP for Kilkenny, took his place. Mr William Robert Grove QC and Messrs Kenealy and Gray assisted Shee.

The trial opened with a powerful four-hour speech by the Attorney General, who outlined with precision the case against Dr Palmer to a hushed courtroom.

Palmer's case was the first occasion in which someone was tried for poisoning using strychnine. With very little published information on the drug, witnesses were divided on whether or not it had actually caused death. The defence argued vigorously that the symptoms in the demise of Mr Cook did not match clinical and experimental experience and postulated that death was actually caused by an epileptic convulsion, angina pectoris or some ill-defined spinal irritation. In fact, tetanus is the only naturally occurring condition that resembles strychnine poisoning. Both act on the nervous system and cause painful and lengthy spasms of the voluntary muscles throughout the body. It is usually easy to distinguish between the two, as a wound or injury is almost always present with tetanus and it progresses over days, strychnine acting much more swiftly. It was established beyond doubt that Palmer had bought strychnine. When asked about this, he said it was to 'Poison a dog'. Few were convinced.

For the prosecution, Ishmael Fisher, wine merchant; Thomas Jones, law stationer; George Read, sporting housekeeper and Dr William Scaife Gibson all testified that Cook had complained of a drink 'burning his throat' in Shrewsbury and that he fell ill soon after. Elizabeth Mills, chambermaid at the Talbot Arms, recounted the 'poisoned broth' destined for Cook she later consumed and the effect this had upon her. Lavinia Barnes, waitress at the Talbot Arms, told how she saw Palmer rifle Cook's pockets after his death. Dr Jones, Cook's doctor, recalled his patient's demise in detail, adding somewhat unnecessarily that Cook believed himself to be suffering from secondary syphilis.

Charles Newton, the assistant chemist who sold Palmer the three grains of strychnine on 19 November, admitted he had not entered the sale in the poisons book nor informed his employer Mr Salt, because the chemist did not like Dr Palmer. Another Rugeley chemist, Charles Joseph Roberts, told the startled court that he too had sold strychnine to Palmer only a few hours before Cook died. Six grains of strychnine were purchased, along with a solution of opium and two drachms of prussic acid. Like Newton, under cross-examination, he admitted none of this had been recorded.

Further witnesses recounted the 'stiffness' of Cook's body on being laid out, the haste of Palmer in attempting to burying his friend, the disappearing ledger and Mr Steven's demand for an autopsy. Some 20 more prosecution witnesses were called before the medical evidence, the crux of the case, commenced. These witnesses gave evidence regarding Palmer's attempt at bribing the coroner, tampering with the Royal Mail, forgery of letters, insurance frauds and dire financial circumstances.

Mr Shee's response was to cross-examine, scoring points against the chemists' failure to keep a record of poisons sold and showing that Palmer could not have purchased strychnine at the time Newton said, as his train from Euston

did not arrive in Stafford until 8.45am on the morning of 19 November and Palmer could not have travelled the nine miles by road in 15 minutes. He th presented five witnesses of his own who stated that Cook had suffered bilio attacks for years and had long endured ulcers and throat infections.

A key defence witness was Jeremiah Smith, who provided an alibi for Palmer at the time he was supposed to have purchased strychnine and other poisons from Newton. Cockburn did not counter his testimony directly but easily discredited him as a witness. Smith was accused of being the lover of Palmer's mother, admitting to sleeping in her home 'two or three nights a week' for 'several years', but denying an 'improper relationship'. This the jury found hard to believe. Smith was single with his own house in Rugeley only a quarter-of-a-mile away by his own admission. More damagingly for Palmer, Smith proved evasive and stumbled through his answers when asked to explain his involvement in the doctor's numerous insurance scams. Smith categorically denied having attested to the proposal to insure the life of Walter Palmer for £13,000 in return for a £5 fee despite signed documents clearly proving to the court that Smith was indeed involved. Smith proved so inept and shady when facing questions from the Attorney General that, if anything, he damned his friend further. No one believed Smith's signature had been forged and Smith left the court with his reputation shattered.

Two thirds of the trial's time was taken up with the medical evidence. Had Cook been poisoned by strychnine or had he not? The foremost medical experts of the day were called to give their opinions. For the prosecution, an astonishing 20 physicians, surgeons, professors, a nurse and a 'lady's attendant', amongst them four Glasgow medics and a surgeon from Leeds, all gave evidence that Mr Cook could not have died as a result of a tetanus infection. In detailed testimony, it was categorically stated that a tetanus infection or idiopathic tetanus would not have killed so quickly. Neither could syphilis, apoplexy, epilepsy or any other naturally occurring illness. Both prosecution and defence agreed that 'tetanic convulsions' had killed Cook however and so the defence clung tenaciously to the 'death by naturally occurring tetanus' argument. At the time, there were believed to be three types of tetanus – the familiar type caused by wounds or trauma, an idiopathic or unknown type and the convulsions caused by strychnine. All acted on the nervous system. Since 1889 it has been known that strychnine has no connection to chostridium tetani (tetanus), whatsoever, except in relation to some of its symptoms.

Professor Taylor spoke for almost an entire day. He was forced by the defence to admit that he had studied strychnine, but never seen the drug act on a human subject before, although Cook's symptoms were consistent with those seen in poisoned animals. He also stated that Mr Cook's stomach had been contaminated by the 'throwing together' of all the contents. The 'fine mucous membrane, on which any poison, if present, would have been found, was lying in contact with

the outside of the intestines'. He was attacked by Shee for believing at first that Cook had died of antimony poisoning and later changing his opinion to strychnine, a drug with which professor clearly had little direct experience. The character of Taylor was also called into question by Shee, who accused him of trying to influence the jury pre-trial by writing to the *Lancet* to set right 'several misstatements regarding the medical evidence'.

After Taylor had spoken, the defence called in its own medical witnesses, 17 in number. In all, eight different explanations were offered by the usual assortment of surgeons, physicians, chemists and toxicologists who again travelled to London from parts distant to give forth their views. One thing was certain and that was the complete confusion of the medical profession, who divided almost down the middle as to what caused the late Mr Cook's demise. Of course, they were not only called to hypothesise about what they believed had killed Cook, but to debunk the opinions of the prosecution witnesses.

Eminent men such as Professor of Surgery at Leeds, Thomas Nunneley, Professor of Toxicology at Bristol Medical School, William Herapeth and Dr Henry Letheby, Medical Officer to the City of London, an avid student of poisons, were among the distinguished defence witnesses. Each of them made clear that, in his expert opinion, a key part of the prosecution evidence was wrong. For example, Professor Nunneley argued, as someone with a large practice who had seen much idiopathic and traumatic tetanus, that 'Death was caused by some convulsive disease'. Mr Cook 'had disease of the lungs ... felt himself for years to be ailing ... suffered syphilitic inflammation of the throat'. Nunneley thought 'excitement' and 'a weakened constitution' brought about Cook's entirely natural death.

Professor Herabeth argued that death from strychnine must leave a trace, 'unless a body had completely decomposed', boasting that he, at least, could find as little as one 50,000th of a grain if unmixed with organic matter, one-tenth of a grain if in water. Herabeth was a professional rival to Professor Taylor and desperate to prove the man he considered his personal adversary incompetent in public. The Attorney General shrewdly observed this enmity towards Taylor. As a result, Herabeth's credibility suffered and the impact of his testimony on the jury proved minimal.

Dr Henry Letheby had 'no hesitation in saying that strychnine is, of all poisons, either mineral or vegetable, the most easily detected'. When asked what killed Cook, Letheby was unhelpful, stating, 'It is irreconcilable with every disease I am acquainted with, natural or unnatural'. So it went on. The defence tried to sow doubt and confusion in the jurors' minds. Possibly they did, yet by offering between them so many different conclusions as to the cause of death, none in Letheby's case, they made the conviction of the prosecution witnesses that strychnine had killed Cook all the more credible.

After ten days of evidence giving Cockburn took six hours to deliver his comprehensive closing speech, one that riveted the court's attention throughout. So detailed was his contribution that every aspect of the defence was examined and comprehensively taken to pieces, showing how Palmer's team had signally failed to effectively counter the circumstantial evidence. Smith in particular came in for harsh criticism. He was Palmer's best hope and yet was exposed as a liar, fraud and possible accomplice to murder. His attempt at discrediting Mr Newton failed miserably. Yes, Newton may not have sold the strychnine at 9.00am on the day in question. It may have been a few minutes later. In any case, Palmer had probably bought the fatal dose from Mr Roberts the following day.

The defence was not allowed to sum up, as this was not permitted until the Denham Act 1865 was introduced nine years later.

Lord Chief Justice Campbell in his summation castigated Jeremiah Smith. 'Can you believe a man who so disgraces himself in the witness-box?' Campbell was clearly hostile to the defendant and made it clear he considered him guilty.

On the facts as presented it looked as if Palmer would soon walk free. Reasonable doubt should perhaps have secured his acquittal. Many scoffed at the evidence of Taylor and it appeared for a time to observers that Palmer would cheat the noose. In the final analysis, the sheer weight of circumstantial evidence and masterly flourish of Cockburn's closing oration weighed against the defendant. Justice prevailed and on the 12th day of the trial the jury pronounced Palmer guilty. They had been out for only an hour and 17 minutes.

Lord Chief Justice Campbell passed sentence in the traditional way. 'That you be taken to a place of lawful execution and be there hanged by the neck until you are dead.' The judge had the choice of having Palmer executed in London or Staffordshire. He thought it appropriate that the punishment be administered near the scene of his crimes – Rugeley. That evening, 27 May 1856, at 7.40pm, Palmer was taken by two officers in a cab, bound hand and foot in chains, to Euston Station.

The press had a field day. For months they had bayed for Palmer's blood. The fourth estate was still more than a century away from the restrictions imposed by the Contempt of Court Act 1981 that curbed publication of 'background material' in a case that a jury had not heard until after the trial verdict. Thus, for months all sorts of hearsay tales regarding the dishonesty and depravity of Palmer, occasionally mythical, sometimes apocryphal, frequently true, were printed and possibly read by the jurors. Such was the extent of the sensational and wholly prejudicial reporting that even the prosecution had felt the need to ask the jury to discount it and convict on the details brought forth in the trial itself.

Not everyone was happy with the outcome. The *Staffordshire Advertiser* on 14 June reported that a Mr Fisher, coachman to Colonel Smyth, MP for York, had bet heavily on a Palmer acquittal. On hearing the verdict, Fisher killed himself, leaving a penniless wife and four children.

Palmer appealed. As the Court of Criminal Appeal was not established until 1907, the only hope was directly to the Home Secretary, Sir George Grey. It was based on the grounds that no strychnine was found in the body of Mr Cook and, rather feebly, that as Britain would celebrate the ending of the Crimean War and the baptism of France's Prince Imperial on the day set for Palmer's execution, 14 June, an execution would 'spoil the festivities'. The appeal was ignored and Palmer doomed.

Although he hinted that he might have killed his wife, brother and Cook using brucine, not strychnine, Dr William Palmer refused to confess. He repeatedly told Stafford's prison governor, Captain Fulford, that 'Cook did not die from strychnine'. When asked if he had poisoned Cook he equivocated, answering 'The Lord Chief Justice summed up for poisoning by strychnine'. To Palmer it was the type of poison that was fundamental, not the act of murder itself. Indignant, feeling sorry for himself, he claimed to have been sent to the scaffold 'a murdered man', as he told Captain Fulford. In fact, it is believed he killed at least 14 people, possibly more.

Not everyone accepted Palmer's guilt. One or two people considered the entire courtroom drama a 'show trial'. A coroner, Mr Thomas Wakeley, distributed a 16-page pamphlet attacking the press for hounding Palmer, who was forced to accept trial by reputation and was convicted only on circumstantial evidence. The motives of some witnesses were called into question too. Elizabeth Mills admitted to meeting Mr Stevens, another prosecution witness, 'ten times' in the months leading up to the trial yet denying, somewhat implausibly, ever having discussed Palmer with him. Mr Wakeley also pointed out that there was considerable disagreement among the host of medical witnesses as to whether strychnine had killed Cook.

Looking at the case a century-and-a-half later, it is hard to believe in the 'innocence' of Palmer. All his life deaths surrounded him from which he clearly benefited. His bizarre antics after Cook's death, not least during the postmortem, his heavy debts and Cook's own belief that Palmer had poisoned him, when considered, are in harmony with the symptoms of death being consistent with strychnine poisoning. In the end, it is hard to believe that the known fraudster, rogue and scoundrel was not for much of his adult life also a devious and accomplished murderer. Justice was served.

What kind of a man was Dr William Palmer? Avaricious, self-centred and without conscience, Palmer was utterly unscrupulous and amoral. A man who could kill his wife, children, brother and friends for money with almost casual indifference, he was undoubtedly a sociopath. At the same time he was charming, if facile, popular with a public that warmed to his superficial appeal, charisma and magnetism. It was such fascination that undoubtedly tempted so many women to give themselves to him, despite his fairly ordinary appearance and demeanour. Notoriety, rather than respect, was Palmer's reputation among his social peers who offered him little, if any, sympathy during his plight. As for the poor, they liked his everyday pleasantries and that he did not talk down to them. His occasional generosity at the inn and willingness to give them free medical advice and treatment along with a few bob with which to try their luck at the track, also endeared him to many in Rugeley.

Two brothers and a sister visited Palmer the night before his death. Whether they tried to find out the truth about their brother Walter's fate is unknown. Once they left, the prison chaplain, Reverend RH Goodacre, tried for most of the night, unsuccessfully, to get Palmer to confess his sins. After the condemned man was given brandy, water and tea for breakfast, Goodacre tried again, asking Palmer if he considered his sentence just. When Palmer emphatically replied no Goodacre exclaimed, 'Then your blood be on your own head!'

It was 7.53am on the morning of 14 June 1856 when the prisoner, shaven-headed, was led out to his execution. A huge and excited crowd of 30,000 had gathered in Rugeley, a town of only 4,500 souls, as people from miles around and as far away as London turned out to see Palmer hang, despite a heavy downpour of rain. As he appeared, Palmer was greeted by a storm of catcalling. The prisoner was calm throughout, stepping out of the way of the numerous puddles that lined the walk to death. Nonchalant until the end, on looking at the gallows trap-door he asked hangman George Smith, 'Are you sure it is safe?' Receiving no reply, he shook hands, said nothing and with the noose around his neck the bolt was slipped. In a second, Palmer fell to his death. As his body jerked for a few moments the crowd booed, cheated of a more thrilling spectacle.

Palmer's body was left hanging for an hour, as per regulations, and then taken to the prison mortuary where a plaster death mask was made. This now resides in Staffordshire County Museum at Shugborough. Palmer was then placed naked in a sack and buried in the prison grounds, the last prisoner in the UK ever to be buried without a coffin. It was perhaps a fitting end for a man who killed even his nearest and dearest without sympathy, sorrow or compunction.

CHAPTER 12
Dr Marcel Petiot: House of Horror

'I ask you not to look. This will not be pretty'

MARCEL ANDRÉ HENRI Félix Petiot was one of the most despicable serial murderers ever to emerge from France. Using the confusion and chaos of war, he preyed on those who feared a terrible fate, posing as a patriot and saviour. Petiot entered the world in the early hours of 17 January 1897. His parents, Félix and Marthe, lived in Auxerre, a pretty Burgundian town 160 kilometres southeast of Paris.

The life of the young Marcel is the stuff of conjecture. It is alleged he had a kitten that he adored until, at the age of five, he discovered it would be more amusing to dip its paws in boiling water. Later the same day he strangled the kitten. Moving on to greater cruelties, he revealed his true nature by blinding young birds with a needle and cheerfully watching as they threw themselves at the bars of a cage in which he kept them.

Throughout his childhood Petiot was cruel to animals, but he developed in many other remarkable ways. Extremely intelligent if diffident, by the age of 11 Marcel could throw knives with astonishing accuracy, occasionally using a terrified classmate as an outline target to demonstrate his prowess.

Marcel's parents worried about their son, not least because of his sleep-walking, fits and habit of not only wetting the bed but, until the age of 12, his trousers too. Doctors could only assure the Petiots that their son would grow out of his strange behaviour.

At 15, Marcel's mother died and his father, a post and telegraph worker, moved the family to Joigny, 25 kilometres away. The young Petiot did not settle and his behaviour led to expulsion from two schools in rapid succession. Returning to Auxerre, he was again expelled and began to embark on a career of petty crime, resulting in charges being brought for mail theft and damaging public property in February 1914. A psychiatric evaluation followed at which Marcel was diagnosed as mentally ill, suffering from 'personal and hereditary problems that limit to a significant degree responsibility for his acts'. The charges were dropped due to the boy's sickness. Marcel's father was less sympathetic. Deciding enough was enough, he washed his hands of his unstable and delinquent son.

After a brief stint at school in Dijon, Marcel was again expelled from another school in Auxerre. Tiring of his behaviour, the authorities transferred him to a special school in Paris from which he graduated in July 1915. By this time, war was engulfing Europe and France was fighting for her very survival. Marcel Petiot was conscripted in January 1916 and saw action later that year. On 20 May 1917, he was gassed and a hand grenade exploded near his left foot.

While recovering from his wounds, Petiot once more showed signs of mental illness and was unable to return to his unit. Eventually he was diagnosed as suffering from 'mental disorder, neurasthenia, depression, melancholia, obsession and phobia'. Despite this, was sent back to the front in June 1918. Suffering a nervous breakdown, Petiot shot himself in the foot and suffered fits when sent behind the lines. Returning to the front once more, he could not adapt to military life and, after yet more time spent in psychiatric care, was finally discharged from the army on 4 July 1919.

More than a year later while living in a psychiatric hospital, Petiot had his case reviewed. He was now considered to be 100% psychiatrically disabled and unable to perform any work physically or mentally. It was recommended that he remain in psychiatric care indefinitely. Incredibly, Petiot, seemingly confused and indifferent to his future, had decided on his future profession and was already studying to be a doctor. Postwar France was reeling. Having suffered over 4.3 million casualties from a total population of less than 39 million, the nation was keen to help its 'heroes' return to civilian life. Former soldiers could therefore take degrees shortened to a few months. In Petiot's case, his medical degree would take not five years but a mere eight months and his internship two years. Thus, despite his psychiatric disability, he would soon switch from patient to practitioner. The Petiot family, even Félix, was proud that Marcel achieved such a prestigious qualification. His father tried to welcome him back into the fold. Marcel dined with Felix, accepted his father's regrets for having misjudged him and then walked brusquely out of the house. He never returned. In later years, at the Petiot trial and beyond, the insanity of Marcel Petiot would be obvious to all. In the early 1920s no one who entered the circle of Dr Petiot could yet see the monster lurking beneath the seemingly pleasant exterior.

Dr Petiot needed a job. Setting up home in the town of Villeneuve-sur-Yonne, 40 kilometres from Auxerre, the practice he started soon attracted patients from those unhappy with the service given by the two existing, older and complacent local physicians. Young and dynamic, Petiot charmed the sleepy town of 4,200 souls and quickly developed a reputation as a sympathetic and diligent healer. Seemingly a workaholic, the understanding young medic would charge little for his consultations, work nights to help the sick and old and listen to the worldly cares that his patients brought to him.

Of course, Petiot was no saint and his competence was questionable too. He would sign up patients to Medical Assistance without their knowledge, ensuring the French taxpayer reimbursed him for the small fees he charged. Prescribing was erratic. Occasionally Petiot recommended nothing. At other times he would prescribe a lethal dose of drugs that the pharmacist would have to alter. On one occasion, when chastised for prescribing a child a deadly dose of narcotics, he replied to the pharmacist: 'What do you care? Is it not better to get rid of a child that exists only to annoy its mother?' Still, he remained popular and most of his patients remained in good health.

Although superficially recovered from his mental illness, odd behaviour manifested itself in little ways. Petiot soon became known as a kleptomaniac and no visit to the home of a patient was complete without the minor theft of some utterly valueless trinket. In later years, his wife and son would return such objects, the removal of which hinted at the inner turbulence in Petiot's mind, an acquisitive one that strove to accumulate and hoard, almost for the sake of it. The villagers tolerated the unorthodox behaviour of their doctor, which they considered for the most part amusing, if baffling. Yet greater crimes were just around the corner.

Petiot rented a house for a year from the Mongin family on the understanding that after the 12-month lease was up they would return. Petiot refused to move out on the expiry of his lease and had to be evicted by court order. The Mongins then threatened to sue on finding that ornaments and furniture had vanished and an antique stove worth 25,000 francs replaced by an imitation. Claiming he was a certified lunatic who could not be held accountable, Petiot forced them to let the matter drop. They believed he had robbed them just for his amusement, as the items (with the exception of the stove) were of no value whatsoever. This minor incident was followed in 1926 by a much more serious one.

Louisette Delaveau was a beautiful 26-year-old employed by Petiot as his cook and housekeeper. She had previously worked for an elderly lady, Madame Fleury. Louisette quickly became the doctor's mistress, to the general surprise of the locals who believed Petiot uninterested in the opposite sex, having spurned the advances of the many young women who had pursued him. A few days after she moved in, the house adjacent to Madame Fleury's was burgled and soon after the Fleury home was not only broken into and robbed but also set ablaze. No one was ever held to account, although Petiot was certainly suspected.

Petiot always appeared agitated, distant and was a night prowler who rarely slept yet was so energetic, vibrant and full of life that he appeared almost 'possessed'. With Louisette in his life, Petiot changed, becoming calmer, more relaxed. After a few short months, Louisette vanished in mid-May 1926. Petiot asked the police if they were worried. His manner was such that the officer concerned reported it to his superior. An anxious citizen then reported seeing Petiot suspiciously loading a large trunk into his car. A few days later a trunk matching that exact description was found in the river containing the body of a headless young woman. She was never identified.

As Petiot was highly regarded and, of course, a doctor, no one seriously suspected that he was connected to the dead girl. As for Louisette, Petiot wept and wailed that she had left him. She was never seen again and her former love moved on with his life.

By now a respected pillar of society and revelling in his prestige, Petiot entered politics. Standing for mayor on a Socialist ticket, he was elected on 25 July 1926 by a landslide. It had been a hard-fought campaign and the new mayor was accused of dirty tricks. At one hustings his opponent was about to speak when a crony of Petiot short-circuited the village power supply, blacking out the hall. Unable to address the villagers, his campaign petered out. Petiot remained popular with most of the people in his new fiefdom for many years. Others saw him as a strange, sinister and thoroughly dishonest opportunist. During his election campaign, Petiot boasted of fooling the army into discharging him with a pension by faking insanity. Monsieur Gandy, an opponent, wrote to the Commission de Réforme to complain of this, only to be informed that Petiot was genuinely ill, despite his boasts. Furthermore, although the doctor's illness was deemed incurable, it could go into remission for long periods of time so when the 'madness' would return was anyone's guess. Villenueve now had a mayor who was sick enough not to be held fully responsible for illegal behaviour, yet sane enough to run the town. Of this bizarre set of circumstances Petiot would take full advantage.

From the outset, Petiot behaved strangely. He stole municipal funds, the drum of a band he disliked and removed a 600-kg stone cross at the entrance to the town cemetery he considered 'ugly'. On one occasion, he threw himself from the Paris express train, ostensibly to protest that his village had no station of its own. Such actions might be expected to turn folk against their mayor. In fact, Petiot's quirks were overlooked because he was actually a very effective politician. Villeneuve would benefit from the installation of a sewer system, the overhaul of its school and the constant lobbying of the state for further resources and improvements, all at the behest of their hard-working and innovative young mayor, Dr Marcel Petiot.

Villeneuve had a 20-member municipal council who seemed in awe of their new leader. When Petiot supported a project they acted as a virtual rubber stamp. When, capriciously, he changed his mind, they did too. Their mayor acted like an absolute monarch and his 'courtiers' went along with him. Why? It was rumoured he had a hypnotic influence. Others simply remarked on his forceful personality and powers of persuasion undoubtedly boosted by his supreme self-confidence and vitality.

On 4 June 1927, Petiot married Georgette Valentine Lablais, the beautiful 23-year-old daughter of a wealthy and influential landowner. On 19 April the following year, Georgette gave birth to a son, Gerhardt Georges Claude Félix Petiot, who was to be the couple's only child. As the months and years passed, the mayor/doctor was involved in a number of unsavoury incidents. On 29 January 1929, he was sentenced to three months in prison and fined 200 francs for fraud. He had stolen some cans of oil from a railway platform. Pleading insanity, Petiot had the sentence suspended. On 6 February his conviction resulted in his removal as mayor for a month. He appealed and, taking his 'fragile mental state' into account, the entire sentence was quashed.

On 11 March 1930, an incident that later pointed to the involvement of Petiot occurred in the town. Armand Debauve, director of a local dairy co-operative, returned home at 8.00pm to find his house on fire and his wife lying in the kitchen, her head smashed in by heavy blows. As the fire brigade struggled to extinguish the fire, the Petiots drove by and stopped for a while to stare. The locals were stupefied when the couple drove on, expecting Petiot to rush in and assist in dealing with the tragedy. Instead, the Petiots headed to the theatre where the doctor was seen to be nervous, distracted and agitated.

The assault on Madame Debauve was an extremely vicious one. Blood spatter showed how she was beaten to a pulp and the house doused in petrol and set on fire to eliminate evidence that could identify the culprit. Footprints led towards the town of Villeneuve and it seemed certain a local must have carried out the crime, someone who knew that Monsieur Debauve did not return home before 7.30pm (the fire stopped the kitchen clock at 7.13) and that the entire takings for the month (235,000 francs) would be in the house. The money was not stolen, having been hidden in the kitchen rather than the family safe. Bloody prints were found on the safe and a hammer covered in blood.

Villeneuvians, convinced a killer lived among them, were shocked that such a murder could take place only a few years after the headless woman's torso was found. Numerous people were accused and denounced by anonymous letters. Dairy staff were fingerprinted and many bemoaned the decline in law and order in recent years that had not only resulted in murder but also a whole spate of unsolved burglaries. Local newspaper *Le Petit Regional* published a series of anonymous articles denouncing the police, casting aspersions on the character and moral fibre of the deceased and describing in precise detail the injuries she suffered, even though such information had never been made public by the police or the coroner.

Monsieur Léon Fiscot, himself a suspect, told friends he had seen Petiot, rumoured to be the lover of 45-year-old Madame Debauve, near the house the evening of the murder and was going to inform the police. Before doing so, he visited Dr Petiot to have his rheumatism treated. The doctor had just taken possession of a new miracle drug from Paris that would cure Fiscot. Three hours after being injected, Fiscot was dead of an unknown cause. Petiot then quickly signed his death certificate and burial authorisation.

No one thought to investigate the mayor or take his prints. The Debauve case remained unsolved. Long after Petiot had been guillotined, the prints were checked. Unfortunately, they were taken from different fingers and so the mystery was never conclusively unravelled.

Complaints about Petiot steadily increased in the early 1930s. Municipal property disappeared, public works commenced without funding or authorisation, expense forms were rewritten, there were irregularities in Medical Assistance application payments and town records were found to be in chaos. The mayor's hand was seen in everything and discrepancies of one kind or another invariably led back to him. Auditors were sent to investigate and, after making a 'strong protest', on 27 August 1931, Petiot resigned. The Yonne Departmental Prefect had actually removed the mayor for a month the previous day. He then petitioned Pierre Laval, Government Minister of the Interior (who would be shot as a traitor after the war), for a permanent deletion.

Petiot was not going to surrender his privileged position so easily. New elections were set for 15 and 22 November. Winning in the first round (a process that in France then reduces the field to the two most popular candidates if no one wins outright) Petiot lost to Dr Eugene Duran in the second. He was not too perturbed, having already been elected on 18 October as the youngest of 34 councillors serving the entire Yonne.

In his new role Petiot excelled. Diligent, relentless, intelligent and driven, he could have gone far. Alas, his innate criminality refused to subside. On 20 August 1932, criminal charges were laid against him for the theft of electricity. As mayor he had been provided with electricity free of charge. After his office was revoked Petiot publicly renounced this free service. It did not take long for the authorities to discover he had a private generator and had tapped into the local grid. No crime was too big or too small for Petiot.

Tried for the theft of electricity, Petiot defended himself ferociously, claiming to be a victim of 'conspiracies' against him, petty jealousy and vindictiveness by political rivals. Such histrionics cut no ice with the court and on 19 July 1933 Petiot was fined 300 francs and sentenced to 15 days in prison. He appealed and the sentence was reduced to a fine of 100 francs. The conviction was upheld and, as a felon, he was deprived of voting rights and removed from office on 17 October. He had already pre-empted this by again resigning, this time a week before his removal. The political career of Petiot was now over.

In truth, Petiot had become bored with politics and life in the Yonne. In January 1933 he found it expedient to move with his family to an apartment at 66 rue Caumartin in the busy commercial district of Saint-Lazare, Paris. He had to find a new list of patients and did so by extravagant claims that he could relieve pain caused by anything from cancer to childbirth, remove everything from tattoos to tumours and cure diseases ranging from sciatica to syphilis. He announced a range of impressive qualifications and, once again, built up a large, loyal and devoted following. Perhaps this was due to his bedside manner or apparent self-sacrifice because later in 1944, when 2,000 of Petiot's former patients were interviewed about him, not one had a bad word to say. Even in the 1960s, former patients refused to believe that the wonderful man who seemed to slave away day and night on their behalf for scant reward could possibly be a mass murderer or capable of any crime at all.

But not everyone was fooled. Famed for 'curing' drug addicts, it was soon suspected Petiot was actually a supplier. In 1935 a Madame Anna Coquille reported to the police that her 30-year-old daughter had died following a visit to Dr Petiot, simply to have a mouth abscess lanced. Under anaesthetic, she never regained consciousness. An autopsy found large quantities of morphine and the coroner believed the death to be suspicious. Eventually the case was dismissed. Madame Coquille tried to re-open it seven years later without success.

Again in 1935, Petiot was investigated for dealing in narcotics. Charges were eventually dropped and a year later he successfully applied for the position of medecin d'état-civil for the ninth arrondissement of Paris, a prestigious post that gave him authority to sign death certificates. That year proved a difficult one for Petiot. On 4 April, he was caught stealing a book from the Joseph Gilbert bookstore on Boulevard Saint-Michel. Producing papers that proved his identity, Petiot tried to pretend the theft was an absent-minded mistake. Store detective René Cotteret thought otherwise and began dragging Petiot to the police station. Petiot threatened to 'bash his face in', tried to strangle Cotteret and then ran off. The incident was reported to the police, who now sought Petiot for assault.

Petiot showed up at the police station on 6 April at 4.00pm. He was weeping and claimed to be depressed and stated that he had previously spent time in psychiatric hospitals. At the time of the 'incident', he had been pondering about how to develop a machine he was inventing to help cure constipation. To show his inventive genius, he provided blueprints of this and a 'perpetual motion machine' he had also designed. Extravagantly, Petiot explained away the assault in a highly convoluted way and even provided his army discharge papers to prove he was mentally ill.

The police considered Petiot to be a rather strange individual, wholly unsuited to looking after the sick and vulnerable and ordered a psychiatric evaluation. The psychiatrist, Dr Ceillier, found Petiot to be deeply disturbed, unbalanced, neurotic and 'dangerous to himself and others'. He ordered Petiot to be detained, against his will, in a psychiatric hospital. The assault charges were dropped on the grounds of Petiot's insanity. Georgette Petiot arranged to have her husband incarcerated in a private sanatorium in the care of Dr Achille Delmas, a famously lax psychiatrist. The court accepted this only if its own doctors could regularly check Petiot.

Petiot was interned on 1 August 1936 and immediately declared himself sane and eager to be discharged. Delmas readily agreed. Other doctors did not. Months passed and eventually, after bombarding the authorities with letters, including the President of France, three doctors were asked to assess Petiot. They found him to be 'amoral, without scruples or moral sensibilities and unbalanced', but also 'free from delirium, hallucinations, mental confusion, intellectual disability, pathological excitation or depression'. He was set free with concerns expressed that 'should Petiot return to criminality, the nature of his criminal responsibility should be examined in detail from the beginning'.

Released on 20 August 1937, Petiot must have grown tired of pleading insanity, perhaps fearing that the next time the authorities would lock him up permanently. He never used such a defence again, even when the alternative was 'Madame Guillotine'.

Petiot now tried to act as a model citizen. His only crime over the next few years appeared to be tax evasion, declaring only a tenth of his estimated annual income. For this, he was fined 25,000 francs but not before making all sorts of ridiculous claims as to his poverty. House calls were made on foot; he took no holidays or bought new clothes for three years nor even entered a café in five. In fact, Petiot owned several properties and would regularly bid for expensive jewellery at auction. At his postwar trial, Petiot finally admitted to tax dodging, claiming, 'It's a medical tradition. I didn't want to seem like some kind of dope. Besides, it proves I am a patriot; the French are notorious for tax evasion'.

Germany's defeat of France in 1940 presented Petiot with an opportunity to feed his avarice by profiting from the death of people seeking to flee from Nazi terror. The German state made its enemies disappear. Why, in the spirit of free enterprise, should Dr Marcel Petiot not do the same?

It took Petiot some months to locate the ideal location to design and build his mini-murder factory. No one would suspect him. He was an upright citizen and family man, a regular church-goer, well respected in Paris. The future charnel house was found at 21 rue Le Sueur, a fashionable old villa in the 16th arrondissement that once belonged to Princess Maria Colloredo de Mansfield and by 1941 had been empty for over a decade. The house had a high wall surrounding it, a large garage and, to Petiot's fascination, a strange, windowless, triangular room with one door. What the princess had used the room for was unknown. The use it was allegedly put to by Petiot would, in a few short years, reverberate around France.

Petiot's new house cost him 495,000 francs and was purchased in his son's name. Even more money was spent converting the house to a very specific use. Most of the work was carried out on the triangular room. A false door and spyholes were installed and the walls were made sound-proof. It was small, with walls only two metres or so long and contained eight heavy iron rings fixed to one wall.

The room was lit by a single naked light bulb. The builder Petiot employed was curious, but satisfied when the doctor informed him it was to house 'mental patients'. A large pit was excavated in the floor of the garage and a furnace placed in the cellar. By the end of 1941, 21 rue Le Sueur was ready for its first victim.

Jacob Guschinow was a Polish Jew and furrier. As both a Jew and a foreigner, he was high up on the list of those for whom Gestapo was combing Paris. Guschinow had no illusions about his fate should he fall into their hands. Desperately, he wanted to escape the city and occupied Europe altogether. It seemed his luck was in. He had heard that a Dr Petiot had contacts with the Maquis and could organise his escape.

Petiot was glad to assist Mr Guschinow. As a patriot, he would gladly help the man for nothing and explained he would secure safe passage to Cuba. Unfortunately, not everyone was as patriotic as the doctor. Bribes would have to be paid to obtain a visa, arrange passage, safe houses etc. Petiot simply did not have the money required. The fugitive understood, liquidated his assets and paid him 50,000 francs, the rest of his money being sewn into his clothing.

The first stop on the furrier's flight to safety was in the rue Le Sueur. There, Petiot informed him he would require a routine inoculation before the Cuban authorities would let him enter their country. Obligingly, Guschinow agreed. He was believed to have been given a lethal injection in the triangular room, fell into a coma and died. Petiot could perhaps watch his victim expire through his spyhole and then prepare for disposal of the body, although, to the bafflement of investigators, the spyhole was found papered over, somewhat weakening this theory. Was injection even the cause of death? It has been thus conjectured mainly because it seems the easiest and most logical way for a doctor to kill, especially if a victim is strong, tough and resourceful as some of Petiot's undoubtedly were. Did the victims even die in the triangular room? Guesswork again. It was never confirmed for certain that those murdered were done to death in the strange little room or even, definitively, in the rue Le Sueur.

Was Petiot was a sadist who enjoyed watching his prey die in agony and fear? It's possible, but more likely he favoured a speedy, painless death that improved the efficiency of his 'enterprise'. Panic would not deliver quicker results. The German method of scientific, organised killing was more effective.

Once Guschinow was dead, he was treated with quicklime, supplied by Petiot's brother Maurice. The quicklime masked the smell of burning flesh from the furnace into which Guschinow was shoved after being dismembered. Word got around quickly that Guschinow had escaped and Petiot soon had plenty of applicants, convinced that his 'underground network' would spirit them to safety. No one ever got further than 21 rue Le Sueur but not all of those who ended their days at the hands of Petiot were seeking escape. Some were murdered for an entirely different reason – the self-preservation of Dr Petiot.

Jan-Marc Van Bever was a well-educated scion of a celebrated family of artists and poets, fluent in four languages and in possession of a baccalaureat degree. Despite such a promising background, education and a half-million-franc inheritance, he lived an adult life of penury, having squandered his legacy on failed business ventures and endured years of poverty, living on welfare. He did not get his first job, delivering coal, until the age of 41, the age at which he disappeared.

On 19 February 1942, Van Bever and his mistress, Jeanette Gaul, a registered prostitute in a licensed brothel, were arrested on drug offences. The collaborationist government of Marechal Philippe Pétain had replaced the cry of the French Republic from 'Liberty, Equality, Fraternity' to 'Family, Fatherland, Work'. Drug abuse had weakened the fabric of the nation and was considered an attack on the state itself. To eliminate it and knowing the borders of wartime France to be virtually sealed, with most dealers now exploiting the black market in other goods, the police were aware that only doctors had regular access to narcotics. The pharmacists of Paris were therefore raided to see who was prescribing drugs to excess and/or illegally. A record was kept by pharmacists of dangerous drug usage and this pointed to Dr Petiot as the supplier of narcotics to Van Bever and Gaul. Doctors could only supply addicts if attempting a cure. Van Bever was no addict, but his mistress was. Although she 'retired' from prostitution on meeting her beau in November 1941, 34-year-old Gaul could not give up heroin. Five doctors believed her their patient, whom they were trying to wean off drugs. Only Petiot was prescribing for Van Bever.

In early 1942, Petiot wrote five prescriptions for Gaul and two for Van Bever, who wanted his mistress to kick her habit but felt obliged to obtain drugs on her behalf until she was able to do so herself. Gaul's receipt of narcotics from a number of doctors, who all thought her their exclusive patient, led to her arrest. As Van Bever lived with her and he too had obtained narcotics, he was hauled in with Gaul. Both immediately revealed that Petiot had illegally supplied drugs to Gaul via Van Bever, knowing full well he was not a junkie. To the authorities this was no surprise. Petiot was one of only 25 Parisian doctors still treating addicts and had 95 on his books, supposedly treated with ever-declining dosages that would steadily wean them off. Petiot was already suspected of infringing the law and this time would be charged. He was not jailed. A trial date was set for 26 May. Meanwhile, Van Bever was released on 15 March while his mistress remained incarcerated.

At 9.30am on the morning of Sunday 22 March 1942, Van Bever was drinking coffee with a friend in the café of the building where he lived, when a man of around 45 came to see him. Van Bever left with the stranger, whom he clearly knew, saying he would return that afternoon. He was never seen alive again. Four days later, Jeannette Gaul's lawyer received two letters by hand, supposedly from the missing man. One letter asked him to Inform Van Bever's lawyer that his services would no longer be required, the other that Jeanette Gaul should 'tell the truth', that Van Bever was a junkie. It seemed obvious the letters were not from him. The identity of the man who took Van Bever away and delivered the letters was never discovered, despite a thorough police investigation. Ten days after his patient's disappearance, Petiot 'found' Van Bever's medical file, 'proving' he was a junkie. So detailed was the file that even a measurement of his penis was included.

Petiot and Gaul went on trial as scheduled. The doctor was fined 10,000 francs, subsequently reduced on appeal, and given a one-year suspended sentence. Gaul was imprisoned for six months and received a fine of 2,400 francs. Van Bever? He reappeared two years later – at 21 rue Le Sueur.

On 5 March 1942, Raymonde Baudet, a young heroin addict, was arrested for fraud. She had been given a prescription for the tranquilliser soneryl. She erased it and substituted it with '14 ampoules of heroin', a crude forgery that caused the pharmacist to alert the police. Baudet was a patient of Petiot, who had already prescribed heroin for her on four previous occasions. Petiot took drastic action.

Madame Marthe Khait, the 51-year-old mother of Raymonde, received a visit from Petiot who tried to persuade her to falsely inform the authorities she was a junkie and that two of Raymonde's prescriptions were for her. Khait thought such a proposal utterly ludicrous, but Petiot gradually browbeat, inveigled and coaxed her into agreeing that it would lessen the charges against her daughter and protect him. To maintain the pretence, he even persuaded her to endure a dozen puncture marks, adding authenticity to her story should the police examine her. Petiot then left.

A few days later, Madame Khait informed her son, who had opposed Petiot's scheme from the start that she would not go along with it. At 7.00pm on Wednesday 25 March just two days after Van Bever disappeared, Madame Khait told her husband she was off to visit her daughter's lawyer to pay his fee. Petiot had altruistically offered to pay 1,500 francs towards it and even recommended the lawyer concerned, Maître Pierre Veron. Ironically, four years later Veron would be a key player in the prosecution against him. Madame Khait said she would be back shortly and even left a pot boiling on the stove. She vanished completely. Again, two letters appeared, delivered the next morning on the same day as those to Maître Francoise Pavie, Jeanette Gaul's lawyer. One was addressed to her son, claiming she was fleeing to the unoccupied zone until her daughter's trial was over the other was to her husband, purportedly confessing that she had been a secret junkie for years. Both letters appeared to be in Madame Khait's handwriting and her husband, David, was certain she delivered them in person, as the Khaits had a large dog that barked furiously at strangers. The dog did not make a sound when the letters came through the door. In addition Madame Khait had frequently talked of going into hiding in the previous few days.

That same busy day, at 10.00am, Veron's maid was handed two letters addressed to her employer and Raymonde Baudet. Confusingly, the maid later claimed to recognise Madame Khait and, on another occasion, that a young man delivered the letters. Both announced Madame Khait's intention to flee to the unoccupied zone and the letter to Veron included 300 francs towards his fee. Handwriting experts analysed the writing on all the letters supposedly sent by Madame Khait and agreed she had written them, albeit under duress. The letters appeared dictated, using names and language unfamiliar to her.

Both Petiot and Veron said Madame Khait had discussed her escape plans with them and her husband remained convinced that is what happened. The police found the circumstances of her disappearance deeply suspicious and similar to those of Van Bever's. Both cases involved narcotics, letters, a sudden vanishing and the rather unsavoury Dr Marcel Petiot. A search turned up nothing but Inspector Roger Gignoux, in charge of both cases, believed the handwriting in all the letters to be by the same hand.

Petiot and Baudet were tried on 15 July 1942. Baudet was sentenced to time served, four months, and Petiot received the identical sentence as in the Gaul case. His lawyer, Maître René Floriot, managed to have both fines reduced to 2,400 francs in total. Petiot could continue practicing medicine.

The investigating magistrate in both cases, the juge d'instruction (examining magistrate), was Monsieur Achille Olmi. His role was to gather evidence, interrogate witnesses, instruct police investigations and compile a dossier from which a decision to prosecute (or not) would then be made. Both Veron and Gignoux wanted Petiot charged with kidnapping and murder. Olmi resisted. Not until a year later did he even allow 66 rue Caumartin to be searched. By then it was doubtful if anything would be found. In fact, a drawer full of jewellery and gold was discovered, along with papers referring to 21 rue Le Sueur. Petiot complained about the invasion of privacy to which Olmi joked prophetically, 'Don't worry, I am not accusing you of killing people and burning them in your stove!'

From the French surrender until November 1942, France was divided in two; an occupation zone controlled by the Germans that included Paris, northern France, the Atlantic and Channel coasts and an unoccupied one, ruled by a collaborationist regime based in Vichy and controlling central, southern and Mediterranean France. It was dangerous to cross the line and papers were issued only in extenuating circumstances. Once in unoccupied France, people in flight required safe houses, food, transport, guides to take them across the Spanish border and a ship to take them overseas from Spain. Those who helped escapees did not always do so for patriotic reasons. Money was all-important and stories abounded of refugees being robbed, handed to the authorities or even murdered. The going rate for safe passage out of France was initially 50,000 francs per person, increasing as the war progressed.

Thousands of French citizens and foreigners found themselves stuck in the occupied zone, fearing arrest, deportation and death. Jews were particularly vulnerable and many would do almost anything to escape. It was from the desperation of such people that Petiot used to line his pockets and, probably more important to him psychologically, accumulate their belongings.

Dr Paul-Léon Braunberger, a 62-year-old Jewish doctor, received a telephone call at his home, 207 rue du Faubourg, St Denis, on the morning of 20 June 1942. It was just 8.30am in the morning. The doctor was instructed to meet a patient in need of urgent medical attention at the metro station Étoile at 11.00am. Carrying only his medical bag, Braunberger set out just before the appointed hour and promptly vanished for ever. Only half-an-hour later, a letter was delivered to the home of Raymond Vallée, a patient and supposed friend of Dr Braunberger. Taking it to the doctor's wife, Marguerite, it was then handed to the police who noticed the letter was written on the doctor's stationery and, while apparently in his handwriting, appeared to have been written under duress. The letter stated that the doctor would not return and urged Madame Braunberger to 'Put all her most valuable possessions in two suitcases and prepare to leave for the free zone', while telling no one of her intentions. The police smelled a rat. Madame Braunberger informed them that she and her husband had already sent all their valuables to Cannes, as they prepared to head south. Only a few days previously, the Germans had informed the doctor that he was to be banned, as a Jew, from his practice and the couple considered flight essential.

On 22 and 23 June, Madame Braunberger received two similar letters in her husband's hand, imploring her to leave that forthcoming Saturday. Vallée then received further correspondence asking him to move all Braunberger's property to the home of Vallée's cousin 'the doctor', near the Bois de Boulogne. Who might this be? Vallée's wife's cousin was none other than the ubiquitous Dr Marcel Petiot.

The whole thing made no sense. Braunberger detested Vallée and would never have confided in him. On 30 June, Madame Braunberger's maid picked up the telephone to hear an unidentified male caller declare that Braunberger was safe and en route to Portugal. The caller, sounding exasperated, declared he would not 'pass' Madame as he 'had not been well paid'. Despite the maid's protestations that this matter could be resolved, the man hung up. Yet another letter arrived the following day, demanding that Madame Braunberger follow the person who delivered it. This was impossible, as the letter had been mailed. On 12 September, Dr Braunberger's wife formally reported him missing. Searching for a missing Jew at that time was not considered a priority for the Paris police and there was no investigation.

Petiot had met Braunberger only once, at Vallée's house, a decade earlier. After their meeting, the latter told his wife that Petiot was, 'Either a genius or a lunatic'. Undoubtedly, the letters sent to Vallée referring to Braunberger were because this was the only connection to the older doctor Petiot had. This connection would be confirmed 18 months later at 21 rue Le Sueur.

On 16 and 17 July 1942, 12,884 Jews were rounded up during a huge swoop in Paris and corralled into the Vélodrome d'Hiver. After three or four days with no food and only a little water, they were moved to Drancy, the camp from which they would be sent east to their deaths. Of 150,000 Jews deported from France, less than 3,000 survived. Parisian Jews were only too aware of the noose tightening around them. Since commencement of the occupation, laws directed exclusively at them were implemented, depriving them of their rights and livelihoods. In June 1941, Jews were banned from cafés, cinemas, libraries, parks, racetracks, restaurants and swimming pools; they had to obtain permission to use a telephone. From 8 July 1942, Jews were not permitted to enter shops except between 3 and 4pm when most were shut. German propaganda continually sought to poison French minds against the Jews, portraying them as 'swindlers, parasites and aliens, sucking the lifeblood from the French people'. Such laws brought forth great opportunities for the criminal fraternity to benefit from the Jews' plight.

At 6.00pm on 18 July 1942, Kurt Kneller, a German Jew, met his doctor, Marcel Petiot, who had promised to help him and his family escape the Nazi depredations. Born in Breslau (now Wroclaw, Poland) in 1894, Kneller left his homeland on 10 June 1933 soon after Hitler's accession to power. Emigrating to France, he married another German-Jewish refugee, Margaret Lent, four years his junior, in 1934. In France, Kurt Kneller worked in the home appliance and radio industries, joined the French Foreign Legion at the outbreak of war and served until demobbed, following his adopted country's capitulation. The night he met Petiot, Kneller left his apartment at 4 avenue du General Balfourier with him. Earlier that day, Petiot and an elderly man had arrived with a handcart and carried off the Kneller's possessions in two large and four small suitcases. The doctor wanted to take Kneller's furniture too, until the landlady, Madame Christiane Roart, pointed out that it belonged to her. The following morning, Kneller's wife Margaret and seven-year-old son René were staying in the house of a friend, Madame Clara Noe, when Petiot arrived. Madame Noe stepped out for a few minutes to buy milk for the boy. When she returned, Margaret, René and Petiot had gone.

In the weeks following their departure, Madame Noe and another of Margaret Kneller's friends received postcards, ostensibly from her. The phraseology was strange and her name was signed 'Marguerite', the French way, whereas Madame Kneller always spelled her name 'Margaret'. On 8 August 1942, only three weeks after the Knellers 'escaped', three dismembered bodies were fished out of the Seine near Asnières. The heads of a man and woman in their forties and that of a seven- or eight-year-old child were found, together with their arms, feet, legs and vertically sectioned torsos nearby. In a state of advanced putrefaction, they could not be identified, especially as their fingerprints, faces and scalps had been surgically removed. Over the next few months, six other unidentifiable bodies, disfigured in the same way, would be hauled from the Seine.

Known as Maurice, Moses Maurice Israel Wolff was born to a wealthy timber merchant in Königsberg (now Kaliningrad, Russia), East Prussia. With his wife Lina, he left for France after the Nazi takeover and subsequently settled in Amsterdam. By the summer of 1942, the Nazis were closing in on the Netherlands' Jewish community and so the Wolffs, with Lina's mother Rachel, fled Amsterdam on 12 July. After escaping into Belgium, Maurice was arrested on the French border. The authorities were sympathetic, sentencing him to time served, ten days in prison, and his money and valuables were not confiscated. The Wolffs were then hidden in their lawyer's house and later a convent, for several weeks before reaching Paris. Their lawyer, Maître René Iung, later arrived in Paris with their identity papers, money and jewellery.

Using the alias 'Walbert', the Wolffs moved from location to location around a Paris becoming daily more precarious for Jews. Eventually, a friend put them in touch with a Romanian Jewess, Rudolphine 'Eryane' Kahane. An apartment was found in Kahane's building at 10 rue Pasquier and the Wolffs were put in touch, via her doctor, the convicted swindler and abortionist, Dr Louis-Theophile Saint-Pierre, with Petiot's associate, Francinet Pintard.

Petiot did not meet and arrange 'escapes' on his own. He had a number of accomplices who did much of the dirty work for him. There was Edmond 'Francinet' Pintard, a former song-and-dance man and make-up artist; Raoul Fourrier, a barber who recruited from his shop; René-Gustave Nezondet, a friend of Petiot from his days in Villenueve, as well as Eryane Kahane, who found prospective escapees from within the Jewish community.

The Wolffs met a man calling himself 'Dr Eugene' the same day, who expressed a keen interest in their state of mind and financial situation. Dr Eugene burst into a rage on finding that Fourrier and Pintard had sullied the noble cause of assisting escapees by quoting double the usual price in an attempt to line their own worthless pockets. Kahane spoke enthusiastically about Dr Eugene, as she knew Petiot, and said she wanted to go with the Wolffs, as she too was a Jew in danger from the Nazis. The doctor refused, as only three could go at a time and Kahane was needed to 'assist the organisation further'.

The next day the Wolffs were visited by Petiot, whom they found to be 'highly cultured, magnanimous' and 'of fine sentiments'. Over tea he told them to take two suitcases each, the contents of which should be devoid of any identification labels, and as much money as they wished. They would be taken to a 'safe' house in Paris for a few days and then depart.

At the close of December 1942, the Wolffs told a friend of theirs, Ilse Gang, that a doctor would come for them that evening. He did and they vanished forever. Two months later Madame Gang was called on by Eryane Kahane and asked if she wished to follow them. The kind offer was politely refused.

Two weeks after the disappearance of the Wolff trio, a new couple, the Bastons, were living in their old apartment and had already been contacted by Petiot. They wished to depart beyond German control with four relatives already in Nice. Petiot was only too happy to arrange it. Marie-Anne and Gilbert Baston originally had the name Basch but changed it, like so many Jews fleeing persecution. They originally left Germany for the Netherlands and, some years later headed to France. Marie-Anne's parents, Chaim and Franziska, were living in Nice under the pseudonym of Stevens. Her sister and brother-in-law, Ludwika and Ludwig, used the name Anspach.

The Stevens and Anspach couples had already paid over a million francs to move to Nice the previous August and hoped to reach Switzerland or South America. They stayed in the four-star Hotel Rossini with many other wealthy fleeing Jews and possessed a great deal of money, furs and jewellery, although they dressed modestly so as not to attract unwanted attention. Nice in 1942 was under Italian occupation. Mussolini, Italy's Fascist dictator was not anti-Semitic or racist and at that time had no truck with Nazi policies against Jews, a situation that was to change later. As a consequence, thousands of French Jews fled to the Italian occupation zone where they were protected not only from the Germans, but enthusiastic, pro-Vichy French police, whom the Italians occasionally chased off at gunpoint. The Hotel Rossini even had a number of Italian intelligence officers in residence, sharing the hotel quite happily with Jewish refugees.

One would have thought it prudent for the Anspach/Stevens group to have stayed in Nice or found contacts in that city to assist them in leaving France for nearby Switzerland or Spain. Inexplicably, they took the highly dangerous decision to join the Bastons in Paris, from whence they would then escape together. Using the Thomas Cook Travel Agency, the Anspach/Stevens group travelled to Paris by train on 26 September 1942 and again on 6 January 1943. Why they made the journey from Nice to Paris and back to Nice before returning, finally, to Paris has never been discovered. Their final destination prior to disappearing was 10 rue Pasquier. What happened there is not known. What is certain is that their ultimate fate would be revealed at the rue Le Sueur.

There can be no doubt that while the majority of those murdered by Petiot were innocent and included women and children, a number of unsavoury individuals also disappeared at the hands of Petiot. Joseph 'Jo le Boxeur' Reocreux led one such group. Reocreux was a 32-year-old hardened criminal who had served over five years for numerous thefts and pimping. Extremely tough, he could fight and overcome three men at once. A lackey of the Gestapo, he supplied them with prostitutes and information in return for their protection from the French police, who wanted to get hold of him on a series of outstanding warrants.

The Germans discovered that their creature had carried out a number of robberies dressed in Gestapo uniform along with another rogue, Adrien 'Le Basque' Estebeteguy, wanted on eight counts of assault, theft, fraud, possession of firearms etc. One such robbery, on 14 December 1942, netted them and two others, a hoard of gold, dollars, francs and silk shirts. It would not be long before their enraged former employers hunted them down. Desperately, the gangsters sought to flee France.

Petiot, using the alias 'Dr Eugene', met Reocreux after his accomplices laid the groundwork. The gangsters were told the price was 25,000 francs each. Apparently his colleagues, Fourrier and Pintard, had told Reocreux it would be double this, no doubt hoping to make an extra profit. Petiot lambasted them furiously and they apologised to Reocreux. Having done this previously with the Wolffs, one can only wonder if this was a ruse intended to convince prospective clients of his integrity. If so, Jo 'Le Boxeur' was not impressed. Despite being reassured as to the honesty of his apparent saviour, Reocreux later told friends that the intensity of the doctor's eyes made him feel 'uneasy'. Accordingly, he no longer wished to leave Paris. This was an astonishing admission from such a hardened, professional criminal. Reocreux decided to send another criminal associate, Francois 'le Corse' Albertini, on ahead. The two crooks would swap mistresses, le Corse taking Claudia 'Lulu' Chamoux and Reocreux, Annette 'le Poute' Basset. Both women were prostitutes. Before travelling, Reocreux would wait for information that Albertini had arrived at his destination safely.

Weeks passed and Petiot began to fret that Reocreux knew too much about 'the operation' and should be encouraged to leave. Eventually, he handed a letter to Fourrier that he wanted returned as soon as possible. The letter was apparently from Albertini in Argentina and said he had arrived safely. Confident, Reocreux took the fatal decision to leave, taking with him Basset, an unknown, prostitute, 1.4 million francs sewn into his clothes, some gold hidden in their shoes and a quantity of expensive jewellery. None of them were ever seen again. Fourrier noticed a few days after the 'departure' of Reocreux that Petiot was wearing the pimp's watch. 'A present', Petiot remarked casually, 'to show his gratitude', an emotion hitherto absent in that particular criminal. Fourrier found it curious, but thought little more of it at the time.

Estebeteguy was next. A telegram from Reocreux was passed around one of his old haunts, the rue de l'Echiquier café, stating his trip had gone smoothly. On the last Saturday of March 1943, Estebeteguey set off with Paulette 'la Chinoise' Grippay, the prostitute mistress of a fellow pimp, Joseph 'Dionisi' Piereschi and was followed the next day by Piereschi and his own mistress, Gisele Rossmy. Again, none would ever be seen alive again.

One might assume that the four pimps and five prostitutes had left in the dead of night, but all departed from Pintard's barber shop at 9.00am on a

Saturday or Sunday morning, heading in the direction of 21 rue Le Sueur, suitcases in hand. Curiously, no one ever saw them arrive there, something that should have been noticed in such a busy street. Beady-eyed local residents spotted no other unusual people over the years and, had the house been entered at dead of night after the city-wide 10.00pm curfew, it would sooner or later have caught the attention of an informer or German patrol. How the bodies and the vast array of goods found at the house got there was to remain an unsolved mystery. Perhaps the fugitives in Petiot's power were not murdered at the rue Le Sueur but somehow brought there later. The question would later baffle detectives. In the meantime, the roll-call of victims grew, but not before drawing the attention of the Gestapo itself.

On 8 April 1943 the Gestapo produced a report detailing the workings of an 'escape network' operating out of the rue de l'Echiquier café, where associates of Petiot openly touted for business. The Gestapo had all the details. They knew how much money was to be brought to the first interview, the required ten photographs and the escapee's actual address (to ensure no Gestapo informers were recruited); the escapee being notified three or four days before departure and taken to a secret location in a hotel or doctor's apartment and after two days in hiding taken to a train station and given a false passport, visa and tickets for a ship usually bound for Argentina.

The Gestapo did not know who was at the centre of the 'network', but believed it had connections to a foreign embassy, which supplied documents, and to be 'highly organised and secretive'. To break it, Robert Jodkum, Gestapo Chief of Jewish Affairs in Paris, resolved to blackmail a Jew who would be beyond suspicion into helping them.

Yvan Dreyfus was a wealthy Jew who had headed a large radio and electronics company before the war. When France surrendered, Dreyfus had supplied the Maquis with transmitters and repaired damaged radios dropped from the air. He was arrested in Montpellier while trying to leave France to join Free French forces and now languished in Compeigne prison awaiting deportation to certain death in Germany or, more likely, Auschwitz.

Still at liberty, Madame Paulette Dreyfus did everything she could to free her husband. Eventually, she was informed that her husband's liberty could be purchased at a price: 3.5 million francs. A Gestapo agent, Pierre Pehu, told Madame Dreyfus that her husband would have to sign a form indicating that he was released after offering to work for Germany. She refused at first, but was advised that this was only a formality to allow the Germans to cover themselves, should questions be asked regarding Dreyfus' release.

Madame Dreyfus was bled for another 1.1 million francs before her husband was finally released. Dreyfus met Dr Eugene a few days later on 15 May and on 19 May the two of them left Fourrier's barbershop together, watched by German agents, whom they successfully eluded on the Champs-Élysées, heading in the direction of the rue Le Sueur. The Gestapo were impressed at the way their quarry had eluded them. No matter, another 'escapee' would soon be sent and the organisation broken.

Meanwhile another Gestapo Department, IV-E3, led by Dr Friedrich Berger and responsible for security in occupied France, muscled in. French collaborator Charles Beretta was sent to pose as a possible escapee. He was told to pay 100,000 francs, which he haggled down to 60,000, to cover false papers and instructed to meet Dr Eugene on 21 May, only two days after the disappearance of Dreyfus. He was to bring ten photographs, two suitcases full of belongings, a blanket and 'all the money he owned'. That day, as Beretta, Pintard and Fourrier met in the latter's apartment, the Gestapo burst in, arrested them all and wrung from Fourrier the name and address of Petiot. As his home was searched, Nezondet arrived with theatre tickets and he too was arrested. When Berger discovered he had ridden roughshod over the plans of a colleague, the prisoners were sent to Jodkum for interrogation. Petiot was savagely beaten for several days.

Petiot behaved remarkably bravely under the whip. He admitted being part of an escape organisation but claimed the brains behind it was a fictional 'Robert Martinetti', who could not be contacted. Beaten solidly round the clock for three days, Petiot had his teeth filed down three millimetres, his head crushed in a vice and was almost drowned in freezing water. A dead man was shown to him and another with his head smashed to pulp. The Gestapo said these were members of his organisation. For months, on and off, Petiot was brutally interrogated. Despite the torture, he never changed his story. Sent to prison at Fresnes, to his cellmates he was a hero, hurling insults regularly at the Germans, smuggling messages out of the prison and talking endlessly of his alleged escape organisation – 'Fly-Tox'.

Nezondet was released after a couple of weeks, the Germans believing him innocent. As he left, Petiot whispered a message that Nezandot was to pass on: 'Tell my wife to go where she knows to go and dig up what is hidden there'. He followed the doctor's instructions, although Georgette Petiot seemed baffled by them. The Gestapo searched Petiot's home at 66 rue Caumartin and another property at 52 rue de Reuilly. In a remarkable oversight, although bills and documents attesting to its ownership were scattered all around, 21 rue Le Sueur was not investigated.

On 11 January 1944, Fourrier and Pintard were set free. Terrified, they had told the Germans all they knew, which was very little. Petiot was released a few days later, astonishing other prisoners who thought him so openly contemptuous of his captors that he was bound to be shot. His brother Maurice paid only a relatively modest 100,000 francs for Petiot's release, possibly because Marcel claimed he had terminal cancer and would soon die anyway. In later years, much conjecture was heaped on why the Germans released the leader of Fly-Tox. Perhaps they were aware of his murderous activities and thought of him as doing their dirty work for them. More likely they hoped to find out more by placing Petiot under surveillance. The infernal activities of Dr Petiot were soon to become public knowledge.

On 6 March 1944, dirty, thick, slimy, foul-smelling smoke was witnessed belching from a chimney at Petiot's house at 21 rue Le Sueur. For five days the smoke continued, the lack of even a slight breeze ensured that the evil stench emanating from the chimney continued to pervade neighbouring homes. One of the residents across the street, Madame Andréa Marcais, could stand it no longer and sent her husband, Jacques, to complain. He knocked the door to no avail, eventually observing a note that stated, 'Away for one month. Forward mail to 18 rue des Lombards in Auxerre'. Unwilling to tolerate the stench any longer, Mr Marcais called the police.

Two police officers, Émile Fillion and Joseph Teyssier, arrived and tried to access Petiot's house by door and shuttered window. After enquiring of neighbours, the police discovered who owned the building and were even given the owner's telephone number, Pigalle 77.11. Teysier rang and Madame Petiot answered. Her husband then took the call, asked the police to wait and said he would be along 'in 15 minutes with the keys'. After half-an-hour, Petiot had not arrived and, with the smoke thickening and smell worsening, the fire brigade turned up. Their chief, Avilla Boudringin, climbed in through a second-floor window with some men and headed for the source of the fire and stench in the basement. Within a few minutes, he and his colleagues staggered out of the house, one of the firefighters retching in shock at what he had seen. 'Gentlemen, I think you have some work ahead of you', was Boudringin's understatement, as he ushered the two police officers inside.

Within 21 rue Le Sueur, a vision of ghastly horror greeted the visitors. Gingerly, they headed towards the dark basement and found two stoves, one unlit, the other blazing furiously, with a woman's hand protruding from the open door. Only the eerie light from the stove guided the police as they explored, finding a staircase at the bottom of which was a pile of coal on which were scattered arms, a head, two skeletons, broken rib-cages, feet, hands, jawbones, skulls and a heap of small bones and rotting human flesh. The startled officers left the house almost immediately, bumping into a man in the street just arrived on a bicycle. In his mid-forties, the man had dark, almost black, piercing eyes. It was Petiot.

Petiot was surprised to see his house open and asked to go inside with the police. Calmly viewing the gory scene in the basement, he announced, 'This is serious. My head may be at stake'. Back on the street, Petiot asked the police if they were patriotic Frenchmen and told them the corpses were those of German soldiers and collaborators he had slain as leader of an underground Maquis cell.

He needed time to burn 300 compromising files and asked if, 'in the name of France', he could be allowed time to do so. Believing such a grisly site could only be that of an organised resistance group, the police agreed and Petiot rode off on his bike.

A whole series of officials now descended on 21 rue Le Sueur. The fire was eventually extinguished and the authorities, French and German, attempted to get to the bottom of what had happened there. Entering 21 rue Le Sueur; one came first to a short vaulted passageway. After ten metres a paved courtyard was reached, surrounded on three sides by a building and a nine-metre wall on the other. The yard was thus concealed from outside. The house was large and spacious, with six bedrooms, public and dining rooms and a library. Filthy and covered in dust, the rooms were heaped to the ceiling with a fantastic assortment of furniture, art, chandeliers and all sorts of bric-a-brac. Across from the main building were former stables and servants' quarters. A second library was sited there as well as the only neat and tidy room in the entire complex – a doctor's consultation room. Tiny and wedged in a small L-shaped corridor, it seemed an odd place to have such a room when the size of the house was considered. Next to the consultation room was a garage, containing a mound of quicklime, 12 cubic metres of it, full of human remains including a scalp and jawbone. Adjacent to this were the stables, in which a former manure pit with a ladder to enable access was propped and a block and tackle for lifting heavy objects rigged above. In the pit itself, was yet more quicklime pitted with human debris. On the landing of a staircase leading from the courtyard to the basement was a canvas sack. Half-a-left-sided torso was within, complete except for the foot and viscera. Beside the coal in the basement, an axe with what looked like dried blood on it and a shovel were discovered. A sink in the basement kitchen large enough to hold a corpse and with drainage sufficient to let blood flow without coagulating, was also found.

An amazing assortment of booty was piled around the rue Le Sueur. Included were 83 suitcases, five fur coats, 28 suits, 66 pairs of shoes, 79 dresses, 87 towels, 115 men's shirts and a host of coats, hats, sweaters among 1,760 items discovered. When considering that Van Bever and Madame Khait left with no luggage, one can only imagine the extent of Petiot's nefarious activities. Once Maurice Petiot's two homes in Auxerre and Dr Petiot's at 66 rue Caumartin were searched, a total of three tonnes of clothing and assorted articles were found. The police soon concluded that the number of victims could easily run into hundreds.

Within hours of discovering the bodies, the case was given to Commissaire Georges Massu, a 33-year-old policemen with 3,257 arrests to his name and the model for Georges Simenon's Maigret. Checking out the house, he found the odd triangular room and imagined how it featured in the death of those who met their end in that terrible place. Were they chained to the iron rings, beaten, tortured, drugged, gassed? There was no sign that the spyholes had been used or that victims had struggled. No gas, needles or poisons were found. There were many puzzles relating to the murders that no one, least of all Petiot, would ever properly explain.

The Germans assessed the situation quickly and, describing their former captive as a 'dangerous lunatic', ordered his immediate arrest. On hearing this, Massu concluded that Petiot, whom he intended to arrest early that morning of 12 March, probably was with the Maquis and so he procrastinated. When members of his team went to 66 rue Caumartin, they discovered the Petiot's had left only 30 minutes before. Half-heartedly, the police looked for him, earning a stern rebuke from the Gestapo, who soon realised Fillion and Teyssier had deliberately let Petiot escape. Both then fled France, returning only after the liberation.

The press revelled in the case, publishing ever more lurid tales of speculation as to what had happened to Petiot's victims and the ever-increasing number of those estimated to have been killed. How many were there? Careful sifting of the quicklime to extricate the remains was carried out by four gravediggers before a team of eminent pathologists and anthropologists, led by France's foremost scientist of the day, Dr Albert Paul, who spent a month measuring, labelling and reassembling the bones. Even so, they could only guess that at least five women and five men had been found, out of possibly as many as thirty. In addition were ten complete scalps, 15 kilos of charred bones, 11 of uncharred, five of hair and 'three garbage cans full', as Dr Paul told the newspapers, of fragments too small to identify. As to the ages of the victims, these varied from 25 to 50. Few had any distinguishing features, even the teeth being unrecognisable. Breakages in the bones were so rough and ready that it appeared as if wedging them in a door and pulling had caused the fractures. As for how the bodies had been dismembered, the ribcages had been torn open as one would a chicken. The technique was reminiscent of that used on the nine bodies found in the Seine a year to 18 months previously. Such dissection was professionally done but was thought to be more the work of a coroner than a surgeon.

Analysis of the corpses revealed nothing as to how they had died. All had been dead for several months, apparently murdered prior to Petiot's sojourn with the Gestapo. Identification of the dead would be difficult. Examining the loot helped more in this regard than the bodies themselves.

Among the clothing found were identification tags marked with the names of the victims briefly outlined above. Initials too abounded in the effects left by Petiot. Some had been torn off but so randomly and haphazardly that identification was quite easy. Where possible, relatives and neighbours of the previous owners of the loot were interviewed and eventually the police were slowly able to piece together a list of people they were certain had finished their 'escape' at 21 rue Le Sueur. It was not definitive by any means, but a good starting point.

On 13 March 1944, the search for Dr Petiot finally began. The hunter became the hunted, but despite sightings the length and breadth of France and in North Africa, he was nowhere to be found. Ten people associated with him were arrested, interrogated and, after several months, released. These included Georgette Petiot, Fourrier, Pintard and Maurice Petiot, who it was revealed, had sent 683 kilos of luggage in five suitcases to Auxerre on 26 May 1943, five days after the Gestapo arrested his brother. Maurice claimed he did this at the request of Marcel and that he had seen nothing unusual when collecting the booty from 21 rue Le Sueur. No bodies, no smell filled the house, perhaps because the bodies were submerged in the quicklime he himself had delivered to the house.

As D-Day came and went, Paris was soon to enjoy its liberation from a German army that surrendered the city to General Jaques Leclerc's Free French forces on 25 August. Petiot was temporarily forgotten, as an orgy of revenge was unleashed against collaborators, thousands of whom were lynched, and tens of thousands sacked from their jobs or arrested and either tried or released some months later. The city reeled from the purge, yet Massu never took his eye far from the Petiot case. As the demand for vengeance against those who had betrayed France slowly subsided, Massu decided to take advantage of public opinion to lay a trap for the murderous doctor.

On 19 September 1944, the newspaper *Resistance* published an article headed, 'Petiot, soldier of the Reich', in which the fugitive was denounced as a member of the Parti Populaire Francais, an actively collaborationist organisation that openly supported Germany, accusing him of leaving France in German uniform the previous March to fight against the Maquis. Petiot took the bait. His vanity would not allow such 'outrageous' accusations to go unanswered. On 18 October, the same newspaper published a reply sent by Petiot via his lawyer, in which he utterly refuted allegations of collaboration, claimed to be a Maquis hero and that he had 'lost everything but his life' by 'selflessly risking even that' in an attempt to establish his patriotism, if not his innocence.

The authorities now guessed that Petiot was still living in Paris, not only under an alias but probably serving in the French Forces of the Interior (FFI). To catch him, military security was asked to compare the handwriting of Petiot's with that of their men and to look out for anyone matching his description. Among those given this job was Captain Henri Valeri, the officer in charge of counter-espionage and interrogation, based in Reuilly, Paris. Valeri had been a member of the FFI for only a matter of weeks. His real name, according to his identity papers, was Dr Francois Wetterwald. He was in fact Dr Marcel Petiot.

After fleeing 66 rue Caumartin, Petiot stayed with a number of persons unknown for a few days here and there. Eventually, he found refuge with Monsieur Georges Redoute, a former patient whom he knew only slightly. Redoute was concerned at harbouring someone accused of such heinous crimes, but his fears were assuaged by his highly persuasive guest, who convinced him that he was a patriot, on the run after having killed the enemies of France. Cooped up for months and sharing his patient's rations, Petiot let his imagination run wild, telling Redoute of his frequent operations on behalf of the Maquis in which he fetched weapons dropped by the Royal Air Force, assassinated German troops and collaborators and destroyed them physically either by throwing their bodies into the canals adjoining the Seine or at 21 rue Le Sueur. Apparently, Redoute never thought to ask why it was necessary to dismember, burn or otherwise dispose of enemy bodies in such a way.

After months in hiding at Redoute's, on 20 August Petiot disappeared for the day and returned carrying a drum and some grenades which he claimed to have taken from Germans he and his Resistance comrades had fought and killed that day. A few days later he left without a word, taking all his possessions and went off to join the FFI.

Petiot was an incredibly resourceful individual. He did not just join up under a false name. Wanting to remain a doctor, he sought out members of his profession who were still held by the Germans. Eventually, he came across the name of Dr Francois Wetterwald, incarcerated in Mauthausen, a Nazi concentration camp. Visiting Wetterwald's mother posing as a resistant, he persuaded her that her son's identity papers were required to secure his release. After obtaining them, Petiot adopted the nom de guerre of Dr Wetterwald and left the real owner of that name to rot in captivity, where he stayed until the end of the war. For security reasons, Petiot/Wetterwald then took the new alias of Dr Valeri when joining up.

As a soldier, Petiot initially impressed all who came into contact with him for his patriotism, hard work and ceaseless commitment to rooting out and liquidating those who had betrayed France. As was common in those anarchic times, promotion could be swift and Petiot quickly became a captain. His madness still troubled him and he slept three nights a week for a month in Ivry cemetery, believing German troops and their French stooges were hiding there. It was not long before his innate criminality surfaced and he began abusing his new authority to line his own pockets.

On September 12, a Lieutenant Dubois, an underling of Petiot, searched the home of café owner Madame Juliette Couchaux on an unconvincing pretext and ransacked her home, stealing three million francs worth of jewellery. She complained to Dubois' commanding officer, Captain Valeri, now sporting a beard and in uniform, a couple of days later. Told to withdraw her complaint, Madame Couchaux was advised to 'sell her café and disappear'. She had no intention of doing so and was thrown into prison. Released a couple of months later, Madame Couchaux claimed that another woman, who shared her cell for describing a similar event, had told her that the officer she went to see, Petiot/Valeri, was even wearing the rings she called to report stolen!

Petiot had by then linked up with a vicious gang who joined the FFI to rob vulnerable citizens. On 16 September, two FFI members of the gang, Lieutenant Jean Duschesne and Corporal Jean Salvage, together with a civilian, Victor Cabalguenne, broke into the home of Monsieur Lareugance, Mayor of Tessancourt, supposedly to investigate his alleged collaboration. Instead, they beat him ferociously and shot him in the head before blowing his safe and escaping with 12.5 million francs in cash and valuable stamps. Three youths who saw the killing were themselves arrested after informing Petiot.

On 31 October 1944, at 10.15am Captain Valeri was standing on the platform of the metro station Saint-Mande-Tourelles on the eastern edge of Paris when approached by FFI Captain Simonin and three other army officers, who had awaited him for over three hours. One of them asked Petiot the time. Still wearing the watch of Joseph Reocreux, as he was distracted the doctor was handcuffed, kicked to the ground and then dragged to a waiting car. Petiot was subsequently handed to the military police and then taken to civilian police headquarters. How did Simonin know that Petiot and Valeri were one and the same? No one would ever know. There was no Captain Simonin. He vanished, never to be found. The police did discover his real name was Soutif, a collaborator responsible for the killing or deportation of hundreds of patriotic French citizens.

Cabalguenne and Duchesne were soon picked up. They told the police that Petiot had told them his real identity, claiming to have killed 63 collaborators, including Reocreux. Salvage, who had provided Petiot with an apartment, never re-appeared. He had worked for Simonin/Soutif and when the police sought him they were told he had been sent on a 'top secret' military assignment. No one knew to where or would disclose when he would return. The authorities would never find out. Those who later offered to provide information on Salvage or Soutif met with death. Whoever this mysterious duo were, they had important connections that enabled them to cover their tracks. Petiot must have been an embarrassment to them. Handing him to the authorities must have seemed a good way of getting rid of someone who no longer served a useful purpose. At last, Massu had his man. Now he must build a solid case if the mass-murderer was to pay a visit to Madame Guillotine. It would not be easy.

In custody in Sante prison, Petiot vigorously denied being anything other than a patriotic servant of France who had risked all in serving the nation. He wrote to his former commanding officer, Colonel Ruaux, to enlist his aid, stating that 'Captain Valeri is incapable of having committed acts that would make an honest man blush with shame'. His letters being censored, this one was never sent. Nevertheless, the Petiot defence of calling him a resistant could only cause headaches in French society, splintered as it was by the occupation and its immediate aftermath.

Preposterous as it might seem, the Petiot defence would be difficult to break down. The doctor had sewn the seeds of doubt in many in the months leading to his arrest and a few people were taken in to the extent that they genuinely believed the man a hero. He had told the same tale consistently even from the time he was in the hands of the Gestapo. Was Petiot telling the truth? Those looking at the case in any depth were not so easily fooled.

The juge d'instruction in charge of the case was Ferdinand Goletty. Petiot's story was that from 1940 he provided false medical certificates to Frenchmen who were to be rounded up for forced labour in Germany. He also worked with Spanish Republican guerrillas and was trained by the Maquis in plastic explosives, unarmed combat, weapons etc. Petiot then claimed he was appointed to head his own group of resistants by Pierre Brossolette, a famous resistant conveniently (for Petiot) killed in March 1944. Petiot's group was named 'Fly-Tox', after the slang name for an informer, mouchard (mouche is French for fly) and the name of a fly spray.

While building his resistance group, Petiot still found time to design a secret weapon, so secret it was never discovered. The mad doctor boasted of how he used this incredibly powerful weapon to kill two German motorcyclists, claiming that five tonnes of it could have cleared France of the Boche (Germans). The weapon was so amazing that no cause of death was left on the victims, who were thought to have died of natural causes. The design of the weapon was, Petiot pompously asserted, 'classified' and he refused to describe it even in rough outline.

British agents parachuted into the unoccupied zone provided training for members of Fly-Tox and Petiot asserted that he and his comrades soon became experts in handling weaponry, explosives and hand-to-hand combat. Petiot explained that his victims were selected by observing those who entered Gestapo headquarters. These people were then followed when they left and Petiot's men arrested them, pretending to be Germans. If a person protested that he was a German agent, he was immediately beaten to death with rubber hoses filled with sand, lead and bicycle spokes and buried a few kilometres outside Paris in the woods at Marly-le-Roi. These bodies were never found and probably never existed. Those killed in this way supposedly numbered 63. Thirty-three French collaborators and 30 German soldiers. Petiot would always remain adamant that this was the total number of his victims, yet between 1941 and 1943, 86 dismembered bodies were found in the Seine alone, most of which appeared to be the handiwork of the evil doctor. The thighs invariably had similar pincushion marks, from a dismembering scalpel being stuck in, while the body was being ripped apart. Although most of the bodies taken from the river were beyond identification circumstantial evidence from such as the Knellers, led to Petiot as the culprit.

The escape route was genuine said Petiot, who maintained that many suspected of meeting their demise at 21 rue Le Sueur, such as Guschinow, had actually escaped to South America. Others, Reocreux for example, were killed for trying to expose the route. As for his accomplices, Petiot recruited Fourrier and Pintard as he thought a barber and make-up artist would be useful in creating disguises. The comrades who helped expose traitors, kill them or assist with providing documents, safe houses, transport etc for escapees he steadfastly refused to name, saying either that he was unaware of their true identities or that to do so would put their lives at risk should Germany once again invade. Their codenames and aliases were never proved to relate to anyone who ever existed. One or two real names were offered up, again, of Resistance activists who had met heroic deaths and who could neither support, nor refute the doctor's story. As for the Jews killed, 'all were traitors in the pay of the Nazis', declared Petiot outrageously.

The 'house of horror', as the French press called it, had been in a shambolic state when Petiot was released from Gestapo custody. Fly-Tox had apparently ceased to exist with the lack of a British/American invasion. Feeling ill, Petiot went to Auxerre to recuperate. It was not, the doctor declared, until 8 February 1944 that he ventured back to his house in the 16th arrondissement, where a month later his ghastly crimes would be discovered. On entering, he claims to have found the place in disarray following a Gestapo search. Bodies were piled in the old manure pit in an advanced stage of decomposition and stinking to high heaven. Valuable medical equipment and furniture had been stolen. Petiot resolved to clean up the mess and asked his brother to bring 200 kilos of quicklime from Auxerre, ostensibly to kill cockroaches but in reality to disinfect and assist the decomposition of the corpses. Petiot argued that, had he known the bodies had been there, he would have brought the quicklime himself, thus avoiding the involvement of his 'innocent' brother.

How had the cadavers ended up in Petiot's house asked Goletty? Who were they? The doctor believed it to be the work of his over-enthusiastic comrades. He claimed to have reproached them and they in turn accused the Germans, although it was preposterous that the occupying power would kill people and leave them lying rotting around in a house in the middle of Paris. What to do? Petiot claimed that two of his associates decided, unknown to him, to burn the bodies commencing on 10 March. It was the following day that the fire brigade and police 'with typical impertinence', in the words of Petiot, broke into his property.

Smoke was pouring from Petiot's house from 6, not 10 March, as the doctor stated. No names of comrades were forthcoming, as Petiot did not want to 'get them into trouble'. In all probability there was no one else directly involved in the destruction and disposal of so many people. Investigators concluded that those who participated in Petiot's scam probably believed their victims did escape. Only Petiot knew the grim truth. Only he was involved in burning the corpses at 21 rue Le Sueur.

As the authorities planned their next move, Petiot busied himself in prison, taking up smoking, writing poetry and even a 300-page manuscript he entitled *Le Hasard Vaincu* (Chance Defeated), detailing how to maximise one's chances at poker, lotteries, the roulette wheel etc. The book, published by Roger Amiard in 1946, was a fascinating, flowery work of numerous digressions exploring such bizarre subjects as God's relationship to Satan. Strangely, the dedication of the book was to Dr Eugene, Captain Valeri and Dr Petiot, ie himself and two of his aliases.

Resistance members were interviewed to ascertain their knowledge of Petiot's wartime activities. Despite exhaustive investigations, not a soul was found who could verify his tall tales of heroic resistance, Spanish Republicans, Fly-Tox, secret weapons, contact with the British or his 'assassination' of the two German motorcyclists. On 3 May 1945 lieutenants from the Direction Generale des Études et Recherché (military security or DGER) produced a report stating quite categorically that the doctor was a fraud. He had no connection whatever to the Resistance and named as associates only those whose names were commonly known as having died in the service of France. The report detailed 25 points where the deposition of Petiot conflicted with reality and they concluded with the statement, 'We formally reject the hypothesis that the accused played even the remotest part in the Resistance'.

Petiot rebuked his accusers and settled down to further months of questioning as the dossier against him grew and grew. Eventually he tired of it all and, on 30 October 1945, declared he would answer questions only in open court. Goletty informed his superiors of the strong accusations Petiot had to answer. A trial was now inevitable.

No one wanted to try the case. It would be huge and inevitably recount issues many felt uncomfortable with in the immediate aftermath of war. Vichy, the Resistance, collaboration and the role of those directly involved in the case could surface. Honour and career considerations meant few wanted the dubious privilege of taking on Petiot. The Procureur Général, who would normally handle such a complex and high-profile trial, passed the case to an assistant, who also passed it on to someone who did likewise until eventually Avocat Général Pierre Dupin was instructed to prosecute the case. He had only six weeks to study and master the thousands of pages that comprised the Petiot dossier. The doctor stood accused of murdering 27 people for financial gain, having stolen an incredible 200 million francs in cash, gold and jewellery that was never found, even by treasure hunters who searched through the rubble of 21 rue Le Sueur after it was demolished a few years later.

The trial of Dr Marcel Petiot was one of the most enthralling and extraordinary events to take place in France in the immediate postwar era. The public were fascinated and the Palais de Justice was packed throughout, with hundreds of curious citizens, scores of journalists, 80 witnesses, numerous relatives of the victims and their legal representatives. French law allows the victims of a crime to have their own lawyers present their case and, if the accused is convicted, seek financial recompense. The court was thick with members of the legal profession and their clients glowering at the accused.

On Monday 18 March 1946, the trial opened with Michel Leser, President of the Tribunal, taking charge of proceedings. He was flanked by a magistrate on either side, with a total of seven jurors next to them, with three alternates. Together, this group would decide the defendant's guilt or innocence. For the prosecution, the state had selected Advocats Généraux Dupin and Elissalde. Petiot had Maître René Floriot, his long-standing legal representative and the greatest criminal attorney in France, to defend him.

The clerk to the court read out 27 indictments, followed by a biography of Dr Petiot outlined by the president. He was often corrected by Petiot, bored, arrogant and sarcastic, who complained that: '80% of the dossier is false'. Shouting, interrupting and showing contempt for proceedings that would never be permitted in an American, English or Scottish court, Petiot continued to find the recounting of his life tiresome and erroneous, as he was accused in the dossier of all sorts of petty crime, ranging from the theft of the antique stove and electricity to practising as a quack and graduating to mass murder. 'Keep your opinions to yourself ... please let me continue, this is my trial ...' and 'I don't care to be treated like a criminal', were some of Petiot's rude and frequent interjections. He went on to proudly admit tax evasion, a 'medical tradition', in his view, but denied any other illegalities.

The president had great difficulty keeping the accused in check and the trial degenerated into farce at times, as Leser traded insults with the defendant. Eventually, Leser got to the crux of the matter and raised the issue of the sinister happenings at rue Le Sueur. To Petiot, the temerity of the judge in raising this was tantamount to believing 'German lies'. Petiot declared that he was a Resistance hero, who was merely burning the bodies of unknown Germans the Resistance had killed and were disposing of in the house. After all, said Petiot indignantly, 'Would I have returned to the house when contacted by the police had I been guilty?'

Of course, no one was surprised when Petiot refused to name his supposed comrades. According to him, they had volunteered to attend but he had refused, believing he said that they would be arrested too. Dupin responded that he would ensure they were each awarded the Liberation Cross if an appearance was made. This, said Petiot, was impossible whilst 'men who pledged their allegiance to Pétain are still free'. Petiot then made the fantastic assertion that he had developed a 'secret weapon' in the rue Le Sueur. Of course, as with Goletty, in the interests of 'national security' he could not go into details in court.

As Leser lost his command of the court, Petiot was repeatedly questioned by the lawyers acting for the victims on how much he knew about explosives, firearms etc. Not much it seemed. Still, the accused remained confident and unfazed by anything thrown at him and bragged of blowing up enemy trains and killing German motorcyclists with his mysterious secret weapon. It all proved hugely entertaining for the people in the public gallery. When Petiot claimed to have killed a mounted German in the Bois de Boulogne, a wag shouted, 'Call the horse to the stand!'

Maître Pierre Veron, lawyer for the Khait and Dreyfus families, asked how long it took a grenade to detonate. Petiot replied, 'Thirty minutes'. Gleefully, Veron pointed out it was seven seconds and denounced Petiot as an imposter, who had never been in the Resistance. Angered, Petiot yelled at Veron, accusing him of defending 'traitors and Jews'. When, on the second day of the trial Petiot repeated the smear, Veron lost his temper, shouting, 'Take that back or I'll knock your teeth in!' The crowd roared with laughter and the journalists had great head-lines for next morning's newspapers.

Pressed to reveal the names of anyone who could corroborate anything he said, Petiot refused, saying he would do so 'only when acquitted'. Showing a complete lack of impartiality but understandable exasperation, Leser replied, 'I doubt you will be'.

Petiot then owned up to killing French civilians he had tricked. Of course, Petiot claimed they were not frightened people desperate to save their lives, but 'traitors and collaborators' who got their just deserts. Petiot then told the court of his arrest by the Germans, the torture he endured whilst in their custody and finding his house full of bodies when released upon his brother handing over a modest 100,000-franc bribe. Apparently unfazed, if irritated by the cadavers in his home, the doctor proceeded to explain how, when and why the corpses were burned.

The day after Petiot's latest fantastical recollections, the newspapers appeared almost to admire his bombast and egoism. The prosecution certainly seemed incapable of tying down the numerous contradictions in Petiot's ludi-crous tales that appeared to be made up virtually on the hoof. There was a mountain of evidence and Dupin was struggling to cope with, let alone turn the defendant's lies against him. Petiot was enjoying being centre stage and frequently contradicted the evidence he had supplied to the Goletty dossier that Dupin had before him. Floriot taunted Dupin, telling him to learn the difference between 'always' and 'sometimes' and 'yes' and 'no'. His client was unimpressed, complaining, 'Don't I have the right to say anything? I'm involved in this too you know'. To which Veron sarcastically yelled, 'Poor fellow. Are you bored?'

Monsieur le President sank into sarcasm frequently too, wearying of the farcical goings on in a court he singularly failed to control. After denying he had ever heard the name of a particular victim, Denise Hotin, whom he may not actually have killed, Petiot 'allowed' Leser to continue, for which Leser replied, 'How gracious of you to permit me'. Later that day, Leser denounced the accused to David Perlman, reporter for the *New York Herald Tribune*. 'Petiot is a demon, an unbelievable demon, a terrifying monster and an appalling murderer'. A juror chipped in, 'He (Petiot) is mad, with a terrible intelligence. He is a monster. The guillotine is too good for him!' Another juror added, 'We are only hearing of the bodies found. How many more were killed and how many bodies are still hidden? We shall never know'.

Floriot demanded a mistrial. Leser simply replaced the jurors with alternates. He then proceeded with more caution, striving to ensure the trial progressed as smoothly as possible thereafter. On the third day of the trial, some of the victims' stories were detailed. When Dupin mentioned the sanctity of human life, the 'audience' roared with laughter, causing him to shout that, 'Those who wish to amuse yourselves should go to the theatre'. Petiot remained impervious to Dupin's questioning. Asked where Guschinow was now, he simply responded, 'In South America. Have you searched it? It's a big place'. Floriot interjected and showed that only two people had been contacted regarding the whereabouts of the missing furrier. Of course, neither had seen the missing man. Petiot's lawyer then pointed out that if the same question asked of two people in Paris regarding any missing person it would probably provide the same answer. It was 'ridiculous' yelled Floriot. Dupin, not Petiot, was now on the defensive. Asking why identifying labels were removed from clothes, Dupin was caught out by Petiot replying: 'If you knew anything of the Resistance ... '. Haughtily, Dupin said he did, to which Petiot cattily remarked, 'Yes, but not from the same side'.

Dupin began to outline other individuals who had vanished at the doctor's hands: Dr Braunberger, Reocreux and other victims. Petiot began to invent and elaborate stories of how the 'collaborators' met their end, some bravely, some begging for their lives. It was all fantasy.

The sarcasm continued. Dupin suggested that Petiot had stolen millions of francs from Estebeteguy alone, money allegedly stitched into the victim's shoulder pads. When questioned about it Petiot denied having found any money but asked for a 10% 'finders fee' if any money was discovered.

Petiot did not help his case by insisting that his Jewish victims, the Basches, Stevens and Wolffs were traitors who deserved to die. This strained the court's credibility, but Floriot pointed out that the Wolffs had entered France with legitimate German passports. The Nazis had requisitioned the hotel they had hidden in. Dupin's lack of detailed knowledge prevented him from interjecting that the Wolffs had entered France in 1933 not 1942 as Floriot misleadingly implied.

Petiot scoffed that the Wolffs had hidden as he had on his honeymoon. 'I hid under the sheets and asked my wife to try and find me'.

On day four of the trial, Petiot attempted to besmirch the memory of Yvan Dreyfus, claiming he was responsible for Petiot's incarceration by the Gestapo. In this he showed his anti-Semitism by asking the court, 'Who cares if a Jew has disappeared?' They certainly cared about seven-year-old René. How could this little boy possibly be accused of treason? 'The boy was a lovely child', recounted Petiot. Was? Why did Petiot use the past tense? Dupin thought he had him but Petiot sidestepped. Dupin then made another error, accusing Petiot of refusing to sign an inventory of clothing found in his house. Floriot leapt to his feet and threatened 'to give up practising law right now' if the prosecution could prove his client had ever seen the list. He hadn't and Floriot scolded Dupin once more for his ignorance as to the contents of Petiot's dossier.

The following day, the court visited Petiot's sinister house in the rue Le Sueur. Thousands lined the streets to get a glimpse of the 'monster' and 300 policemen held back the crowds. A mêlée developed as journalists and citizens jostled for a peek. Soon the public burst into the house and Petiot's library was ransacked as others gawped luridly at the stove and pit. Lawyers even posed for photographs holding thighbones aloft. The situation was farcical.

Eight members of the court including Dupin, Petiot, Leser and Floriot found their way inside the triangular room. It was eerie and pitch black. Candles were lit but repeatedly went out. Utter darkness lasted for seemingly endless minutes until a gendarme lit up the room by torch. Everyone sensed the cold, dank horror of the place and began to chatter nervously. Dupin tried to speak, was ignored and petulantly threatened to leave if not heard. He stormed out as the rest of the court was gradually ushered in one at a time. Professor Charles Sannie pointed out where half-a-corpse was found in a cement bag. Petiot insisted it was a mailbag. Floriot was outraged to discover no one knew even where the sack was. Apparently it had not been retained as evidence.

Back at the Palais de Justice, Sannie was forced to admit that the fingerprints of the accused had not been found anywhere in the rue Le Sueur. Following him, Commissaire Massu was asked about the sack containing the body. 'A potato sack', thought Massu. On being asked specific questions he tried to deflect responsibility saying that, 'Inspector Poirer was in charge of this', or 'Inspector Batut was in charge of that … '. Despite having overall responsibility of the investigation, like Dupin and unlike Floriot, he showed only a haphazard knowledge of the case. The court realised the slapdash way in which the entire prosecution case had been cobbled together.

On the sixth day, a Saturday, Prince Rainier of Monaco attended. That day the defence was less able to counter the witnesses before it. As always, Petiot attempted to interject. He was caught out when Veron exposed him as being ignorant of the appearance of, and how to detonate, plastic explosives. Petiot claimed he knew about detonators when Veron was 'breast feeding' and accused Veron of never having seen any. Veron was able to retort he had travelled with up to 150 kilos in his car while working for the Resistance. The doctor was then caught out as having falsely claimed to have killed two Gestapo agents and burying them in Marly woods. In fact, they had been killed months later and the police knew their killers, all 11 of them. A Captain Henri Boris, a former aerial operations director for de Gaulle during the war who had shared a cell with Dreyfus, testified that Dreyfus supplied the Maquis with radios and would never have betrayed France. He added that no plastic explosives were in France when Petiot claimed to have used them. Petiot hurriedly asserted that a man parachuted in from London delivered them. When asked his name, Petiot said he did not know but the man had 'fled to Corsica and there committed suicide'. Laughter erupted at this unlikely scenario.

The next day was Sunday and so court was not in session. The following Monday, 25 March, a tentative, pale and sad Madame Guschinow appeared and explained her husband's disappearance. Petiot had told her he had received letters from her husband in Argentina, saying that Mr Guschinow had arrived safely but then destroyed them for 'security reasons'. To everything she said, Petiot shouted out, 'She's lying!'. His bullying riled Leser and lawyer, Maître Jaques Archeveque, who stepped in to question her attacker about the details of Guschinow's disappearance. Petiot took on the mantle of victim and accused Madame Guschinow of having a young lover, knowing her husband was still alive and, astonishingly, criticised her for not availing herself of Petiot's services during the war. Floriot then remonstrated with Dupin for failing to organise a search of Argentina for Monsieur Guschinow, stating his belief that he was still alive. No one in the court believed it, but it was an important point that once more undermined the prosecution's lack of attention to detail.

Monsieur Michel Cadoret de l'Epingham gave evidence. He had intended to escape using the Petiot 'network' but changed his mind when Petiot told him he would require injections, saying, 'These will make you invisible in the eyes of the world'. Petiot shouted out, 'I see it all now, the mad doctor with his syringe. It was a dark and rainy night, the wind howled under the eaves and rattled the windowpanes of the oak-panelled library ... '. Cadoret was also upset that Petiot asked for money, which resistants did not do and by the grime beneath his fingernails, unusual for a physician. He had paid some money to Petiot but before he could ask for it back, Petiot returned it to him, explaining curtly that he could not help. It seemed that both parties were equally suspicious.

On day eight, the 'experts' had an opportunity to specify their often grisly findings in court. Dr Albert Paul detailed the remains discovered at 21 rue Le Sueur. The skulls, shoulder blades, collar bones, arms, legs vertebrae, five kilogram's of hair, scalps and face skin expertly removed in one piece. The gendarme next to Petiot was visibly horrified at the gruesome minutiae, while Petiot simply whistled and looked bored.

In response to Dupin's questioning, Dr Paul could not specify when the victims died, how, their exact ages and in some instances their sex. Fire and lime had caused too much damage. No bullet wounds or skull fractures were found, but their deaths could have been caused in numerous other ways. The similarity of the pincushion thigh wounds to those on bodies fished from the Seine was emphasised, as was the expertise of the dissection. Floriot quickly interrupted to say that Petiot had never taken a dissection course. 'That's a shame, because he dissects very well', retorted Dr Paul.

Professor Henri Griffon, a Director of Toxicology for the Paris police, had examined the remains for poison, finding nothing. He hypothesised that the triangular room was used as a gas chamber or the victims killed by morphine. Floriot pointed out that neither gas nor morphine was discovered at the rue Le Sueur, although 504 ampoules of morphine were found in Petiot's rue Caumartin apartment.

Next up was Dr Genil-Perrin, a psychiatrist who had examined Petiot both in 1937 and before the trial. To the amusement of the court, he found Petiot to be highly intelligent with 'an extraordinary gift for repartee'. Yet Petiot was also 'morally stunted and responsible for his actions'. His colleague Dr Gouriou described Petiot as 'perverse, amoral and devious'. Floriot asked Dr Gouriou if he had examined Petiot's sister. He had and found her 'quite normal'. Floriot then revealed that Petiot had no sister, as Gouriou shambled off the stand, his credibility in pieces, the courtroom laughing at him.

Edouard de Rougemont, a graphologist, then testified. He had examined the many letters purportedly from victims and announced all were written under duress and that, 'Monsieur de Rougement is a great scholar who never makes mistakes'. He could even tell 'with certainty' if a man writing on a piece of paper was lying or telling the truth. Floriot sarcastically pointed out that, had Petiot simply written his story down, de Rougemount could have decided if he was being truthful and saved France the expense of a trial. An embarrassed de Rougemont then shuffled off.

Monsieur Jacques Ibarne, journalist for with the newspaper *Resistance* and Military Security officer, informed the court that his investigations revealed no one in the Maquis who had heard of Dr Eugene or Fly-Tox. Petiot never knew any Maquis heroes, played no part in the Resistance and gained any information he had from a former Fresnes cellmate, Robert Lateulade, now deceased. He added that he believed Petiot to have collaborated. Otherwise, the Germans would never have released him. Petiot gave Ibarne a deathly stare throughout his testimony.

Veron used the Ibarne evidence to pin down the accused on the 28 German soldiers he claimed to have killed, apart from the two allegedly slain by 'secret weapon'. Petiot declined. He would only do so 'when acquitted, which is already a certainty'.

Wednesday, 27 March found Petiot's gang in the witness box as one by one, Fourrier, Pintard, Porchon, Nezondet and Petiot's brother Maurice testified. They said little, afraid of incriminating themselves. Only Nezondet said anything of significance, recounting that while Dr Petiot was in German captivity, Maurice had told him fearfully that, 'The journeys begin and end at the rue Le Sueur'. Under oath, Maurice Petiot, dying of throat cancer and trying to save his brother, denied ever having said such a thing.

Day ten saw Eryane Kahan enter the witness box. With strawberry-blonde hair, dark glasses and beige suit she was wrapped in fur hat and gloves, oblivious of the heat of the courtroom. She was 50 but looked much younger and spoke, quivering with sentiment, in a strong Romanian accent. Her testimony flatly contradicted Petiot's rants about those devoured by the rue Le Sueur. The Jews who hoped to escape through 'Dr Eugene' were terrified of the Gestapo, trusted their 'saviour' and were patriots, not collaborators. She was perhaps in a good position to judge. Just before his execution, former collaborator and Floriot client Henri Lafont, attempting to clear his conscience, detailed Kahan's life accurately and denounced her as a Gestapo informant happy to betray fellow Jews to the Gestapo in return for her own survival. She had vanished the day Petiot's photograph appeared in the newspapers for the first time. Claiming to have been a resistant which she was after March 1944, she could prove nothing before then, having apparently switched sides when the writing was on the wall for her former employers.

Floriot revealed that Kahan had taken money when procuring escapees for Petiot. She denied it or that she had a German lover. 'He was Austrian', said the witness. 'Just like Hitler!' exclaimed Floriot. She even had a dossier revealing her collaboration and Dupin said he had never heard of it. 'Number 16582' replied Floriot. Kahan was discredited.

Three witnesses who knew Dreyfus swore to his exemplary patriotism. One of de Gaulle's ministers, Pierre Mendes-France, sent a telegram to declare his 'stupefaction' that Petiot was attempting to dishonour the 'noble memory', of Dreyfus. Madame Dreyfus gave evidence sadly and quietly, still distressed at her husband's fate. Petiot was silent throughout, as she detailed her efforts to buy him out of prison and then France. Monsieur Fernand Lavie, son of Madame Khait, who described his mother's disappearance and the strange circumstances surrounding it, followed her. Madame Braunberger then testified, explaining how she identified clothing from Petiot's house that had been worn by her husband the day he vanished. Petiot was asked to answer questions on this, refused and swore at his guards. After more witnesses, regarding the Knellers this time, the court became bored, with even President Leser gazing at his watch, fidgeting. The trial seemingly dragged on and on, even though few doubted the eventual verdict. Maître Dominique, representing the Piereschi family, asked Petiot how he came to be released by the Germans. 'Good grief', remarked Leser. At this point Petiot shouted to the lawyers, 'You are all bastards'. Spontaneously and in unison they replied, 'Thank you!' After several lawyers began droning on, Leser, fed up, got up and walked out.

The thirteenth day, 1 April, it was rumoured Judge Robert H Jackson would take time off from the Nuremburg war crimes trial to attend the more entertaining case of Petiot. It was an April fool. As the prosecution rested, it was time for the defence to bring forward its own witnesses, mostly to attest the 'noble character of the accused.

Defence witnesses from Villenueve-sur-Yonne painted a glowing picture of Petiot's near saintliness. Former patients, admittedly afraid of his 'intense eyes', nevertheless denounced the trial as a politically motivated slur against their former mayor, revealing the 'astonishing things' he had done to improve the lot of his constituents and his devotion to the sick. He had vastly improved the local school from being a 'virtual leper colony', built the sewer system and improved transport links. The doctor was a '200% Frenchman' who had saved many lives, was sadly missed and would 'never be forgotten'. A deaf witness could not take the oath due to his hearing impairment. He said he had 'heard nothing' of Petiot since he left. 'I am not surprised', said a caustic Leser.

Patients of Petiot from his Paris practice rallied round him too. He had cured one of constipation using a 'strange machine', provided identity papers for two British pilots shot down in France and paid from his own pocket for an exhausted patient to take a vacation. The undoubted star turn was Lieutenant Richard Lhertier, who marched into court wearing the uniform of the French paratroopers. He had been dropped behind enemy lines, was caught and placed in a cell with Petiot. The doctor was a 'man of integrity" who told him in detail about Fly-Tox, how to resist torture and reveal nothing under interrogation. Petiot had shown only contempt for the Germans and proven an inspiration to his fellow prisoners. The court was impressed. Lheritier said he was 'proud to have shared a cell with Dr Marcel Petiot'.

Another former cellmate, Roger Courtot, backed up Lheritier's testimony and denied it was 'possible' for Petiot to have been motivated by money. The doctor had never worried about his personal safety. As Cortot spoke, Petiot wept in silence.

Mademoiselle Germaine Barre had volunteered to appear. She had been caught working for the Allies and was in the office of Robert Jodkum when he offered Petiot his freedom for 100,000 francs. Petiot had contemptuously rebuffed him, was insolent and condescending, refusing to sign a document stating he would do nothing against Germany if released. It was 'impossible' that Petiot was a traitor she announced. It was a positive note on which to end the defence.

On day 14, lawyers acting for the families of the deceased questioned Petiot and much evidence was repeated. As they droned on, both Petiot and Floriot fell asleep. The following day was much the same and again Petiot, Floriot and many in attendance slumbered. Veron woke them up. Denouncing the accused as a psychopath, he alluded to Petiot being a false saviour who exploited people's trust in the same way as wreckers lured ships onto rocks by lantern. Petiot had turned the survival instincts of the terrified, desperate and hunted people who sought his help against them for loot. In doing so, in hiding behind the skirts of the Resistance, the murderer brought only shame on France.

Dupin summed up for the prosecution with a flourish. He could do little else, having such a poor command of the facts. Petiot had outdone Landru, France's 'Bluebeard', who had 'only' killed 11 people, with 27 victims, although Petiot himself boasted of 63 killings. Again, Dupin repeated that the memory of the Resistance could not be stained by a creature as foul as Petiot, a pathological liar and cold-blooded killer who had concocted a 'fictional drama' to save his own skin.

Thursday 4 April, day 16, was the last day of the trial. Dupin, who had spoken for two hours previously, did so for another 90 minutes in similar vein, recounting the hideous crimes of the accused. He insisted that only the death penalty would suffice. Justice demanded that Petiot join his victims. As he sat down, Petiot remarked, 'Thank God that's over'.

Floriot opened his remarks at 3pm having drunk a glass of champagne. He would drink another halfway through a speech that went on without interruption for more than six hours. In doing so he avoided the emotion of the prosecution. He focussed only on hard facts, making no comment or plea that could not be ascertained directly from the Petiot dossier.

Everything against Petiot was false. His reputation was destroyed even before entering court, portrayed as he was by the media as a heartless fiend, obsessed with plunder. He would never have been accused at all, but for the bodies in the rue Le Sueur. Originally, the police had accused his client of over 100 murders but dropped most of them when their real murderers were caught, it was discovered they had been deported or had vanished while Petiot was in prison. Any murders the police could not pin elsewhere were dumped at Petiot's doorstep. In fact, reasoned Floriot, over 60,000 non-Jewish Parisians remained missing almost two years after the liberation. The police could easily find a connection between the accused and some of those people to frame Dr Petiot. The huge number of missing Parisians mentioned by Floriot did not help his client, having the effect of convincing the jury that the number of Petiot victims must surely have been much greater, such as the bodies in the Seine perhaps?

The police had interviewed 2,000 of Petiot's patients and not one had said anything against him. On the contrary, all stressed his dedication to them. It was political jealousy and spite that had brought Petiot to the dock.

Floriot continued to paint an exemplary view of his client as a patriot who, when war engulfed his homeland, risked his life for others, for France. He had killed only traitors. He denied killing only eight of the 27 people he was accused of murdering: Braunberger, Guschinow, Denise Hotin (possibly murdered by her own husband), Khait, the Knellers and Van Bever. If the prosecution could prove Petiot had slain even one of these people, he deserved to die.

Petiot's link with Hotin was weak. Her husband said she had gone to see him by train from their village of Neuville-Garnier outside Paris on 5 June 1942 and vanished. There is no evidence she did. She was not a patient of his. Monsieur Jean Hotin made no reference to Petiot regarding his 'missing' wife before the doctor's arrest. Indeed, her identification papers were found at his home 18 months after her disappearance. During the occupation it was extremely unlikely that anyone would leave home without papers.

Floriot had difficulty in disposing of the charges against other victims by trying to persuade the jury that clothing labels relating to victims were mis-identified and so should be discounted. He was not persuasive. So what did happen to Dr Braunberger et al? The Germans were blamed of course. Dr Braunberger and Madame Khait were Jews, probably swept up in the Holocaust. The other victims may have been liquidated by the Gestapo too or might still be alive somewhere.

Maître Floriot now turned to the 19 dead that Petiot accepted responsibility for. All, Floriot argued, were connected to the Germans. They were pimps, prostitutes, thieves and informers. The Jews proved difficult to malign but an heroic effort was made. After all, had not the Basches shared a hotel with the Italians and crossed demarcation lines seemingly at ease? He now concluded by demanding the acquittal of his patriotic client. When he finished, the court was so impressed that he was given a standing ovation.

Petiot had little to add, saying only that he was a Frenchman who had killed collaborators and that the jury would 'know what to do'. He was then taken away where he cheerily discussed oriental carpets with Floriot's assistants.

As the seven jurors, Leser and the other two magistrates deliberated, one can reflect that Floriot's brilliance and prosecution incompetence would have led to acquittal in many jurisdictions. The farcical nature of the trial itself and the comments of jurors and President Leser should have led to a mistrial. As it was, five questions had to be asked concerning each of the 27 deaths. These were:

Was each specified victim killed by Petiot?

Was there malice aforethought?

Was the killing premeditated?

Were the victim's possessions and valuables stolen?

Was the victim killed for the purpose of financial gain?

At least six votes were required to condemn on each of the 135 questions asked in total. Few doubted Petiot's guilt, but proving that Guschinow was not at that moment sipping coffee in a Buenos Aires café for example opened the door to 'reasonable doubt'. Dupin had been poor, circumstantial evidence haphazardly presented and Floriot's defence detailed and systematic. What made the difference was the sheer scale of what was presented and the figure of Petiot himself, who came across as arrogant, cocky, bullying, mocking, sarcastic and totally without remorse for the dead or pity for their families. He enjoyed being the centre of attention while relatives of the deceased wept. Petiot certainly did not come across as either a caring doctor or dyed-in-the-wool patriot. Rather he was seen as a cruel, ruthless, efficient and devious murderer who probably laughed, joked and reassured his victims up until the moment they rolled up their sleeve to receive a lethal injection.

It was 35 minutes past midnight when they jury came back. The 135 questions had been asked and answered in barely three hours, having spent an average of only 80 seconds on each question. The defendant was found not guilty of all charges in connection with Denise Hotin and not guilty of stealing or intending to steal the possessions of Madame Khait and Monsieur Van Bever. He was convicted on the remaining 126 charges, including 26 murders.

President Leser now asserted the dignity and authority of his office that had been so lacking until that point. As the courtroom remained silent and transfixed on his words, he sentenced the 49-year-old defendant to die by the guillotine. Petiot seemed unperturbed. He had enjoyed himself, amused others and seemingly cared little beyond that. As he was taken away he shouted, 'I must be avenged!' By whom and for what was not clear. The civil-suit lawyers claimed compensation on behalf of their client's families. The three magistrates gave awards, based on the victims estimated worth, ranging from 880,000 francs for Dreyfus to 10,000 for Piereschi. Surprisingly, the relatives of the Knellers and Wolffs were awarded nothing. In total, 1,970,000 francs were paid out. This was estimated to be less than 1% of the 200 million francs Petiot stole from his victims. Georgette Petiot paid half the court costs of just over 300,000 francs.

Floriot appealed his client's sentence on 13 May. It was rejected ten days later. Petiot spent his last days smoking and writing. Only Floriot and the prison's doctor and chaplain were allowed to visit. Under French law, the condemned were only allowed to know when their day of execution had arrived at 18.00 the previous evening. In Petiot's case, there were delays because 69-year-old Henri

Desfourneaux, his executioner who held the post went on strike for higher pay. Known as 'Monsieur de Paris', the executioner owned his own guillotine and claimed Allied bombing had damaged it. After the authorities agreed to pay him 65,000 francs per year to carry out executions and 10,000 to maintain his guillotine, he agreed to carry out his appointed task.

In the early hours of 25 May, just after dawn, Petiot was woken from his peaceful slumbers. He anticipated the moment, as Dr Paul Cousins, assistant to Floriot had nervously informed him the previous evening. Dupin uttered the traditional words. 'Have courage, the time has come'. Petiot swore back at him as he blearily watched the removal of his manacles and exchanged his prison uniform for the suit he had worn at the trial. He quietly wrote letters to his wife and son and spoke to Floriot. 'My friend, if anything about me is published after my death, please ask the author to include photographs of those I have been accused of killing. Then perhaps they will appear and my innocence proved'. To a rather queasy Goletty and Dupin, Petiot merrily said, 'Gentlemen, I am at your disposal'.

Petiot was offered the usual glass of rum and a cigarette, declining the former. He heard mass, though insisted his conscience was clear and signed the executioner's register. After having the nape of his neck shaved and his hands bound behind his back, Petiot was led outside and saw Madame Guillotine for the first and last time. Erected swiftly and quietly earlier that morning by Desfourneax, she stood five metres tall. The oblique blade weighed seven kilograms alone. With a 30-kilogramme weight attached, it would soon descend its well-oiled tracks and do its clinical business in a fraction of a second.

Witnesses later remarked how incredibly calm and nonchalant Petiot was. He showed not the slightest trace of fear as he lay down to expect the blade. 'Gentlemen', he shouted to the watching group of officials and lawyers, 'I ask you not to look. This will not be very pretty'.

The courtyard of La Santé prison was almost silent. The police had placed a cordon around the place. Seven years previously, the execution of German serial killer Eugene Weidmann had appalled the French authorities when citizens rushed to dip their handkerchiefs in the murderer's blood. There would be no repeat. Executions were now carried out in private.

At 5.05am the blade cleaved the head from Petiot's shoulders. At the moment of impact, a photograph secretly taken captured the expression on Petiot's face; he was smiling serenely.

CHAPTER 13
Dr Edward Pritchard: Walter Mitty

'Come back, my dear Mary Jane, don't leave your dear Edward.'

DR EDWARD PRITCHARD was apparently a 'Walter Mitty' character, who not only lived in a world of boastful fantasy but was mentally unstable, lecherous and fundamentally dishonest. He was the son of a Royal Navy captain, brother of a naval surgeon and nephew of two admirals. From an early age it was clear he would follow in his father's footsteps and those of his seafaring naval family. Born in Southsea, Hampshire in 1825, at 14 he began to train as a naval surgeon, going Surgeons and commissioned at 21 as an assistant naval surgeon aboard HMS *Hecate*, where he served for five years.

In appearance, Pritchard was almost completely bald, with heavy sideburns and a full but neatly trimmed sand-coloured beard. He was tall, handsome, with aquiline features and bright, intelligent eyes. Certainly, he was aware of the favourable impression he made on the opposite sex.

While stationed in Portsmouth he married a Scottish girl, Mary Jane Taylor, daughter of a retired Edinburgh silk merchant, by whom he would father five children. Tiring of Portsmouth, in March 1851 the family moved to Hunmanby, a small community near Filey in Yorkshire. Here, Pritchard established a practice, eventually becoming medical officer for the whole district, centred on Bridlington. Pritchard enjoyed publicity and wrote articles for local newspapers and published a couple of books on the attractions of the neighbourhood. However, he was a notorious spendthrift who quickly gained a reputation as untrustworthy and a relentless womaniser.

In Yorkshire Dr Pritchard's unctuous, incorrigible, lying and philandering character soon made his position untenable as his practice shrank and he began to neglect it. Pritchard began to seek an escape from his professional failure. Aspiring to what would, on paper, seem impressive qualifications he bought a Doctor of Medicine degree from the German University of Erlangen, in absentia, in 1857. A year later he became a Licentiate of the Society of Apothecaries in London.

A freemason, Pritchard used his membership of that organisation to advance himself wherever possible. Nevertheless, he became so unpopular in Yorkshire that he felt obliged to sell his practice in 1858, leaving a mountain of unpaid debts behind and becoming for a year the private physician to a gentleman, travelling, according to Pritchard, all over Europe in the process while his dutiful wife stayed with her children at their grandparents' home in Edinburgh.

Upon returning to England, Pritchard felt the necessity to vainly brag to all he met of his adventures, many of which seemed obviously to be mere figments of the doctor's imagination. He claimed to have 'plucked the eaglets from their eyries in the deserts of Arabia and hunted the Nubian lion in the prairies of North America' and to have risked death on the 'cannibal-infested islands' of Fiji. Profoundly self-absorbed, Pritchard bizarrely began to offer photographs of himself to all and sundry, including total strangers. He also claimed to be a 'personal friend' of Italian nationalist hero Garibaldi, whom he had never met, going so far as to carry a walking-stick engraved, 'from his friend General Garibaldi'. Applying for eminent surgery professorships, the references Pritchard used were blatant fabrications, as he claimed familiarity with distinguished members of his profession who had never even heard of him. As a result of such brazen antics, no such appointment was offered.

In 1859, Dr Pritchard moved further north, this time to Glasgow where he would be close to his wife's family and seek their financial assistance to establish his practice afresh. Such proximity to his in-laws did not inhibit Pritchard's amorous adventures and he had numerous affairs. His professional reputation suffered as he continued to exaggerate his importance to anyone who would listen. Scottish doctors of the time were proud of their well-earned and highly regarded status throughout the world of medicine and an English braggart of dubious talent and repute would hardly be welcomed with open arms. The Faculty of Physicians and Surgeons refused him membership. Unperturbed, he became a director of the Glasgow Athenaeum Club and set up a practice that grew steadily and provided him with ample opportunity to proposition his female patients. On one occasion Dr Pritchard only narrowly avoided prosecution, having made advances to the wrong woman. Alas, if his behaviour had remained merely unsavoury, two (possibly three) lives would not have been taken.

On the night of 4 May 1863 a fire broke out in the Pritchard's home at 11 Berkeley Terrace. Elizabeth McGirn, a young servant girl, died in the conflagration. Horribly burned, her arms completely consumed to the elbows, a postmortem suggested she had been unconscious in her bed and died soon after the fire started, presumably from smoke inhalation. Mrs Pritchard and her other maid were not at home. Dr Pritchard was and when a policeman knocked on his door at 3.00am on the morning of 5 May to report the glare of firelight from an attic window he answered the door fully dressed. The doctor explained that he had just been woken by the smell of smoke and was about to call out the Fire Brigade. His insurers were suspicious, particularly when Pritchard claimed for the loss of some expensive jewellery, not a trace of which was found after the blaze.

A fraudulent claim was declared. Eventually, the insurers paid out in part after a verdict of death by misadventure was returned. Pritchard did not dispute it, perhaps not wanting to draw attention to the falsity of his claim. This did not stop damage to Dr Pritchard's reputation. Rumour abounded that the dead girl had been drugged prior to death or would otherwise have been alerted by the fire. The blaze had been conveniently restricted to her room and although the authorities believed the dead girl had fallen asleep reading and the fire had commenced when the curtains caught alight from the gas jet, many had their doubts.

The inquest into the death of Miss McGirn left Dr Pritchard in the clear. It was never explained why, if the girl died reading a book as the doctor claimed, no trace of one was found at the scene or how the girl could have been overcome by smoke before she could raise the alarm. The gossip of the day suggested she was pregnant and blackmailing her employer. A hypothesis of this kind can now only be conjecture. Following his later, murderous career it is not implausible that Elizabeth McGirn was murdered and Pritchard simply got away with it.

A year after the Berkeley Terrace fire, the Pritchard's moved first to 22 Royal Crescent and, a few months later, in 1864, to a new home at 131 (now re-numbered as 249) Sauchiehall Street, adjacent to Clarence Place. The house was bought partly with money from Mrs Pritchard's parents, who paid the full £400 deposit, leaving Pritchard to pay up the £1600 mortgage. Despite his in-laws generosity Dr Pritchard remained 'up to his eyes' in debt. As he was not a gambler and by now had a lucrative practice and was known to be less than generous, the reason for this remained a mystery.

In the summer of 1864, Mrs Pritchard happened one day upon her husband kissing 15-year-old servant girl Mary MacLeod in one of the bedrooms. Miss MacLeod offered to leave the household but her mistress would have none of it, declaring her husband to be a 'nasty, dirty man'. The doctor had seduced Miss MacLeod while her mistress was staying at her parents' home during the summer of 1863. The relationship lasted some 18 months, during which she became pregnant and Dr Pritchard subsequently performed an abortion. Later she would swear Pritchard promised to marry her once his spouse passed away. Relations became strained between husband and wife following the discovery of his 'romance' and Mrs Pritchard fell ill in November that year.

Previously in excellent health, 38-year-old Mary Pritchard never had a serious illness in her life. Now she felt continuously nauseous, suffered headaches, aches, pains, was depressed and frequently bedridden. Life became even more impossible due to some pupil-apprentices of Pritchard living in their home, making the successful running of the household more arduous for Pritchard's wife.

Despite the dutiful attendance of Dr Pritchard, his wife preferred to recuperate at her parents' home in Edinburgh, a move originally resisted by her husband who believed his household 'unable to cope' without her. Mary Pritchard appeared to make a full recovery in Scotland's capital city. Unfortunately, upon returning to Glasgow on 22 December to spend Christmas with her family, having gained weight and 'eaten her parents out of house and home', she fell ill once more. Vomiting every time she ate or drank, Mrs Pritchard herself remarked how strange it was that she was 'always well in Edinburgh, always sick at home'.

On 24 November 1864 Dr Edward Pritchard had purchased an ounce of Fleming's tincture of aconite and in the following three months purchased five more. Aconite, more commonly known as wolfsbane or monkshood, is a plant extract used to treat arthritis, fever, inflammation, neuralgia and skin disease. While the pulp of the plant above ground is effective and non-toxic when diluted, its root is extremely poisonous with only a teaspoon enough to cause cardiac arrest and respiratory collapse. Eight days earlier, Dr Pritchard began to stock up on tartar emetic, containing antimony potassium tartrate. Purchasing an ounce, some 435.5 grains, Pritchard now had enough for more than 200 times the dose required as an emetic.

On 6 February, a retired doctor and cousin of Mrs Pritchard received a letter at his home in Edinburgh from Dr Pritchard expressing anxiety at his wife's deteriorating health. The following day, Dr JM Cowan visited Glasgow and prescribed a mustard poultice for her stomach, together with some champagne and ice to relieve her exhaustion. That night, Mrs Pritchard had a severe attack of cramp and demanded the attentions of another physician, Dr Gairdner.

Professor of Medicine at Glasgow University, Dr William Tennant Gairdner, was asked to examine the patient, as was Mrs Pritchard's own brother, Dr Michael Taylor, who hurried from his practice at Penrith to attend to his sister. Both were highly suspicious as to the cause of the symptoms, were unhappy at the treatment she received from Dr Cowan and wanted Mrs Pritchard removed from the house. She was too ill unfortunately and so 70-year-old Mrs Taylor, urged to do so by Dr Cowan, arrived to nurse her daughter.

Mrs Taylor found her daughter confined to bed and suffering from incessant vomiting and cramp. Assuming command of the household, Mrs Taylor shared her daughter's bed and prepared her daughter's meals. The cook, Catherine Lattimer, was dismissed by Dr Prichard a couple of days later supposedly on the grounds of 'old age' and Mary Patterson, a younger woman, engaged as her replacement.

On 16 February Mrs Taylor ate some tapioca, later found to contain antimony, and became violently sick, believing she had 'caught' the same illness as her daughter. On 24 February Mrs Taylor, who had previously been in excellent health, retired at 9.00pm. Half-an-hour later she rang a bell for Mary MacLeod to bring hot water to make her vomit as she felt desperately ill. When the maid returned she was asked by Mrs Pritchard to fetch her husband. When he entered the room, Mrs Taylor had obviously had some kind of seizure and was gripped by what her son-in-law later called 'catalepsy,' a theory Pritchard had already pro-pounded with regard to his wife. This was apparently on account of muscular cramp that affected her entire body spasmodically. Dr Gairdner had already rejected Pritchard's catalepsy theory with regard to Mrs Pritchard, believing she would recover if simply given plenty of rest.

Another physician, Dr James Paterson, Professor of Midwifery at Glasgow and a near neighbour, was asked to assist with the treatment of Mrs Taylor. Dr Paterson was convinced that the woman was under the influence of a narcotic, probably opium. Dr Pritchard stated that he thought both alcohol and opium to be the cause. No trace of alcohol was noted by Dr Paterson, who was pedantic, cautious and who rejected the suggestion of Pritchard that his mother-in-law was an incorrigible drunkard. Mrs Pritchard was still sharing the same bed as her mother and, fully conscious, witnessed her mother's sudden, shocking demise.

Dr Paterson informed Pritchard that Mrs Taylor was dying. He also took a quick look at Mary Pritchard and thought her very weak. The Englishman seemed incredulous. After Dr Paterson made Mrs Taylor and her daughter as comfortable as possible given the circumstances, he headed home around mid-night.

Mrs Taylor passed away at 1.00am on the morning of 25 February 1865. As Mary Patterson and a charwoman by the name of Mrs Nabb laid out the body, in the pocket of Mrs Taylor's dress a bottle of the opium-based 'Battley's Sedative Solution' was found. Dr Pritchard expressed shock at such a discovery he deceit-fully claimed had been intimated to him by Miss MacLeod.

Dr Paterson was asked to sign the death certificate. He refused, suspecting that the narcotics involved in Mrs Taylor's death were not self-inflicted. He wrote to the District Registrar on the 2 March that the death was 'sudden, unexpected and mysterious'. His motivation, later stated in court, was that he 'wished to save Mrs Pritchard's life, guard my professional reputation and detect the poisoner'. The District Registrar took no notice of Dr Paterson's letter and inexplicably destroyed it. Dr Pritchard, diagnosing 'apoplexy' as the cause of death, wrote the death certificate himself. He then proceeded to finish murdering his wife.

With Mrs Taylor deceased, Dr Pritchard took sole command of everything his wife ate or drank. On 13 March he gave Mary MacLeod a piece of cheese for Mrs Pritchard's supper. Perhaps suspecting at last that she was being poisoned, Mrs Pritchard offered a little to her maid who found it 'hot like pepper', burning her throat and inducing thirst. The cook tried some the following day, with the result that she not only burned her throat but suffered from cramp and had to take herself to bed for five hours. Such symptoms were consistent with those one would expect of someone suffering from acute antimony poisoning.

There was to be no respite for Mrs Pritchard. On 15 March Pritchard sent a jug of camomile tea to his wife. Drinking it, she threw up immediately. Between

10.00 and 11.00pm that night, he took her egg-flip (raw egg, sugar and whisky), to which he added some extra 'sugar'. Tasting it, the cook found it horrible, bitter and burning and vomited until 4.00am. Unperturbed by Mary Patterson's response, Dr Pritchard took the egg-flip to his wife who suffered a similar reaction.

Valiantly, Mrs Pritchard had survived some four months of her mystery illness. Her system could hold out no longer. At 7.45pm Dr Pritchard called Dr Paterson who was struck by Mrs Pritchard's wasted, sunken-eyed appearance. She told Dr Paterson that had been vomiting for days, a comment her husband passed off as 'ravings'. After explaining that his wife had not slept for five nights, Dr Pritchard was asked by his colleague to prepare a sleeping draught of chlorodyne and morphia, only to reply that he kept no drugs in the house other than chloroform and Battley's Solution. At this, Dr Paterson left. At 1.00am Mary MacLeod and the cook were summoned by Pritchard to apply a mustard poultice to his wife. Mary Patterson refused, on the grounds that her mistress was already dead. The tormented Mary Pritchard had finally passed away earlier that morning of Saturday, 18 March 1865. Pritchard cried out,'Come back, my dear Mary Jane, don't leave your dear Edward.' That same day he wrote some letters and informed the cook on returning from posting them that the ghost of his late wife had 'kissed him on the cheek' and 'bade him look after the children'. He again wrote the death certificate and this time certified the cause of death as 'gastric fever'.

It seemed obvious that the two deaths in Dr Pritchard's home had resulted from poisoning, especially when the household cook and housemaid both fell ill after eating food prepared for the late Mrs Pritchard. Hastily, the widowed doctor took his wife's body to Edinburgh for burial where a macabre incident took place. Mrs Pritchard's appalled relatives witnessed him, as the coffin was leaving for the railway station, opening the lid, kissing Mary repeatedly on the lips and expressing his boundless, heartfelt love. His 'beloved' was buried on Wednesday 22 March.

Returning to Glasgow, Dr Pritchard was arrested by a police force alerted to the possibility of murder through receipt of an anonymous letter received by Mr William Hart, Procurator-Fiscal of Lanarkshire. The letter was damning. Signed *Amor Justitae* (lover of justice), it directly accused Dr Pritchard of the double murder of Mrs Taylor and her daughter. Dr Paterson was assumed to be the author but he flatly denied all knowledge of it.

The corpses of Mrs Pritchard and her mother were exhumed and autopsied by doctors Andrew MacLagan and Henry Littlejohn. As the cause of death could not be ascertained by their appearance alone, the organs of both women were sent for chemical analysis. The body of Mrs Pritchard was laced with antimony. The stomach of Mrs Pritchard itself contained no poison, implying that the deadly agents were slowly administered over a period of time. Mrs Taylor's body showed evidence not only of antimony but also aconite and opium, all three of which were subsequently found in the bottle of Battley's Solution she imbibed on the night of her death.

Dr Pritchard expressed shock at his arrest and later, somewhat ungallantly, tried to place the blame on his recent amour, the young Mary MacLeod. Mary was also arrested but released shortly after, having agreed to testify against her employer and former lover.

*   *   *

Pritchard went on trial in Edinburgh on 3 July 1865, before the High Court of Justiciary, having expressed his innocence with enough charm, guile and sadness at his wife's demise to encourage many to believe he was genuinely innocent. Even her relatives were fooled. The trial was to prove them wrong.

In his evidence, Dr Paterson showed himself very hostile to the accused, greatly assisting the formidable prosecution team of Solicitor-General Mr George (later Lord) Young, assisted by Messrs James Arthur Crichton and Adam (later Lord) Gifford. Although he proved of great assistance to the Crown, Dr Paterson's own reputation was utterly destroyed in the process.

The defence team, Messrs David Brand, Andrew (later Lord) Rutherfurd-Clark and William (later Lord) Watson tried in vain to deflect the guilt onto Miss MacLeod. They also attempted to have the deaths of Mrs Pritchard and Mrs Taylor heard independently, believing that two acquittals would be easier to achieve than one, given their belief that not enough evidence was available to secure separate convictions. Putting all the evidence together it might be a lot easier for a jury to see the whole story and secure the conviction of their client. It was. The judges ruled that each death was intertwined with the other and, over five days, the prosecution team won their case. The vicious and cold-blooded way in which Pritchard had slain his victims provided some juicy headlines, although the trial itself was almost a procession of damning evidence.

Throughout the trial and following the publication of the autopsy results, the press were baying for Pritchard's blood. Portraying him as a 'handsome, dashing, cool and unconcerned' monster ensured the courtroom was full to bursting on every day of the trial. The evidence of Mary MacLeod proved the most salacious for the press, covering as it did her seduction, pregnancy and abortion. As she spoke a look of malice transformed the previously complacent and unworried occupant of the dock. Drs MacLagan, Littlejohn and a plethora of medical witnesses dealt a fatal blow to the defence by explaining the agony of each victim's death, in the case of Mrs Pritchard through antimony poisoning and in the instance of her mother, antimony, aconite and, from the Battley's Solution, a trace of opium. The Pritchard team could barely respond, unable, as they were to find a single medical expert to refute the evidence of the prosecution witnesses.

Dr Paterson hammered a nail into not only Pritchard's coffin, but also his own public and professional standing. Under oath, he rather haughtily declared himself convinced that Mrs Pritchard was being poisoned by antimony when he had called on her. Despite this conviction, to the astonishment of the court, Paterson declined to visit her again. She was 'not his patient' and it was 'not his duty' to do so, he obdurately and pompously stated. Rutherfurd-Clark pressed on, to be again told that Dr Paterson did not consider himself 'under obligation' to save the life of a woman being poisoned to death in a cruel and agonising manner. The court was aghast that his warped sense of ethics had allowed him knowingly to let an innocent woman die. With absolute conviction, Paterson blustered that his 'conscience was clear'. He then cast doubt on his own professional competence by obstinately insisting that opium, not antimony and aconite, had caused the death of Mrs Taylor, despite all evidence to the contrary. Eventually forced to concede that all three drugs had contributed to her death, Paterson left the stand with his reputation in tatters. Refusing to accept that his neglect and obdurate, arrogant behaviour had contributed to this state of affairs, after Pritchard was executed Dr Paterson wrote a lengthy letter, published in the *Glasgow Herald*, in which he tried to explain that his conduct was deliberately misunderstood by the Edinburgh legal establishment at the trial merely because he was a Glaswegian and thus considered inferior to his Edinburgh betters. Having dug himself into a hole, Dr Paterson had just kept digging.

Desperate to sway the jury, Rutherfurd-Clark stooped to call two of the Pritchard children to the stand to say how much their parents adored each other, how kind their father was and how much they loved him. Endearing as 14-year-old Jane Frances and her 11-year-old brother Charles Edward were, it smacked of barrel-scraping in the absence of anything concrete to exculpate his client and reverberated badly with the jury. At this point the defence, as she was the only other possible culprit, accused Mary MacLeod. The girl was still only 16 and no one believed her capable of such horrendous crimes.

When it came to making his final statement of the trial, the Solicitor-General did not have much difficulty in focusing the jury. The evidence made clear that the victims had not died of gastric fever, apoplexy, accidentally or by suicide. Murder by poison was certain and not disputed even by defence counsel. The culprit(s) could not include the children or the cook as the former had not always been there and Mary Patterson had replaced Catherine Lattimer, the original family cook, only on 16 February. Mrs Pritchard's murder, said Mr Young, was one 'in which you almost detect a doctor's finger'. It was carried out slowly, deliberately, painfully, with the sole intention of undermining the victim's constitution. One day she would be fine and then for a couple of days deteriorate. Only Mary MacLeod and Dr Pritchard were ever-present. Was it not ludicrous to suggest a servant girl had the skill to carry out such a misdeed before her medically trained employer? Only Pritchard could have carried out this foul endeavour and the cruel slaying of Mrs Taylor.

Addressing the jury, Rutherfurd-Clark began by looking at his client and stating that, were his client guilty, 'he would be the foulest man who ever lived', having cold-bloodedly murdered the loving woman who bore his children and the mother-in-law who 'idolised' him. Pritchard was not such a man. Laying it on thickly, Rutherfurd-Clark continued, 'The mind of a man can barely conceive of a wretch so devoid of human feeling in perpetrating such crimes'. He did his client no favour, as it was clear to all that Pritchard had method and means, even if motive was obscure. After all, no food or drink had passed her lips without his direct intervention.

In summing up, the Lord Justice-Clerk went over the testimony of each witness step-by-step, meticulously detailing every shred of evidence while also taking the opportunity to denounce Dr Paterson's 'lack of consideration for the rule of life' in favour of a misguided sense of professional etiquette. In concluding, he hinted strongly to the jury that the prosecution had proved its case, hinting that even if Miss MacLeod had contributed to the deaths of Mrs Taylor and Mrs Pritchard, the jury could have 'very little doubt' that Pritchard had provided and prepared the poison.

Faced with overwhelming evidence, it took only an hour's deliberation for the 15 Scottish jurors to find Dr Pritchard guilty. The judges, the Lord Justice-Clerk, Lord Glencorse, Lord Ardmillan and Lord Jerviswoode provided an experienced and formidable array of judges. Their chair, Lord Glencorse sentenced Pritchard to be hanged on the morning of 28 July, prior to which he was to be fed only on bread and water.

Dr Pritchard at first thought a reprieve possible, giving off the air of a loving husband misjudged and facing martyrdom. Seemingly devoted to his bible he anticipated a rising tide of public anger at his sentence only to find not a single person willing to lift a finger to save the egocentric and deluded murderer.

Perhaps to redeem his soul, Pritchard admitted in prison that he did indeed carry out the murders of Mrs Taylor and his wife. Malevolently, he also initially tried to implicate Miss MacLeod. Eventually, he recanted and admitted he alone carried out the deeds for which he was convicted. And what were his motives? A delegation of notaries including three clergymen, three policemen and his executioner, Calcraft, visited Pritchard at dawn on his day of execution to ascertain them. They left disappointed. So we can only speculate.

Dr Pritchard was unpopular, a sociopath and undoubtedly psychotic. Perhaps with his wife out of the way he could begin a new life with someone else. Curiously, one area that was not pressed home by the prosecution was the financial circumstances of the accused. At the time, money was considered the prime motivation, even though Pritchard, in debt to be sure, was not being pressed to repay and could probably have looked forward to continue milking the Taylor family for the foreseeable future, had Mrs Taylor lived. Perhaps he did not realise he was better off than he thought. He had insurance policies that the two banks he had overdrafts with would have accepted as security. Certainly, greed appears in retrospect to have been less significant than thought at the time, as Pritchard would not have gained from his wife or mother-in-law's deaths financially. His real motivation was possibly malice, otherwise why draw out the poisoning of his victims in such a cruel and painful way? Yet he appeared to hold no hatred for them that could possibly justify, even in his own convoluted mind, the agonising and callous treatment meted out. Perhaps he murdered to satisfy some malignant sadistic impulse or merely killed for the thrill of 'getting away with it'.

Emboldened by what appears to have been the murder of the unfortunate Elizabeth McGirn, he may have wanted to carry out a slaying that would seem, to him at least, even more 'daring'. He never did provide a reasonable explanation and took his secret to the grave with him. Perhaps he himself did not know.

Trying to appear contrite while remaining centre stage, Pritchard with his last words offered his thanks to over 40 people by name. These ranged from family and friends to the judges at his trial, although his defence team were noticeably omitted. Taken to the scaffold, Pritchard met his death with a quiet dignity that stilled the jeering mob. Vexed at being denied the right to address the crowd, Pritchard was hanged in Jail Square near Hutcheson Bridge at Glasgow Green just after 8.00am. Such was the excitement generated by the case that members of the public gathered a full 24 hours before the sentence was to be carried out. A record gathering of over 100,000 attended, and cheered, the execution of Dr Edward William Pritchard. His body was buried in the precincts of the prison in Jail Square.

In 1910 Pritchard was, in a manner of speaking, resurrected. The justiciary buildings in Jail Square were demolished. In the process the body of Pritchard was exhumed. The skeleton and skull were examined and two years later formed the basis of an article by Dr George Edington published in the *Glasgow Medical Journal*. The skull and bones were well preserved as were the clothes and a pair of elastic-sided boots Dr Pritchard wore at his execution. Eventually, their curiosity sated, the authorities quietly re-buried the remains. This time, one hoped, permanently.

CHAPTER 14
Dr Buck Ruxton: The Jigsaw Murderer

Red stains on the carpet,
Red stains on your knife,
Oh Dr Buck Ruxton you murdered your wife!
The nursemaid saw you and threatened to tell
Oh Dr Buck Ruxton you killed her as well!

JUST NORTH OF the popular Borders town of Moffat, on the morning of Sunday 29 September 1935, a vacationing Miss Susan Johnson was out for a morning stroll. Walking across a bridge on the A701 Edinburgh road over the Gardenholme Linn ravine, she happened to glance down at an unusual looking package at the side of the river flowing beneath the bridge. It seemed to contain a protruding human arm. In a state of shock, she returned to her hotel and persuaded her brother, Alfred, to investigate further. It soon emerged that a number of parcels of cloth and newspaper were in the river each containing human remains. The police were called.

One package contained two heads wrapped in a baby's romper suit. Another held 17 pieces of flesh in a sheet along with a human torso. A blouse contained four portions of flesh and two upper arms. The last was a pillowcase enveloping two thigh bones, two upper arm bones and yet more human tissue. Fingers and thumbs were found amidst the ghastly remains, all with the skin removed, as an obvious attempt at preventing identification.

From the state of decomposition of the remains, it was clear that the packages had been placed in the river only recently. As the murderer had made strenuous attempts at disguising the identity of the victims, they must have been originally placed elsewhere. Heavy rain had caused flash floods in the River Annan and Rushholme Linn on the 18 and 19 September, throwing the parcels and other body parts discovered later onto the riverbanks. The police could focus on tracing people who had disappeared before 18 September. A stroke of luck soon enabled them to direct their attention much more narrowly.

Over the next few weeks a plethora of body parts were found, including a pelvis, left thigh, left forearm and hand, a left foot and finally, on 4 November, a right forearm. Three female breasts, a uterus and exterior female sex organs revealed the gender of the dismembered. All were sent to Edinburgh University to be analysed by James Couper Brash, Professor of Anatomy, Sydney Smith, Professor of Forensic Medicine and John Glaister, Professor of Forensic Medicine, Glasgow University, from whence he was co-opted. The rotting state of the human debris, infested with maggots and in a state of partial decomposition, helped to pin down the infamous day when the murders occurred.

All obvious identifying marks had been deliberately obliterated, including facial features, fingertips, scars and sex organs. Teeth had been wrenched from the two skulls. It appeared that one victim was male, around five feet, six inches in height, the other was female, some five inches shorter. Re-examination on finding the third breast proved conclusively that the 'male' skull belonged to a heavily built woman. The bones and teeth showed the corpses to be around 20 and 35-45 years old respectively. Such accuracy would greatly help to convict the killer, the victims being, in fact, 20 and 34 years old. It was what the pathologists did not find that aided identification. Prominent birthmarks and scars, known to be on the victims, were removed from the remains. Why, if not to obscure marks unique to two specific individuals?

Part of a bed sheet, a seemingly innocuous find amongst myriad remains, would later prove decisive in securing the conviction of the culprit. Meanwhile another piece of evidence was to prove invaluable in finding out just who the perpetrator was. With the cadavers were parts of the *Sunday Graphic* from 15 September 1935. This publication helped the police immensely, as its circulation was confined to Lancaster in north-west England. Enquiries soon revealed that a woman by the name of Mary Rogerson had recently vanished. Mary was a 19-year-old nursemaid who worked for a Dr Buck Ruxton, a local GP. The suspicions of the police were soon aroused when they discovered that Dr Ruxton's wife had, he claimed, recently left him.

Dr Ruxton was 36, Indian by birth and had anglicised his name from Bukhtyar Ruttomji Ratanji Hakim. He was the scion of a rich Parsee family in Bombay and first moved to England to study medicine. Returning to India, Ruxton qualified as a Batchelor of Surgery, becoming an officer in the Indian Medical Corps, serving in Iraq. After leaving the service, Ruxton graduated in London as a Batchelor of Medicine, moving to Scotland where he failed the examination to become a Fellow of the Royal College of Surgeons in Edinburgh. It was in Edinburgh in 1927 that Ruxton met his future common-law wife, Isabella Van Ess, the divorced wife of a Dutch sailor she had married at 18. Born Isabella Kerr, the future Mrs Ruxton managed a restaurant her future husband frequented. She was 26, he 28 when they met. From 1928, they lived together in London before moving to Lancaster in 1930. It did not appear to be a happy 'marriage'. Dr Ruxton, who had a legal wife in India, had participated in a pseudo-marriage ceremony with Isabella. Perhaps because he was insecure in this aspect of his relationship with her, it intensified feelings of violent jealousy. He was prone to hurling threats and abuse to such an extent that on two occasions police were called to his house. He continually suspected Isabella of having affairs and took to following her, after which a confrontation usually took place. As his behaviour became more unusual, even friends stated that Dr Ruxton occasionally 'lost control' and became 'unbalanced'.

Mary Rogerson, a petite girl of 18 when she entered her doctor's employ, was nanny to Isabella's daughter Elizabeth Kathleen. Cheerful in disposition, she stayed with the Ruxtons despite the comings and goings of other household staff, the endless arguments between Mr and Mrs Ruxton and her pitifully low wages. She wrote constantly to her parents in Morecambe and when her letters stopped after her disappearance, it prompted police to suspect the worst.

The Ruxtons lived at 2 Dalton Square, Lancaster, in a house with a ground floor, two upper floors a basement and back yard. Outside, it was painted a rather florid green and red, inside green and yellow. It stood out like a sore thumb from the rather drab homes in the neighbourhood. Dr Ruxton was vain, egocentric, bombastic and self-assured. While superficially charming, it did not take much for him to explode with anger, especially where Isabella was concerned. As for his 'wife' she was plain and physically unattractive for which she compensated by way of an outrageously flirtatious nature.

The relationship was an explosive mismatch. Neighbours often complained of the racket the Ruxtons made during their frequent screaming matches. To make matters worse, Isabella found Ruxton's jealousy to be both passionate and exciting. She deliberately picked arguments with her 'husband', goaded and teased him in order to enjoy the delirium of 'making up'. Clearly, 'Mrs Ruxton' was playing an increasingly dangerous game. The doctor did not appreciate being toyed with and in front of numerous witnesses, verbally abused his spouse and sometimes assaulted her when not threatening to kill her with knives, a revolver he kept in the house, or using his bare hands. Comments like, 'She will not come back alive' and 'she will end up in the mortuary' were often uttered and heard. They loved and loathed each other in seemingly equal measure. Eventually, Isabella Ruxton became tired of the abuse she endured and her husband's relentless possessiveness. She wanted to return to Edinburgh.

By late 1931, the Ruxtons were living apart in the same house, sleeping in separate bedrooms on the upper floor. Their children were with their mother and Mary Rogerson occupied a third bedroom. Downstairs Dr Ruxton held his surgeries and had a waiting room for patients. At around that time a telegraph arrived from Ruxton at the home of Mrs Jeanie Nelson, Isabella's widowed sister, informing her that Isabella had tried to gas herself. Arriving in Lancaster Isabella told her sister that what Ruxton considered to be a suicide attempt was actually 'accidental'. Ruxton, furious at this suggestion struck his bed-ridden wife and demanded that she 'tell the truth'. After being aggressively and continually harangued for some time, Isabella, who stuck by her rather unlikely story, asked Mrs Nelson in exasperation to take her and the children back to Edinburgh. At this understandable suggestion, Ruxton threatened that, should they leave he would 'cut the throats of the lot of them'. The following day he had mellowed, Isabella went to Edinburgh with the children and returned to her husband soon after.

In 1934 Isabella appeared at the door of Mrs Nelson in Edinburgh exclaiming that this time she would 'not be going back' to Lancaster, a town she was bored with and had learned to despise along with her husband. The children were not with her and Dr Ruxton soon came in pursuit. He pleaded that he would be ruined without her and the children needed their mother. Regrettably, in view of what would happen the following year, Isabella did go back.

On Saturday 14 September 1935, Isabella Ruxton drove to Blackpool to meet her sisters, Jeanie Nelson and Eileen Madden and see the illuminations. After a meal, Isabella left her siblings at 11.30pm to begin the 20-mile journey back to Lancaster. She was last seen alive outside her home in Dalton Square a short time later. What happened to Mrs Ruxton after returning home and being confronted by her volcanic, temperamental and uncontrollably jealous husband can only now be conjecture. With certainty, a ferocious argument ensued that claimed the lives of two people.

Perhaps this time Dr Ruxton lost all vestiges of self-control? Possibly his wife mocked him once too many times, only there would be no rage followed by calm soothing words? Furiously, Ruxton undoubtedly assaulted his wife, halting her screams by squeezing the life from her. He had threatened murder before. Here was a promise fulfilled. And what of young Mary Rogerson? The shouting, threats and screams she had heard countless times before? What made this occasion different? Did silence fall suddenly, prompting her to check on her mistress? Or was it that she came upon the soon to be lifeless body of Isabella while Ruxton was in the last throes of her murder? What is now certain is that Mary witnessed the scene of a crime Dr Ruxton wanted no one to know of, then or ever.

It must have crystallised in the mind of Dr Ruxton then and there that, were Mary Rogerson to live, the hangman's noose would soon be round his neck. She must have realised it too. Attempting to flee the scene, the hapless and innocent young Mary was brutally slain, her head mashed to a pulp by a heavy blunt instrument. Senseless but alive, she was soon finished off by her now frenzied employer who viciously stabbed her to death.

The three Ruxton children, Elizabeth (six), Diane (four) and two-year-old Billie slept through the carnage. For Dr Ruxton himself, he had to restore the scene of death to normality and make the bodies disappear. Throughout the night the murderer laboured feverishly, with only a two-inch scalpel blade to help him render the two women with whom he shared a home into shapeless chunks of meat. Dismemberment took place in both his bedroom and the bathroom and work continued well into morning. Throughout the ghastly task, Ruxton, whatever else went through his mind, was gripped by a strong survival instinct that ensured a considerable element of cool thinking and full utilisation of acquired surgical skills and training. Any identifiable marks or features on either body the doctor sought to brutally erase. Gouging out her eyes obliterated an eye defect that Mary Rogerson had and Isabella, the woman whom he once professed he 'could not live without', was vilely mutilated. Slicing open her breasts, sex organs and cutting flesh from her calves, he tore 14 teeth from her head with pliers to ensure that her skull, if found, would not be identified from dental records.

Such slaughter was bound to leave its mark. When Ruxton finished his horrific night's work, the house was awash with blood, resembling more an abattoir than a family home. Ruxton himself provided some of it, having cut himself deeply while engaged in the destruction of his victims. Before trying to clean the bloodstains, Ruxton drained the human debris of blood as best he could and took it into the bedroom. He had to be quick – signs of his butchery would be evident to Mrs Agnes Oxley, his charwoman, destined to arrive at 7.15am.

It may have been a Sunday, but Dr Ruxton liked his char to clean for him day-in and day-out. That morning he realised that the Herculean task of cleaning the house had to be carried out by him alone. To head Mrs Oxley off at the pass, he first locked his sleeping children in their room and then hurried to the Oxley home. Arriving at 6.30am Ruxton told a bleary-eyed Mr George Oxley that the services of his wife would not be required as his wife and Mary had gone to Edinburgh on holiday and he would take the children to Morecambe for the day. The following day, Mrs Oxley was to call as usual. Both the Oxleys were surprised at Ruxton's appearance. He had never called that early, nor asked Mrs Oxley not to call and she had never missed a day in his employ.

Back home, Ruxton had to work strenuously, feverishly, to clean the house. Was he sane? Panicking? Methodical? Who can say? Whatever his state of mind, his instinct for self-preservation ensured that no matter how exhausted or traumatised by the deeds of the previous few hours, he stuck to the job of meticulously scrubbing away the despoliation that had gone before.

It was to be a quite frantic morning for Dr Ruxton. First of all Miss Winnie Roberts called to deliver the Sunday papers and collect two-weeks money. After ringing the bell for several minutes, a rather dishevelled and agitated Dr Ruxton answered the door, explaining that his wife and maid were in Scotland. An hour later Mrs Margaret Hindson arrived and delivered four pints of milk. This time he said that Isabella and Mary had left with the children, a different story from that he told Miss Roberts. Miss Hindson always put the milk in the scullery but this time was asked to place it on the hall table. No doubt with his nerves now badly frayed, Dr Ruxton was again disturbed only 15 minutes later. Mr John

Partridge, from another newsagent, called to deliver the *Sunday Graphic*. Receiving no answer, he pushed the newspaper under the door.

After these interruptions, Ruxton drove to two garages in succession, where he purchased four gallons of petrol from each. He thought he was unknown at either, yet everyone knew him. In those days, Asians were few and far between and a doctor from India would be familiar to all in such a relatively small town. Back at the house, Mrs Isabella Whiteside, her son Ronald and friend Mrs Gilbert arrived for an appointment at which Dr Ruxton was to operate on Ronald's foot. Dr Ruxton apologised. He could not do the operation as his wife was in Edinburgh and he only had his maid to help lift the heavy carpets in expectation of the decorators arriving the following morning. Once again, he offered a different explanation that day for the absence of his wife and maid.

Removing his children from the house to enable a further clean up, Dr Ruxton took them to the home of a dentist friend, Herbert Anderson. Mr Anderson was told that, 'Isabella and Mary had gone away for a few days'. Anderson noticed that Ruxton's hand was bandaged. Taking a look at it he noticed the wound was 'cut clean through to the bone.' Ruxton claimed it was the result of a slice from a tin opener.

For a further four hours, Ruxton struggled to clean the house. The task before him was a monumental one; he decided to call in some help. The woman asked, Mrs Mary Hampshire, had been a Ruxton patient since he moved to Lancaster. She had never worked for him before. He told her he needed help having cut his hand. To explain why the two women of the household could not assist, he said, 'Isabella is in Blackpool and Mary is on holiday'. He was obviously not thinking straight and was inadvertently sowing the seeds of his own downfall.

Arriving at 2 Dalton Square, Mrs Hampshire was taken aback by the scale of the task before her. The bath was stained a heavy yellow colour and, try as she might, she just could not get the stains out. Reluctantly, Ruxton agreed to let Mr Hampshire assist. While the Hampshires were cleaning the house beyond the rooms where the hunks of meat and bone of his victims were secreted, Ruxton collected his children.

Mrs Hampshire took the opportunity presented by her employer's absence to look around the house. She saw straw peeking out from beneath the door of the locked bedroom and tried to clear it up without success. Going into the yard, she saw carpets stained with blood, one very heavily. A bloodstained shirt and towels partially burned with petrol were also found.

Ruxton was relieved when the Andersons agreed to let the children stay overnight. Driving home to collect their nightclothes with Mrs Anderson in the car, he stopped off at the home of Mary Rogerson's parents in Morecambe. They were not in. Their lodger, Mr William Risby, was informed that Mary had gone to Scotland on holiday, Ruxton having given her wages to her sister.

Arriving home, Ruxton offered the Hampshires a suit and some carpets he kept in his waiting room free of charge. They were happy to accept but shocked when they saw the extent of the bloodstains on the jacket. 'It was from my cut hand', Ruxton explained. It was now after 7.00pm. As the Hampshires worked on until 9.30, Ruxton left them the keys and headed back to Morecambe. On the way he asked Mrs Anderson to buy 2lb of cotton wool on his behalf, possibly to absorb blood from the bodies. Amazingly, considering recent events, Ruxton then took Mrs Anderson and his two oldest children to see the Blackpool illuminations. After he dropped them off at 9.30pm. Dr Ruxton was not seen again until the following morning.

It is only conjecture now, but Ruxton, still full of adrenalin and the urge to cover up his misdeeds, may have taken the opportunity to head for Moffat, a hundred or so miles to the north, where he dumped the body parts that had been concealed in his home.

The following morning, Mrs Oxley arrived for work a few minutes early to find no one at the Ruxton residence. After waiting a while she went home. At 9.00am the Hampshires were astonished to see the usually immaculate Dr Ruxton career into their home unshaven and unkempt without so much as a knock on the door. Declaring he had not slept and was ill because his hand was infected, Ruxton tried to persuade the Hampshires to give him back the suit for 'cleaning'. Failing to convince them to hand over a valuable suit they might not see again, Ruxton demanded that his name tag be cut from the suit and immediately burnt before his eyes. Alarmed at his odd behaviour, Mrs Hampshire suggested Mrs Ruxton be recalled from holiday to look after him. Ruxton did not want to interrupt her break and asked Mrs Hampshire to help him herself. She agreed.

At 2 Dalton Square, Mrs Oxley was waiting. She noticed the hall light was on, thinking it strange that someone should leave it on in broad daylight. She immediately surmised that no one had been home the previous night. Mrs Oxley cleaned the house apart from the locked bedroom. After carrying out her duties, she left just after noon. Mrs Hampshire arrived soon after, whereupon noticing that Mrs Oxley had cleaned the house already, remarked that there was nothing for her to do. Ruxton replied, 'You are here to give me courage'. Such an unusual response should perhaps have set Mrs Hampshire thinking. She had in her possession three carpets, one of which was soiled with so much congealed blood it could not be washed out. She had Ruxton's suit, with a waistcoat so bloodstained it was ruined; Ruxton had turned up dishevelled and distraught at her house and the women of the house were nowhere to be seen. Her suspicions were not of murder, but she knew something was amiss. Ruxton told her his wife was in London. 'You are not telling the truth doctor', Mrs Hampshire announced. Shocked, Ruxton made up a story about his wife leaving him. 'I'm the unhappiest man in the world. My wife has left me for another. I could forgive extravagance but never infidelity.' He burst into tears. Comforted by Mrs Hampshire, Ruxton eventually pulled himself together and treated some patients.

That day, Monday 16 September, the refuse collectors called. Dr Ruxton asked the crew of five to remove the rubbish in his yard and clear it up afterwards. Included was a bloodstained, partially burnt shirt, loads of charred debris, bloodstained carpets, a hamper of straw, a blue silk dress and some oilcloth. Mrs Hampshire arrived to claim the carpets, bloodstained or not.

That night Dr Ruxton put his car in for servicing. His Hillman was too small for the job he had in mind. A four-seat Austin was the very dab. On the way home he met Mr Robert (Bobby) Edmondson, a friend of the family and for some reason needlessly told him Isabella and Mary were on holiday in Scotland with the children and had gone there in his Hillman. That night Ruxton slept at home. The next day he was involved in a car accident with a cyclist, Mr Bernard Beattie, in Kendal, 20 miles north of Lancaster, while heading south. Ruxton sped away from the scene of the accident, leaving Mr Beattie to nurse some minor injuries. Taking the number of the car, Mr Beattie contacted the police and Constable James Lowther stopped Dr Ruxton at Milnthorpe, seven miles further south. On being cautioned, Ruxton became almost hysterical, claiming he visited Carlisle, 67 miles north of Lancaster, on business. Seen dropping his older children off at school at 9.00am that morning, he would have had little time to conduct it, given the condition of the roads in 1935 and the car he was driving. He would, however, have had time to drive a few miles north of Carlisle, over the border to Moffat. Shockingly, if disposing of more body parts, he would have had his youngest child Billie with him.

That night Ruxton lit a huge fire in his yard. No one knows what was burned, but it blazed on brightly for hours. One can only assume that bedding, straw and other incriminating evidence was incinerated. Despite the fire being seen by half the town, Ruxton later denied ever lighting it that evening. He also claimed his children stayed with him that night while the Andersons stated that they were with them and collected only the following morning.

As the week wore on, a Mrs Mabel Smith, another char who worked part-time and Mrs Curwen, a full-time cook taken ill the day before the murders, came to work and noticed the huge changes to the house that had transpired over recent days. Bloodstains were found in numerous locations and when bloodstained curtains were pointed out to their employer, he burned the offending parts, asked them to use the remainder as cleaning rags and joked that he would 'now be a suspect in the murder of Mrs Smalley', a woman recently found dead in Morecambe. That afternoon he returned the Austin and picked up his now serviced Hillman.

The following day, Mrs Oxley saw Ruxton move several heavy bags from the previously locked bedroom downstairs into his car. In retrospect, it seems the bags contained the last of the bloody remains Dr Ruxton had been distributing near Moffat over the past few days. Why over several days? The sheer bulk of the two dissected corpses and the packaging in they were wrapped in made one trip virtually impossible. He had to get rid of them piece by piece and quickly, before the smell of rotting flesh pervaded the entire house. That day, he set off at 8.00am, ostensibly to see a specialist about his hand, intending to return for his surgery at 3.00pm. Thus, Ruxton had plenty of time to drive nervously to Moffat. Would he escape detection? Could he get away with his mission, unseen and undiscovered?

In Dr Ruxton's absence, his servants noticed that the previously locked room was now unlocked and a foul stench pervaded the landing and upper floor. The charred remains of three travelling cases and bloodstained cotton were also discovered. Curious they may have been but, despite the bloodstained clothes carpets and curtains, the fires, smell, sudden disappearance of two women, Ruxton's behaviour and the well-known history of threats and violence between the doctor and his wife, as yet no one suspected anything untoward.

That evening another blaze lit up Ruxton's yard. It was the belongings of his wife and maid now being torched, probably so he could make their disappearance seem more plausible if it appeared they had taken their belongings with them. For three hours the bonfire crackled. As the last embers were flickering, Ruxton received a call from midwife Miss Beryl Beckett, requiring his urgent assistance. Inexplicably, he told her he could not come, having hurt his hand in his car, a pointless lie that deviated from explanations given before to others. When she called on him the following morning, he fled from the room in yet another display of irrational behaviour.

The trying week now drew to a close. It was Friday. Mrs Curwen complained about the pervasive smell in the house and was asked to buy some cologne spray to conceal it. Bobby Edmondson passed by and saw Ruxton's Hillman. Ruxton casually told him his wife was in London with her sister. Possibly with his mind foggy at the traumas, frequent deceptions and panic that had gripped him that week, the doctor forgot that he had told Edmondson Isabella was in Edinburgh, having travelled in the car now obviously in situ outside 2 Dalton Square. Had she driven from Edinburgh just to head straight for London by train? It seemed unlikely. Visiting a patient and friend of Miss Rogerson, Miss Bessie Philbrook, he mentioned that Mrs Ruxton had taken young Mary to Scotland to arrange an illegal abortion. This showed the depths to which he had sunk and also the thought given to explaining her disappearance. With abortion being socially unacceptable, he may have assumed it would stop further enquiries about Mary's whereabouts. The opposite was the case and rumour and gossip circulated. Isabella was even suspected of having a lesbian affair with Bobby's sister Barbara with whom Mrs Ruxton, who had thick ankles and masculine looks, was known to be 'close'.

The hearsay about his wife, reported sightings of her and Bobby and tittle-tattle regarding their alleged liaisons must have driven the already near-demented Ruxton to the brink of a complete breakdown. Nevertheless, he struggled on. Miss Philbrook agreed to baby-sit the Ruxton children in the absence of her friend. As she did so, Mary's brother Peter Rogerson called at the house to enquire after his sister. Returning home, Ruxton said rather curtly, 'He is only after her wages'.

By 23 September it looked now to Ruxton that he had 'got away with it'. His phrenetic activity appeared to have paid off. Occasionally, the odd event triggered a question in the mind of someone who visited or worked in Dalton Square, such as when Mrs Smith found a nightgown with a huge bloodstain on the shoulder in the linen basket. Of course, the police would soon ask questions and when Mrs Smith intimated that they had called her in for an interview, Ruxton temporarily lost control, ranting and raving in front of her, Mrs Oxley and Mrs Curwen. Regaining his composure, later that evening he allowed Peter Rogerson into the house and explained his sister was in Scotland with the mistress of the house 'for a week or two on holiday'. Ruxton expressed surprise that Mary had not told her brother. He was even more surprised, it seemed, when Rogerson informed him he had since heard nothing from her. At night, Ruxton rounded off a tiring day with a trip to see Clive of India at the cinema. If he was a man with a troubled conscience it did not show.

The lack of contact with his wife began to 'worry' Ruxton. Suspecting that he was the subject of local rumourmongers, Ruxton visited the town hall on the afternoon of 24 September to complain that he was the subject of malicious gossip. Ironically he burst in on Inspector John Moffat in a state of near hysteria and accused all and sundry of asserting that he had killed the aforementioned Mrs Smalley. Ruxton had taken Moffat so unawares that the inspector could not begin to write down his haverings. The best he could do was calm the doctor and explain that he was neither under suspicion nor would the police want to interview him in connection with the Smalley case. Of course, Moffat did recall soon after that Ruxton had said a number of rather odd things; mentioning that his carpets had been uplifted, that the police could search his house and that his wife had left him a note before vanishing, a note that Ruxton could not then or later produce.

The next day Ruxton again visited the police, this time he was more circumspect but mentioned the Smalley case again. Trying to be too clever, Ruxton thought he could double-bluff the police. If they investigated him for the Smalley case, for which he undoubtedly had a cast-iron alibi and no connection, he assumed that any rumours that subsequently emerged regarding Isabella and

Mary would be quickly discounted. He was to be sadly disappointed. As has happened in countless murders, drawing attention to oneself only creates more interest and the gamble Ruxton was taking was not going to pay off.

The Rogersons soon had their daughter's employer at their door. He informed them of Mary's 'pregnancy', a mythical 'laundry boy' being announced as the putative father and cause of her flight from scandal. He even told them he had declared Mary to be pregnant in the presence of Mrs Anderson, something she strenuously denied later in court. The Rogersons were dubious in the extreme. Who was the 'father', where did he live and why had they not heard of such a liaison before? Mary was a quiet girl and when Ruxton implied that she was living it up in a fancy hotel in Edinburgh with Isabella, the whole story seemed too preposterous to be believed. Struggling to retain credibility, when Mr Rogerson said he would report her disappearance to the police, Ruxton dissuaded him by saying he would return her 'safe and sound' on Sunday. Raising the dead was beyond Ruxton's talents as he well knew, and the hole which he was digging for himself continued to deepen.

Sunday came and Mary unsurprisingly did not re-appear. That very day the first body parts were found in Moffat, causing headline news around the UK the following day. As Mrs Oxley cleaned the house as usual, Ruxton read of the discovery in bed. He was laughing and excitedly called Mrs Oxley to his bedside. Reading aloud, he declared that a man and a woman had been found, or so the police believed at the time (the third breast still awaited discovery), and Ruxton declared, 'It could not be our two'. Relieved, he was ecstatic in believing that, despite their discovery, the authorities in Scotland's initial belief that they had found the remains of a couple would put them off the scent and leave him off the hook. It was not to be.

On the first day of October the Rogersons, refusing to be placated by Ruxton's feeble stalling – the most recent story being that the wayward women had robbed his safe of '30 or 40 pounds' and would return when it was spent – went to the police. After a few days of contemplation, Ruxton reported his wife missing on 4 October. Detective Constable John Winstanley called at his home and sat while Ruxton poured invective on his 'callous' wife who had abandoned her children and did not have the consideration to bother sending even a postcard to tell her worried spouse of her whereabouts. Becoming excited, Ruxton accused Mr Edmondson of having an affair with Isabella; of knowing of her whereabouts and demanded the police intercept his letters. Ruxton then suggested the constable search his home to prove he was innocent in the Smalley case, the murder he continually harped on about. The constable became more and more exasperated as Ruxton went on and on making ludicrous accusations about his wife's behaviour. She had kept photographs of herself and Bobby Edmondson together under his mattress, not her own in her own room and he had asked the post office to keep a record of calls from his house to Edmondson's after he had heard 'silly love talk' on the line.

On Saturday 5 October, Ruxton called at Bobby Edmondson's home. His father, Robert, explained his son was in Edinburgh. A stoke of luck, thought Ruxton explaining, 'It could only be with Isabella'. Bobby arrived home that day and with his father visited Ruxton to sort out the 'misunderstanding'. After confronting the doctor and asking if he was accusing him of involvement in Isabella's disappearance, Ruxton backed down immediately and was warned to stop slandering him. Eventually the three men shook hands and parted amicably but Ruxton then visited an acquaintance, Mr Thomas Harrison and asked him to tell Bobby Edmondson to, 'keep away from my wife'.

Deeper and deeper Ruxton dug himself into his pit of lies as reality drifted further and further from view. He wrote a convoluted letter to Mrs Nelson in Edinburgh asking if Isabella had decamped there, reminding her that it was not the first time she had gone missing. Accusations were made of gambling debts left behind by Mrs Ruxton and that the last he heard she was in Birmingham. Of course, while written in the accusative, the letter was fulsome in its declarations of love for a woman who, despite having 'heartlessly' left him and the children in the lurch, still kept a special place in his heart.

Police enquiries revealed no train tickets had been bought and there were no sightings of the two women anywhere. They had apparently vanished into thin air. Soon however the pieces of the jigsaw would fall neatly into place.

The discovery of the *Sunday Graphic* of 15 September, no doubt the very copy shoved under Ruxton's front door the morning he spent frantically cleaning up evidence of the bloodbath in his home, compelled the authorities to concentrate their investigations as to the identity of the victims in the vicinity of Lancaster. Narrowing the search even further, the publishers confirmed that only 3,000 copies of that edition had been printed. It was a 'slip' edition, meaning that, by switching a particular plate during printing, a publisher could slip in stories of interest only to the local, rather than general readership. That slip edition carried news of a beauty pageant in Morecambe and only there and in Lancaster had it been distributed.

The Chief Constable of Dumfries liased closely with his Lancashire counterpart and ensured that photographs of clothing found with the remains were printed in northern English newspapers. Mrs Rogerson immediately identified the clothes as belonging to her young daughter Mary.

The net was closing in as Ruxton determinedly continued with the charade. He planned a trip to seek his errant wife in Edinburgh. On 9 October, the very day that Mrs Rogerson contacted the police, he asked Mrs Curwen to empty his wife's wardrobe of her clothes, or rather those he had not burnt, to take the best to her. They were packed in a suitcase and the rest, along with Mary's, offered to the staff, although he had no right to give away his maid's clothes, even if she was not coming back. As for his wife's, why would he give her clothes away if she was returning? Leaving the house for the station, Ruxton was reminded by Mrs Curwen that he had forgotten his wife's suitcase. 'I can't be bothered with it', he replied, clearly in a confused state of mind.

By the time Ruxton arrived at the Edinburgh home of Mrs Trench, sister of Isabella and Mrs Nelson, the latter had read about the Moffat discovery. It was now known that the body parts were confirmed as belonging to two women. She asked Ruxton if he had 'done anything to them'. Immediately rebuffed by a man who declared only undying love for his lost wife, she then had to endure hours of Ruxton's meandering talk about the missing women during which he made the usual accusations and suppositions. After several hours he left asking both women to 'say nothing' if questions were asked.

Arriving at Lancaster Castle railway station at 3.50am on Tuesday, 10 October, Dr Ruxton was stunned to see Inspector Thomas Clark meeting the train. It was normal procedure for an inspector to meet all early hour trains at Lancaster but Ruxton did not know that, panicked and began babbling to the inspector. He informed the officer that he had been in Edinburgh to ascertain the whereabouts of his wife, accused Bobby Edmondson of knowing where Mrs Ruxton was and then scurried off home. A few hours later he barged into the Hampshire's home and asked about the bloodstained suit and carpets. Advised by Mrs Hampshire that the suit and one of the carpets were still stained, he begged her to 'burn them' and told her he would make a statement to the police. That night he duly did but first of all he demanded of the duty constable Detective Winstanley that he act to 'stop the talk' he decried was ruining his practice. The constable responded that he had no power over the press but accepted a statement that described the missing Isabella, confirmed her date of disappearance as 15 September and accompanied the doctor home to obtain her photograph.

The behaviour of Ruxton had been noticeably odd in recent weeks and he continued to do all he could, inadvertently of course, to draw attention to himself and, ultimately, put a noose around his neck. On 11 October he wrote a note of his 'movements' and handed them to Detective Sergeant Walter Stainton. The sergeant knew Ruxton of old, having visited his house five and 18 months previously following threats he made, overheard by Stainton, to murder his wife. Wearily, the sergeant listened to a typical paranoid tirade in which Ruxton demanded that he be 'accused directly of the Moffat murder' and asked preposterously for 'a dead baby to be put on my doorstep so I can be accused of killing it'. Repeating that rumours were ruining his practice and giving a long unprompted explanation of how he injured his hand, Ruxton was stopped in mid-rant when asked if he had given away any carpets. He had, as the carpets were worn.

Twice more on 11 October Ruxton visited the police. Once to give Captain Henry Vann permission to publish a photograph of Mrs Ruxton and later to remonstrate over a story in the *Daily Express*, a copy of which was then flashed at the officer. The story merely described the find and the state of the Moffat remains. Ruxton declared that the teeth of Mary and Isabella 'in no way' resemble the Moffat assemblage. He demanded that the captain publish a statement that there was no connection between the Moffat remains and the two women missing from the Ruxton household. Vann replied that he would, only 'if it was proven that was the case'.

Thursday 12 October saw a panic-stricken Dr Ruxton scurrying around Lancaster and Morecambe talking to a whole array of people from the Anderson's servant to Arthur Howson, his hairdresser, to Frank Eason, his decorator. To all he alluded that 'they' were out to get him for the murder of Isabella, Mary and that old chestnut, Mrs Smalley. He even had the gall to quiz Mary's father on her dental history before returning to his surgery to meet a *News of the World* reporter. He handed over a letter that was to be opened only in the event of his death or handed back unopened if arrested, tried and acquitted. The request was honoured.

The police could not but act upon the rather outlandish conduct of Dr Buck Ruxton. His arrest was inevitable. At 9.30pm that evening, Ruxton went to the police station and 'helped the police with their enquiries' until 7.20am the following morning. Specifically, the doctor was asked to retrace the events of 14-30 September in detail. After dictating and signing a statement, Ruxton was charged with the murder of Mary Rogerson, a charge he immediately repudiated. Remanded in custody, on 5 November he was further charged with the murder of his wife.

Ruxton urged the police to thoroughly search what he hoped was a house now 'cleansed' of any evidence. They took up his invite. After tearing up the floorboards and inspecting the plumbing, their hunt proved much more productive than Ruxton had anticipated. The police quickly found evidence of human fat in the drains and numerous bloodstains everywhere. Although charged with two murders, the Crown tried him only for the killing of his wife, for which they had stronger forensic evidence. Had he been acquitted of Isabella's murder, he could subsequently have been tried for the homicide of Mary Rogerson.

Described in the press as a 'Mohammedan of mixed French and Indian blood', Ruxton would provide an exotic distraction to the media, who nicknamed him: 'The Jigsaw Murderer'. His history was investigated and he was found, on a positive note, to have a pleasant bedside manner, with numerous patients grateful for the skills he used to treat them and the modest fees he charged. They rallied round and scores of them wrote letters to the authorities and to Ruxton himself declaring their belief in his innocence. Many believed he was the scapegoat of a conspiracy by other Lancaster doctors, jealous of Ruxton's popularity. Ruxton urged his patients to stick by him, appealing for them to, 'Stay loyal in my hour of trouble. I am an innocent victim of circumstance. Please do not leave my panel or private list'.

* * *

The trial began at Manchester Assizes on Monday, 2 March 1936 before Mr Justice Singleton. The case for the Crown was led by Mr JC Jackson assisted by Mr Maxwell Fyfe KC (later Lord Kilmuir) and Mr Hartley Shawcross (later Lord Shawcross), who also became Attorney General and served with distinction on the prosecution benches of the Nuremberg war crimes trials. Mr Norman Birkett KC defended Ruxton.

Reading this case so far, one might be forgiven for concluding that the conviction of the erratic Dr Ruxton would be a foregone conclusion. That was not the situation. The burden of proof remained with the Crown and they had to prove not only the identity of the bodies found at Moffat but that Ruxton had killed and dismembered them at 2 Dalton Square.

In opening for the Crown, Mr Jackson described the horribly mutilated finds at Moffat, the violent deaths of Isabella and Mary, the copious quantities of blood left from their brutal dismemberment and the callousness and cowardice of their murderer, Dr Buck Ruxton. Prosecution evidence was so voluminous that Jackson called 113 witnesses who took eight-and-a-half days to testify. The only defence witness was Ruxton himself.

Identification of the bodies was a lot easier that might be supposed from their condition when found. Despite the slicing off of some fingertips, others inexplicably remained to provide fingerprint evidence. Clothing fragments belonging to the missing women were found on the bodies and easily identified. Professor Brash of Edinburgh University had used skull reconstruction, then still in its infancy, to build a picture of how the victims would have looked when alive. He also took photographs of the skulls and compared one to a photograph of Mrs Ruxton wearing a tiara taken from the same angle to the same scale. It was a perfect match.

Professor Glaister had pieced together much of the remains and explained that it would have taken at least eight hours for a person highly skilled in dissection to dismember both corpses to such an exceptional degree. He informed the court of the scars and birthmarks, such as Mary's appendix scar and a mark on her thumb, that were excised. A fingerprint corresponded with one from 2 Dalton Square – Mary's. Isabella's prominent nose was completely missing, as were her protruding teeth. The cause of her death was obvious, due to the condition of her tongue and lungs. Isabella Ruxton had been asphyxiated. Other areas of the body that would show up asphyxiation, such as the eyes, ears and lips had been removed, implicating someone who had medical knowledge. Mr Birkett asked if the bloodstains at the Ruxton abode could have been due to Ruxton's wounded hand? 'Yes', replied the professor, giving Ruxton a glimmer of hope. However he added that, 'The volume of blood indicated another source'.

Dr Shannon, Medical officer at Strangeways Prison had examined Ruxton's cut hand. It could have been from a tin opener but more likely a knife. A doctor would know how to stop such a cut swiftly. In any case, the clots formed in the drains could only have formed from blood dripping straight down them without any attempt to stop the bleeding. It was a crucial point.

To confirm when the victims were murdered, Dr Alexander Mearns of Glasgow University, in a pioneering work analysed the maggots found in the victim's flesh and compared it with those found on the riverbank next to where they were discovered, pinpointing their deaths almost exactly to on or around 14 September 1935. As a procession of witnesses gave strong, unprejudiced evidence, corroborating the prosecution's contentions, it looked bleak for Ruxton.

Mr Birkett had his work cut out. He fought a strong rearguard action and tried to obfuscate by occasionally challenging the medical experts on their assignment of particular body parts to one or other woman. He also strongly suggested that the body of Mary Rogerson had shown signs of pregnancy, hinting therefore that she had been in Scotland seeking an illegal abortion when slain along with her mistress by a person or persons unknown. Unfortunately for his client, the mutilation of the bodies strongly hinted at their death by someone known to them and trying to hide the fact and that the murderer was an individual of considerable surgical skill. No evidence appeared of a pregnancy, such as the one Ruxton alleged Mary had.

The prosecution had proven the identity of the bodies fairly conclusively. The place where the murders were committed and the bodies of the victims destroyed had to be proven next. Luckily for the prosecution, the evidence showed overwhelmingly that 2 Dalton Square was both the scene of the crime and the hideous dismemberment. Witness after witness came forward to report the countless contradictory statements volunteered by Ruxton as explanation for the whereabouts of the missing women. The bizarre events of 15 September and beyond were recounted step-by-step by those most closely acquainted by the doctor on those days. The bloodstained suit, carpets, shirt, the cut hand, the three fires, the locked room, the stained bath and so on combined with Ruxton's incongruous actions on the days in question pointed the finger straight at the doctor. His counsel put up a valiant defence but police reports of blood found in disparate locations such as in the bathroom, on the stair handrails, in the drains and on the carpets impacted strongly on the jury. Mr Birkett claimed that it was 'normal' for blood to abound in a doctor's house-cum-surgery. He tried to claim that blood on the staircase carpet was either from a miscarriage Isabella Ruxton had had a year before her murder when she fell on the stairs, or from Ruxton's own hand when he ha dcut it opening a tin of fruit. The suit? It was damning. Mr Birkett expressed the view that it was stained with so much blood because his client wore it while conducting dental extractions and circumcisions that Dr Ruxton apparently undertook without wearing a white coat. It was an explanation that cut no ice.

Then there was the circumstantial evidence. The umpteen different explanations Ruxton volunteered to a quite bewildering array of people as to why Mary and Isabella had disappeared came back to haunt him with a vengeance, as did his obviously mendacious meanderings when asked to explain his movements during the days in question. Quite devastating for Ruxton's crumbling defence, were the often frantic demands he had made to witnesses in the days and weeks between the murders and his arrest that they lie on his behalf if questioned by the police.

The existence of the *Sunday Graphic* and the child's romper suit in which a head was wrapped was identified as belonging to one of the Ruxton children and could not be explained away by Mr Birkett. Finally a Mr Fred Barwick, director of testing at Manchester Chamber of Commerce, testified that a bed sheet containing remains was 'identical in composition, weave, thread and yarn count, direction of yarn twist and the class of cotton to other sheets on Ruxton's bed'. While one might consider that thousands of sheets may nonetheless be exactly the same, Mr Barwick pointed out that the 'selvedge' that makes a sheet stronger should have had 26 threads but was three short on both the sheets covering the remains and the Ruxton bed. In other words, the sheets must have come from one uniquely faulty loom. It was virtually as good as a fingerprint.

To stem the tidal wave of evidence against him, Ruxton took the stand, taking the oath on the New Testament, despite not being a Christian. In retrospect, testifying was not a good idea. For almost two full days the prosecution systematically and comprehensively dismantled the defendant's testimony. It was pitiful to watch as tears, hysteria and anger welled up time and again from the accused as he shrieked at witnesses, denouncing them as liars when his recollections clashed with their evidence, heard earlier in the trial. Shouting excitedly one minute, speaking moderately the next, the court was shocked at his wretched, cowardly attempt at self-preservation. At one point he addressed the judge, apologising with: 'Sorry, but I am fighting for my life. MY LIFE! I humbly, most humbly beg your pardon for interrupting'.

Ruxton was unable to account satisfactorily for his suit, on which he claimed the bloodstains had accumulated over two or three years. He obviously forgot, although Mr Jackson reminded him that the same suit was thoroughly dry-cleaned only on 17 August 1935, less than a month before the disappearance of Mary and Isabella. Ruxton could not account for it.

In his closing speech for the Crown, Mr Jackson asked the jury to satisfy themselves that the bodies found in Gardenholme Linn were those of Mary Rogerson and Isabella Ruxton. He reminded them again of how the bodies found did indeed resemble those two unfortunates to a remarkable degree. For example, Mrs Ruxton had a bunion on her big toe; the remains had flesh removed from that precise location. Perversely, the defendant had helped recognition of the bodies by destroying what would identify them as the missing women and only them. In detail, he repeated the evidence, that 'proved beyond all shadow of doubt', Ruxton's guilt.

In closing for the defence, Mr Birkett talked of the evidence being 'circumstantial'. Even if the jury were convinced that Isabella and Mary had been found in Gardenholme Linn it did not, alone, make the defendant their killer. No witness saw Ruxton commit murder or deposit the remains. The bloodstains from 2 Dalton Square were from Ruxton's injured hand. No blood was found in his car or the one he hired as might be expected. The victims themselves, Mr Birkett suggested, purchased the *Sunday Graphic* as they headed north to a dastardly fate at the hands of a person or persons unknown. The jury should acquit.

Friday 13 March 1936 was the last day of the trial. Mr Justice Singleton summed up, making clear that the defendant should have the benefit of the doubt, if the jurors had any. For his part it appeared he did not, speaking of the 'amazing coincidence' regarding the bed sheet, for instance. Ruxton, meanwhile, sat in the dock with his head in his right palm and his left arm wrapped round his knees.

The jury retired at 3.58pm. and returned at 5.20 with the verdict everyone in court expected. Guilty. The second count of murder was formally presented and he was found guilty on this count too.

Ruxton meekly and in an apparent daze sat dumbstruck as the judge sentenced him to hang on the morning of Tuesday, 12 May 1936. The night before his execution, Ruxton wrote to his counsel asking him to 'do his best' for his children, providing him with a 'small token' of his esteem and gratitude – a set of silver forks with mother-of-pearl handles. Birkett refused the gift but did all he could to aid the care and education of the unfortunate children.

Buck Ruxton's trial created such interest that it entered local legend. His crimes were even put to verse. In Lancaster the children sang in the school playgrounds:

> *Red stains in the sunset,*
> *Red stains on the knife,*
> *Old Dr Ruxton you murdered your wife.*

> The maid came and caught you,
> You murdered her too,
> Now Dr Ruxton what are we to do?
>
> They'll hang you tomorrow,
> They'll not spare you 'tis sure,
> And then Dr Ruxton will murder no more.
>
> Red stains on the carpet,
> Red stains on the knife,
> Why Dr Ruxton did you murder your wife?

And in Glasgow:

> Red stains on the carpet,
> Red stains on your knife,
> Oh Dr Buck Ruxton you murdered your wife!
>
> The nursemaid saw you and threatened to tell,
> Oh Dr Buck Ruxton you killed her as well!

Despite the grisly nature of his crimes and his tempestuous behaviour, Dr Ruxton remained popular in Lancaster. Almost 6,000 people signed a petition demanding a reprieve. The Home Secretary duly ignored it and he was accordingly executed on the appointed date at Strangeways Prison, Manchester.

So what of the letter Ruxton had given to the *News of the World* on 12 October? On Sunday 17 May 1936 the handwritten letter was published. It read:

> '*I killed Mrs Ruxton in a fit of temper because I thought she had been with a man. I was mad at the time. Mary Rogerson was present at the time. I had to kill her.*'

CHAPTER 15
Dr Harold Frederick Shipman: Pillar of the Community

'You wake up and you receive a phone call – Shipman's topped himself. You have got to think for a minute: is it too early to open a bottle?'

David Blunkett MP

SUCH WERE THE comments of the Home Secretary, on hearing that the most prolific mass-murderer in British history, Dr Harold Shipman, had hanged himself in his prison cell in the early hours of Tuesday, 13 January 2004.

For the relatives of Shipman's victims, the news was not so welcome, for while many were happy to see Shipman rot in hell, any explanation of why he had killed and exactly whom, would go to the grave with him. He had, in the words of Jayne Gaskill, whose mother, 68-year-old Bertha Moss was among Shipman's victims, 'taken the easy way out'.

Shipman had been jailed for life in January 2000 at Preston Crown Court for the murder of 15 of his patients by morphine injection. In 2002 Mr Blunkett decreed that Dr Shipman would spend the rest of his life behind bars. Nevertheless, Shipman never accepted his guilt and he had lodged an appeal. The fourteenth of January 2004 was to be his 58th birthday yet the previous day he had fashioned a noose out of bed sheets which he then tied to the window bars of his cell and then strangled himself. Shipman was found unconscious at 6.20am. Resuscitation attempts failed and he was pronounced dead at 8.12am.

Professor Ian Stephen, one of Britain's leading forensic psychologists, speculated that the murderer died because he realised the futility of carrying on, only to face further court appearances and more anguished and angry relatives of his victims. 'Shipman has played god again, this time defying a justice system that put him away. He was manipulative, controlling and saw himself as beyond criticism. He would have considered taking his own life preferable to facing another court telling him he is guilty'. As a doctor Shipman would know how to hide the signs and symptoms prison staff look out for in potentially suicidal prisoners.

To the end, Shipman showed no remorse and made no confession. At his former surgery, the word 'justice' was daubed 12 times across the metal shutters. The picture the world has of Dr Shipman was one of a bespectacled, bearded, middle-aged man of medium build with slicked-back, greying, brown hair, usually seen photographed next to his battered old maroon Renault Espace. It was because he was seen as the epitome of ordinariness that makes his appalling crimes seem even more horrific.

*   *   *

It was on a cold night in the early hours of 1 August 1998. A digger struck at the hard-packed soil in Hyde Cemetery as the body of 81-year-old Kathleen Grundy was exhumed. An autopsy revealed morphine in her muscle tissue. A former mayoress of Hyde, known for her dedication to helping the elderly and numerous charitable causes, Mrs Grundy was lively, well known and much loved. She was visited by Shipman at 8.30am on 24 June 1998, just a week before her 82nd birthday, supposedly on the pretext of taking a blood sample. On arrival, he gave Mrs Grundy a lethal injection of morphine instead. He then scurried back to his dingy surgery and altered her medical records to imply she was a codeine addict who regularly overdosed. His undoing, if not his motive, was greed. Her friends, John Green and Ronald Pickford, found Mrs Grundy dead on the settee at 11.55am.

Apparently, Shipman had never before tried to make financial gain from his victims. This time it was different. He crudely and stupidly forged Mrs Grundy's will on his surgery typewriter to read, 'I leave all my estate, money and house to my doctor. My family are not in need and I want to reward Dr Shipman for all the care he has given to me and the people of Hyde'. He then forged her signature. Why did he risk exposure at this juncture? Perhaps the £386,402 left in Mrs Grundy's will offered the chance of an escape from his mundane life and high-risk hobby and so he could not pass up the possibility. In the event, it was a stupid mistake.

Unfortunately for Shipman, Mrs Grundy's daughter, Mrs Angela Woodruff, was an experienced solicitor of 25 years standing and doggedly refused to believe that the shoddy will, typed in upper case, was conceived and signed by her mother. To Mrs Woodruff it was 'inconceivable',that this could have happened or that her mother would leave her worldly possessions to her GP. She began an investigation into her mother's untimely death.

Mrs Grundy had a prior will that left all her money to her only child, Mrs Woodruff. A new will had been drafted and signed on 9 June, only a fortnight before her death, using a different firm of solicitors, Hamilton Ward. Mrs Woodruff nervously visited the 'witnesses' to her mother's will, Mrs Claire Hutchinson and Mr Paul Spencer. Both, as they later confirmed to the police and at Shipman's trial, had been asked to sign an innocuous 'document' while at Shipman's surgery. They were unaware of what they had attested to. Mrs Grundy's own diary, meticulously detailed, would reveal that she had not known either, believing she was signing up to a 'survey' Shipman was conducting on behalf of Manchester University. No such survey existed. Mrs Woodruff was now faced with the realisation that her mother had been murdered by her GP for personal gain.

On 24 July Mrs Woodruff went to the police and Shipman's world began to crumble. Mrs Grundy would be the last of his numerous victims.

Shipman was born on 14 January 1946 to a respectable working-class family in Nottingham. His father had been called Frederick but changed his name to Harold, as his wife did not like it. Nonetheless, Harold junior was given Frederick as his own middle name and known as 'Fred' throughout his life. A clever but unexceptional pupil, Fred passed his 11 plus and entered the distinguished High Pavement Grammar School. While sitting his A-levels, Shipman's devoted mother Vera died of lung cancer after a long and painful illness on 21 June 1963. She was only 42 and the only relief she obtained from her suffering was from the daily injections of diamorphine administered by her GP. It can be no coincidence that her son chose this very drug to dispatch his own victims. Fred was absolutely devastated at his mother's death. He bottled up his grief and few were to know the heartbreak he felt at losing his mother. Grief at the premature death of a loved one is an emotion Shipman would make sure was felt by hundreds of others in the years ahead.

It was a proud moment for the Shipman family when Fred won a place at Leeds University to study medicine. He originally had no interest in becoming a doctor. Vera's death suddenly thrust on him a desire to make medicine his vocation. His studies began in 1965, at a time when only 7% of school students went on to university, an even smaller proportion from Shipman's modest background. Nevertheless, as a student Shipman was fairly ordinary and had to spend almost every waking minute studying, as he struggled to pass his exams. A keen rugby player as a boy, sport and a social life were neglected in favour of medicine. Until his future wife emerged on the scene.

The joy of university life, such as it was, was cut short for Fred when he met 17-year-old uneducated window-dresser Primrose Oxtoby, the daughter of the landlady at his student digs in Wetherby. Soon she was pregnant. In those days the proper thing to do was marry and on Guy Fawkes Night, November 1966, 20-year-old Shipman and his young bride tied the knot. It was a low-key registry office wedding witnessed only by the new Mrs Shipman's mother Edna and Fred's dad. Not a single photograph of the event has ever come to light. Sarah, the first of their four children, was born four months later on St Valentine's Day. Fred now had a young family to cope with as well as the burden of relentless study and he suffered frequently from exhaustion. Former colleagues from Leeds University Medical School have since suggested that Shipman had a macabre fascination for dead bodies at this time. Perhaps death was already permanently etched on his mind. Possibly he felt calm, or more alive, in the presence of people who had ceased to be.

The Shipmans had another child, Christopher, on 21 April 1971 and Fred graduated soon after. Upon qualifying, he began work as a house officer at Pontefract General Hospital and registered as a doctor on 4 August 1971. He took a Diploma in Child Health and a Royal College Diploma in Obstetrics and Gynaecology. After three years, Shipman decided hospital medicine was not for him. A career in general practice beckoned.

Accepting the offer of a job in Todmorden, a Yorkshire market town of 15,000 souls, Shipman started work as a junior GP on 1 March 1974. In Todmorden he appeared to blossom. The group practice run by Dr Michael Grieve was impressed by his hard work, dedication and enthusiasm. He also became a pillar of the community, helping to clean out Rochdale canal at weekends in the company of Primrose and some local volunteers, who were greatly impressed that a doctor would dirty his hands on their humble venture. In only a month he was promoted from assistant to principal GP. Shipman seemed destined for great things, with his flair for new ideas and growing reputation as an excellent administrator. He was popular too with partners and patients alike, rapidly developing quite a following.

Yet there can be no doubt that even as a young doctor, Shipman was a haunted man. He may have appeared to others as a dynamic, self-confident go-getter but the reality was different. To deal with his inadequacies, fears and miseries, he began to self-inject the synthetic opioid painkiller pethidine hydrochloride. Used as an analgesic primarily in childbirth, the short-lasting euphoria it gave Fred allowed him an escape from the stresses of everyday life.

To cover up his addiction, Shipman wrote prescriptions in the name of patients who never received the drug and were unaware it had been prescribed for them. He topped up his supply by 'recycling' pethidine left over through deliberate over prescribing, from those who had actually taken it. He was taking 6-700 mg daily, injecting upwards of a dozen times a day.

The signs that something was amiss became apparent when Fred began to suffer blackouts and falls. His devoted wife, who worshipped her husband, took to driving Shipman to house calls. His partners worried but Fred lied that he suffered from epilepsy. He was soon caught out.

In Todmorden village, the local chemist was worried at Shipman's pethidine use. Rather than raise the issue directly, he deliberately left the 'drug book' open when a receptionist came to collect some dressings. The receptionist was horrified to read pages and pages of entries in Shipman's name, all for pethidine ampoules, a drug seldom used in general practice. A partner, Dr John Dacre, was informed and after checking the book himself, he and his colleague Dr Brenda

Lewin decided to confront Shipman directly. Without informing Dr Grieve, they spoke to Shipman on Monday 29 September 1975, at the end of his weekend shift.

Shipman flew into a fury. His partners were taken utterly aback. They had never witnessed such behaviour in their colleague who denied nothing, said he would stop and demanded another chance. Eventually, Shipman stormed out saying he had resigned. Dr Grieve was shattered that his young protégé was a junkie. An hour later, Primrose barged into the surgery and told the partners that her husband would never resign. They would have to sack him. Sack him they did but it took six long weeks while he stayed at home on full pay. The grounds he was dismissed on were, 'Breaking practice rules through misuse of drugs'.

Shipman admitted to police that he had taken pethidine for six months prior to the discovery and blamed depression caused by overwork. He was prosecuted at Halifax Magistrates' Court the following year and pleaded guilty to eight charges of obtaining drugs by deception, asking for 67 similar offences and seven counts of forgery to be taken into consideration. Fined £600 by the GP Magistrate, Dr Maurice Goldin, Shipman also had to reimburse the NHS £57.78 for the cost of drugs taken illegally. Sent to The Retreat psychiatric unit in York, he never worked in Todmorden again.

The recommendation Dr Goldin gave to Fred was to 'Get better and get out of medicine'. He also recommended that Shipman 'never have access to drugs again'. Sound advice, though sadly for Shipman's victims, it was not taken. He kicked his habit and voluntarily resigned from the Controlled Drug Register, which would have left him open to checks on how he stored morphine, pethidine and other controlled substances. Shipman was never again allowed to retain or carry in his medical bag controlled drugs. He did of course. For their part, the General Medical Council (GMC) took no action and Shipman was not struck off.

Moving with his family to a new council house on the Burnhill Estate, Newton Aycliffe, County Durham, and seemingly out of medicine, Shipman, with Primrose right behind him, was determined to bounce back. There was a feeling in the medical profession that Shipman 'deserved another chance'. He took it and became a children's clinical medical officer for the South-west Durham Health Authority. Just 18 days later, on 12 September 1977, he began working again as a GP, this time with the Donneybrook House group practice in Hyde, a former mill town and close-knit community in Greater Manchester of 22,000. The Shipmans rented a pretty semi-detached house in Lord Derby Road. Two years later they bought their final home, another semi in Roe Cross Green, in the quiet suburb of Mottram. On the 20 March that year, their son David was born and on 4 April 1982 their family was complete with the arrival of Sam. On 5 January 1985, Shipman's father died aged 70, of a heart attack. Although not close to his father, who believed his son's marriage to Primrose had brought scandal on the family, Shipman was deeply upset at his father's demise, barely avoiding a nervous breakdown. He became even more detached and aloof, retreating further into his own private world of resentment, anger and frustration.

Shipman was very strict with his children, a control freak, just as he was at work. On one occasion, when his two younger sons were six and nine, Primrose phoned Fred to inform him the children were at the table ready to eat. He instructed her not to feed them until he returned. When he did so, hours later, his boys had fallen asleep hungry at the table. It was even alleged that he struck his sons on occasion.

The GPs in the seven-strong Donneybrook House practice were aware of Shipman's past. Through hard work he gained their trust but became equally well known for his aggression and violent mood swings. He brooked little opposition from colleagues at practice meetings, snapped at the staff and would go pale with fury when he did not get his own way but he rarely raised his voice or lost his cool. The apparent internalising of their co-employer's rage would sometimes unnerve the staff. On other occasions he would shout and bully receptionists and the atmosphere in the practice soon deteriorated. The practice manager, Vivien Langfield, who had over 25 years experience there, soon clashed with him, noticing his obsequiousness to other doctors and aloofness and arrogance towards employees. He was, she recalls, 'a divisive, despicable man'. If he took a dislike to a staff member, he would demand the practice manager sack that person, as he was too cowardly to do it himself. Shipman used his qualifications to belittle those he considered beneath him. If one queried his methods he would retort: 'I am a good doctor, I qualified at Leeds Medical School and passed my exams'.

Shipman became involved in a number of organisations, ranging from the Local Medical Council and Parent Teacher Association to the St John Ambulance Brigade, becoming their Area Commissioner, Divisional and Area Surgeon. Abruptly and for no apparent reason, he would leave these organisations after years of commitment and never return.

In November 1989, the GMC received a formal complaint from the Family Health Services Appeal Unit. Shipman had prescribed the wrong dose of epilepsy treatment, epilim, to his patient, Derek Webb. Mr Webb suffered brain damage as a result and never fully recovered. His family sued Shipman who accepted his error and was found to be in breach of his terms of service. The case rumbled on for a further decade. The GMC did not check Shipman's record.

February 1992 saw Shipman fined by the GMC for failing to visit a patient who had suffered a stroke. Upon investigating such professional misconduct, his previous record was again ignored.

In August 1992, after 15 years at Donneybrook, Shipman struck out alone and began to work from his own solus practice in Market Street, opposite the Age

Concern charity shop, ironically the one Kathleen Grundy often helped at. He took 2,300 of his loyal Donneybrook patients, three receptionists and a district nurse with him. He said the reason for leaving was that his old-fashioned approach to medicine was at odds with colleagues' plans to computerise their records. When he moved, Shipman did just that. The real motive for relocating was to create his own fiefdom. In Market Street he had no medical colleagues or senior partners, no one looking over his shoulder, leaving him free to carry out his cold-blooded killings, confident of avoiding discovery.

His partners had no inkling that Shipman would move out. Deviously, he found a loophole in his contract that enabled him to take his patient list. His partners had always behaved honourably towards him and were aghast when he refused to pay £30,000 towards the tax bill as his share of the previous year's profits. As the practice was a company, they could not claim it from him. Former colleagues were also embittered that they were left to pay his £20,000 a year share of staff and ancillary costs and buy out his £23,000 share in the building. As he had taken his patient list, they could not even replace him. A sense of bitterness and betrayal festered between Donneybrook and Shipman from this point onwards.

Shipman was considered at this time by many to be 'the best doctor in Hyde'. He seemingly could not do enough for his flock, making impromptu visits to the elderly, being kind and patient with them. He had an outstanding bedside manner and also made sure his patients received the best of medicines. Frequently he was over budget with the local prescribing adviser, fighting his corner tenaciously to defend his prescribing habits. Rather than refer patients to hospital, Shipman insisted on treating them himself whenever possible. Long hours were the norm and, until the enormity of his crimes became evident, he was highly spoken of. He nursed two neighbours and patients, Alan and Jane Smith, through nervous breakdowns, insisting that rest not medication would help them recover and when Jane became distressed at the death of her father Stanley, both Primrose and Fred insisted on running her to Tameside Hospital. 'He is absolutely marvellous; I can't speak well enough of him', she said after Shipman's arrest. Other patients took the opposite view. Lorraine Leighton remarked that: 'He gave me the creeps'.

Some patients disliked the often brusque and condescending way Shipman spoke to them, others revered him. Soon, Shipman had a waiting list of admirers wishing to join his practice, a list eventually swollen to 3,100, two-thirds of whom remained on it six months after his conviction. He was unlike other GPs, who would write a prescription almost as soon as a patient arrived. Shipman would listen intently, inform the patient of his diagnosis and explain why he would embark on a particular course of treatment. As a result of such consideration, when he was accused, many of Dr Shipman's patients simply refused to believe it. Cards, letters and floral tributes from well-wishers flooded into the surgery, telling him to 'keep his chin up' and the like. Comments to reporters were made such as, 'He ensured I got the life-saving heart surgery I needed, I owe my life to the man', or 'he was a saint, nothing was too much trouble' and 'he was kind, reassuring and so dedicated'. Others had a different view.

On 19 September 1997, 55-year-old Jim King visited his doctor's surgery. An unusually ebullient Shipman greeted him with the words, 'Congratulations, you've won the lottery'. Mr King was told he did not have the cancer Shipman diagnosed eight months earlier. He had never had it. Relieved and upset, having endured three months of painful chemotherapy and eight months of injecting morphine, he blamed the hospital. Yet, his GP was told on 22 November the previous year that King was free of cancer and probably had kidney disease. Perhaps for his own sadistic pleasure, he had nevertheless informed King that he had only 18 months to live. In the meantime, he became addicted to morphine and his family life deteriorated. His father, also Jim King, was angry at Shipman and wanted to find another GP. He never got the chance. On Christmas Eve, Shipman called at 2.30pm to give the 83-year-old a flu jab. Mr King was found dead half-an-hour later. Shipman called it 'old age', even though King snr had been as fit as a fiddle, walked five miles a day and had just redecorated his home. Possibly he was murdered with morphine 'harvested' after being prescribed for his son. Jim King's aunt, Irene Berry, was to die in similar circumstances, as had another aunt, Molly Dudley, in 1997.

It was soon discovered that while Shipman was highly regarded by many, he also had the nickname of 'Dr Death'. Elderly women were heard to say, 'He is a good doctor but you don't last. Lots of old ladies have died with him'. Made almost in cheery innocence, such comments are somewhat chilling in that if rumours about Shipman were abroad in the community, why were the authorities unaware of what was going on until, for so many, it was too late? As the Shipman case unfolded on television, millions watched incredulous that such a seemingly bland individual was such a prolific killer.

Mrs Woodruff had taken her concerns to her local police station in Warwickshire, who passed them on to Stalybridge CID Detective Inspector Stan Egerton. Detective Superintendent Bernard Postles was placed in charge of the investigation and Shipman's subsequent interrogation. He checked the details given to him by Mrs Woodruff and was convinced she had been murdered. To prove it, an exhumation order was required. Coroner John Pollard provided it. Forensic pathologist Dr John Rutherford examined the body of the late Mrs Grundy. Liver and muscle tissue samples were taken and sent for examination to Dr Julie Evans, forensic toxicologist, in Chorley and Professor Hans Sachs of the University of Munster, Germany.

Detective Superintendent Postles set up an incident room on 21 August in Ashton-under-Lyme station. He was 46, had 27 years on the force and served 22 of those in the CID. Some 59 officers were part of the team, working night and day, under the leadership of Postles and his subordinates detective inspectors Mike Williams and Stan Egerton, who instigated much of the hard work that brought Shipman to justice.

On 2 September 1998, Dr Julie Evans confirmed that large doses of morphine existed in the body of Kathleen Grundy. Five days later Shipman was arrested at 9.18am at Ashton-under-Lyne police station. The police had been in no rush. Shipman wasn't going anywhere and they did not want to start a commotion. A locum doctor took Shipman's place at the surgery he had continued to work in almost to the moment of his arrest. Shipman was charged not only with the murder of Mrs Grundy, but with theft by deception and three counts of forgery.

To investigating officers, Dr Shipman was cold, arrogant and displayed an air of intellectual superiority and calculated indifference towards them. He scoffed at their lack of medical knowledge, 'You don't understand medical matters, you are only plods', he said to the police. He was contemptuous of their incredulity at his insistence that Mrs Grundy was a drug addict at the ripe old age of 81.

Shipman's arrogance was partly based on ignorance. He had no idea that his computer would betray the times and dates he input data, changing the medical histories of patients he had recently murdered. He therefore readily admitted that he and he alone had access to patients' computer records. Unfortunately for him, the police were able to show a direct correlation between the deaths of patients and the retrospective altering of their records hours or even minutes later. They were also able to prove that, on at least one occasion when Shipman claimed to be 'treating' Mrs Grundy, she was miles away with her daughter. When this was revealed to him, his aloof demeanour cracked. Detectives questioning him also proved he had altered the medical records of other victims to make it look as if their deaths were due to natural causes. At this juncture he seemed to break down completely and fell weeping and gibbering to the floor. Perhaps at that moment, when his world came crashing down, he knew he was finished. Subsequently, Shipman never said a word. In interviews he turned his back to the police and closed his eyes when shown victims' photographs.

Checking the number of deaths among Shipman's patients soon convinced the police, to their horror, that they were dealing with someone who had killed many times before. The police had so many potential victims they did not have the resources to investigate them all. Sixty of the most likely were investigated, with the police developing a five-point methodology for choosing which ones to progress. Firstly they would ascertain if a body was cremated or buried, the latter giving the opportunity for an exhumation and examination to find traces of morphine, scoring one point if the deceased had been interred. Secondly, they would then check if the family of the deceased had any suspicions regarding the death of their loved one, awarding another point for 'yes'. Thirdly, another would be scored if the cause of death was inconsistent with the medical history of the deceased. Fourthly, a point was given if the medical records of the departed had been tampered with and, lastly, an extra point was scored to those cases that had a total of four points from the above categories, making them top priorities for investigation. By scrupulously sticking to their formula, the police were able to fully investigate 15 cases that they would be able to take to court including Mrs Grundy. Gruesomely, another 11 exhumations would be ordered in the coming weeks and months, all of them carried out in the dead of night. The deceased were then quietly reburied a day or so later, usually after a short, dignified religious service.

Not all the families of the dead wanted to assist the police. It was too distressing for them. Much time had to be spent and a great deal of sensitivity shown by the police. Counselling of family members helped. Such was the adverse emotional impact of the case that soon a number of stressed officers availed themselves of the service too. Shipman's victims were often those one would least expect to die suddenly. Not all were old and many vigorous and in fairly robust health.

Elizabeth 'Lizzie' Adams was killed on 28 February 1997. She had just turned 77. A former dance teacher who had retired only the previous year, she still took to the floor with regular partner Bill Catlow several times a week, was fit and full of vitality. Lizzie was in high spirits when she told her daughters, Sonia and Doreen, that Dr Shipman would call and give her some antibiotics for a 'bug' caught on a recent holiday to Malta. When Mr Catlow came to her home at 2.00pm he was surprised to see Dr Shipman looking at her dance trophies while Lizzie lay slumped in a chair. Examining her, Bill found a pulse. 'It's your own', said Shipman coldly, explaining that Mrs Adams had 'gone'. Her iron was on and a meal was cooking on the stove. She had succumbed, said her doctor, to pneumonia.

Joan Melia was an independent and spirited woman of 73 when slain by Shipman, his second to last victim, only 12 days before Mrs Grundy. A divorcee, she remained close to her ex-husband and six nephews and nieces. Found dead in a chair by her fiancé, Derek Steele, she was another active pensioner, all hustle and bustle, who died after a visit from her GP. Her engagement ring, which she never removed, disappeared the day of her death.

Mother of five Winifred Mellor was Shipman's third to last victim. Although aged 73, on occasion she played football with her grandsons. On the day she died, Mrs Mellor had been shopping and chatted to friends on the phone. That fateful day, 11 May 1998, Shipman had also called on her friend, Mrs Gloria Ellis, after supposedly finding Winifred dead in an armchair. According to him, she had suffered from angina for months and refused admission to hospital. It did not ring true. Nevertheless, family and friends had no reason to doubt a doctor whom they knew and trusted.

Only 49 when Shipman poisoned her, on 10 December 1997, Bianka Pomfret was one of his youngest victims. Having suffered from manic depression over many years, she placed great faith in her doctor. Quiet and religious, Bianka was probably killed because Shipman considered her dependence on him and frequent visits to his surgery a 'nuisance'. In the summer of 1997 she promised to leave her worldly possessions, £100,000 in money and property, to her GP. After a fierce argument, when Shipman realised he was not the only person of importance in her life, Bianka threatened to cut him out. Shipman tried to give her a 'sedative'. She refused the injection, temporarily saving her life. In the days that followed Mrs Pomfret changed her will, leaving everything to her son and grandchildren.

Maureen Ward was 57 when killed by Dr Shipman on 18 February 1997. Only two years previously he had killed her mother Muriel at the same address. Whilst Muriel's death was supposedly caused by 'heart failure', her daughter's demise was brought about by a 'brain tumour', which does not kill quickly. Muriel Ward had been cremated so police did not have enough evidence to charge him with that murder. They did with Maureen, a retired college lecturer who had only recently fought off cancer.

Marie West was 81 when she met her death on 6 March 1995. She was not alone with her murderer at the time. Her friend, Mrs Marion Hadfield, was in the next room. Of this, Shipman was unaware. He was startled to see Mrs Hadfield emerge from the kitchen where she had enjoyed a cup of tea. 'She collapsed on me', he stammered. 'Can't you do something?' Her friend pleaded. Lifting her eyelid, Shipman retorted, 'See, no life there!' A widow, Mrs West had lost her daughter to cancer eight years previously. Grandchildren were her life and she doted on them. Marie was a character, always in good spirits and seemingly excellent health until the assassin came to her home.

The people of Hyde, most of whom had only the highest regard for Shipman, often rationalised his actions by considering the doctor an advocate of euthanasia, nothing more. He had killed perhaps, but only to put some frail, terminally sick persons out of their misery. Such attitudes made the job of the authorities difficult as many locals shunned their investigations.

Dr Shipman was placed on remand after appearing before Tameside Magistrates Court on 7 October, breaking down in the dock when new charges of murdering Joan Melia, Winnie Mellor and Bianka Pomfret were read out. Initially he was placed in Walton Prison, Liverpool, 50 miles from Hyde, for fear of attack by relatives of his victims among both prisoners and staff if he was incarcerated in Manchester Strangeways. Eventually he was moved to Manchester Prison (as Strangeways is officially known) after his solicitor, Ann Ball appealed that Walton was too far away for Primrose and the children to visit. As a 'first timer' he was placed on 'suicide watch'. The authorities feared he might kill himself, as the other Fred - Fred West - a confessed serial killer, had done in Birmingham before he could be tried.

Although 12 women were exhumed, the police did not proceed in the cases of Sarah Ashworth, Alice Kitchen and Elizabeth Mellor. Morphine was found in all of them and Shipman was almost certainly their killer, but the state of decomposition could allow the defence to challenge police findings. On the other hand, cases involving six cremated victims where the police had phone and computer records, plus strong eyewitness testimony, were progressed to show the indiscriminate nature of the murderer.

Shipman was brought to trial at Preston Crown Court, 35 miles from Hyde, as it was believed Manchester could not provide an impartial jury. It was a fitting venue for such an important trial as it was architecturally similar to the Old Bailey in London with Victorian fixtures and fittings. Media interest was intense and 38 seats were set aside for press use. Outside the court, the streets thronged with reporters and television crews buzzing with anticipation.

The trial of Dr Harold Frederick Shipman began on Monday 11 October 1999 before Mr Justice Thayne Forbes, renowned for being scrupulously fair. For the Crown was Richard Henriques QC, the most respected and senior barrister in north-west England, assisted by Peter Wright QC. Defending was Nicola Davies QC, a specialist in medical cases from Wales, assisted by Mr Ian Winter.

Shipman faced 16 charges, from 136 cases investigated back to 1984. One count of forging Mrs Grundy's will and the murders of fifteen women: Elizabeth Adams, Muriel Grimshaw, Kathleen Grundy, Pamela Hillier, Jean Lilley, Ivy Lomas, Joan Melia, Winifred Mellor, Norah Nuttall, Bianka Pomfret, Marie Quinn, Irene Turner, Kathleen Wagstaff, Maureen Ward and Marie West.

Mr Henriques' opening remarks lasted over eight hours. He at once asked the jury to discount any thought of euthanasia. None of the victims had been prescribed morphine or its derivatives prior to being 'executed' by the doctor they knew and trusted. The doctor had killed not to relieve pain but for his own twisted pleasure.

Angela Woodruff was the first witness heard. Despite her legal training she found the experience an ordeal. Nevertheless, she gave a vivid and emotive account of her mother's life and death that impacted immediately on the jury. Scores of other witnesses followed over 25 days of prosecution evidence. The decent, dignified and plain-spoken people of Hyde came first, including Mrs Grundy's best friend, 91-year-old Mary Clark, detailing the rich and fulfilling lives led by the victims with friends and loved ones until cruelly and mercilessly cut short by their family doctor. Occasionally, the defence tried to swoop on an elderly witness who muddled times and dates. The witness seldom yielded and attempts to discredit their evidence lost Shipman ground with the jury.

Damning testimony came from the defendant's district nurse, Marion Gilchrist, who told the court that Dr Shipman had said to her just before his arrest, 'I read thrillers and on the evidence they have, I would find me guilty'. In the dock, Shipman looked crushed.

The Crown's experts followed the citizenry in giving evidence. They included pathologist Dr John Rutherford, who described his examination of the exhumed bodies. Dr Hans Sachs from Munster, (the home town of Bianka Pomfret), explained the result of morphine overdose. Dr Julie Evans, detailing her analysis of the exhumed bodies, was asked by the defence if it was not true that morphine existed in some non-prescription medicines such as codeine or kaolin and morphine diarrhoea treatments. Her client was not helped by the retort that over a litre-and-a-half would have to be consumed to attain the body levels found in Shipman's dead patients.

Mr Ian Borthwick, fingerprint expert, explained that while none of Mrs Grundy's prints were on the document that purported to be her last will and testament, a Shipman fingerprint was.

Professor Henry McQuay of Oxford University described the effect of morphine on the body and Dr Steven Karch of Stamford University explained that the hair of the victims showed no trace of morphine, showing that they were not regular users, seriously undermining statements by Shipman that Mrs Grundy was.

Three pharmacists from Hyde specified the morphine Shipman prescribed for 28 patients, many of whom were still alive. Shipman had callously used the morphine ostensibly for some patients to kill others. This showed the cruel, calculating and premeditated nature of the accused. Close family members of patients who had died in agony told how their nearest and dearest received no morphine, despite being named on prescriptions. Mrs Ann Brown, daughter of Muriel Grimshaw, told the court that her late husband had actually been prescribed morphine for cancer. When he died, Dr Shipman arrived soon after and removed unused boxes of diamorphine. The jury was left with the distinct impression that it was deliberately stockpiled by Shipman to kill others, including Mrs Brown's own mother, who died four years later, possibly from morphine harvested from another terminally ill patient.

On 8 November, an inebriate sneaked into the public gallery. 'Murderer!' he yelled at Shipman, who alone did not look up as the man continued yelling before being dragged away. Further excitement was added on day 22 when a bomb scare emptied the court.

Shipman had informed the police that he retained no morphine at home, yet 93 tablets of morphine and four ampoules of diamorphine were found when it was searched. An examination of Shipman's prescribing habits revealed that he had prescribed 22,000mg of morphine in his six years as a solus GP. A fatal dose can be anything up to 100mg, depending on the age, health and weight of the patient. 50-60mg is normally deadly.

Despite the damning testimony presented, the defendant remained stoic throughout. To many rather grey and small, Shipman thought himself a superior intellect in a drama with himself in the starring role, as he betrayed in letters to former patients with whom he corresponded. Nicola Davies fought valiantly on his behalf. Prior to its commencement, she even tried to have the trial stopped as it 'Could not be fair', given the 'unremitting, extensive, inaccurate and misleading' reports on the case. Mr Henriques explained that the publicity was 'reasonable, given the enormity of the crimes being investigated and the huge number of suspected victims'.

When Shipman took the stand on Thursday 25 November, it was day 26 of the trial. The courtroom was silent and tense with a sense of expectation that the defendant's testimony, under oath, would be the most crucial yet heard. He outlined his life and career as Primrose, short, plain and obese, sat loyally with her children in the gallery, giving him their full support.

Shipman seemed out of place, giving off the air of a quiet academic rather than a ruthless serial killer. But looks can be deceptive. He spoke quietly at first, apologising for slurring his words. Looking for sympathy, he said it was because of the tablets he was taking for his nerves. Gradually he spoke more authoritatively but with a curious mixture of homespun accents perhaps intended to give him the air of a simple, hard-working and innocent local GP. Davies built up a solid picture of vocational dedication and family life. Unfortunately for Shipman, the humble posture was a difficult one for him to maintain and his true, arrogant self was made apparent to press, public and most importantly, the jury.

It was revealed by the police that the 'will' supposedly written by Mrs Kathleen Grundy had been typed in Shipman's surgery. His feeble and incredulous account of how Mrs Grundy 'frequently borrowed' his typewriter was believed by no one. That he had committed fraud was a certainty. Soon murder would be proven beyond doubt too.

Shipman did not help his case by describing his former patients in less than glowing terms. He coldly stated that a smoker with heart disease, like Bianka Pomfret, 'is silly and looking to die'. He hinted at patients 'going downhill' and that, if resuscitated, he was afraid of 'what we would end up with'. Why did the victims need to be revived in the first place? Shipman had difficulty explaining, especially after he admitted he had simply 'cold called' on some of the elderly victims in passing and that few had even requested his attendance. That most of the 15 had died in front of him, or within minutes of his call, struck the jury as more than coincidence. That he changed all of their records, backdating them to the time he said the patient had first noticed her symptoms, was also considered strange. Asked directly on 15 occasions if he had killed a specific patient named in the charges against him, in every instance he simply replied, 'No', or 'no I did not'.

In the case of Ivy Lomas, who died in his surgery, ostensibly from 'heart disease', Shipman was forced to accept that the toxicology report made it clear she had died of a massive overdose of morphine within five to ten minutes of it being ingested. How this could happen if self-administered, Shipman simply could not say. 'I have no explanation', he muttered. No one else was present and he had 'no idea how it got into her body'. Weakly, he denied any responsibility.

With regard to Norah Nuttall, Shipman admitted he had not called on her in eight years, yet within minutes of his cold call she was dead. Mr Henriques tore into him, accusing the beleaguered doctor of failing to call an ambulance, admit a patient to hospital or allow an autopsy in the instance of anyone he was accused of killing. Why? Because he had murdered them.

On day 40 of the trial, Monday 13 December, with all the evidence heard the court was recessed until 5 January 2000. On that date Mr Henriques delivered his closing speech, reminding them that more than 120 witnesses had spoken for the Crown, each adding to the mountain of proof that Shipman was a heartless slayer of defenceless, trusting, harmless old women who had placed their faith in him until their untimely end. The accused was also manipulative, duplicitous and determined. There was no limit to his evil and he would cajole, comfort and bamboozle relatives into cremating or burying their relatives without the 'trauma' of a postmortem. Ambulances and hospitals were strenuously avoided as travelling along that road lay the certainty of detection. Such was the weight of evidence against Shipman that Henriques was on his feet all day and resumed again the following, finishing only at lunchtime. Nicola Davies now had to address the jury on behalf of her client.

Shipman was portrayed as old-fashioned, eccentric, dedicated and caring. He loved his patients and cared little for record-keeping and other 'modern' bureaucratic niceties that kept him from his calling. To those who found him cold and unsympathetic, this was an expression of his 'calm, professional attitude'. No motive was unearthed by the prosecution and his stockpiling of morphine was simply 'routine', medical practice. He simply carried with him a medicine that could prove 'useful at any time'. The toxicology report said Ms Davies, was, 'inherently unreliable', the evidence having been gathered using new scientific techniques. As for the forged letter, it was dismissed as being 'obviously' from someone who was not a skilled letter writer, like her client.

In his summing up, Mr Justice Forbes asked the jury to consider each of the murders separately, to look at the case dispassionately and he outlined in detail all the evidence before the jury, taking four days to do so. Eventually, the jury retired on 24 January to deliberate. It took a long, long week before they were ready with their verdicts, asking even then for a further ten minutes. Finally, at 4.33pm on Monday 31 January 2000, the jury foreman stood up, announced that the verdicts were unanimous and, to each charge, pronounced the defendant guilty.

Shipman remained emotionless. The gallery, packed to the gunnels with journalists and victims' relatives, was shocked when the judge informed the court of Shipman's previous convictions for forging prescriptions 25 years earlier. He then read out the sentence, expressing his horror at the wickedness of a doctor who betrayed the trust of so many vulnerable people who had put their faith in him. Shipman received 15 life sentences, one for each murder and four years for forgery. A recommendation was made that, 'Life must mean life', and Shipman spend his remaining days behind bars.

The police announced after Shipman's conviction that he would be tried with 23 more murders. Bearded, ordinary, respectable, Shipman was a silent killer both in methodology and in his obstinate refusal to say anything about the number or identity of his victims. He claimed innocence, even to the 'old lags' who became his new 'patients' after he was sent to Frankland Prison, County Durham. Primrose and the family believed in him still and moved to Whitby, North Yorkshire, to make visiting easier. On 10 February 2000, the GMC finally struck Shipman off the Medical Register.

In prison, Shipman began to exert some influence on fellow inmates and was moved to the sex offender's wing, in the prison hospital, which deeply offended him. He translated *Harry Potter* into Braille, was put in solitary confinement 'for his own safety' and placed on suicide watch. Shipman was adamant he would not take his own life. He was 'determined' to prove his innocence. He had a funny way of doing it, refusing to co-operate in any enquiries.

In January 2001 the Baker Report, commissioned by the Department of Health and chaired by Professor Richard Baker OBE of Leicester University, was published, detailing Shipman's career in murder. It would be swiftly followed by Dame Janet Smith's DBE's public inquiry. Meanwhile Shipman became more and more despondent in jail, with rumours of suicide attempts emerging as his health deteriorated. He became increasingly frail, suffering from eye problems and depression.

His first proven victim was Marie West who died on 6 March 1995, the last, Kathleen Grundy on 24 June 1998. The first 'officially' suspected victim from Hyde was Sarah Hannah Marsland, who died on 7 August 1978, aged 86. A widow living alone, Mrs Marsland was found by her granddaughter, Mrs Celia Anne Saxton, after her grandmother had ostensibly died of 'coronary thrombosis. Mrs Marsland was in good health until Shipman appeared, 'to see if she was alright'. Mrs Saxton's aunt, Mrs Celia Chapman, was also to die at the hands of her doctor.

However, much more was to follow. Two days after Shipman committed suicide, Mrs Sandra Whitehead, a student nurse at Pontefract General Hospital from October 1971 to October 1974, contacted the public inquiry stating that she believed he was killing patients even then. A number of suspicious deaths had occurred on Shipman's watch when he was a young house officer at PGI between August 1970 and March 1974.

Dame Janet Smith's inquiry investigated 137 deaths at PGI involving Shipman. In 133 cases he signed the death certificate and was present at four more deaths. An appeal for evidence in the local *Pontefract and Castleford Express* newspaper resulted in a number of other witnesses coming forward. Unfortunately, medical records at the hospital were lost or destroyed during four major management restructurings and hospital expansion in the intervening decades. Only 28 records, whole or in part, still existed. Many witnesses were dead and the full extent of Shipman's guilt was almost impossible to prove, if indeed he was a murderer so early in his career. At best, guilt could be surmised 'statistically' ie if the number of death certificates signed by Shipman significantly exceeded that of other doctors dealing with similar patients over an equivalent time period. Obviously, this was wholly unsatisfactory and distressing for the relatives of potential victims and, it can be argued, served little purpose other than further inflating the scale of crimes committed by Shipman. It should be recalled that many, if not all, of those among the 137 were seriously ill and would have died even without the attentions of the murderous doctor, even if one assumes not all their deaths were natural. In fact the inquiry rejected this approach. After looking at the records available and interviewing witnesses, they became convinced that Shipman killed at least three patients, all male, at PGI.

The first PGI victim was Thomas Cullumbine, 54, who died on 12 April 1972. In his notes, Shipman showed himself 'hostile' to Mr Cullumbine, a smoker who suffered from emphysema yet still craved cigarettes. On the night his patient died, Shipman acted suspiciously. Drug notes were altered to delete a 10mg shot of morphine administered, prior to which Shipman had dissuaded the Cullumbine family from carrying out a night vigil by Thomas' bed, as they had done on the previous night. The doctor was alone when Mr Cullumbine died and Shipman lied about prescribing aminophylline to his patient. He had not. He also said his patient 'fell asleep', which was unlikely given the man's condition. Mr Cullumbine 'officially' died of 'ventricular failure due to emphysema'.

Shipman's other 'confirmed' PGI murders were of Mr John Brewster on 28 April and Mr James Rhodes on 22 May that same year. In total the inquiry considered there were 21 further cases where there was 'cause for suspicion', 45 where there was 'insufficient evidence' and in 68 instances the patients died naturally.

The first person Shipman was suspected of killing was 62-year-old Wilfred Arnold Sanderson on 18 March 1971. His family are adamant Mr Sanderson died naturally. Dr Julian Boon, a leading criminal profiler who has examined the Shipman case, believes Shipman's compulsion to kill would have begun to 'build up' while unsupervised and with vulnerable patients in his care. It would then be his choice who in his care lived or died. On entering general practice, he would have had to proceed with much more caution. In Todmorden, Shipman's first victim was Eva Lyons. She suffered from cancer of the oesophagus and was killed on, 17 March 1975, the day before her 71st birthday.

Incompetence may have led to further deaths among Shipman's patients. During his brief stint in Todmorden, he signed 22 death certificates, more than double that of any other local GP. Included was one for prematurely born Christian Orlinski. Shipman, probably high on pethidine at the time, visited the baby's parents, Mark and Susan, took a cursory look at the newborn and said the child was okay. He did not suggest any routine check-ups or that the little boy should be taken for observation to hospital. Sadly, he died the next day. Shipman described the death as being from 'Sudden Infant Death Syndrome' on the death certificate. Had he done his job, Christian Orlinski might still be alive today.

Ten months after he began his career as a GP, on 21 January 1975, three of Shipman's patients, Lily Crossley, Robert Lingard and Elizabeth Pearce died suddenly that same day. All expired within minutes of him visiting, all were ill to varying degrees, although none were previously considered at risk of an abrupt end. Did Shipman kill them? It seems probable. Without more evidence than the inquiry had available, no one will ever know for sure.

Shipman's modus operandi followed a set pattern. The victims, the vast majority of them elderly women living alone, would be visited at home. He would betray the trust of his patient by examining him/her and then advising that an injection was required to treat some malady or other. The patients sleeve would then be rolled up, the fatal dose administered and soon the victim would calmly drift into a drugged sleep, their breathing becoming shallower and more depressed until it stopped altogether a few minutes later. Shipman then rearranged the body to suit him, often leaving them propped up in an armchair. Before leaving for his surgery to alter his victim's medical records, he took 'trophies', no doubt to later remind him of the 'thrill' just experienced. Usually nothing too valuable was taken, just trinkets, rings, and odds and ends. Primrose found them stashed in a cardboard box, accepting her husband's plausible explanation that they were gifts from grateful patients.

As time went on, Shipman no longer needed to be with a dying patient. He could save time by leaving them to die while driving away, enjoying in his mind the scene of death that was soon to follow – a scene he had arranged so many times.

What drove Shipman to murder on such a massive and, ultimately, reckless scale? Sexual or physical abuse suffered as a child are often precursors to a life as a serial killer but there is no evidence that such abuse was ever suffered by him. He was socially inadequate though. In his youth, prior to meeting Primrose, he was unable to cultivate friends or girlfriends. In his childhood he felt powerlessness and developed an inadequacy that remained in adulthood. This undoubtedly helped form his cold and calculating personality, yet the most decisive moment in shaping his murderous destiny could only have been the agonising death of his mother. Why had she been taken when so many 'inferior' beings continued to walk the Earth? Shipman decided he would play God. Who would live, who would die would be his choice and his alone. A warped form of altruism may have gripped him. After all, did his victims not endure a death much less painful than his beloved mother?

Of course, as a true psychopath, Shipman had no empathy whatsoever for his victims or their families. They were there to provide an outlet for his own manipulative psychosis. He undoubtedly gained pleasure not only from ending the lives of others but from 'getting away with it' too. Whereas his early crimes were usually committed several months apart, his need to kill became greater and greater as time passed. The high obtained from each murder gradually wore off more and more quickly. In 1997, the last full year of his killing spree, he killed 37 people, as he became more and more convinced he was 'untouchable' and needed ever increasing numbers of victims to satisfy his craving for death. In the first half of 1998 a further 18 patients were dispatched. So focussed was he on killing that the rest of his life was a shambles. His house was a squalid tip and his practice was deteriorating. He suffered from anxiety and insomnia, believing himself to be infallible, while at the same time fearing imminent discovery. Near the end, he took such risks that perhaps part of him wanted to be caught, to end the charade his life had become. For what other reason did he stupidly forge Mrs Grundy's will?

Why were certain patients chosen rather than others? It has been suggested that 'difficult' patients, such as Ms Pomfret, were prioritised for death. He could often be irritable and intolerant of other people, especially if he considered himself at the fringes of their thoughts rather than the centre of their universe. Shipman was also embittered that his medical 'genius' remained unrecognised as he failed to win enough respect and admiration from colleagues, community and patients. Certainly his patients did like him but they were considered too insignificant to massage his fragile ego. In the end, he regarded his victims as less than people with lives, hopes and fears; they were merely objects for his warped gratification.

Opportunity was a factor in selecting a victim. Called out on a house visit to a vulnerable patient, he sometimes could not resist the chance to kill. He even murdered six patients in his own surgery. Perhaps Shipman gained even more euphoria from these 'in your face' murders than the others.

What astonished so many of those who looked into the Shipman case was how he got away with it for so long. The nearby Brooke clinic had three times the numbers on Shipman's patient list with only one-tenth of the sudden death rate, yet GPs from this practice continued to countersign their colleague's death certificates. A new partner in the practice, Dr Linda Reynolds did become suspicious. She was to pass away from cancer on 6 March 2000 but not before she had initiated action. Alan Massey and his daughter Debbie, Hyde funeral directors, grew concerned at the number of bodies they were called to that were found alone in exactly the same position. Mr Massey visited the doctor, who seemed so unfazed that his suspicions were temporarily allayed. Local pharmacists noted the huge quantities of diamorphine used by Shipman. Even taxi driver John Shaw noted the number of his customers who had died on Shipman's list. For seven years Mr Shaw kept a list of people he believed had died suspiciously. One of them, Joan Harding, had actually died after he had delivered her to Shipman's surgery. Mr Shaw told the police the 24 names on his list after the doctor was in custody. To do so before, he believed, could have led to his accusations being ridiculed. As a doctor, trained, employed and supposedly dedicated to saving lives for many Shipman was above suspicion. As one former patient said, 'You don't expect Santa Claus to steal your presents do you?'

For years nothing was done. Eventually, on 24 March 1998, the police, following a complaint by Dr Reynolds to Coroner John Pollard, carried out an investigation. Dr Reynolds had only been at her current practice for three years, yet noticed the unusually high amount of 'ash cash' generated by her partners for co-signing death certificates of Shipman's cremated patients. She talked to members of the community, associates of Shipman and checked death rates for his practice compared to that of other local doctors. In doing so she knew her career could be destroyed if her assumptions proved false.

The police despatched only one officer, Detective Inspector David Smith, to investigate. The investigation was to be subtle, giving no clue to Shipman that he was being probed, or who had complained about him. DI Smith interviewed doctors, including Linda Reynolds and undertakers such as the Masseys. Medical records were checked, although at the time the police were unaware they had been literally 'doctored'. Nothing was found to incriminate Dr Shipman and there was no apparent motive as to why he would harm his patients. Inspector Smith asked for copies of death certificates of Shipman's patients for the previous six months. He received 19. Unbeknown to him, there were 11 more. No check was made on whether Shipman had a criminal record, his prescribing habits or if he was ever called out with police officers, routinely, to investigate sudden deaths.

The investigation was carried out half-heartedly. It was no surprise then when no discrepancies were found between patient's medical histories and their death certificates. Without sufficient evidence, no exhumation of possible victims could be carried out. After several weeks, the investigation was terminated. Dr Reynolds asked for autopsies on the bodies of two more of Shipman patients at Massey's funeral parlour. The police did not act. Shipman continued as before, killing a further three women before his arrest: Winnie Mellor, Joan Melia and Kathleen Grundy. The investigation was not in vain however, as without it, Mrs Grundy might not have been exhumed, because when Mrs Woodruff came forward, the police were much more ready to take complaints about Shipman seriously.

What lessons could be learned to prevent another 'Shipman?' In future prescription drugs will be much more tightly monitored, including the disposal of those that are unused. GP death rates will be cross-checked and solus doctors subject to greater scrutiny. It will now no longer be considered 'unthinkable' that a doctor systematically and methodically might kill his/her patients.

At the time of Shipman's death he was not on suicide watch. He had even spoken to Primrose the night before. Perhaps he knew how to hide his suicidal feelings just as he hid so many other emotions for so long. Possibly the enormity of his crimes dawned on and overwhelmed him. This is unlikely. He never displayed a hint of remorse for what he did. The relatives of former patients who had died under his 'care' wrote to the doctor in prison. He never replied to a single one. His death was a final act of control, a last hurrah.

Dame Janet Smith's inquiry produced six detailed reports, the first on 17 July 2002 and the last on 27 January 2005, the inquiry being wound up that Easter. Looking into so many unexplained deaths over so many years from so many witnesses had been a difficult, harrowing and gruesome task. No one will ever know the exact number of Shipman's victims. Over 24 years in general practice, in Todmorden and Hyde, 526 patients died sudden deaths. Of these, 174 were considered 'natural', 60 'probably natural', 43 appear to be 'probable' victims, 212 'definite' and in 37 instances there was 'insufficient evidence' one way or the other. Including PGI, Shipman killed a minimum of 215 people. There were almost certainly more.

CHAPTER 16
Dr Levi Weil: The Apple Dumpling Gang

'Lord have mercy on me! I am murdered.'
Mr John Slow

THE LONDON OF the mid-18th century was a foul-smelling, dirty and danger-ous place in which to live, if also bustling and exciting. Disease was rife and com-petent doctors were at a premium. One might suppose therefore that an ambi-tious and talented young doctor arriving in town might soon make a positive impact.

Dr Levi Weil was born in the Netherlands and educated at the prestigious University of Leyden. A Jew with a strange accent, few were willing to submit themselves to his skills. Tall and thin with dark eyes, olive skin and full lips, Weil's charming, polite and urbane manner could not compensate for his alien appearance. His clientele were of modest means consisting of, for the most part, employees working in London's shops and warehouses, whom he secured as patients only by charging half the fee of his fellow physicians. With his practice too small to provide a reasonable income and the expenses of a gentleman so high, Weil sought out other avenues for his undoubted abilities, ones that would bring in a healthier financial return.

One day Weil was called out to Enfield, then a small community outside London surrounded by fields. He was to treat the sister of a wealthy merchant whose regular physician was ill. Weil was delighted at the chance to treat a better class of patient and successfully ministered to the lady. Invited to supper by her brother, Weil was paid in cash. Impressed by the opulent surroundings of their mansion house, Weil returned to the city in the company of his host, with whom he had struck up an instant rapport. Although his companion was tipsy from hav-ing drunk too much wine, Weil was not. He began to fixate upon the wealth in money and jewels he suspected was secreted within an old bureau he had spotted in the house he had just visited. Returning that very night, Levi Weil quietly crept into the house and stole £90, a tidy sum in those days and more than he had earned in months. When the crime was discovered five hours later, no one sus-pected that the charming physician was in any way connected to it. Dr Weil now realised that burglary, not medicine, was his true calling. He would have to be careful, discreet and ensure that he was not 'coincidentally' in the vicinity of too many burglaries that might take place. Tongues might wag and investigations ensue. Even if they did not, while he might not be suspected directly of any crimes, no one would want a doctor considered 'unlucky' to look after them.

Weil formed a gang with his unscrupulous brother, Asher. Asher was told to keep a wide berth of Levi's medical practice. To ensure the gang would remain close-knit and could be trusted, Levi recruited poor fellow Jews from Amsterdam, informing them of the rich pickings available should they join him in England in a career of theft. Soon the prospective burglars secured a passport from the British consul and embarked for England on the Harwich packet-boat.

Maintaining his medical practice as a 'front', Weil would visit wealthy patients, 'case' their property and pass on information to Asher. Or at least, that was the plan. A major flaw was that Weil had no wealthy patients. Had it not been for the fact that the lady in Enfield's family doctor was indisposed, even his first robbery would not have taken place. Eventually, the lady recommended Weil rather gushingly to a retired admiral who lived near to her. Weil was astonished at the wealth seemingly oozing from every pore of his new patient. His house was crammed with gold and silver artefacts and rare works of art. The admiral proud-ly showed Weil an antique gold workbox studded with diamonds and a massive gold dish worth hundreds of pounds. He discussed these and other treasures with Weil who talked about them as if he was a highly cultured connoisseur of such objects.

While enjoying the admiral's hospitality, Weil not only took note of the items he wished to purloin, he also checked out doors, windows, the servants quarters and anything else that might prove useful in a burglary.

Some weeks passed before the admiral's home was robbed. As with the Enfield lady, no one suspected Dr Weil. His patience and meticulous attention to detail had paid off. So well had it been planned that Weil involved only his brother, who carried out the burglary quickly and effectively, taking only the choicest items. A receiver of stolen goods with contacts in Europe disposed of the booty and the brothers divided up their ill-gotten gains. Asher took one third, his brother the rest.

With his financial position set to dramatically improve, Dr Weil decided to enhance his reputation by becoming something of a philanthropist. As well as giv-ing modest sums to the poor, he would treat them free of charge. On occasion he would be seen to stay up all night by the bedside of a sick urchin. One such night was the one on which the admiral's mansion was burgled. It was a perfect alibi.

By this time Dr Weil's reputation as a competent doctor was spreading fast, thanks ironically to his first two burglary victims who were keen to tell all and sundry of his superb skills and excellent bedside manner. Dr Weil's practice final-ly began to prosper. No matter. By now he was addicted to crime, becoming ever greedier and with no intention of stopping. Nevertheless, Weil was no fool. He did not live an opulent lifestyle. To outsiders he seemed better off than before, but only in keeping with his increasingly wealthy clientele. Annoying though it might be to work all day for a few pounds when much more could be earned thrillingly and illegally, Dr Weil's practice did provide excellent cover and he always kept his eyes and ears open for new victims. One of his poorer patients, a carter, mentioned in passing that he had a rich uncle. The doctor pretended not to take much notice. In fact, he had the man in question checked out and found that he was indeed in possession of a fortune.

Mr Johnny Stripe was an aged caretaker of a large building he had looked after for over half-a-century situated near St Paul's Cathedral. It was rumoured that Stripe, who had always lived frugally, kept his life savings hidden in his garret home. Other criminals had broken in, ransacked the house, lifted every floorboard and tore plaster from the walls only to find nothing. In fury they had beaten him and Weil generously offered to treat the old miser's injuries free of charge. Stripe was in need of hospital care. His vehement insistence on staying at home convinced Weil that the money he sought was there somewhere. Sedating his patient, Weil thought the loot must be in the ceiling, which was crossed by a great beam. The ceiling and beam were the only places not previously searched. A cavity was found, not in the ceiling but in the beam itself. Two nights later, Asher Weil and an accomplice stole £2,789 from the hiding place in the beam. This represented the vast bulk of Stripe's life savings. The caretaker never discovered the crime. Waking up the next morning he was visited by Dr Weil who continued to 'care' for him until he died a week later. Given an overdose of sedative, he died a victim of Levi Weil's greed. As for his family, they found nothing of the late Johnny Stripe's fortune. Given that he had never been seen to spend money, they assumed they had been wrong. There was no money after all.

Levi Weil's practice could now justify his upward mobility from cramped to more amenable surroundings. He left his lodgings and rented a house. He could have bought one outright but would have sown the suspicion that he always tried to avoid. Rather, he moved commensurate with the increased prosperity gained from treating his increasingly affluent patients. Not for him a horse-drawn carriage and servants, which the £500 or more he was stealing each month could easily pay for. Still, the secret of his double life, the thrill it gave him and the fact that he and his gang of ruffians never failed to bring home the booty they sought filled Dr Weil with a confidence his patients found reassuring. Many more patients confided in him than could possibly have been taken advantage of and he could pick and choose from a host of rich, potential victims.

As the gang became increasingly successful, it soon grew to an unwieldy nine in number, including Dr Weil but information on their activities was more likely to leak as more people became involved. Group and self-discipline were imposed and Weil was generous, even treating their afflictions. All could swing if the authorities rumbled even one of them. Each man knew too much about his fellows to risk breaking ranks, even if he wanted to leave such a successful 'crew'. This assumption was to prove the gang's undoing. One of the members, a German Jew named Isaacs, was caught stealing from his colleagues. To Isaacs there was no honour among thieves. His associates thought differently and he was first unceremoniously beaten and then flung, humiliated, out of the gang. This act would come back to haunt them.

Although the gang took part in numerous burglaries each week, Levi Weil did not generally participate. After supplying all necessary information his confederates carried out each crime. On occasion however, when the gang thought a job too risky, a disguised Dr Weil came along to help restore their faltering courage. One such event led to murder.

In the autumn of 1771, Levi, Asher and their accomplices battered loudly on the door of a prosperous house in Kings Road, Chelsea Fields, another area that is part of modern London, yet at that time lay outside its boundaries. The owner was a widow, Mrs Hutchings, who supposedly kept a large sum of money and some valuables on the premises. Weil had helped her recover from some minor ailment, insisting on calling on her repeatedly until convinced she had fully recovered. It was 10pm and the household, with the exception of Mrs Hutchings and two female servants, was asleep. The bleary manservant of the abode woke up startled and sought to find out the reason for the commotion. He was instantly knocked to the ground. The entire gang rushed in, seized the maidservants and threatened to murder them on the spot unless they were given what they came for. Mrs Hutchings, a powerfully built woman, fought ferociously but was overpowered and tied up with her own petticoats. Her two young sons, daughter and the three servants were also bound.

Ransacking the house, the gang broke into an apartment within the house occupied by two farm labourers, John Slow and William Stone. Believing them a threat to their entire criminal enterprise, Weil shot wildly at Stone's chest. The bullet only stunned him. Slow now joined the struggle and cries from the gang went up. 'Shoot him! Shoot him!' the desperados shrieked. A pistol shot was heard and Slow fell, yelling, 'Lord have mercy on me! I am murdered!'

The wounded man was dragged out of the room onto the stairs, while Stone, recovering his senses, leaped up, climbed out of the window and frantically escaped over the roof.

The house was ransacked and looted of its silver plate but no money was discovered. Mrs Hutchings was threatened with torture and murder if she did not reveal the hiding place. After being repeatedly assaulted, she eventually told them and the gang fled with her watch, the plate and £65. The household soon broke free from their bonds and found Mr Slow. He declared himself to be dying. Sure enough, the following afternoon he died of his wounds.

Following the slaying of Mr Slow, a furore arose and a reward was offered for the capture of what was now known bizarrely and inexplicably as 'The Apple Dumpling Gang'. Wealthy homeowners already shaken by the recent spate of burglaries now feared murder too. Many took no chances, hiring servants to sit up at night fully armed to await any robbers who might trespass.

Amidst the public outcry, Isaacs saw a chance to get revenge for being thrown out of the gang, be pardoned for his own misdeeds and gain a reward. Thus, he turned King's Evidence, a controversial device whereby, when murder was involved, a criminal informed on his former partners in crime in exchange for immunity from prosecution. Essentially he became a 'supergrass'.

The Weil brothers had no idea that their crime spree was soon to end. Levi was planning his biggest caper yet, the robbery of a diamond jeweller expecting a shipment worth the then astronomical sum of £40,000. It would be an easy task. Dr Weil dined with the jeweller who spoke effusively of his riches, when they were arriving and where they would be kept. Dr Weil was so convinced that the diamonds were as good as in his possession he decided the robbery could be carried out by himself, his brother and only one other gang member. Alas, for Weil and the short-lived if temporarily successful Apple Dumpling Gang, Isaacs had alerted the Bow Street Runners to their misdeeds before they could carry off their last big 'score'. All eight remaining gang members were arrested.

At the Old Bailey six of the gang were tried, two having died soon after their arrest, supposedly in terror at what lay before them. While Marcus Hartagh and Lazarus Harry were acquitted for lack of evidence, Dr Levi Weil and his brother Asher, Jacob Lazarus and Solomon Porter all swung. Isaacs had his revenge in full.

The trial had taken place on a Friday. The following day was the Jewish Sabbath and the gang were declared an anathema by London's rabbis, aware of the hostility and suspicion heaped on London's small Jewish community by the depredations of their co-religionists. Two days later, one rabbi visited the condemned as they languished in Newgate prison, presenting each with a Hebrew book. The rabbi declined to pray with them or accompany them to the gallows, such was the shame they had brought on their people.

At Tyburn Gallows an immense crowd gathered that day, 9 December 1771, to witness the execution. The damned prayed together in Hebrew before being sent into oblivion one by one.

CHAPTER 17
Dr Carl Weiss: Improbable Assassin

'God, don't let me die, I have so much to do.'
Senator Huey Long

IT WAS A hot, balmy evening, 8 September 1935, when a 'crazed' assassin, Dr Carl Weiss, came forth from the shadows and gunned down the Louisiana Senator Huey Pierce Long jnr in the State Capitol of Baton Rouge. Huey Long was a fiery, populist Southern Democrat with an eye on no less a prize than the presidency of the United States. Tall and charismatic, with dark curly hair and a ruddy complexion, he was dynamic, outspoken and consumed with belief in his own destiny. Few historical figures in America have had a greater impact on politics, the press, literature and even film than Long. Included in works that encapsulated his career are the Pulitzer Prize-winning novel *All The King's Men* of 1946 by Robert Penn Warren and the 1949 Oscar-winning film of the same name, whose central character, Willie Stark, was based very much on Huey Long.

Long had many enemies, who nicknamed him 'the Despot of the Delta' and 'Caesar of the Bayous'. Long preferred to call himself 'Kingfish' after a wily character in the popular radio programme Amos 'n'Andy even answering the phone with, 'This is the Kingfish'.

* * *

Dr Carl Austin Weiss was one of history's least likely assassins. He was born on 6 December 1906 in Baton Rouge, Louisiana, the son of Dr Carl Adam Weiss. Studying at Tulane University Medical School in New Orleans, Dr Weiss worked initially at the city's Turo Infirmary before heading to France, where he found employment at the American University in Paris. He then worked in New York's Bellevue Hospital from May 1930 before finishing his postgraduate studies in Austria. By 1932 Weiss' wanderlust had waned and he returned to Baton Rouge and found employment in his father's medical practice. The following year Weiss married Yvonne Pavy, the daughter of Judge Benjamin Henry Pavy, a man who hated Huey Long with a passion.

Originally Jewish, Weiss' family had converted to Roman Catholicism many years previously. Yvonne Pavy was descended from a long line of Catholic French Bourbon planters.

By the age of 28, Dr Weiss was the most renowned ear, nose and throat specialist in Louisiana. Tall and handsome with a thin, angular, inquisitive face and bright eyes, bespectacled Dr Weiss looked every inch the highly intelligent and respected man he was, which makes what happened all the more inexplicable.

Judge Pavy's relentless opposition to Huey Long led to the senator launching undeclared war against him, as he did against any who dared oppose his dictats. Pavy could not be unseated from his stronghold of St Landry's Parish in the 13th Louisiana judicial district, some 33 miles west of Baton Rouge and so Long vindictively used his influence to have two of his daughters sacked from their teaching posts. The tension between the two men rose further when Long began to threaten Pavy with rumours that his family contained 'coffee blood', a reference to Pavy's father-in-law supposedly having had a black mistress. It was even rumoured that Long was preparing a bill to remove Judge Pavy on the grounds of his 'defiled ancestry'. In fact Senator Long was moving against his long-standing opponent, but race was not a factor. Pavy's independent mind was.

On the morning of 7 September 1935, Senator Long announced that he would convene a special session of the Louisiana legislature that evening in Baton Rouge. In all, 42 bills would be considered. One of these would transfer the predominantly Catholic parish of St Landry's to the predominantly Protestant 15th judicial district, a Long stronghold. Without St Landry's, the 13th would be open to a takeover by Long supporters.

The transfer of St Landry's created tensions even among Long's allies, so blatant was the proposed gerrymandering involved. The Kingfish therefore drove from New Orleans to ensure his view prevailed. The following evening, Sunday 8 September, after supper, Senator Long entered the legislative chamber. He chatted to colleagues and held the floor until the meeting adjourned just before 9.20pm. Senator Long then headed towards the governor's office along with the Lieutenant Governor, Justice John Fournet of Louisiana Supreme Court (who 30 years later was to be involved in investigating the Kennedy assassination) and seven armed bodyguards, or 'Cossacks' as they sometimes called themselves, walking to where his nemesis was waiting.

That Sunday evening, Weiss was supposedly enraged by the rumours circulating that his wife was of partial black descent. This meant the family would be considered black socially and Weiss feared the impact that would have upon his practice. He determined to visit Senator Long in the State Capitol building and intended, it is speculated, to also raise the issue of Long's gerrymandering against Judge Pavy.

Senator Long was outside the office of his handpicked successor, Governor Oscar Kelly Allen. Allen was a man so devoted to his master that it was alleged he not only signed any bill Long placed before him but even a leaf that blew in through his window.

Weiss lurked behind a marble pillar dressed in his Sunday-best white linen suit, somewhat curious attire for an 'assassin'. He approached the senator and appeared to raise his hand to shake Long's. Weiss then drew a .32 automatic revolver and Fournet tried to deflect his arm but the gun still went off and a bullet hit Long in the abdomen. Bodyguard Murphy Roden leapt on Weiss, wrestling him to the ground. After a second shot tore Roden's wristwatch from his arm, he struggled free of the assassin, Weiss' gun jammed and a hail of bullets engulfed him as Long's bodyguards opened fire. At least .31-, .38- and .45-calibre bullets struck Weiss, whose body was later found to have 61 entry and exit wounds. One of the bullets from the bodyguards ricocheted off a pillar and struck Long painfully in the lower spine.

Long staggered from the building unaided and was taken to Our Lady of the Lake Sanatorium. He was operated on at 11.20pm by a reluctant Dr Arthur Vidrine, who would have preferred the operation to be carried out by a more experienced surgeon. A bullet had penetrated below Long's ribs and pierced his colon. His pulse rose and his blood pressure fell, a sure sign of internal haemorrhaging. He lost a lot of blood but the prognosis looked positive when the senator was patched up. However, a second bullet was then discovered lodged near his kidney and the internal bleeding continued. As the second bullet had remained undetected by the surgeons until it was too late, they could not operate on a patient too weak to survive further surgery. Long died at 3.30am on 10 September 1935, 30 hours after being shot. He had just turned 42.

Fifty years after the Long assassination, John Fournet was interviewed for an eponymous documentary on the life of Huey Long. According to Fournet, as he stepped out of the governor's office a man 'with a strange look on his face' was coming towards them, gun in hand. A bodyguard, Mr Murphy Roden, grabbed the gun and it went off hitting Senator Long on his right side. Later, Fournet visited a seemingly still robust Kingfish in hospital. The doctors at first would not let Fournet in. Long insisted. When told who had shot him, perplexed, he said, 'What does he want to shoot me for? I don't even know him'. A few hours later, realising his death was imminent Long uttered his final words, 'God, don't let me die, I have so much to do'. Later it was speculated that Weiss had slain Long because he 'reminded him of Hitler'. Having worked in Europe and being of Jewish origin, this theory seemed to be rather too neat an explanation.

Long's body lay in state in the Memorial Hall of the Louisiana State Capitol for several days, watched over by national guardsmen who banned the cameras of mourners walking past in silent procession. Over 175,000 people watched the funeral procession, the biggest turn-out for a funeral in Louisiana's history.

* * *

Dr Carl Austin Weiss was unique among assassins. He was not embittered, socially hostile or a loner. In fact, he was a seemingly contented man with a newborn son, Carl jnr (who would later become a distinguished doctor himself), a loving wife, a stable family background and a highly respected and thriving career. He had no history of mental illness, violence or extreme political views and seemingly had everything to live for. His family and the general populace were equally perplexed by what had happened and there was no universal public condemnation of the 'murderer'. No one vilified the Weiss family or Carl, his family were treated sympathetically by the press and Carl was given a hero's send off at his funeral. Bewilderment was the feeling most apparent among friends, colleagues and his shocked family. Why had he done it? Judge Pavy thought the racial slurs against his family trivial, unlikely to be believed and, as for the gerrymandering, well he would retire soon anyway.

The Weiss family did not accept the official story of the Long/Weiss killings or the media's interpretation of it. There seemed no rational motive and the scepticism of the Weiss family was shared by thousands of others across Louisiana and beyond. An unpublished report claimed that one of Long's bodyguards had killed the senator, 'confessing' while drunk that he had killed his 'best friend' and planted Weiss' gun on the doctor to frame him. So was Weiss a killer or a patsy for treacherous or incompetent and reckless bodyguards?

Astonishingly, neither Huey Long nor Carl Weiss had autopsies conducted on their bodies. Suspiciously, Dr Thomas B Bird, East Baton Rouge parish coroner, was under such pressure from Long's associates not to hold an inquest into Weiss death that it was postponed from 9 September. It did not take place until 16 September, eight days after the shootings. By then General Louis F Guerre of the Bureau for Criminal Investigation, a Long ally, had de-briefed all who had been in the vicinity of the incident and whose stories since had clearly coalesced. A report he alone had access to regarding the shootings subsequently disappeared, as did all the physical evidence collected at the scene. One thing the witnesses could not agree on was the number of shots Weiss fired. One or two was as close to a consensus as could be reached. Two witnesses alleged that when they first saw Weiss he appeared to be 'chambering a round', ie placing a bullet in the chamber of his gun. Surely, if one was planning an assassination, especially someone as meticulous as Dr Weiss, ensuring one had a bullet ready to fire would be a basic prerequisite for the success of the venture?

The official 72-page record of the Weiss inquest was made public only on 10 September 1985 when entered into the Congressional Record by Huey Long's son, Senator Russell B Long. In contrast to the Weiss inquest, the inquest into the death of Senator Long took place almost as soon as he had died, being held without testimony at Rabenhorst Funeral Home, Baton Rouge, on 9 September.

On the fateful day it transpired that Carl and Yvonne had gone to Mass, dined at his parents' house and then the entire family had enjoyed a riverside picnic in the warm summer sunshine. At 7.30pm they returned to the city and Carl took his wife home, situated near the State Capitol. He phoned a colleague, Dr J Webb McGehee, at 8.15pm to confirm the details of an operation he was to carry out the following day and its change of location from Our Lady of the Lake Sanatorium to Baton Rouge General Hospital. These were not the acts one would expect of someone planning an assassination immediately thereafter. At 9.00pm he received a telephone call to visit a patient. Within minutes he was in the State Capitol. Nothing in his demeanour that quiet day had given any clue that the young doctor was contemplating murder. Could he have been under the influence of drink or drugs? An autopsy might have given us an answer.

The inquest into Weiss' death showed the savage way in which he died. Half his face was blown away and the 61 exit and entry wounds were found on his mutilated, broken body. If Dr Carl Weiss had planned an assassination, why confirm the operation for the following day? Why was he not restless or agitated that Sunday and how did he manage to walk into the building with a gun, unmolested by guards always on the alert for an attack? Why did he shoot Senator Long in the abdomen when success was more likely to result from shooting his victim in the head?

Opponents of his crude and aggressive political style have long reviled the memory of Huey Long, while for many of the poor in Louisiana he is remembered as a Robin Hood-style folk hero. He was born the seventh child in a family of four boys and five girls on 30 August 1893 to Huey Pierce Long Snr and Caledonia (Tison) Long, in the poor farming community of Winnfield, Winn Parish, north-central Louisiana. Winnfield was without paved roads, livestock roamed through the streets and stores and shops were often erected in tents. His family were middle-class Baptists but Long absorbed many of the strong populist traditions of the area he grew up in to become an avowed socialist, populist and, some claimed a 'neo-Bolshevik'.

Long was educated locally at public schools but left before graduation, having quarrelled with the school authorities who expelled him in 1908 for circulating a petition calling for the principal to be sacked. He worked successfully as a salesman for four years, selling canned goods and patent medicines while gaining the reputation of being able to 'sell anything to anyone'. His early career taught him the importance of advertising, sales promotion and product marketing.

On 21 April 1913 Long married Rose McConnell, whom he met three years earlier when she won a cake-baking contest he was judging. They would go on to have three children and, from the start, he told her of his intended path to political greatness. In September 1914 Long enrolled at Tulane University Law School in New Orleans. For the next eight months he rarely ate or slept, cramming for his bar examination, which he sat and passed in May 1915. Highly intelligent with a photographic memory that ensured he never forgot a name or a face, Long was now the youngest certified lawyer in the state. Initially he practiced law in Winnfield before earning enough to open a prosperous practice in Shreveport.

Huey Long was always determined to have a career in politics and in 1918 he was elected to the fairly modest post of Louisiana Railroad Commissioner, defeating wealthy landowner Burke A Bridges by 7,286 votes to 6,651. As one of three commissioners regulating the railways, oil and gas pipelines, he built a strong reputation as a friend of the workers, enhancing their pay, benefits and working conditions while provoking the ire of big business. Anyone opposing him was attacked as 'feeding out of the hands of Standard Oil', a company that he opposed throughout his life. In 1921 the commission gained new powers and was renamed the Public Service Commission. Becoming chairman in 1922, Long was twice unsuccessfully indicted for challenging Standard Oil regarding the regulation of pipelines, enhancing his profile and status among the constituency he targeted. He raised oil company carriage rates and opposed the Cumberland Telephone and Telegraph Company's plan to hike their telephone charges by 25%.

A rich, landed Bourbon class of French ancestry known as the 'Old Regulars' effectively controlled Louisiana in the 1920s, then as now one of America's poorest states. Impoverished white sharecroppers and factory workers were exploited, patronised and bore the brunt of taxation and, in time of war, military service. Wages were low because the huge black underclass could always undercut the wages of their white counterparts. Should the poor whites get too 'uppity', the threat of black unrest could always be used against them. Quite simply, the ruling hierarchy were content with life and brooked no change that would upset their apple cart.

In 1924 Long ran unsuccessfully for Governor of Louisiana in the Democratic Primary against the candidate of the Old Regulars, Hewitt Bouanchaud, and Henry Luce Fuqua on a platform of free schoolbooks, road construction and building state warehouses for farm crops. He wanted to reduce corporate influence on government, increase state involvement in the economy and reduce the wealth of the 'bloated plutocracy', the two percent of the population who controlled 65% of Louisiana's wealth.

Although less well known than his opponents and with no established political organisation, Long was an innovative campaigner, pioneering the use of mailed circulars, posters, radio speeches and brutal personal invective designed to appeal to the masses who believed themselves to be excluded from wealth, privilege and power. At this time he began to wear a white linen suit to distinguish himself from the common weal.

He won 73,935 votes on election day, 15 January 1924, against 84,162 for Bouanchaud and 81,382 for Fuqua. Although eliminated from the race Long had won an outright majority in 21 of the state's 65 parishes and his supporters ensured Fuqua would go on to become governor, as the Democrat candidate was virtually guaranteed victory.

Long now built a political machine across Louisiana. He was strongest in the north but weakest in New Orleans. In 1926 he supported the re-election of Catholic Joseph Eugene Ransdell and two years later French Catholic Edwin Broussard, building his support in previously hostile Catholic and Cajun areas. In 1927 Long began a 600-speech, 15,000-mile campaign to become governor, attacking his fellow Democrat opponents as 'trough feeders, low-down dirty thieves and liars'.

Huey Long was nothing if not egocentric, power-hungry and ruthless, convinced he was a man of destiny. In his own words he was 'suis generis (one of a kind) just leave it at that'. He would become a master of manipulation in office and a brilliant machine politician who dominated a system in which bribery and corruption, patronage, bullying and extortion would become almost routine. That he was highly complex, a brilliant political strategist and a boor were beyond doubt.

In the Democratic Primary Long won 126,842 votes (43.9%) against two opponents. Although this should have meant a run-off, rival Oramel Hinckley Simpson pledged his support to the Kingfish in exchange for a lucrative state post. The feeble Republican candidate was defeated in the actual election in April 1938 by 92,941 votes to 3,733 and Huey P Long was elected Governor of Louisiana. During the campaign, he honed his previously poor oratorical skills, knocked on thousands of doors and reached out to parishes he had little support in previously.

At the relatively young age of 34, Long was to have an immediate, electrifying and long-lasting impact on his state. To Long the moderate Democrats that preceded him were incapable of taking the radical steps necessary to eliminate the desperate poverty into which so many in the state were born, lived and died. Race was important but not the massive issue it was in neighbouring Alabama and Mississippi and Long was the first to campaign in Louisiana without playing the race card. Like other southern Democrat states with de-facto one party rule, people were mired in poverty, accepting the rule of those who controlled the Democratic political machine. In Louisiana, within the Democrats the voters at least had a choice of fiscal conservatism from the Democrat establishment or Long's populism, a state of affairs that lingered on for a quarter of a century after Long's death.

In power, only 9 of 39 senators and 18 of 100 members of the House of Representatives initially backed Long. To secure his base, he took the unprecedented step of deciding who sat on which committees and was able to ram his legislative programme through. Using patronage Long gained control of the State Health Board, State Transportation Board and the Public Services Commission. All managerial employees, including Lieutenant Governor Paul Cyr, were required to sign undated resignation letters to intimidate them.

As Governor of Louisiana, Long developed what he called his 'Share the Wealth' programme to court public support. Infrastructure was prioritised, with the redevelopment of New Orleans port and the construction of its first airport. Swamps were drained and 3,000 miles of paved road and 111 bridges built by raising tax on gasoline from two to four cents a gallon. To improve educational attainment in a state where many children were illiterate because their parents could not afford books, all schoolchildren were given free schoolbooks funded by a severance tax paid by oil and gas companies. Louisiana State University saw a quantum leap in funding and the opening of a medical school. Investment in health was increased too through expansion of the charity system and the opening of New Orleans Charitable Hospital to treat poor people who lacked medical insurance.

Even prisons and mental institutions were reformed in the myriad of changes imposed by the workaholic, phenomenally energetic and ambitious Kingfish who seemed to devote himself 24 hours a day to Louisiana. Chain gangs and straitjacketing were abolished and dental care introduced along with prisoner rehabilitation. An adult literacy drive helped the black community raise its literacy levels from 62% to 77% at a time when few whites sympathised with their plight and endemic poverty.

Long sought to expand his political base and increase voter participation among blacks and poor whites by abolishing the poll tax as a voter registration qualification. To allow poor blacks to vote, the National Guard was used to protect polls.

Long's fiscally conservative adversaries opposed him every step of the way, whether it was his policy of taxing wealth and businesses or his plan to build a new State Capitol. The oil, sugar and lumber companies, particularly Standard Oil, the biggest corporation in the old Confederacy, resented the increased taxation the Kingfish imposed on them.

State spending was almost tripled from $28 to $83 million per annum and the state debt grew from $11 to $125 million during Long's tenure. Judge Cecil Morgan, a former state legislator commenting many years later on both the dynamism and corruption of the Huey Long era said that, 'He provided about $100 million worth of good roads. And it only cost $150 million. There was a cushion for other people's fraud'. When Representative Morgan refused to support a piece of Long legislation his father was immediately fired from his state job, leading to Morgan bringing forward an attempted impeachment of Long in 1929.

On 26 March 1929 Long defeated the attempt which was backed by Standard Oil because of a five-cent tax he had imposed on refined oil. Standard Oil threatened to close its refineries and leave the state, costing thousands of jobs. In Louisiana's House of Representatives a group calling itself the 'Dynamite

Squad', in protest at Governor Long's unauthorised demolition of the gubernatorial mansion, grouped to oppose their governor. The impeachment accused Long of having tried to induce a former bodyguard to kill a Long opponent in exchange for money and legal immunity. Nineteen charges were levelled and eight accepted as grounds for impeachment. Included were accusations of incompetence, corruption, gross misconduct, misappropriation of funds and using 'vile, obscene and scurrilous language'.

Long's use of circulars to show himself to the public as a victim and 'negotiations' with fellow politicians, 15 of whom signed a round robin that they would not vote to convict regardless of the evidence, led to his acquittal. Two-thirds of the 39 senators were required to impeach. With 15 on his side, Longs opponents were two votes short.

Riled by the impeachment attempt, the Kingfish became more of a demagogue and behaved increasingly ruthlessly towards enemies whether real or imagined. His more visceral opponents, who he intimidated by calling out the Louisiana National Guard on occasion, considered him a 'Fascist'. He controlled both the police and the judiciary, which he used to his own ends. His practices were undoubtedly anti-democratic and his power was such that he would call special sessions of the state legislature to rush through new laws without proper debate or committee scrutiny. Between August 1934 and September 1935 alone, some 236 bills were enacted in this way. Some of these included measures previously rejected but incorporated in another piece of legislation to get it through.

That Long abused his power is beyond dispute. Political allies were awarded state contracts, appointing family members and cronies to well-paid state jobs. All state employees had salary deductions in order to fund a pro-Kingfish newspaper *Louisiana Progress* he founded in 1930. At the same time Long sought to muzzle existing publications that did not kowtow to him or criticised the governor, his allies or his policies. His biggest enemy was Louisiana's lively press, the one democratic institution he failed to dominate or control. Some 163 daily, weekly and monthly publications existed in Louisiana in the early 1930s. While some supported Long, the hatred of urban newspapers for him was implacable.

In June 1930, legislation denounced by the American Newspaper Publishers Association as 'the boldest and most flagrant measures ever aimed at the freedom of American newspapers', was introduced in Louisiana. A 15% tax was imposed on advertising revenue. Further to this, the governor could impose a court-issued injunction to suppress any newspaper that was 'lewd, obscene, lascivious, malicious, scandalous or defamatory'. If the courts failed to act, private citizens could initiate proceedings themselves.

Long was temporarily defeated in his assaults on the Louisiana press which had the vociferous backing of newspapers the length and breadth of the United States. The implications of Long's assault on press freedom were obvious: any newspaper that was hostile and which the Kingfish deemed to have broken the new law could face legal action and possible closure. Likewise the newspaper tax could be raised until the offending publication was driven into bankruptcy. Publishers fought ferociously in the courts to derail Long's plans. A war of attrition commenced, finally being won by Long in 1934 when the newspaper tax was imposed and Alice Lee Grosjean, alleged mistress of the Kingfish, was installed as its collector. Grosjean, beautiful and only 25 years old had previously been Long's personal secretary when he appointed her Secretary of State in October 1930 on the death of incumbent James J Bailey.

Long called his tax proposal, 'a tax on lying at two cents a lie'. On 2 July 1934 Long announced, 'I believe in freedom of speech but it's got to be truthful speech, and lying newspapers should have to pay for their lying. I'm going to help these newspapers by hitting them in their pocketbooks. Maybe then they'll try to clean up'. On 10 July 1934, the New Orleans *Times-Picayune* responded to this implied threat, denouncing the new law as, 'The rape of representative government and the assault upon a free press ... driven ... by the openly wielded lash of a dictator without principle, honest conviction or scruple, constitute the blackest chapter in Louisiana's history'.

The press took legal advice and the courts eventually invalidated the tax law on the grounds of its illegitimacy and punitive nature. The case, American Press Company v Grosjean, eventually reached the US Supreme Court in January 1936 when the late Huey Long's legislation was thrown out, ironically on the very day his widow was sworn in to succeed him in the US Senate. The Supreme Court decision helped to actually broaden the constitutional guarantee of press freedom beyond the prohibition of prior restraint.

Long's controversial policies and occasionally eccentric behaviour, such as meeting the captain of a visiting German cruiser in his pyjamas, soon pushed the Kingfish onto the national stage.

Using a sound truck for the first time in US politics to address huge crowds, in 1930 Long was elected to the US Senate after defeating the incumbent Joseph Ransdell in the primary by 149,640 votes to 111,451. As one of Louisiana's two senators, he now considered himself to be bigger than the 'Kingfish' name he had given himself years before, saying, 'I ain't no fish, I'm gonna pick another name, maybe one with a lion or a tiger on it'. Kingfish stuck and Long did not head to Washington until January 1932, retaining his gubernatorial status until his political allies were secure. This was in defiance of the Louisiana constitution, which stated that two powerful political offices should not be held simultaneously. To aid his hold on power, he created a new police organisation, the Bureau of Criminal Identification (BCI), responsible to him alone. This sinister organisation was empowered by Long to arrest and detain anyone without warrant at his behest.

Lieutenant Governor, Paul Cyr, had fallen out with Long who announced he would not accept Cyr as governor, 'even for a minute'. After much wrangling, in October 1931 Cyr took the oath as governor, stating that Long had vacated the post upon his election to the Senate. The Kingfish called out the police and National Guard and had them surround the governor's mansion and office. Declaring Cyr's appointment null and void, the Kingfish declared that Lieutenant Governor Cyr had vacated his own office and replaced him with the President of the Louisiana Senate, Alvin Olin King, a Long supporter, who became governor in January 1932. In May 1932 Governor Allen, Long's choice as his successor, was installed, albeit with the Kingfish still calling all the shots.

Arriving in Washington on 25 January 1932 Long shook up the US Senate just as he had his own domestic legislature back home in Louisiana. He produced long lists of fellow Democrats whose legal firms had the largest corporations as clients, denouncing them as being in the pockets of big business interests. He allied himself with progressive Republicans to force through an extension of bankruptcy privileges to farmers hit hard by the Depression. After attacking his old foe Standard Oil for supporting Bolivia in a war with Paraguay for control of Latin American oilfields, the Paraguayans named a stronghold 'Senator Huey Long Fort' after him. More outlandishly, Long wasted energy on absurd legislation, such as a bill requiring all Jew's harp manufacturers to make them to the same specification.

Formerly a staunch supporter of President Roosevelt, Long had given an impressive speech at the Democratic National Convention in Chicago but broke from the President in June 1933 in protest at not being given federal patronage. This he knew undermined his own monopoly of power in Louisiana, especially when Roosevelt's own men began distributing New Deal money in that state. Senator Long became a nuisance, insulting his own party colleagues at every turn. He also believed that the president was not doing enough to ameliorate the Depression.

Long's boorishness almost caused his downfall. Drunk at a party in Long Island on 27 August 1933, Long insulted an obese woman and urinated on a man. The press laughed at him, calling him 'Huey Pee Long'. Back in his home state on a speaking tour, he was pelted with rotten fruit and eggs. To save his political career and move towards fulfilment of his presidential ambitions, he launched himself at the nation.

Huey Long enunciated his 'Share the Wealth' programme on the floor of the Senate, unveiled his new 'Share Our Wealth Society' on 23 January 1934. By July 1935, Long's initiative would have 7,682,768 million members, roughly one in 15 Americans, organised into 27,431 chapters in every state of the Union. Tourists to Washington wanted to see the 'White House, Monument, Capitol and the Kingfish'. He was becoming a serious potential threat to the establishment, and after one radio speech attacking the president's administration, Senator Long received over 30,000 letters a day for 24 consecutive days.

A man in a hurry, Long made it clear he intended to run against President Roosevelt for the 1936 Democratic Party Nomination. He appeared at speaking engagements across a country racked by the Depression offering simple, perhaps simplistic, solutions, supported by Louisiana Progress which he had renamed American Progress in 1933. His slogan, as he denounced oil companies, speculators and the 'idle' rich, was the somewhat preposterous, 'Every Man a King but no one wears the Crown'. An autobiography, or rather hagiography, *Every Man a King* was published. Ultimately Long believed that even if he lost the nomination he could launch a third party and win through in either 1936 or 1940.

Long wanted strict controls on incomes with a ceiling of $1 million a year and no American to have a net worth of more than $10 million. These were vast sums in the but Long also showed he was a defender of the 'little man'. He promised a guaranteed income of $2,000 a year when 18.3 million American families survived on less than $1,000 per annum and promised pensions for the elderly and free education, up to and including college, for the young. Egalitarianism and fairness were his watchwords and his oratory, blunt manner and apparent honesty appealed to many of the rural and small-town poor he primarily reached out to. So confident was Long that his message would resonate with the American people that he began a book in his last year of life, modestly entitled *My First 100 Days in the White House*, in which he proposed relegating President Franklin Delano Roosevelt to Secretary of the Navy!

Back in Louisiana, towards the end of 1934 and in 1935 the Kingfish took steps to tighten his grip. As well as taking on the press, Long's rubber-stamp legislature passed laws to give control of all police forces and fire stations to the governor, who could hire or fire any police officer or firefighter. Municipalities could no longer appoint teachers, councillors or officials. The state government took on this power. The New Orleans Tax Act prevented the city from collecting any taxes, effectively bankrupting the city. This was repealed when the administration agreed to support Senator Long. The State Board of Censors Act allowed the governor to prohibit any films, including newsreels, from being shown in Louisiana. The State Elections Board was given the power to count and confirm all ballots cast in a Democratic primary, placing elections and selections in Long's hands. The State Printing Board was empowered to decide which newspapers were to become the 'official printer' for a district, printing parish, school and municipal notices. For many small publications this could mean the difference between staying in and going out of business. As a consequence, many anti-Long newspapers did an immediate volte-face.

The public grew restless at Long's relentless attacks on their rights and centralising of power in his own hands. On 25 January 1935, an estimated 300 protestors, most of them armed, seized East Baton Rouge Courthouse. Long reacted by placing Baton Rouge under martial law, forbidding crowds from gathering and the 'carrying, transporting, selling or buying of firearms'. This was a breach of constitutional rights. Nevertheless, the city was renamed the 'First Military District', and placed under the command of the BCI commander, General Guerre. Martial law remained in place for six months.

Senator Long knew the hackles he was raising across America with his open challenge to vested interests. Forces were mobilising against him, ranging from the 'Square Deal Association' in Illinois to the 'Minutemen of Louisiana'. After Chicago Mayor Anton Cermak was killed in a botched assassination attempt on the president in 1933, Long surrounded himself with bodyguards, saying 'Some crazy galoot's liable to be behind any one of those telephone poles and take a shot at me'. In July 1935 his Louisiana opponents held a large convention in the DeSoto Hotel in New Orleans to decide their slate of candidates for the upcoming state elections. A by-now paranoid Long claimed that a plot was formulated at that meeting to assassinate him. Indeed, Judge Morgan later stated that, 'The tension was so high that in any gathering of more than three people, someone would say "Long ought to be shot".' If a plot ever existed to kill Senator Long, Dr Carl Weiss had no part in it. He was treating patients in Opelous, St Landry's parish on the day of the convention and those who attended would later deny ever having met him or even known who Dr Weiss was.

Since the events of 8 September 1935, an alternative theory has emerged as to what actually happened that night. Living so close to the State Capitol and visiting a patient anyway, it is likely that Dr Weiss decided to remonstrate with the Kingfish about Judge Pavy on impulse. He did not hide behind a marble pillar but waited in full view of Senator Long, attempting three times to speak to him. Each time Weiss was told to wait. During this time Weiss had ample opportunity to kill had he wanted to. He did not, probably because he was not a murderer and was in any case unarmed. After being brushed off for a third time by a tired, rude and probably irritable Long, Weiss lost his temper and punched him on the face, splitting the senator's lip. In fact, when asked in hospital when he had cut it, the Kingfish replied, 'that's where he hit me'.

The punch landed by Weiss enraged Senator Long's inexperienced and trigger-happy bodyguards who now fired wildly at Weiss, hitting their boss by mistake in the process. To cover up their incompetence, Weiss' gun, a Belgian .32 Fabrique Nationale, was retrieved from his medical bag and dumped beside his bloodied corpse. The two bullets taken from Long were .38 and .45 slugs, the same as those that had killed Weiss. The story of Weiss raising his gun arm and shooting Long was an invention to cover up what had really transpired.

Almost immediately on hearing on the radio of the incident, Weiss' brother Tom and his cousin Jim raced to the State Capitol. There they found Carl's car locked with his medical bag inside. Returning home to find keys, when they revisited the car's location it had vanished. It was found soon after behind the building unlocked, with Weiss' medical bag opened and disordered. His gun, usually kept in the glove compartment, had gone. It had been taken after the killing and placed at the scene of the shooting.

In 1985 a reporter looking into Long's insurance policy discovered that the insurance company, Mutual Insurance of New York, had quietly investigated the death and concluded that it was due to an accidental shooting by one of his own bodyguards. Bodyguard Joe Messina was considered by another, Delmas Sharp, to have fired the fatal shot and was referred to by Sharp as 'the killer' thereafter. Why was the alternative theory of how Long met his death not properly investigated? A cover-up seems highly likely, as ballistics alone would have proved Weiss was not the killer. In fact, shortly after the alleged assassination all the official records of the case and Weiss' gun disappeared. In September 1991 they were found in a safe deposit box owned by Mrs Mabel Binnings, daughter of General Louis Guerre, the man who had conducted the 'investigation' into the assassination and had then obviously decided to appropriate some of the evidence afterwards. The official records were released into police care. They commented that 'nothing worth mentioning' had been discovered.

Long's programme of public works had proven very popular in Louisiana and he was not forgotten either by friend or foe. In office he was aided by a press he had ruthlessly suppressed and muzzled almost from the commencement of his period as governor. In fact, many of Long's successes could have been enhanced had he accepted Federal Relief. This he blocked to emphasise how his state was being 'ignored' by Washington. After his untimely death, federal relief funds were instrumental in lifting Louisiana out of the Depression.

After his death American Progress blamed Long's press foes for his demise. On 24 October it pronounced, 'Of all the forces that conspired, incited and urged the removal of Huey P Long from politics in Louisiana, there is none whose hands are so stained with blood as the daily newspapers of Louisiana'. His enemies did not respect him even after Long's death. Said the Chicago Tribune on 12 February 1936, 'Huey Long was a Hitler in every sense but one: Hitler controls the press of Germany. Huey Long did not control the press of Louisiana'.

Rose Long, the senator's wife, was appointed to succeed him on 31 January 1936 and was subsequently elected on 21 April 1936 in a special election to fill the vacancy until 2 January 1937. Senator Long's younger brother, Earl Kemp Long, who had been estranged from his sibling until just before Huey died, took over his brother's political faction and controlled it until 1960. Earl Long served three years as Lieutenant Governor and then three terms as governor from 1939-1941, 1948-1952 and 1956-1960 when he died of a heart attack. Huey Long's son, Russell Billiu Long, had an even more impressive political career. He became a senator the day before his 30th birthday and served continuously from 31 December 1948 until he retired on 3 January 1987.

However, the story of Long's 'assassin' Carl Weiss had not ended yet.

* * *

On 20 October 1991 the remains of Dr Carl Austin Weiss were removed from Roselawn Cemetery in Baton Rouge after the exhumation was denounced by numerous Louisiana politicians who wanted to 'let sleeping dogs lie'. It was subsequently flown to Washington DC and examined by a team led by Professor James E Starrs, Professor of Law at the National Law Centre, George Washington University, Washington DC and a professor of forensic science. Professor Starrs writes, publishes and distributes *Scientific Sleuthing Review*, a quarterly publication that encourages the use of up-to-date scientific techniques to investigate controversial and often 'closed' cases. He had already helped to locate Weiss' missing gun.

Professor Starrs had long been intrigued by the circumstances surrounding the deaths of Long and Weiss and was given permission by the Weiss family to exhume the body. Professor Starrs did not plan to exhume the body of Huey Long. Although that might be beneficial to solving the case, the Long family were strongly against it. In fact, Starrs' purpose was to see whether Weiss' remains supported the testimony given by Long's bodyguards at the Weiss inquest in 1935 or if they cast a doubt over their evidence and therefore the probable guilt of Dr Weiss.

The bones of Dr Weiss still retained some flesh that would enable Dr Alphonse Poklis of the University of Virginia to carry out a toxicological investigation of the remains. Dr Douglas H Ubelaker, Curator of the Museum of Natural History at the Smithsonian Institute intended to examine the remains anthropologically and Dr Irvin M Sopher of the University of West Virginia planned to carry out an autopsy to check if there was a physiological or pathological reason for the actions of Dr Weiss on that fatal night in 1935. Mr Lucien Haag, a criminologist and firearms expert from Phoenix, Arizona had the task of evaluating any bullets or bullet fragments found in or near the remains.

In preparation for taking the skeleton of Weiss to Washington for forensic analysis, Starrs washed the bones and placed them on a bed next to him to dry. Staying up all night to turn the bones, the following morning members of Starr's team asked him how he slept. 'I can't say I slept in peace, but Dr Weiss slept in pieces', was his jocular retort.

The investigation of Weiss' remains was carried out in the Department of Anthropology at Washington DC's Smithsonian Institute. Toxicology showed, as far as was possible given the decomposition of the tissues that Dr Weiss had not been under the influence of any identifiable drugs. Dr Ubelaker proved that at least two bullets had struck Dr Weiss in the head while he was in a prone position. A further 12 had hit him in the back and three other bullets struck him on the right side. Two shots had been fired from the left and seven from the front. This was weighed together with ballistics tests on a spent .32 calibre bullet from the scene of Long's death found in the Binnings collection that compared it with one test fired from Weiss' gun. The spent bullet was not fired by Weiss' FN .32 handgun. So who did fire it? Probably no one will ever know. Undoubtedly it was a bodyguard who carried a .32 for 'back up', but which one? Messina? Roden? Sharp? It could have been any one of the seven.

After concluding his investigations, Professor Starrs presented them at a meeting of the New Orleans Academy of Forensic Science in February 1992. It was a presentation that a local judge, aware of the sensitive topic, tried unsuccessfully to gag. After detailing his analysis of the evidence, Professor Starrs announced to a hushed audience that it was 'highly improbable' that Weiss had killed Senator Huey Long.

Whether Dr Carl Austin Weiss killed Senator Long or not, it is clear that it was his visit to the State Capitol that fateful evening that led to the Kingfish's death. One can speculate whether Weiss meant to assassinate or merely remonstrate. However, what is not open to conjecture is that his intervention ultimately proved fatal both for Senator Huey Pierce Long and himself. How much American and world history was changed that day can now only be postulated.

Bibliography

ARTICLES

Sitford, Mikaela, Addicted to Murder, The True Story of Dr Harold Shipman, *Manchester Evening News*, Manchester 2000

BOOKS

Allay, JB, *Famous Trials* Richards Ltd, London 1899

Annals, George J & Groin, Michael A, *The Nazi Doctors and the Nuremberg Code: Human Rights in Human Experiments*, Oxford University Press, New York 1992

Bedford, Sybille, *An Account of The Trial of Dr Adams*, Simon & Schuster, New York 1959

Blasdell, RH and Wilson, GH, *The Trial of Buck Ruxton*, William Hodge, Edinburgh 1950

Boswell, Charles and Thompson, Lewis, *The Girls in Nightmare House*, Fawcett Publications, New York 1955

Burleigh, Michael, *Death and Deliverance, Euthanasia in Germany 1930-1945*, Cambridge University Press, Cambridge 1994

The Third Reich: A New History, Macmillan Publishers, London 2000

Clarkson, Wensley, *The Good Doctor Blake*, London 2001

Cortner, Richard J, *The Kingfish and the Constitution: Huey Long and the First Amendment and the Emergence of Modern Press Freedom in America*, Greenwood Press, Westport, Connecticut 1996

Cullen, Tom, *Crippen The Mild Murderer*, Bodley Head, London 1977

Devlin, Lord Patrick, *Easing the Passing, The Trial of Dr John Bodkin Adams*, Bodley Head, London 1985

Dew, Ex-Chief Inspector Walter C, *I Caught Crippen*, Blackie & Son, London 1938

Diederich, Bernard and Al Burt, *The Truth About Haiti Today*, McGraw-Hill, New York 1969

Evans, Colin, *Killer Doctors*, Michael O'Mara Books, London 1993

Fest, Joachim, *The Face of the Third Reich*, Pantheon Books, New York 1970

Foran, David R et al, *The conviction of Dr. Crippen: New forensic findings in a century-old murder*, Journal of Forensic Sciences, volume 56, issue 1, 2011

Franke, David, *The Torture Doctor*, Hawthorn Books, New York 1975

Franklin, Charles, *The World's Worst Murderers*, Odhams Books Ltd, London 1965

Friedlander, Henry, *The Origins of Nazi Genocide. From Euthanasia to the Final Solution*, University of North Carolina, Chapel Hill & London 1995

Geyer, Frank P, *The Holmes-Pitezel Case*, Philadelphia Publishers Union, Philadelphia 1896

Gilbert, Martin, *Descent into Barbarism, A History of the 20th Century 1933-1951*, HarperCollins Publishers, London 1998

Gilbert, Michael, *Dr Crippen*, Odhams Press Ltd, London 1953

Glaister, John and Brash, James Couper, *Medico-Legal Aspects of the Ruxton Case*, E & S Livingstone, Edinburgh 1937

Gold, Herbert, *Best Nightmare on Earth, A life in Haiti*, Prentice Hall Press, New York 1991

Graves, Robert, *They Hanged My Saintly Billy, The Life and Death of Dr William Palmer*, Doubleday, New York 1957

Greene, Graham, *The Comedians*, Bodley Head, London 1966

Gutman, Yisrael & Berenbaum, Michael, *Anatomy of the Auschwitz Death Camp*, Indiana University Press, Bloomington and Indianapolis 1994

Hallworth, Rodney & Williams, Mark , *Where There's A Will ... The Sensational Life of Dr John Bodkin Adams*, The Capstan Press, Jersey 1983

Haydon, Colin and Doyle, William, *Robespierre*, Cambridge 1999

Hedley, Thomas, *Sick to Death*, Allen & Unwin, Sydney 2007

Hofmann, Werner, *Une époque en rupture 1750–1830*, Gallimard, Paris 1995

Howse, Geoffrey, *North London Murders*, Sutton Publishing, Stroud 2005

Iverson, Kenneth V, *Demon Doctors, Physicians as Serial Killers*, Galen Press Ltd, Tucson 2002

James, CLR, *The Black Jacobins*, Penguin Books, London 1938

Johnson, Dorothy, *Jacques-Louis David: New Perspectives*, University of Delaware Press 2006

Kane, Harnett T, *Louisiana Hayride, The American Rehearsal for Dictatorship*, William Morrow & Company, New York 1949

Kingston, Charles, *Law-Breakers*, John Lane The Bodley Head Limited, London 1930.

Le Neve, Ethel, *Ethel Le Neve – Her Life Story*, Daisy Bank Printing & Publishing Co, Gorton, Manchester 1910

Legrand, Jacques, *Chronicle of the French Revolution*, Chronicle Communications, London 1989

Lengyel, Olga, *Five Chimneys*, translated by Paul Weiss, Granada Books, London 1972

Levy, Alan, *The Wiesenthal File*, Constable & Co, London 1993

Bibliography

Lifton, Robert Jay, *The Nazi Doctors: Medical Killing and the Psychology of Genocide*, Basic Books, New York 1986

Maeder, Thomas, *The Unspeakable Crimes of Dr Petiot*, Atlantic-Little, Brown Books, New York 1980

Marks, Alfred, *Tyburn Tree, Its History and Annals*, Brown, Langham & Co, London 1910

Marquis, Max, *Deadly Doctors*, Macdonald, London 1992

Matalon Lagnado, Lucette, *Children of the Flames, Dr Joseph Mengele and the Untold Story of the Twins*, Sidgwick & Jackson, London 1991

Nyiszli, Miklos, *Auschwitz: A Doctor's Eyewitness Account*, translated by Tibere Kremer and Richard Seaver, Granada Books, London 1973

Perl, Gisela, *I was a Doctor in Auschwitz*, International Universities Press, New York 1948

Posner, Gerald and John Ware, *Mengele, The Complete Story*, Queen Anne Press, London 1986

Rowland, John, *Poisoner in the Dock, Twelve studies in Poisoning*, Arco Publications, London 1960

Roughead, William, *1870-1952 Classic Crimes*, New York Review, New York 2001

Russell, Guy, *Guilty or Not Guilty*, Hutchinson, London 1931

Schechter, Harold, *Depraved: The Shocking True Story of America's First Serial Killer*, Pocket Books, New York 1994

Seth, Ronald, *Petiot, Victim of Chance*, Hutchinson, London 1963

Starrs, James E & Ramsland, Katherine, *A Voice for the Dead: A forensic Investigators Pursuit of the Truth in the Grave*, Putnam Adult, New York 2005

Thompson, John CJS, *Poisons and Poisoners*, Barnes & Noble, New York 1993

Twiss, Miranda, *Evil Men*, Michael O'Mara, London 2003

Varaut, Jean-Marc, *L'Abominable Dr Petiot*, Balland, Paris 1974

Waddell, Bill, *The Black Museum, New Scotland Yard*, Little, Brown & Co, London 1993

Warren, Robert Penn, *All The King's Men*, Harcourt, Brace & Company, San Diego 1946

Watson, Eric R, *Trial of William Palmer*, William Hodge, Edinburgh 1952

Watson, Katherine, *Poisoned Lives, English Poisoners and their Victims*, Hambledon & London, London 2004

Whittle, Brian and Ritchie, Jean, *Prescription for Murder, The True Story of a Mass Murderer*, Warner Books 2000

Wyndam, Horace, *Consider Your Verdict*, WH Allen, London 1946